EVERY DAY WITH Jesus

A DAILY DEVOTION FOR PERSONAL REVIVAL

WITH UPDATES AND INTRODUCTIONS
BY ANDY PECK

Copyright © Waverley Abbey Trust 2025

Published 2025 by Waverley Abbey Trust, Waverley Abbey House, Waverley Lane, Farnham, Surrey GU9 8EP, England. Registered Charity No. 294387. Registered Limited Company No. 1990308.

Excerpts in this compilation were taken from issues of *Every Day with Jesus*, previously published as Jan/Feb 2007, Mar/Apr 2013, May/Jun 2019, Jul/Aug 1988, Sep/Oct 2009, Jan/Feb 1980.

All rights reserved. No part of this publication may be reproduced, stored in a retrieval system, or transmitted, in any form or by any means, electronic, mechanical, photocopying, recording or otherwise, without the prior permission in writing of Waverley Abbey Trust.

Unless otherwise indicated, all Scripture references are from the Holy Bible, New International Version® Anglicised, NIV® Copyright © 1979, 1984, 2011 by Biblica, Inc.® Used by permission. All rights reserved worldwide.

Other versions are marked:

Mof: Scripture quotations marked (Mof) are from the James Moffatt, A New Translation of the Bible, Containing the Old and New Testaments. New York: Doran, 1926. Revised edition, New York and London: Harper and Brothers, 1935. Reprinted, Grand Rapids: Kregel, 1995.

NKJV: Scripture taken from the New King James Version®. Copyright © 1982 by Thomas Nelson. Used by permission. All rights reserved.

REB: The Revised English Bible with the Apocrypha. Oxford University Press and Cambridge University Press, 1989.

TLB: The Living Bible copyright © 1971 by Tyndale House Foundation. Used by permission of Tyndale House Publishers Inc., Carol Stream, Illinois 60188. All rights reserved. The Living Bible, TLB, and the The Living Bible logo are registered trademarks of Tyndale House Publishers.

AMPC: Amplified Bible, Classic Edition (AMPC). Copyright © 1954, 1958, 1962, 1964, 1965, 1987 by The Lockman Foundation.

NASB: New American Standard Bible®, Copyright © 1960, 1971, 1977, 1995, 2020 by The Lockman Foundation. All rights reserved.

Concept development, editing, design and production by Waverley Abbey Trust.

Printed in the UK.

Paperback ISBN: 978-1-78951-538-1

THE STORY OF *EVERY DAY WITH JESUS*

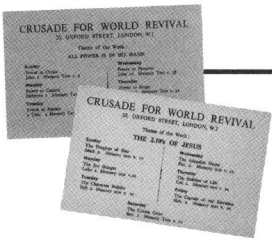

1965
When Selwyn Hughes was asked to help his congregation study the Bible, he wrote notes on postcards.

1967
Shortly after, the first official monthly *Every Day with Jesus* was printed and given away for free.

2006
After the passing of Selwyn Hughes, the organisation continued to disperse his writings.

2012–2021
Email subscription and ebooks were introduced, along with new contributors.

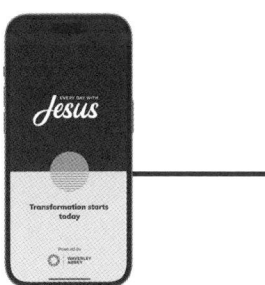

2024
To make *Every Day with Jesus* available to every person on the planet, the app is launched.

CONTENTS

5   FOREWORD

6   JANUARY & FEBRUARY
       The Character of God

68   MARCH & APRIL
       Eat, Pray, Share

132   MAY & JUNE
       God's New Society

196   JULY & AUGUST
       Armour of God

262   SEPTEMBER & OCTOBER
       Perfect Balance

326   NOVEMBER & DECEMBER
       Sharing Your Faith

FOREWORD

Every Day With Jesus has been helping people around the world to encounter God in a simple, accessible way every single day for more than fifty years.

Its author Selwyn Hughes – a son of the Welsh Revival – was a humble coal-miner who became a pastor and began writing these notes on postcards for the members of his church. Word spread, demand grew, printing became necessary, and before long *Every Day With Jesus* had become one of the very first daily devotions of its kind, reaching more than a million people each day.

The impact was astounding. Somehow these simple reflections, quietly composed in leafy Surrey at Waverley Abbey, and printed for many years as hard copy, reached the very ends of the earth. For example, in Nigeria so many people used *Every Day With Jesus* that, when Selwyn landed at Lagos airport, the president met him with a marching band! But the most moving stories are the testimonies from prisons where this resource is used to this day.

It's remarkable that Selwyn Hughes continued writing these notes every day for the rest of his life, even when his wife tragically died, followed by both of their sons. This is hard-won wisdom compiled for the first time in a single volume containing many of Selwyn's best, most insightful reflections.

If you're looking for something cool and contemporary, this book may not be for you (there are plenty of trendier devotionals out there on the market today). But if you're looking for accessible, seasoned wisdom from a humble, faithful friend of God, here in this book you are holding a time-tested guide to personal, daily revival.

Pete Greig
24-7 Prayer International, Waverley Abbey

JANUARY & FEBRUARY

THE CHARACTER OF GOD

INTRODUCTION

Today many of us have got our priorities wrong. We think that life revolves around us – our interests and our problems. In these two months of daily notes, Selwyn Hughes turns our focus instead to God.

Here we read about God's immense power, His longing for us to relate to Him, His love, His holiness, His complete faithfulness, His intolerance of sin, His kindness to the undeserving and His infinite knowledge and wisdom. When we start to contemplate this wonderful God and realise just how great and dependable He is – and what He expects of us – our whole outlook will be changed. We will lose all sense of self-sufficiency and instead will trust and adore Him as we should.

The Primary Focus

1 JAN

FOR READING AND MEDITATION – GENESIS 1:1–12

'In the beginning God...' (v1)

We begin a new year by focusing on what without doubt is the most noble of themes – the character of God.

The choice of this theme was prompted by my travels in different countries and my observation that all over the world, generally speaking, Christians seem to be preoccupied with knowing more about themselves instead of being anxious to know more about God. Ask any Christian publisher, 'What are the bestselling books?' and you will discover it is not those that unfold for us the nature of God, but those that deal with matters such as how to get a better self-image, how to manage money, how to find inner healing, how to get more excitement out of life. It is not that these subjects are unimportant, but they are explored in a self-absorbed way that gives us the impression that the most important thing in life is knowing ourselves better. It isn't. The most important thing in life is knowing God better.

John Lancaster, a minister in Cardiff, South Wales, in an article entitled, 'Where on earth is God?', asks the question, 'Given a choice between attending a seminar, say, on 'The Glory of God in Isaiah' and one on 'The Christian and Sex', to which would you go?' The point he is making is that though the Church attempts to answer the questions people are asking, the problem is that frequently people are not asking the right questions. In today's Church we are far too people-centred, and not sufficiently God-centred. It is not by accident, I believe, that the Bible opens with the thunderous acclaim, 'In the beginning God...' I tell you with all the conviction of which I am capable that if God is not our primary focus then everything else will soon get out of focus.

O Father, on this first day of a new year help me determine to make You my primary focus. And give me the grace and strength to maintain this focus through all the changes and uncertainties of another year. In Jesus' name I pray. Amen.

Exodus 20:1–6; Mark 12:28–30; 1 Corinthians 1:10–12
1. What is the greatest commandment?
2. Who were the Corinthians following?

A Lost Art

2 JAN

FOR READING AND MEDITATION – ROMANS 11:25-36

'Who has known the mind of the Lord?
Or who has been his counsellor?' (v34)

A subject which is of great interest to many today is anthropology – the study of humankind. Although this subject is of importance, for a Christian there is something far more important – the study of God. It was the famous nineteenth-century preacher, C.H. Spurgeon, who said, 'The highest science, the loftiest speculation, the mightiest philosophy that can ever engage the attention of a child of God is the name, the nature, the Person, the work, the doings, and the existence of the great God whom he calls his Father.'

The contemplation of God seems to be a lost art these days. We appear to be more concerned about subjects such as the emerging Church, signs, wonders and miracles, and the end times. I am not suggesting that these issues are irrelevant or unimportant, but they must not be allowed to replace the supremely important matter of the eager and constant investigation into the great subject of the Deity. The more we know of God, the more effective will be our lives here on earth. Those who have given themselves to the study of God tell us that the rewards are mainly threefold: it humbles the mind, expands the soul, and consoles the heart.

Take the first – it humbles the mind. When our minds master other subjects we feel a degree of self-content, and start to think, 'I'm wise.' But when our minds engage with thoughts of God we discover that there is no device that can sound His depth, and we come to the conclusion, 'I know nothing.' In an age which stresses the supremacy of the human mind, it is no bad thing to learn that there is something far greater. Indeed, Someone far greater – the infinite and eternal God.

Gracious and loving heavenly Father, teach me how to focus on You and contemplate You so that all my vanity and pride dies, and I go on my way no longer caught up with how wise I am but how wonderful You are. In Jesus' name. Amen.

Job 11:7-9; Isaiah 40:12-18; Hebrews 12:2-3
1. Why does studying God humble our minds?
2. What are we to consider?

Quiet Contemplation

3 JAN

FOR READING AND MEDITATION – PSALM 92:1–15

'For you make me glad by your deeds, Lord…' (v4)

Yesterday we said that contemplation of God has a threefold effect: it humbles the mind, expands the soul, and consoles the heart. We have looked at how it humbles the mind, and now we examine briefly how it expands the soul.

'The soul,' commented one theologian, 'is at home only when it is in God.' By that he meant that because the soul was made for God, it functions effectively only when it is indwelt by Him. Contemplation of God is like breath to the soul: it inflates it and invigorates it. 'My whole body functions better when God is in it,' said a doctor to me some years ago. I replied, 'And so it is with the soul, dear Doctor, so it is with the soul.'

The third benefit of contemplating God is that it consoles the heart. But how? It does so by focusing the heart's attention on the greatness and goodness of God, and also on His amazing mercy and compassion. The more we know of God, the more we will realise that when He permits us to pass through deep and dark waters, it is not because He is powerless to deliver us, but because a beneficent and eternal purpose is being worked out in the process. And what is more, we discover that God is interested not merely in working out His purposes in us, but in imparting to us a richer sense of His presence. In God there is a balm for every wound, a comfort for every sorrow, and healing for every heartache. All kinds of remedies are on offer in today's Church to help those who are hurting (some of them more secular than sacred), but I know nothing that relieves the anguish caused by great tides of sorrow and grief as does the quiet contemplation of the Godhead.

My Father and my God, forgive me if in times of trial and distress I look for comfort in the wrong places. You, and You alone, are able to meet my needs. Please help me to become completely convinced of this. In Jesus' name. Amen.

Psalm 147:1–3; Isaiah 43:1–5
1. How does God relate to the broken-hearted?
2. Why do we not need to fear deep and dark waters?

'Eccentric' Christians

4 JAN

FOR READING AND MEDITATION – ISAIAH 40:21–31

'He sits enthroned above the circle of the earth,
and its people are like grasshoppers.' (v22)

The people-centred focus that is creeping into the Church these days must be resisted at all costs. I am not suggesting that we should close our eyes to the fact that men and women need help on such matters as parenting children, marital problems, and establishing proper priorities. These issues should be addressed, but we must be careful that 'market forces' do not mould our theology. We may want to know about these issues, but what we need, primarily, is to know God.

It could be argued that our problems have become acute because we are lacking in our knowledge of God. The context in which we think and feel is so limited that it is no wonder our souls feel stifled and claustrophobic. One preacher describes our condition in this way: 'We are like Peter trying to walk on the water but becoming so engrossed in the winds and the waves that we lose sight of the all-sufficient Christ who is right there beside us. Our immediate environment has blotted out the sense of the eternal.'

This is why I have chosen today's reading from the magnificent book of Isaiah. The prophet does what a doctor would do when visiting a patient with a minor sickness and finding all the windows closed and the room lacking in oxygen. He or she would throw open the windows and invite the patient to inhale the purer air. 'Take a deep breath of the oxygen of the Spirit,' Isaiah is saying in effect. 'See how great and powerful God is. Set your problems in the context of His might and omnipotence.' We become like the thing we focus on. If we centre on human beings rather than on God then we should not be surprised if we end up off centre – eccentric.

O God, save me from being a Christian who is off-centre and thus an eccentric Christian – in the true meaning of that term. May my primary focus be always on You. Grant it, dear Lord. In Jesus' name I pray. Amen.

Numbers 13:17–33; 14:24
1. How did the spies view themselves?
2. Why did Caleb think differently?

Stirred – But Not Shaken

FOR READING AND MEDITATION – PSALM 16:1–11
'With him at my right hand, I shall not be shaken.' (v8)

Today we stay with the theme we touched on yesterday – the danger of allowing our faith to become more people-centred than God-centred. When I have had the opportunity to address Christian counsellors I have always tried to urge them to put the glory of God before their client's wellbeing. A great deal of 'Christian' counselling today follows the client-centred approach in which the person being counselled is all-important. The inevitable result of this approach is to pay more attention to how the person has been hurt by others than to how he or she may be 'hurting' God by being unwilling to trust Him. This is a very sensitive issue, of course, and I tell counsellors in training that it must never be raised until other issues have been explored and understood. Ultimately, however, this is an issue we must all face, whether or not we are in counselling.

Ask yourself this question now: Do I allow myself to become more obsessed by the wrong people have done to me than the wrong I might have done (and may still be doing) to God by my unwillingness to trust Him? The thought of putting the glory of God before our personal wellbeing is rather alien to Christians who have been brought up in the 'Me' generation. It means we have to break away from the idea that life revolves around our desires, our ambitions, our self-image, our personal comfort, our hurts and problems, and recognise instead that it revolves around the glory and will of God. When we do as the psalmist tells us he did in our text for today, and set the Lord always before us, then no matter what happens, though we may be stirred, we will not be shaken.

Father, thank You for reminding me that though I cannot avoid my soul being stirred by life's problems, when I set You before me then I can avoid being shaken. Please help me to grasp this truth today. Amen.

Exodus 14:10–14; Psalm 62:1–12
1. Contrast the attitudes of Moses and the Israelites to danger.
2. Where did the psalmist find rest and what was the result?

God Marginalised

6 JAN

FOR READING AND MEDITATION – JEREMIAH 9:17-24

'But let the one who boasts boast about this:
that they have understanding and know me...' (v24)

A minister speaking at a conference held by a large denomination made this remark: 'The reason why there is such depletion of spiritual energy in people nowadays is because of the rush of modern-day life.' But is this really true? Is it right to argue that the blame for our condition lies outside of us rather than inside us – the place (in my opinion) where the difficulty really lies? No, the real reason for the spiritual dullness evident in so many lives is that we have lost our sense of priority. One of my favourite poets is William Wordsworth, and I simply love the following lines:

> *The world is too much with us; late and soon*
> *Getting and spending, we lay waste our powers;*
> *Little we see in Nature that is ours;*
> *We have given our hearts away...*

The world is too much with us! Therein lies our problem. Other things, other issues, other problems, other priorities have been allowed to press in upon us, and the consequence of all this is that God has become marginalised. If we were to pay as much attention to the things that pertain to God as we do to the things that pertain to the world then the spiritual health of the Church (generally speaking) would not be such a cause for concern.

Through the prophet Jeremiah God speaks to us and shows us that His greatest desire is that we should come to know Him. When we lose God we lose touch with reality, for reality, as one great Christian defined it, is Jesus' other name.

O God, forgive me that so often my desires conflict with Your desires. My desire is to know more about me; Your desire is for me to know more about You. Help me to bring my desires in line with Your desires. In Jesus' name. Amen.

Isaiah 1:2-4; Luke 14:15-23
1. What was God's message to Israel?
2. How did people excuse themselves from the feast?

Take Delight in God   7 JAN

FOR READING AND MEDITATION – HOSEA 6:1–11

'Your love is like the morning mist,
like the early dew that disappears.' (v4)

A danger we must become aware of as we discuss the need to contemplate God more deeply is that of becoming more interested in godliness than in God Himself. The theologian Jim Packer comments that he is often troubled by what he finds among his fellow evangelicals. Many believers are extremely keen to become godly, but show little direct interest in the God whom they are seeking to follow. When they study the Bible they do so to discover the principles that will enable them to develop their spiritual lives – not to take delight in their heavenly Father. He says, 'It is as if they should concentrate on the ethics of marriage and fail to spend time with their spouse! There is something narcissistic, and, to tell the truth, nutty in being more concerned with godliness than about God.' I think 'nutty' is the right word.

Some years ago I did indeed come across a man who attended every seminar he could find on the subject of marriage, and whenever he was presented with a new idea he would make a note of it and spend time reflecting on it. The only trouble was that he never got past the stage of reflection. So, because he was more taken up with the mechanics than the dynamics of marriage, while he indulged himself in new and interesting ideas, his wife was left languishing at home.

How sad that a man can take more interest in the principles that undergird his marriage than in the marriage partner whom he has pledged to love, honour, and cherish. Let's be watchful that we don't care more for the principles of godliness than for the God we are called to praise and please every day of our lives.

Gracious and loving Father, forgive me I pray if I have been caught up more in the mechanics of my faith than in the dynamics of it. May nothing ever become more important to me than my relationship with You. Amen.

Matthew 15:7–14; 23:23–28
1. How did the Pharisees put godliness before God?
2. What would be the result of their spiritual blindness?

Seeing the Invisible

8 JAN

FOR READING AND MEDITATION – HEBREWS 11:17–29

'He persevered because he saw him who is invisible.' (v27)

Today we ask ourselves: What is it that prompts some people to show more interest in the principles of godliness than in God Himself? Why would a person become more taken up with what we might call 'the nuts and bolts' of their religion than with their loving heavenly Father? One reason, I think, could be that we are more comfortable when we are dealing with the visible than we are with the invisible. Rather than launch out into the unseen and simply trust, we prefer to work with things we can touch, or handle and apply, since we feel an immediate impact.

During the days when much of my time was spent in personal counselling, I often saw people come up against this problem. My strategy was to bring these people to the point where they could accept that the roots of their problem lay in a failure in their relationship with God. However, when I told them that what was called for was a movement towards Him of simple basic trust, alarm would appear for a moment in their eyes and they would say, 'Give me some steps I can take to deal with my problem, some principles I can follow.'

All of us find it easier to do than to be – to have a plan to follow rather than a Person to trust. What our carnal nature hates to be faced with is the challenge of throwing ourselves in utter dependence on a God who is invisible and intangible. Yet this is what a relationship with God entails. The thing that marks Moses out as outstanding in the passage we have read today is not his works but his faith: 'He persevered because he saw him who is invisible.' It is possible to see the invisible, but it is possible only to those who have the eye of faith.

My Father and my God, help me recognise this terrible tendency in myself to be more comfortable with working than with trusting. Let Your Word reach deep into my heart today. Please teach me how to be. In Jesus' name I pray. Amen.

2 Kings 6:8–17; 2 Corinthians 4:16–18
1. What could Elisha see that his servant could not?
2. Where do we fix our eyes?

Balanced Christianity

9 JAN

FOR READING AND MEDITATION – GALATIANS 3:1-25

'After beginning by means of the Spirit,
are you now trying to finish by means of the flesh?' (v3)

It is important for us to think a little more about the issue we raised yesterday – the tendency to focus on doing rather than being. The Church has always struggled to get the balance right between faith and works. Take, for instance, the New Testament books of Romans and James. Romans is the great book on 'faith', while James is the great book on 'works'. Some Christians known to me never read the letter of James, taking sides with Martin Luther, who called it 'an epistle of straw'. Martin Luther was right about so many things, but he was wrong when he referred to the letter of James in this way. We need to study both Romans and James if we want to be properly balanced Christians.

The difficulty with faith and works is this. We become Christians by depending on the innocent sufferings of our Lord Jesus Christ on Calvary as the ground for our acceptance by God, and then, when we learn the principles of Christian living, we can turn from dependence on Christ to dependence on them. This was the problem in the Galatian church, and it is still a problem here in the Church of the twenty-first century. Showing that our repentance and faith are real by doing good works is extremely important, but we are not to depend on works for our salvation.

We tend to focus more on works than faith because, as I said yesterday, works result in something visible and tangible. It is possible to see what we are doing and assess it. Faith is different. It requires of us a degree of helplessness – something the carnal nature abhors. But if we are to know God better and avoid falling into the trap of pursuing godliness more keenly than God Himself then our faith is absolutely vital.

O Father, help me to get this right. I am saved to do good works, but I am not saved by good works. Prevent me from falling into the trap of being more preoccupied with Your principles than with You Yourself. In Jesus' name. Amen.

Matthew 17:1-5; Galatians 2:11-21
1. What was Peter's response to revelation?
2. Why did Paul reprimand Peter (Cephas)?

Meeting the Person 10 JAN

FOR READING AND MEDITATION – PHILIPPIANS 3:1-14
'I want to know Christ – yes, to know the power of his resurrection...' (v10)

We spend one more day setting the stage before lifting the curtains on this most important subject of the character of God. It must not be assumed from what has been said over the past couple of days that the study of Scripture and contemplation of the principles which God has set out in His Word are of little consequence. They are tremendously important. What I am saying is this: let us be on our guard that we do not fall into the trap of giving more consideration to the principles which God has laid down than we do to God Himself.

Often I have observed students of Scripture make this mistake. While they are reading their Bible the only things that catch their eye are the principles that relate to Christian living. They underline these principles in their Bible, mark alongside them other scriptural references, and think that by doing so they are growing spiritually. The problem is that only the principles of daily personal godliness capture their interest; their heavenly Father does not.

Imagine treating a love letter in that way – identifying and underlining the principles, reflecting on the profundity of some of the insights, marvelling at the clarity of the language, and yet missing the main purpose in the letter – to communicate romantic passion and love. Yet this is the way some people approach the Bible. Our aim in studying the nature and character of God must be to know God better (not merely to know His Word better), and we must seek to get better acquainted not simply with the characteristics of His nature, but with the living God whose characteristics they are.

O God, may I never approach the Bible content to understand only the written Word. Give me a passion that is not satisfied until, through the written Word, I discover more of the living Word. In Jesus' name I ask this. Amen.

John 5:39-40; Revelation 2:1-5
1. Why did Jesus rebuke those who studied Scripture?
2. Why were the Ephesians' deeds insufficient?

God's Self-Revelation   11 JAN

FOR READING AND MEDITATION – ISAIAH 42:10-17

'But those who trust in idols...
will be turned back in utter shame.' (v17)

Now we are ready to start focusing on our subject, and together we will contemplate as far as we are able the nature and character of the God we worship. Most of what we know about God is from His self-revelation in the Scriptures. We know something about Him as we look out through the lattice of nature, but because the world of nature has been affected by the Fall, we cannot expect to find a full revelation of Him there. Scripture, however, is different. The Bible, I believe, has been supernaturally protected from the effects of sin, and in its pages we have a clear revelation of who God is and what He is like. This is why all human ideas about God, His will, and His work, both traditional and contemporary, must be ruthlessly brought in line with what Scripture says.

Those who think that they can get a clear picture of God apart from Scripture are deceived. A young Christian once said to me, 'I don't need to read the Bible to know God. I simply sit and meditate on Him and He reveals Himself to me.' He thought that he could know God in this way, but he was mistaken. When we try to get to know God using our own imagination, we run the risk of knowing an imaginary God.

The Bible is God's revelation of Himself, and unless our thoughts are guided and constantly corrected by God's thoughts we will soon go off at a tangent. I can look into my own heart to see what I am like, but I have to look into the Bible to see what God is like. And we need to remember that idolatry – which really is forming unbiblical notions of God and thus worshipping unrealities – is the sin that is most frequently denounced in Scripture.

O God, help me understand more fully that the entrance of Your Word gives light, and the neglect of Your Word produces darkness. May I take Your light as my light, and thus walk through life with a sure and steady tread. Amen.

Isaiah 44:9-20; Colossians 3:5; 1 Timothy 6:9-10
1. Why are human ideas about God deluded?
2. What is a modern form of idolatry?

The Great Creator

12 JAN

FOR READING AND MEDITATION – ISAIAH 42:1–9

'The Creator of the heavens, who stretches
them out, who spreads out the earth...' (v5)

Today we ask the question: what is the first thing we learn about God as we open up the Scriptures? It is that He is omnipotent. The Bible never argues that there is a God; everywhere it assumes and asserts the fact. Majestically, the opening verse of Scripture states, 'In the beginning God...' (Gen. 1:1). Its paramount concern is not to persuade us that God exists, but to tell us who God is and what He does. And the first thing we see Him do in the Scriptures is to act creatively.

I love the story which I first read in a paper called *The Welsh Churchman* concerning a group of researchers who set out to discover what really happened when the earth was created. They spent months gathering information and feeding the data into a computer. Finally, when everything was ready, they hit the printout key and waited. Soon a message appeared with these words, 'See Genesis 1:1.'

Many think the only reference to God's creative act is the one described in the first two chapters of Genesis, but the truth is woven inextricably into both the Old and the New Testament. One example is found in today's text. We cannot have a right conception of God or contemplate Him correctly unless we think of Him as all-powerful. He who cannot do what He wills and pleases cannot be God. As God has a will to do good, so He has the necessary power to execute that will. Who can look up at the midnight sky and not echo the words of the psalmist, 'When I consider your heavens, the work of your fingers, the moon and the stars, which you have set in place, what is mankind that you are mindful of him...?' (Psa. 8:3–4). A great and powerful God brought them into being simply by saying, 'Let them be.'

Father, I sense that the more enlightened my understanding, the more my soul responds with thanksgiving, adoration, and praise. Enlighten me still more, dear Father. In Jesus' name I pray. Amen.

Isaiah 45:12; Acts 17:22–31; Hebrews 11:3
1. What does God declare about the universe?
2. What did Paul explain about the world?

Not From Me!   13 JAN

FOR READING AND MEDITATION – PSALM 33:1–22

'By the word of the Lord the heavens were made,
their starry host by the breath of his mouth.' (v6)

In today's society the idea that God created the world is scoffed at by many. Modern astronomers, probing into outer space with their gigantic telescopes, favour two theories as to the origin of the universe. One is the so-called Big Bang theory, according to which 'The cosmos started with a titanic explosion and as a consequence has been expanding ever since.' The other is the Continuous Creation theory which maintains that 'The universe is self-creating and is constantly making itself out of nothing and falling back into nothingness again.'

What many scientists are not prepared to admit is that the ultimate energy behind the universe is not a Big Bang but a Big Being – an intelligent Being of indescribable majesty and power who is able to do whatever He chooses. And because what He chooses is always good, He can be trusted to have the best interests of His creation at heart. Some time ago I read that when Joseph Haydn, the famous Austrian composer, had finished his great oratorio, 'The Creation', he is said to have cried, 'Not from me! Not from me! From above it has all come!'

Our text for today reminds us that by God's word the heavens were made, and by His breath the stars were formed. I once heard my father, a local preacher, picturesquely describe the creation in this way: 'It was no harder for God to create the world than it is for my son to blow soap bubbles into the air out of his clay pipe.' Frequently my mind goes back to that lovely image, and when it does and I contemplate this awesome, mighty, all-powerful God, my soul instinctively cries, 'How great Thou art.' I hope yours does too!

Yes, Father, as I contemplate Your majesty and Your power my soul cries out also, 'How great Thou art.' It can do nothing else, for contemplation of You inevitably leads to adoration of You. Amen.

Psalm 148:1–5; 2 Peter 3:3–5
1. How did God create the world?
2. What do some deliberately forget?

Sustained and Secure   14 JAN

FOR READING AND MEDITATION – PSALM 104:1–35

'All creatures look to you to give them their food at the proper time.' (v27)

We have considered God's might and power in the act of creation; now we consider His might and power in the act of preservation. No creature has the power to preserve itself. 'Can papyrus grow tall where there is no marsh?' asked Job, and 'Can reeds thrive without water?' (Job 8:11). Both humans and animals would perish if there were no food, and there would be no food if the earth were not refreshed with showers of rain. In the words of one preacher, 'We came from God's hand, and we remain in His hand.'

Think, for example, of the marvel of life in the womb. How a baby can live for so many months in such a cramped environment is unaccountable except for the power of God in preservation. It was divine preservation Daniel was thinking of when he said to the godless Belshazzar, 'You did not honour the God who holds in his hand your life and all your ways' (Dan. 5:23). Everywhere in the Scriptures God is presented not only as the Creator of the world but also as its Sustainer and Preserver.

God has not wound up the universe like a clock and then separated Himself from it; He is active in sustaining it, and were He to remove Himself from it, it would cease to exist. The writer to the Hebrews reminds us that He is *upholding* all things by the word of his power' (1:3, KJV, my emphasis). If a cabinet-maker who produced a bespoke piece of furniture were to die, his death would make no difference to the object he had made. It would continue to exist just as it did before. Not so with God and His world, however. If God were to die the universe would fall to pieces. But don't worry – God cannot die. The universe is quite secure.

O God, when I consider how You are my Sustainer and my Preserver, my heart is humbled. You cannot die, and because I belong to You, I shall always live. I know my body will die, but my soul is Yours – for ever. Thank You, dear Father. Amen.

Psalm 8:1–4; 147:5–9; Isaiah 46:3–5
1. What does God care for?
2. Of what did God remind Israel?

This God is Your God

15 JAN

FOR READING AND MEDITATION – EZEKIEL 22:1-16

'Will your courage endure or your hands
be strong in the day I deal with you?' (v14)

Today we look at another aspect of God's great and mighty power. God is powerful not only in creation and preservation, but He is powerful in judgment also. When He acts no one can resist Him, as our text for today makes absolutely clear. The flood of Noah's day is one example of God's intervention, when the entire human race – with the exception of eight people – was wiped out (Gen. 6:1-9,18). A shower of fire and brimstone from heaven destroyed Sodom and Gomorrah and all the cities of the surrounding plain (Gen. 19:1-29). And Pharaoh and his army were impotent when God swept them into the Red Sea (Exod. 14:1-31).

Now what does the contemplation of God's great power do for us? First, it causes us to tremble before Him. The trouble with many modern men and women is that they do not tremble before God. To treat with presumption the One who can crush us more easily than we can an ant is, as someone has put it, 'a suicidal policy'. 'Kiss his son,' said the psalmist, 'or he will be angry and your way will lead to your destruction… for his wrath can flare up in a moment' (Psa. 2:12).

Another thing the contemplation of God's great power does for us is to cause us to adore Him. Who can consider the might of this awesome God without wanting to worship Him? The rebellious heart will resist this, of course, but the heart cleansed by the blood of Christ will bow in homage and say, 'Who is like you – majestic in holiness, awesome in glory, working wonders?' (Exod. 15:11).

Well may we, as believers, trust such a God. No prayer is too hard for Him to answer, no need too great for Him to supply, no predicament too difficult for Him to solve. Grasp this great and gripping truth: this God is your God.

O Father, I see that contemplation of You tilts my soul in Your direction. I realise that without You I am nothing. May I tremble before You until my trembling turns to adoration and ever-increasing trust. Amen.

Psalm 31:19-24; 99:1-9
1. Why should we tremble before God?
2. Why should we adore God?

The God Who Speaks

16 JAN

FOR READING AND MEDITATION – ISAIAH 55:1–13

'As the heavens are higher than the earth, so are my ways higher than your ways and my thoughts than your thoughts.' (v9)

As we have seen, the first thing we learn about God when we open the pages of the Bible is that He is powerful. This awesome might and power, we said, was demonstrated in the creation of the world.

The next thing we observe about God in Genesis 1 is that He is personal. But what does it mean to be a person? What is personality? The best definition of personality I know is the one given to me by the tutor who taught me theology. He explained that to be a person we have to be able to think, to reason, to feel, to judge, to choose, and to communicate in words that constitute a language. Richard Swinburne, a theologian, observes that people use language not only to communicate and for private thought, but to argue, to raise a consideration, to object to another person. Unlike animals, which show evidence only of wanting things that are essential for life, such as food and drink, people can want not to want something, like a fasting man, for example, wanting not to want food.

Now with that in mind – that one of the elements of personality is the ability to think and speak – read the first chapter of Genesis once again. Notice how many times these words appear: 'God said.' Count them. God is portrayed to us as a speaking God, and as speech is one aspect of personality, this reveals that the Deity is a personal Being. We are not long into Genesis before we are brought face to face with the fact that there is more to God than mere power; the Almighty is a Person. This means, among other things, that He cannot be studied from a 'safe' distance. Because God is a Person, He is someone who wants and waits to be 'known'.

Loving heavenly Father, how thankful I am that You made me like Yourself – to know and be known. May my strongest desire be to know You, and not merely to know myself. This I ask in Jesus' name. Amen.

Genesis 1:1–31
1. How many times does God speak?
2. Who did God speak to?

Plenty of Time For You　　17 JAN

FOR READING AND MEDITATION – PSALM 139:1–24

'How precious to me are your thoughts, God!
How vast is the sum of them!' (v17)

We continue exploring the fact that God is not only powerful, but personal. The different elements of personality are affirmed of God on almost every page of the Bible. Listen to this: 'I will raise up for myself a faithful priest, who will do according to what is in my heart and mind,' said the Lord to Eli in 1 Samuel 2:35. This shows – if it needs showing – that God has a mind with which He thinks.

God has emotions also – another aspect of personality. Some modern-day theologians claim that God is unable to feel, but clearly this view is not supported by Scripture. God can be angry (Psa. 2:12), jealous (Zech. 1:14–15), merciful (Psa. 78:38), and delighted (Deut. 30:9). These are just a few of the emotions which the Bible talks about, but of course, as a comprehensive study of Scripture shows, there are many more. Then again, God chooses and decides. Take this, for example: 'The Lord regretted that he had made human beings on the earth... So the Lord said, "I will wipe from the face of the earth the human race"' (Gen. 6:6–7).

While surveys reveal that the majority of human beings believe in some kind of God, many view Him as being so exalted and remote that they think He cannot possibly take a personal interest in such small and insignificant creatures as ourselves. Dr Henry Norris Russell, a great astronomer and a Christian, gave a talk once on the vastness of the universe. Afterwards someone asked him this question: 'How is it possible for such a great and infinite God to have time for me?' This was his reply: 'An infinite God can dispatch the affairs of this universe in the twinkling of an eye, thus giving Him plenty of time for you.'

O Father, in the midst of every trial and difficulty, help me to be encouraged and reassured by the fact that no matter what my problem, You always have plenty of time to give to me. I am so deeply thankful. Amen.

Luke 12:6–7,22–34
1. What does God know about us?
2. What has pleased God?

Jittery Theologians

18 JAN

FOR READING AND MEDITATION – LUKE 12:13-21

'But God said… "You fool! This very night your life will be demanded from you."' (v20)

Why is it that so many these days are attracted to the notion of a God who is impersonal?

In my opinion, there is a very subtle reason why men and women prefer to think of God as a power rather than as a Person, although most of them will be quite unaware of the unconscious reasoning that underlies this preference. If God is merely a power, or a formless life-force flowing through the universe, there are no demands – we are not challenged to relate to an energy in the same way that we are challenged to relate to a person. As soon as we recognise that God is a Person we are forced to ask: how do I relate to Him? It is the idea of meeting a personal God that causes men and women to tremble.

But deep down in every human heart, placed there by the Almighty, is the conviction that a personal God exists. We have all been made in His image, and His stamp is upon us whether we like it or not. In reality, as we said yesterday, there are very few atheists; most people believe in some kind of God. Someone has described an atheist as 'a theologian with the jitters'. An effective way of dealing with those jitters is to expunge from the heart the idea that God may be personal and that we might be accountable to Him. Better a life-force or a celestial energy, a power that can be tapped rather than a Person we might some day have to meet. How foolish it all is – settling for short-term comfort but facing eternal loss.

Father, I am saddened when I realise how many want to run from You when they should be running to You. I am so glad that I have found You, but I long that others might find You too. Draw many to You this very day, dear Lord. In Jesus' name. Amen.

Ecclesiastes 3:11; Matthew 12:35-37; Romans 14:9-12
1. What has God set within us?
2. What will each of us have to do?

The God Who is There

19 JAN

FOR READING AND MEDITATION – PSALM 14:1–7

'The fool says in his heart, "There is no God."' (v1)

Yesterday we saw why it is that men and women are so reluctant to pass from the notion of an abstract force or deity to acknowledging the living God. The idea of a living personal God gives men and women the jitters. They sense deep within that they are accountable to Him but they just don't know what to do about it.

C.S. Lewis, in his book Miracles*, expressed it like this: 'The Pantheist's God does nothing, demands nothing. He is there if you wish for Him, like a book on a shelf. He will not pursue you. There is no danger that at any time heaven and earth should flee away at His glance.' But Christ the Creator King is there. And His intervening presence is terribly startling to discover. Lewis goes on to compare the shock of discovering that there is a living personal God in the universe to sitting alone in the dark and sensing someone breathing beside you. 'It is always shocking,' he says, 'to meet life where we thought we were alone.'

Listen to this paragraph by Lewis which I quote in full as it puts the truth in a way that cannot be equalled: 'There comes a moment when the children who have been playing at burglars hush suddenly: was that a real footstep in the hall? There comes a moment when people who have been dabbling in religion suddenly draw back. Supposing we really found Him? We never meant it to come to that! Worse still, supposing He has found us? So it is a sort of Rubicon. One goes across; or not. But if one does, there is no manner of security against miracles. One may be in for anything.' No one need worry about getting any shocks when they steadfastly resist believing in a personal God. No shocks, but no salvation either.

Gracious God, how can I ever sufficiently thank You for bringing me to Yourself? The thought of a God who is alive, taking a personal interest in me, is more than I can comprehend. Yet I do believe it with all my heart. Amen.

Psalm 36:1–4; Proverbs 1:1–7
1. What is the nature of the wicked?
2. What do fools despise?

Miracles by C.S. Lewis, copyright © C.S. Lewis Pte. Ltd. 1947, 1960. Extract reprinted by permission.

The Father God

20 JAN

FOR READING AND MEDITATION – LUKE 11:1–13

'When you pray, say: "Father…"' (v2)

For one more day we focus on the fact that God is not only an omnipotent Being who creates, but also a personal Being who longs for a close and intimate relationship with those who are His children.

Samuel Shoemaker, the American Episcopalian preacher who was instrumental in forming Alcoholics Anonymous, pointed out that the whole principle of prayer depends on what kind of Being the Creator is. Listen to what he said to a group of recovering alcoholics: 'If He created the universe and gave everything a primeval push, and then retired beyond, where we cannot get in contact with Him, prayer is a vain effort. But if He be a personal God, as Christians believe He is, then He will have a concern for the people He made, and will want to involve Himself with them in all their affairs.' We are not alone in this universe; a personal God stands behind all things, waiting and longing that we might enter into a relationship with Him.

Two days ago we said that one of the reasons why people desire an impersonal God is because that kind of God is far easier to live with than one who is personal like themselves. It is rather nice to carry inside our hearts a subjective idea of a God of beauty, truth, and goodness. That kind of God demands nothing of us. Better still a formless life-force surging through all of us, a vast power we can tap and use to our advantage. That kind of God is extremely easy to live with. But a God who approaches us at infinite speed – the King, the Shepherd, the Husband – that is quite another matter. Yet whether we believe it or not, that is the kind of God He is.

Gracious and loving God, how thankful I am that You are not some supernatural energy or life-force, but a personal Being whom I can address as 'Father'. Your personality engages with my personality. In that my joy knows no bounds. Amen.

Psalm 23:1–6; Romans 8:13–21
1. How does God relate to us?
2. What have we received?

On This Truth We Stand

21 JAN

FOR READING AND MEDITATION – MARK 1:1–13

'Jesus... saw... the Spirit descending... And a voice came from heaven: "You are my Son..."' (vv10-11)

Those who accept the Scripture's teaching concerning God must be prepared to say that He is not only personal, but that He is a plurality of Persons also. In other words, a Trinity. This brings us to the next aspect of God's character we must examine – His triune nature.

The doctrine of the Trinity – that God is One yet three separate Persons – is not easy to understand, but it is a clear doctrine of Scripture nevertheless. The term 'Trinity' does not appear in the Bible (it was first used by Tertullian around AD 210), but the roots of the term are deeply embedded in the Word of God. That God is three Persons is mainly a revelation of the New Testament, but there are glimpses of the truth to be seen in the Old Testament also. Take this: 'Let us make mankind in our image...' (Gen. 1:26). To whom was God speaking at this stage? Some say the angels, but nowhere in Scripture are angels seen as being involved in the act of creation or as being on the same level as God. Read Colossians 1:16 and it will become clear to whom God was speaking. Then again: 'Man has now become like one of us' (Gen. 3:22). Another indication that there is more than one divine Person in the Godhead is found in Isaiah 6:8, when God asks, 'Whom shall I send? And who will go for us?'

'Go to the Jordan,' wrote St Augustine, 'and you find the Trinity.' There at the baptism of Jesus the three Persons in the Godhead are simultaneously in evidence. The Father is heard speaking directly from heaven, the Son is seen being immersed in the river, and John the Baptist beholds the Spirit descending upon the Christ. Three in One, and One in Three. On this truth we must stand, even though we may not fully understand.

Blessed Trinity, Three in One, and One in Three, I worship You this day in spirit and in truth. My spirit joins with Your Spirit, and Your truth brings joy to my heart. Amen.

Colossians 2:9; Titus 2:11–14; 3:1–9
1. Who is our great God and Saviour?
2. How does Paul identify the source of salvation?

The Baptismal Formula

22 JAN

FOR READING AND MEDITATION – MATTHEW 28:11-20

'Baptising… in the name of the Father
and of the Son and of the Holy Spirit…' (v19)

Yesterday we concluded with some words written by St Augustine telling us if we want to see the Trinity in action then all we have to do is to go to the River Jordan. Augustine also pointed out that the Trinity is mentioned in the verse that is our text for today, which we call 'the baptismal formula'. Notice that we are told to baptise in the name (not 'names') of the Father, Son, and Holy Spirit, indicating their essential unity and oneness.

There are many so-called Christians who do not accept the doctrine of the Trinity, and this makes me very sad. How I wish they would look at the matter again. I have found it to be one of the most satisfying of doctrines, and it meets the greatest needs of my soul. George Matheson spoke for me and for millions of other Christians when he said:

Some seek a Father in the heavens above,
Some ask a human figure to adore,
Some crave a Spirit vast as life and love.
Within Thy mansions we have all, and more.

Alfred Tennyson, a man with an incisive mind and great perception, wrote this about the Trinity: 'Though nothing is such a distress of soul to me as to hear the divinity of Christ assailed, yet I feel I must never lose the unity of the Godhead, the three Persons being like three candles giving together one light.' Notice his words, 'I must never lose the unity of the Godhead.' I would simply add: neither must we. Neither must we.

Father, Son, and Holy Spirit, I freely confess my mind finds it difficult to comprehend how You can be Three in One, and One in Three. Yet this is the teaching of Scripture. So I believe; please help my unbelief. In Jesus' name. Amen.

1 Corinthians 12:1-6; Acts 20:28; Hebrews 9:14
1. Where do spiritual gifts come from?
2. Whose blood purchased salvation?

Three Great Errors
23 JAN

FOR READING AND MEDITATION – ROMANS 15:23–30

'I urge you... by our Lord Jesus Christ and by
the love of the Spirit... by praying to God...' (v30)

'God is One, yet God is Three. How can such a strange thing be?' These are the lines of a ditty that supposedly was sung by troops on the march in World War I. Theologians down the ages have tried to illuminate this doctrine for us, but it is an issue that will not be fully clarified until we arrive in heaven (see 1 Cor. 13:12). Basically the doctrine of the Trinity is this: God is One but exists as three Persons, all equally divine.

Over the centuries a number of errors have been propounded. The first is the teaching that there are three Gods. The Jehovah's Witnesses accuse present-day Christians of believing this, and say that we conceive of God as a body with three heads. That might be true of ancient heresy but it is not true of classic Trinitarianism. The second error taught is that God is unipersonal and the other two Persons in the Trinity are simply manifestations of the Being of the one God. The third main error denies the equality of the divine Persons and regards them as being of different rank.

To protect Christians from such erroneous ideas the Church formulated the Athanasian Creed in the late fifth century, which states, 'We worship one God in trinity and trinity in unity – neither confusing the Persons, nor dividing the substance.' What we must see, however, is that no words can fully explain the truth of the Trinity. 'The creed is a safety net to keep us from falling into error,' explains one preacher, 'rather than a verbal net in which to trap the truth.' We use the term 'Trinity' expecting not so much that in that one word the truth may be spoken, but that it may not be left unspoken.

Father, I accept that life often presents me with facts which seem irreconcilable at one stage of knowledge and are then better understood at another. While I wait to understand the Trinity more fully I simply worship and adore. Amen.

Isaiah 44:6–8; 1 Peter 1:1–5; Revelation 1:9–18
1. How did Peter identify different members of the Trinity?
2. Who is the first and the last?

Logically Necessary

24 JAN

FOR READING AND MEDITATION – PSALM 136:1–26

'Give thanks to the God of gods. *His love endures for ever.*' (v2)

If you were totally unfamiliar with the Bible and you started to read it straight through from Genesis to Revelation, you might not discover the doctrine of the Trinity until you reached the New Testament. But once you found it there, on looking back, you would realise that it had been implicit in the whole Book from the beginning.

Ian Macpherson, in his book *The Faith Once Delivered*, says that when the island now known as Trinidad was discovered by Columbus, he initially thought it was three islands as all he could see were three hills silhouetted against the sky. However, when he got closer, he found that what he had seen was not three islands but just one island. From a distance it looked like three, but close up it was only one. Hence he named the island 'Trinidad', Spanish for 'Trinity'.

That is the kind of experience you get when reading the Word of God. At first it seems as if the Bible is talking about three Gods, but as you go deeper into the Scriptures you discover there are not three Gods, but one – one God in three Persons.

It is not only in isolated texts that we encounter the doctrine of the Trinity. The very concept of God's love presupposes plurality in the Godhead. Love, to be love, must have an object. Self-love is love's opposite. Since God (as we shall see more closely in a few days' time) is eternal love, He must have had objects of eternal affection. The objects of His affection are the Son and the Spirit. The doctrine of the Trinity, therefore, is not only theologically but logically necessary to an understanding of the nature of the Deity.

Father, help me understand that a Being who is fully comprehended could not be God. In Your unfathomable depths all my own thoughts are drowned. Symbolically I remove my shoes, for I sense I am standing on holy ground. Amen.

Deuteronomy 6:4; John 10:30; Ephesians 4:1–6
1. What did Jesus claim?
2. How did Paul confirm the 'oneness' of God?

The Great Triune God

25 JAN

FOR READING AND MEDITATION – JOHN 20:19–30
'Thomas said to him, "My Lord and my God!"' (v28)

Dr W.E. Sangster told the story of how one Trinity Sunday he overheard a chat between three children. One of the children remarked to the others, 'I can't understand all this "Three in One, and One in Three" business.' 'I can't either,' said one of the other children, 'but I think of it like this: my mother is Mummy to me, she is Mabel to Daddy, and Mrs Douglas to lots of other people.' Is that the answer then? Is it just a question of names? Are we right in finding the doctrine of the Trinity in the text we looked at three days ago (Matt. 28:19), where the word 'name' is singular but three names are given – Father, Son, and Holy Spirit?

No, that is just part of it; there is much more to it than that. One of the better explanations of the Trinity is this. God, we know, is one God. But there stepped into the world one day Someone who also claimed to be God. He came from Nazareth and His name was Jesus. He forgave sins, disclosed that He had existence before Abraham, and accepted worship as His right. Worship, remember, is for God alone. After Jesus was resurrected and had returned to heaven He sent back the Holy Spirit, who is also seen as God (2 Cor. 13:14). He – the Holy Spirit – came into the disciples and brought with Him the resources of the Godhead, breaking the sin in their nature, moulding them to holiness, pleading in prayer, and exalting the Saviour.

Thus we see that God is One, but also Three in One: God above us, God among us, God within us. The Father in majesty, the Son in suffering, the Spirit in striving. This is the central mystery of our most holy faith. Together, and with all our hearts, let us adore the great triune God.

Father, Son and Holy Spirit, though I cannot comprehend Your essential Oneness and unity, I can worship You nevertheless. This I do now, in humble adoration. Glory, honour, and power be to Your name for ever and ever. Amen.

Isaiah 42:8; John 1:1–14; 5:23; 17:5
1. How did John describe Jesus?
2. What did Jesus say of Himself?

A Watershed Truth

26 JAN

FOR READING AND MEDITATION – 2 CORINTHIANS 13:1–14

'The grace of the Lord Jesus Christ… the love of God…
the fellowship of the Holy Spirit…' (v14)

We continue reflecting on the fact that God is one God yet three separate Persons. That great Christian, Francis Schaeffer, said he would have remained an agnostic if it weren't for the doctrine of the Trinity. It was this, he claimed, that gave him the answer – the only answer – to the theme of unity and diversity.

The question I have been asked most often about the Trinity is this: Why didn't God make clear the truth of the Trinity in the Old Testament? Why did He leave it as something to be deduced in the New Testament? Usually I answer like this. Before God could entrust His people with the knowledge of His Threeness, He had to lay deep in their minds a piercing conviction of His essential Oneness. The Bible begins in monotheism (belief in one God), but soon after the Fall comes polytheism (belief in many gods). The story of Israel is really the battle of the gods – which god is the real God? Not until belief in one God was laid deep in the consciousness of the Jewish nation was God ready to reveal more clearly to humankind the sublime truth of the Trinity.

Dr George Smeaton says, 'The biblical idea of the Trinity is the heart of the unique message of Christianity. To explain this mystery is not our province… ours is simply to conserve the mystery.' In my experience, those who call themselves Christians yet reject the doctrine of the Trinity will soon latch onto some other error. It is a strange thing, but I have observed it as a fact of the Christian life that when this truth is modified or pushed aside, it is as if the door is opened to the inrush of all kinds of absurd ideas, bizarre theories, and half-truths.

Father, help me hold fast to this sublime truth, and enable me to see that though something is above reason, it is not necessarily against reason. Blessed Trinity, Father, Son, and Holy Spirit, I worship You. Amen.

John 5:16–18; 8:56–59; 10:31–33; 14:8–10
1. Why did the Jews try to stone Jesus?
2. What did Jesus reveal to Philip?

The High-Water Mark

27 JAN

FOR READING AND MEDITATION – 1 JOHN 4:7–16

'God is love.' (v8)

Now we move on in order to consider another aspect of God's character – His love. Three things are told us in Scripture concerning the nature of God. First, 'God is spirit' (John 4:24), which means He has no visible substance. Second, 'God is light' (1 John 1:5), which means no darkness can dwell in Him. In Scripture darkness stands for sin, evil, death, and so on. Third, 'God is love', which means the energy that flows out from His Being is that of infinite, eternal beneficence.

Many of my own generation learned the text 'God is love' during childhood, and we have used it as a slick statement yet without much understanding of its meaning. This is not true of everyone, of course, but I think it is true of most. When John wrote the words 'God is love' he was not repeating a slick statement as it was the first time in history that the declaration had been made. People had believed that God was love, and had speculated about His benevolence, but now the categorical statement is laid down for all to see. These words, in my judgment, are the high-water mark of divine revelation; nothing more needs to be said for nothing greater can be said.

Often I create a mental picture for myself of the angels peering down from heaven as John wrote those words and then, when they had been written, I imagine them breaking into rapturous applause and saying to each other, 'They've got it. They've got it! At last they see that God is love.' And a sigh of deep satisfaction and great joy would have filled the portals of heaven because the greatest truth about God had now been made crystal clear. The implied was now inscribed.

O Father, I am so thankful that You have demonstrated categorically that the greatest thing about You is love. My heart gladly rests upon that glorious fact. And I look forward to exploring it for ever. Amen.

Psalm 136:1–12; Ephesians 3:14–19
1. What is the limit of God's love?
2. What was Paul's prayer for the Ephesians?

Amazing Love! 28 JAN

FOR READING AND MEDITATION – DEUTERONOMY 7:1–10

'The Lord did not… choose you because you were…
numerous… the Lord loved you…' (vv7–8)

When the Bible says God is love, it is saying more than that God loves, or that God is loving, or even that God is lovely; it is saying that love is the energy behind everything He does – love is not merely one of His attributes but is His whole nature. God is not only the Author of loving acts; He is love in the very core of His Being. Sometimes you hear people talking rather sentimentally about the love of God as if it is some kind of amiable weakness, a sort of good-natured indulgence patterned after fallen human emotions. Our thoughts of God's love, however, must be built on God's revelation about Himself in the Scriptures, not by projecting our own ideas about love onto Him. Let's focus, therefore, on what the Bible has to say about the God who is love.

First, God's love is uninfluenced. By that I mean nothing in us can give rise to it and nothing in us can extinguish it. It is 'love for nothing', as someone has described it. The love which we humans have for one another is drawn out of us by something in the object of our love. But God's love is not like that; His love is free, spontaneous, and uncaused. The passage we have read today makes it clear that there is no reason behind the love of God for His people. He loves because He would love. If you look for a reason you just won't find one. He loves because… He loves. He is love.

No man or woman can ever explain why God loves us. To 'explain' it would require that He loves us for something outside of Himself, and, as we have seen, He loves us for ourselves alone. And that love has its beginning, not in us, but in Himself. He is love's source as well as its river.

O God, what security it gives me to know that Your love for me will never be diminished and never be taken away. Help me reflect on this and draw from it the inspiration I need to walk tall and strong through every day. In Jesus' name. Amen.

Romans 5:1–8; Ephesians 2:1–10
1. How do we know God's love is not based on what we do?
2. Why can we love others as God loves them?

What a Tranquilliser! 29 JAN

FOR READING AND MEDITATION – JEREMIAH 31:1-12

'I have loved you with an everlasting love...' (v3)

'How little real love there is for God,' comments Arthur W. Pink, a noted theologian. He suggests that the reason for this, and the resulting low level of spirituality in today's Church, is that our hearts are so little occupied with thoughts of the divine love. He says, 'The better we are acquainted with His love – its character, its fullness, its blessedness – the more will our hearts be drawn out in love to Him.' Yesterday we saw that God's love is uninfluenced and unconditional; now we focus on the fact that it is also eternal.

Since God is eternal, it follows that His love also is eternal. This means that God loved us before earth and heaven were called into existence, that He has set His heart upon us from all eternity. This is the truth proclaimed in Ephesians 1:4-5, where we are told that we were chosen in Christ before the creation of the world. What a tranquilliser this is for our hearts! Can you see what is implied by this? If God's love for you had no beginning then it has no ending either. It is from 'everlasting to everlasting'.

Another thing we need to know about the love of God is that it is a holy love. This means that His love is not regulated by whim or caprice or sentiment, but by principle. Just as His grace reigns not at the expense of righteousness but 'through' it (Rom. 5:21), so His love never conflicts with His holiness. This is why John says that God is light before he says that God is love. And this is why, too, the Almighty never lets us go unchanged. He loves us too much for that. His love is pure, holy, and unmixed with maudlin sentimentality. God will not wink at sin, not even in His own people.

O Father, the more I learn about Your love, the more my heart is set on fire. Increase my understanding, for I see that the more I comprehend how much I am loved, the more secure I am in that love. Amen.

Romans 8:28-39; 1 John 3:1
1. What can separate us from Christ's love?
2. What can we be called?

Love Creating Love

30 JAN

FOR READING AND MEDITATION – 1 JOHN 4:17–21; 5:1–12

'We love because he first loved us.' (4:19)

Even though the love of God is clearly evident in the Old Testament, the apostle John was the first to actually declare 'God is love'. So why did humankind have to wait so long to have the message spelt out in such clear terms? The answer is simple. People could not see this sufficiently clearly until they had looked into the face of Jesus. The life of Jesus is the clearest revelation that God is love.

We referred yesterday to the comment made by Arthur Pink concerning how little real love for God there is in today's Church, and one reason for that, as we saw, is the fact that so few of us open ourselves to the love of God. Thus we have more fear of Him than we have love for Him. There is, of course, a godly fear or reverence, but that is not the kind of fear I am talking about here. If we fail to comprehend how much we are loved by God then we will have no energy to live our lives in the way they are meant to be lived.

Whenever, as a young Christian, I doubted the love of God, I was told I should go to Calvary. I never quite understood what that meant. Then one day I complained to God that He couldn't really love me; if He did, I argued, He wouldn't allow the things that were happening to me. He gave me no answer, but instead He showed me the cross. And as I saw His Son dying there for me, the scales fell from my eyes, and I found love for Him flowing out of His love for me. That day I discovered what the verse at the top of this page means: 'We love because he first loved us.'

Love for God is not the fruit of our efforts but the response of our hearts to being loved. It is not something we manufacture; it is something we receive.

O God my Father, save me from believing my problem is that I don't love You enough, when the real problem is that I don't know how much I am loved by You. Let the scales fall from my eyes right now and let me see – really see. In Jesus' name. Amen.

Luke 7:36–48; 1 Peter 1:8–9
1. Why may some people know more of God's love?
2. What is the result of loving Christ?

The Cross's Magnetism   31 JAN

FOR READING AND MEDITATION – JOHN 12:20–33

'And I, when I am lifted up from the earth,
will draw all people to myself.' (v32)

What does focusing on the fact that God is love do for us as Christians? Yesterday we saw that one thing it does is that it causes our own love to flame in response. The love for God that burns in our hearts must never be thought of as the fruit of our labour, as if it is something we manufacture. Seeing the love God has for us, our own heart responds with love. We give love for love. We cannot help it. Let's be done with the idea that love for God is something we work at. It is expressed in good works, of course, but it begins in contemplation of how much we are loved.

Often I tell people that they cannot love until they have been loved, and they cannot serve until they have been served. By this I mean that love is a response. We love because God first loved us. Our souls must receive love before they can give out love. Those who did not receive much love from their parents may protest and say, 'I can't love God because my soul was never properly prepared to love; my parents didn't love me.' That is a problem, I agree. However, it is not an insoluble problem. No one who stands at Calvary and sees Jesus dying for them on that tree can ever argue that because they were not loved by their parents they cannot now receive God's love. If they really believe that then they are saying that God's love is obstructed by the adverse influences of human conditioning.

God's love will flow into us only if we let it and if we really want it. To desire it is like the touch of the hand on a roller blind; instantly the spring rolls up the blind and the sunlight flows in. Just to want His love is enough; He will do the rest.

O God, forgive me if I have used excuses to barricade my heart against Your love. I gaze once more on Calvary. As I do so may its mighty magnetism draw my soul towards You in a way it has never been drawn before. In Jesus' name. Amen.

John 3:14–17; 1 John 3:11–18
1. How do we know God loves us?
2. How do we know we have received God's love?

The Quality Par Excellence

1 FEB

FOR READING AND MEDITATION – ISAIAH 6:1–13
'Holy, holy, holy is the Lord Almighty…' (v3)

The next aspect of God's character we examine is that of His holiness. Even the most casual reader of the Scriptures cannot help but notice that God is portrayed in the Bible as uniquely and awesomely holy. In fact, there are more references to the holiness of God in Scripture than there are to any other aspect of His character. This ought to give us some indication of how important it is.

But what do we mean when we say God is 'holy'? There are three thoughts underlying the word 'holy'. First, the idea of separation, of being withdrawn or apart. Second, brightness or brilliance. Third, moral majesty, purity and cleanliness. It is interesting that those who came into direct contact with God in the Old Testament were inevitably overwhelmed by His moral majesty.

Isaiah went into the Temple to pray at a time when his people were in grave difficulties. Uzziah, the king who had ruled Judah for half a century, had died, and Assyria, an evil power, menaced from the north. I feel sure that whatever answer Isaiah thought he would get as he opened up his heart to God, it was not the one he received. He was given a vision of a holy God that shook him to the core of his being. Why should this be? I think it was because the reality of God's holiness is one of the main lessons we are taught in His school, the divine prerequisite for understanding what is in the heart of God, the most important qualification for learning from the Lord.

Sadly, we don't hear much about the holiness of God in the modern Church. But, just as it was in ancient times, so today, the fear of the Lord is, as the psalmist so beautifully put it, 'the beginning of wisdom' (Psa. 111:10).

Father, I must search my heart this day and ask myself: Do I really know what it is to serve a holy God? Have I ever received a vision of Your moral majesty and purity? Deepen my understanding of all this, I pray. In Jesus' name. Amen.

Exodus 15:1–13; Revelation 4:5–8
1. What did Moses sing about God's character?
2. What is the prime quality of God, worshipped before the throne?

A Prod Towards Perfection

2 FEB

FOR READING AND MEDITATION – DEUTERONOMY 10:12-22

'What does the Lord your God ask of you
but to fear the Lord your God…?' (v12)

Yesterday we said that holiness is one of the main lessons in God's school and an important qualification for learning from the Lord. The first thing God called Israel to do when He announced that they were to be His special people and live the way He wanted them to live was not to love Him, serve Him, or keep His commandments, but to fear Him. Loving Him, serving Him, and keeping His laws were of great importance, of course, but the very first thing God asks of them is reverence and fear.

How does all this relate to the love of God which, as we saw a few days ago, is the essence of His nature? When thinking about God, it is wise to see love and holiness as intertwined; not to do so can lead sometimes to serious error. Many in today's Church present the love of God in such a way that it has given rise to the saying 'God loves me as I am.' When I have heard people say this and have questioned them, I have found the idea in many minds is this: 'God loves me as I am, and whether I go on from here or I stay the same, it makes no difference to His love for me.' That is entirely true, but it is not the entire truth. Because God is love, He loves us as we are, but because He is love and He is holy, He loves us too much to let us stay as we are. We can be secure in the fact that God loves us just the way we are, but the holy love of God calls us to move ever closer to Him, and cries out, 'Be holy, because I am holy' (Lev. 11:44).

Error, as I have said before, is truth out of balance. We need to rejoice in the fact that we are loved as we are and not for what we do, but we must see also that God's love is a holy love and thus will inevitably prod us towards perfection.

O Father, help me keep these two things in balance. May I not let the security I feel as I rest in Your love turn to smugness and complacency. Show me that though I am 'accepted in the Beloved' that does not mean You don't want me to come closer. Amen.

Romans 6:1-4; 1 Corinthians 6:12-20; 2 Corinthians 6:14-7:1
1. How can we honour God?
2. What are we to perfect?

The Consuming Fire

3 FEB

FOR READING AND MEDITATION – HEBREWS 12:14–29

'Our "God is a consuming fire."' (v29)

Today we continue reflecting on the fact that love and holiness must always be intertwined in our thinking. Listen to how the writer George MacDonald puts it: 'Nothing is inexorable but love… For love loves unto purity. Love has ever in view the absolute loveliness of that which it beholds. Where loveliness is incomplete, and love cannot love its fill of loving, it spends itself to make more lovely, that it may love more; it strives for perfection even that itself may be perfected – not in itself, but in the object. Therefore all that is not beautiful in the beloved, all that comes between and is not of love's kind, must be destroyed. And our God is a consuming fire.' Powerful words.

The reason why God is a consuming fire is so that the things that are not of Him might be entirely consumed, and only that which is eternal remain. The nature of God is so terribly pure that it destroys everything that is not as pure as fire. God desires us to worship Him in 'the beauty of holiness' (1 Chron. 16:29, KJV). This means that He wants the purity in us to match the purity in Him. We cannot arrive at this purity by self-effort, of course, but the more we draw close to Him, the more the fire of His purity will burn out the dross within us.

'It is not that the fire will burn us up if we do not worship,' said George MacDonald, 'but the fire will burn us up until we worship.' And the fire will go on burning within us after everything that is foreign to it has been consumed, no longer with pain and a sense of something unwanted being consumed. God is a consuming fire. He always was, and always will be, world without end.

O God, I long with all my heart that my worship might be all You want it to be. May Your consuming fire burn out all the dross within me until everything that is foreign to Your nature is part of me no more. In Jesus' name I ask it. Amen.

Proverbs 17:3; 1 Corinthians 3:10–15; 1 Peter 1:6–7
1. What will God's fire consume?
2. What will be the result of God's fire?

The Fear of God 4 FEB

FOR READING AND MEDITATION – PROVERBS 8:1–21
'To fear the Lord is to hate evil...' (v13)

Over and over again in Scripture we are taught that because God is uniquely and awesomely holy – pure, separated from sin, and shining in His moral majesty – we are to draw near to Him with godly reverence and fear. The vision of God's holiness had a powerful and profound effect on the Old Testament saints, and it will have a similar effect upon us too.

The fear of the Lord, as we said the other day, is the beginning of wisdom. Contemplation of His character, particularly His holiness, will lead to a reverential fear that prepares the soul for profitable service and activity, just as it did for Isaiah. But what does it mean to 'fear' God? There are times in the Bible when we are told to fear, and times when we are told not to fear. There is a fear that helps and a fear that hinders. How do we know the difference?

The fear that helps is the fear that expresses itself in reverence, veneration, awe, a sense of the grandeur and majesty of God. For instance, in Jeremiah 32:40 we read, 'I will inspire them to fear me, so that they will never turn away from me.' The fear that hinders is described for us in 2 Timothy 1:7: 'For the Spirit God gave us does not make us timid, but gives us power, love, and self-discipline.' The Greek word *deilia*, which is translated 'timid' in this verse, is used of someone who is cowardly and lacking in courage. God is not to blame for attitudes of cowardice or timidity; they come from within our own hearts. Timid people are frightened people, and if you want to explore this thought still further ask yourself: what kinds of things frighten me? If we fear them more than we fear God then we are being ruled by the wrong kind of fear.

O God, I bring all those fears that hinder me to You right now and lay them at Your feet. Help me develop such a reverential fear of You that all other fears are quickly swallowed up. In Jesus' name. Amen.

Deuteronomy 10:12–21; Proverbs 16:6
1. How can we be holy and avoid evil?
2. How is it possible to both love and fear God?

The Power of Holiness   5 FEB

FOR READING AND MEDITATION – PSALM 99:1–9
'Exalt the Lord our God and worship at his footstool; he is holy.' (v5)

'No one can know the true grace of God,' said the great Bible teacher A.W. Tozer, 'who has not first known the fear of God.' He continued, 'Always there was about any manifestation of God something that dismayed the onlookers, that daunted and overawed them, that struck them with a terror more than the natural. I do not believe any lasting good can come from religious activities that are not rooted in this fear. Until we have been gripped by that nameless terror which results when an unholy creature is suddenly confronted by the One who is holiest of all, we are not likely to be much affected by the doctrine of love and grace.'

There was a time when the nature and character of God was a theme constantly preached from Christian pulpits, but not any more. There are exceptions to what I am saying, of course, but generally speaking today's preachers and writers tend to give people what they want rather than what they need. This is why we must stop every time we come across a reference to God's character in the Bible and pause to consider it. The Church of the twenty-first century needs a new vision of God's holiness. No one has done anything mighty for God without this vision. Ezekiel tells us of the 'rims' in his vision that were so high they were 'awesome' (Ezek. 1:18), and Jacob, rising from his sleep, said, 'How awesome is this place!' (Gen. 28:17).

We will be of little use to God unless we know how to tremble before Him, for otherwise our own ideas and feelings of self-sufficiency will soon take over. Have we lost the sense of awe when we come into God's presence which seemed to characterise the saints of the past? I am afraid we have.

O God, I am afraid as I draw near to You, but I draw near because I am afraid. No one can dissolve the fears that hinder me but You. Draw me closer, for in You, and You alone, lies both my salvation and my sanctification. Amen.

Habakkuk 3:2–19
1. What was the prophet's physical response to God's glory?
2. What was his spiritual response?

Our Trustworthy God

6 FEB

FOR READING AND MEDITATION – DEUTERONOMY 7:7–20

> 'He is the faithful God, keeping his covenant
> of love to a thousand generations...' (v9)

We move on now to consider another aspect of God's character – His lasting faithfulness. God is utterly trustworthy in all He says and does, and this is the reality on which everything in the universe depends. In an age when unfaithfulness is so commonplace, how good it is to lift our eyes to the heavens and realise that there we have One who will never let us down, never need to apologise for failing us, and never go back on His Word.

I wonder if someone reading this has just discovered unfaithfulness in a marriage partner or experienced the break-up of a relationship because a person you trusted did not keep their word. It's a sad moment when we are forced to acknowledge the inconsistency of the human heart. But we need to look into our own hearts, too, for none of us can claim to be completely free of the sin of unfaithfulness. We may not have broken our marriage vows or reneged on a contract, but we have been unfaithful to Christ In other ways – to His commission to witness or to use the talents He has given us, perhaps.

How refreshing it is, then, to read today's text and focus our gaze on the One who is faithful at all times and in all things. We may let Him down but He will never let us down. A chorus I learned as a young Christian comes back to me time and time again when I am tempted to doubt the faithfulness of God, and I would like to share it with you:

> *He cannot fail for He is God,*
> *He cannot fail, He pledged His Word,*
> *He cannot fail, He'll see you through,*
> *He cannot fail, He'll answer you.*

Gracious and loving God, what inspiration it brings to my soul to realise that of all the things You can do, the one thing You cannot do is fail. May the reality of this remain with me this day and every day. In Jesus' name. Amen.

Joshua 21:43–45; Psalm 89:1–8
1. What was Joshua's testimony to God's faithfulness?
2. What did the psalmist promise?

Great is Your Faithfulness  7 FEB

FOR READING AND MEDITATION – PSALM 36:1–12

'Your love, Lord, reaches to the heavens,
your faithfulness to the skies.' (v5)

How wonderful it is, as we said yesterday, in an age when unfaithfulness is such a regular feature of life, to focus our gaze on those scriptures that point to the trustworthiness of our God. The one before us today is quite wonderful, but consider also these: 'Who is like you, Lord God Almighty? You, Lord, are mighty, and your faithfulness surrounds you.' (Psa. 89:8); 'Righteousness will be his belt and faithfulness the sash round his waist' (Isa. 11:5); 'If we are faithless, he remains faithful, for he cannot disown himself' (2 Tim. 2:13). As you read or hear God's Word, can't you just feel the energy that flows from the Scriptures buttressing your confidence in Him? For God to be unfaithful would be to act contrary to His nature, and if He ever were (we are only speculating because He could never do so) then He would cease to be God.

Focus again with me on the text at the top of the devotion. We are told God's faithfulness extends to the skies. This is the psalmist's picturesque way of expressing the fact that far above all finite comprehension is the unchanging faithfulness of God. Everything about God is vast and incomparable, including His faithfulness. He never forgets a thing, never makes a mistake, never fails to keep a promise, never falters over a decision, never retracts a statement He has made, and has never breached a contract. Every declaration He has made, every promise He has given, every covenant He has entered into is vouchsafed by His faithful character. This is why Christians all around the world can say with confidence, 'His compassions never fail. They are new every morning; great is your faithfulness' (Lam. 3:22–23).

O God, how great You are – great in power, great in majesty, great in love, great in mercy. But, above all, You are great in faithfulness. How I rejoice in that. Amen.

Lamentations 3:19–32; Hebrews 6:18
1. Why could the depressed prophet find hope?
2. What is impossible for God?

The Need to Know 8 FEB

FOR READING AND MEDITATION – HEBREWS 10:19-31

'Let us hold unswervingly to the hope we profess,
for he who promised is faithful.' (v23)

The Bible is a veritable mine of information on the fact of God's faithfulness. More than 4,000 years ago He said, 'As long as the earth endures, seedtime and harvest, cold and heat, summer and winter, day and night will never cease' (Gen. 8:22). Every year furnishes us with fresh evidence that He has not gone back on His Word.

Genesis 15:13-14 records that God declared to Abraham, 'Know for certain that for four hundred years your descendants will be strangers in a country not their own and that they will be enslaved and ill-treated there. But… afterwards they will come out with great possessions.' Did that happen? Turn to Exodus 12:41 and you read this: 'At the end of the 430 years, to the very day, all the Lord's divisions left Egypt.' The prophet Isaiah predicted that a virgin would conceive and bear a son whose name would be Immanuel (Isa. 7:14). Centuries later the prediction came to pass. In Galatians 4:4 we read, 'But when the set time had fully come, God sent his Son, born of a woman…'

How I wish I had the space to take you right through the pages of Scripture and show you how faithful God has been to His Word. But as you have a Bible you can study it for yourself. Read it, as I said earlier, not merely to discover the principles of godliness, but to know God Himself. It is absolutely imperative that we who live in an age such as this – an age when unfaithfulness is commonplace – should acquaint ourselves with the fact of God's faithfulness. This is the basis of our confidence in Him. And this is why the Bible provides so much evidence of this great and gripping truth. The more of God's truth we pack into our souls, the better equipped we are for the road that lies ahead.

Gracious and loving Father, the more I learn about Your nature, the more I want to know. Just these glimpses I am getting make me eager to know You more intimately. Take me deeper, dear Lord. In Jesus' name. Amen.

Genesis 12:1-3; Mark 1:1-4; Acts 15:12-18
1. What do fulfilled prophecies reveal about God?
2. How has God's faithfulness impacted you?

Standing on the Promises

9 FEB

FOR READING AND MEDITATION – 2 PETER 1:1–11

'He has given us his very great and precious promises...' (v4)

It is one thing to accept the faithfulness of God as a clear biblical truth; it is quite another to act upon it. God has given us many promises, which today's text describes as 'great and precious', but do we actually count on them being fulfilled? Do we expect God to be true to His Word?

Of course, we have to be careful that we do not hold God to promises He has not given. Over the years I have seen the heartache suffered by Christians who have been encouraged to take a statement from the Word of God, turn it into a 'promise', and urged to believe that it would come about. When nothing happened, they became deeply discouraged and disheartened. One woman told me that several years before we met she had taken the words found in Acts 16:31 – 'Believe in the Lord Jesus, and you will be saved – you and your household' – and claimed them as a promise. When her husband and son died unrepentant she was devastated and on the point of giving up her faith. Speaking to her, I pointed out that first, even God cannot save those who don't want to be saved, and second, the promise given by Paul and Silas was for the Philippian jailer, not for anyone else.

There are, nevertheless, literally hundreds of promises God has given us in His Word that we can claim without equivocation. 'Never will I leave you; never will I forsake you' (Heb. 13:5) is just one among many. Someone who has counted all God's promises in the Bible numbers them as being over 3,000. That ought to be enough to keep you going even if you live to be 100. Be careful, however, that it is a general promise you are banking on, not one given for a specific situation.

Father, I have Your promise that You will guide me into all truth, so my trust is in You that You will give me the wisdom to discern between a promise which is general and one that is specific. In Jesus' name. Amen.

Matthew 11:28–30; John 7:37–39; Acts 2:38–39
1. What does Jesus promise to those who come to Him?
2. Why can we believe our sins are forgiven?

He Can't Forget!   10 FEB

FOR READING AND MEDITATION – JOHN 6:25-33

'Jesus answered, "The work of God is this:
to believe in the one he has sent."' (v29)

It is because God is so utterly trustworthy and reliable that the Christian life at heart is a life of trust. In the passage we have read today our Lord is asked, 'What must we do to do the works God requires?' (v28). His answer was entirely different from that which you are likely to receive if you pose the question to adherents of different religious systems these days. A Buddhist might answer, 'We must follow the eightfold path of Buddhism.' A Muslim might explain, 'We must follow the five pillars of Islam.' And the response of some followers of the Christian way might be: 'We must engage in regular Bible study, prayer, tithing, and Christian fellowship.' But the answer Jesus gave was this: 'The work of God is this: to believe...'

George Watson, a devotional writer, said, 'To trust the Origin of our existence is the fundamental grace of life. There is one virtue [in God] that stands out forever more conspicuously than friendship, or love, or knowledge, or wisdom... it is fidelity. *God's fidelity is in Him what trust is in us*' (emphasis mine). The understanding of this glorious truth that God is faithful and utterly trustworthy will deliver us from such incapacitating emotions as worry and fear. When you think about it, to be overwhelmed by the concerns of this life reflects poorly upon the faithfulness of God.

An elderly saint who was dying became concerned that he couldn't remember any of God's promises. His pastor said, 'Do you think that God will forget any of them?' A smile came over the face of the dying Christian as he exclaimed joyfully, 'No, no, He won't.' That, too, is our confidence. He won't forget because, being God, He can't forget.

O God my Father, if fidelity in You is what trust is in us, then help us come to a place where our trust matches Your fidelity. We confess we are not there yet, but we long to arrive. Help us, dear Father. In Jesus' name. Amen.

Deuteronomy 31:1-8; Isaiah 49:14-16
1. What did Moses promise Israel?
2. How did God answer Zion's claim of abandonment?

No Blemish in God

11 FEB

FOR READING AND MEDITATION – DEUTERONOMY 32:36–47

> 'I will take vengeance on my adversaries
> and repay those who hate me.' (v41)

Now we move on to focus on an aspect of God's character which for some reason many see as a flaw or blemish in the divine nature. I refer to the matter of God's wrath. This is a theme about which little is said in today's Church, but though the subject may be missing from many sermons that are preached, it is not missing from the Bible. If you take hold of a Bible concordance and look up all the texts that refer to the wrath, anger, or the severity of God, you will find that there are more references to these than there are to His love, His graciousness, or His tenderness. Indeed, I would go as far as to say that a proper understanding of God can never be complete unless consideration is given to the fact that God is not only a God of love but a God of wrath also.

I remember that in the early days of my Christian experience, whenever I heard a reference to the wrath of God, I would feel a deep resentment arise within me, and instead of regarding this aspect of God's nature as intriguing, I looked upon it with disdain. Later, however, when I came to understand it and saw it in its proper light – as something to rejoice in rather than to be resented – I found my love for God and my awe of God grew to new proportions.

Arthur W. Pink describes the wrath of God in this way: it is the 'eternal detestation of all unrighteousness... the displeasure and indignation of divine equity against evil... the holiness of God stirred into activity against sin.' I urge you never, never to view the wrath of God as a moral blemish or a flaw in His character. Quite the reverse. It would be a blemish if wrath were absent from Him.

Father, may I be willing to face all reality – even those aspects that do not fit in with my preconceived ideas. Help me not to balk at the idea that You are a God of wrath as well as a God of wonder. In Jesus' name I pray. Amen.

2 Chronicles 19:8–10; 32:22–26
1. Why would the Lord's wrath come on people?
2. How did Hezekiah incur and then escape God's wrath?

God's Great Intolerance

12 FEB

FOR READING AND MEDITATION – ISAIAH 5:18-25

'They have rejected the law of the Lord Almighty...
Therefore the Lord's anger burns...' (vv24-25)

We pick up from where we left off yesterday with the thought that wrath is not a defect in the divine character; rather, it would be a defect if wrath were absent from Him. Those who think of God's wrath in terms of a grumpy tantrum or a desire for retaliation – inflicting punishment for the sake of it or in return for some injury received – do not understand it. Divine wrath is not vindictiveness; it is divine perfection, and issues forth from God because it is right.

One of the things we must always be willing to face as human beings is our tendency to make God in our own image. He made us in His image but we want to return the compliment, and it is there that so often we go wrong. Instead of reasoning from the divine down to the human, and recognising that sin has marred the divine image within us, we reason from our fallen condition and project our own feelings and ideas onto God. Thus, when thinking of the wrath of God, we tend to look at what happens in our own hearts when we get angry and imagine God to be the same. Divine anger must never be compared with human anger. What goes on in our hearts when we are angry is generally a mixture of unpredictable petulance, retaliation, hostility, and self-concern. God's anger is always predictable, always constant, and always set against sin.

We must never forget that God's nature is uncompromisingly set against sin. Though we may tolerate it, He never does. Sin has been defined as 'God's one great intolerance', and for that we ought to be eternally grateful. No loving mother or father tolerates anything which may harm their child. As God's children, we ought to rejoice that He will not tolerate anything harmful either.

O Father, what a change comes over me when I realise Your wrath is not so much directed at persons but at the sin that demeans and destroys them. You are not against me for my sin, but for me against my sin. And for that I am deeply grateful. Amen.

2 Kings 22:8-13; Psalm 5:4-6; Zechariah 8:16-17
1. Why did God's anger burn?
2. What does God hate?

Righteous Indignation

13 FEB

FOR READING AND MEDITATION - ROMANS 1:8-25

'The wrath of God is being revealed... against all the godlessness and wickedness of people...' (v18)

The issue we touched on yesterday, namely the danger of looking at what happens in our own hearts when we are angry and then projecting those feelings onto God, is so important that we must spend a little longer discussing it.

For many of us, wrath conjures up the idea of being out of control, an outburst of 'seeing red', a sense of wounded pride, or just a fit of bad temper. It is quite wrong to take these ideas and impose them on God. God's wrath is never out of control, never arbitrary, never self-indulgent, and never ignoble. These things may be true of human anger, but never of the divine. God is angry only when that anger is merited. Even among men and women there is such a thing as righteous indignation, though in my opinion it is more rare than we think. I used to believe the difference between righteous indignation and human hostility was this: when someone was angry with me that was human hostility; when I was angry with someone else that was righteous indignation! That 'opinion' disappeared as I grew more mature, I hasten to add. All God's indignation is righteous. In love, as our Creator, He makes demands of us, and when we refuse to accept His way His wrath is the consequence.

How can a God who is holy condone evil? How can the One who established the moral law remain impassive when that law is broken? Such a thing is impossible. It is precisely this adverse reaction to evil that the Bible has in mind when it talks about God's wrath. God cannot treat good and evil alike. He can look over it - look over it to the cross where it can be forgiven - but He cannot overlook it.

O God, the more I understand the reason for Your wrath, the more I want to praise and adore You. What a great and wonderful God You are. And how glad I am that You have forgiven my sin. Amen.

Deuteronomy 9:1-5; 12:29-31; 18:9-13
1. Why was God angry with the Canaanites?
2. What was God's warning to the Israelites?

The Unyielding Judge

14 FEB

FOR READING AND MEDITATION – MATTHEW 5:21-26

'Settle matters quickly with your adversary
who is taking you to court.' (v25)

'God's wrath,' said George MacDonald, 'is always judicial. It is always the wrath of the judge administering justice. Cruelty is always immoral but true justice never.' Those who experience the effects of God's wrath get precisely what they deserve. That may sound hard, but it is true.

What great wisdom there is in the words of our Lord recorded in today's text. Settle matters with an adversary, He says, before he drags you into court. Do at once what you must inevitably do one day. As there is no escape from payment, at least escape from the prison sentence that will enforce it. The point our Lord is making is that we ought not to drive justice to extremities. Duty is imperative; it must be done. God requires righteousness of us, and if that righteousness is not met it is utterly useless to think we can escape the eternal law. Yield yourself rather than be compelled.

To those whose hearts are right with God, the idea of judgment and punishment is right; to those whose hearts are not right with God, the idea of judgment and punishment is wrong. Many people live under the illusion that it may just be possible to find a way of escaping what is required of us in this world. But there is no such escape. A way to avoid the demands of righteousness, apart from the righteousness which God accounts to us at the cross, would not be moral. When a man or woman accepts that Christ took the punishment for their sins and asks for forgiveness, the whole wealth of heaven is theirs; their debt is cleared. Those who deny that debt exists, or acknowledging it do nothing to avail themselves of the payment made by Christ on the cross, must eventually face an unyielding Judge and an everlasting prison.

O Father, how serious and solemn is all this – but yet how true. Sin must ultimately be punished. I am so grateful that You have shown me that in Christ my debt has been paid, and availing myself of Your offer, I am eternally free. Amen.

Genesis 18:25; Judges 11:27; Romans 2:1-11
1. What is one of God's names?
2. What is the basis of God's judgment?

Heaven or Hell   15 FEB

FOR READING AND MEDITATION – LUKE 16:19–31

'In Hades, where he was in torment, he looked up
and saw Abraham far away...' (v23)

The final state of those who die without availing themselves of the forgiveness God offers them at the cross is eternal banishment from His presence. The Bible calls this 'hell' or 'Hades'. 'There is no heaven with a little hell in it,' said George MacDonald, meaning that the God who is passionately for righteousness and implacably against sin must ensure that the two are finally separated.

However, hell is always something that people choose for themselves. It is a state for which men and women opt. Before hell is experienced as eternal, it is always experienced as something temporary, in the sense that as men and women retreat from the light God shines into their hearts to lead them to Himself, they experience in a small way what they will experience in full when they are banished into 'outer darkness' (Matt. 25:30, KJV).

Dorothy Sayers described hell as 'the enjoyment of one's own way for ever'. In the last analysis hell is the full and final consequence of the choices people have made; as His Word reminds us, God is resolute in not being able to overlook sin.

Most people reading this, I know, are already Christians, but no doubt some are not. Let me urge those of you reading these lines who have never surrendered your life to Christ to do so today. Christ has died to save you from God's punishment. Pray this prayer now.

Father God, I come to You now through Your Son, the Lord Jesus Christ. I repent of my sin, ask for Your forgiveness, and receive Jesus as my Saviour and Lord. Thank You, dear Lord, for hearing my prayer. Amen.

If you prayed this prayer for the first time we would recommend you purchase a copy of the booklet *Every Day with Jesus for New Christians*.

Matthew 5:27–30; Luke 13:1–5; Revelation 20:11–15; 21:27
1. How did Jesus emphasise the importance of avoiding hell?
2. How can we avoid hell?

Love with a 'Stoop'

16 FEB

FOR READING AND MEDITATION – HEBREWS 4:1-16

'Let us then approach God's throne of grace with confidence...' (v16)

Today we start to think about an aspect of God's nature which at first seems so close to love that many regard it as simply a synonym for it. I refer to that facet of God's character which we describe as 'grace'.

Grace, however, is not a synonym for love; it is a characteristic of the Deity which is quite close to love (and mercy) but yet deserves to be seen as different and distinctive. On one occasion I heard an elderly Welsh preacher make this memorable remark: 'Grace is a word with a 'stoop' in it; love reaches out on the same level, but grace always has to stoop to pick one up.' An anonymous writer had a similar thought in mind when he said, 'Grace is love at its loveliest, falling on the unlovable and making it lovely.' But it is to the great Puritan preacher Thomas Goodwin we must turn for the best clarification of the difference between love and grace: 'Grace is more than mercy and love. It superadds to them. It denotes not simply love, but love of a sovereign, transcendently superior One that may do what He will, that may freely choose whether He will love or no. There may be love between equals, and an inferior may love a superior, but love in a Superior, and so superior that He may do what He will, in such a One love is called grace. Grace is attributed to princes; they are said to be 'gracious' to their subjects whereas subjects cannot be gracious to princes.'

Grace, then, is God's kindness conferred upon the undeserving; benevolence granted to those who have no merit; a hand reaching down to those who have fallen into a pit. The Bible tells us to believe that on the throne of the universe there is a God like that.

Loving and gracious God, help me understand more fully what it means to be a recipient of Your grace. And as I start to understand more, may my gratitude to You increase also. In Jesus' name I ask this. Amen.

2 Samuel 9:1-13; 2 Peter 3:18
1. What did Mephibosheth think of himself?
2. What did David think of him?

Amazing!

17 FEB

FOR READING AND MEDITATION – ROMANS 11:1–24

'So too, at the present time there is
a remnant chosen by grace.' (v5)

At present we are thinking about the meaning of grace. Illion T. Jones, a famous Welsh preacher, commented that 'The word 'grace' is unquestionably the most significant single word in the Bible'. I agree.

When we read about grace in Scripture it is interestingly always in connection with those who have a special relationship with God. Nowhere in the Bible is grace mentioned in connection with humanity in general. Some theologians, however, use the term 'common grace' to speak of the natural blessings which God showers upon us all in this life – blessings such as the fruit and crops which the earth produces, special talents, the orderly nature of the universe, and the restraint of evil. In my reading I once came across a writer who said, 'The creation of the universe was an exercise of grace.' I understand that he might have been using the word 'grace' as a synonym for love (a mistake often made by Christian writers). But the grace of which the Bible speaks – which is sometimes termed 'special grace' or 'saving grace' – is reserved for the elect – in other words, those God foreknew would be brought into a special relationship with Himself through His Son, Jesus Christ. This is why we should distinguish 'grace' from 'mercy' or 'goodness', which, as Scripture tells us, is given to all: 'The LORD is good to all; he has compassion on *all* he has made' (Psa. 145:9, emphasis added).

Arthur W. Pink says, 'Grace is the sole source from which flows the goodwill, love and salvation of God into His chosen people.' Grace cannot be bought, earned, deserved, or merited. If it could, it would cease to be grace. Grace flows down as pure charity, falling on the unlovable and making it lovely. Amazing!

Yes, Father, it's truly amazing! That love should stoop down to me – an undeserving and even hell-deserving sinner – in such an exhibition of grace is more than I can comprehend. But I receive it nevertheless. And because of Your grace I am saved. Hallelujah!

John 8:1–11; 1 Peter 5:5
1. How did Jesus show grace to the woman?
2. Who does God give grace to?

Sovereign Grace

18 FEB

FOR READING AND MEDITATION – EPHESIANS 2:1–10

'For it is by grace you have been saved,
through faith... it is the gift of God...' (v8)

We are acknowledging that in order to understand 'grace' we must see it in relation to a Sovereign. As one writer puts it, 'Grace is bound to be sovereign since it cannot by its very nature be subject to compulsion.' That is why we often refer to grace in hymns and prayers as free grace. There is no reason for grace but grace.

The old definition of grace that almost every Christian will know is one that I believe cannot be improved upon: 'Grace is the free unmerited favour of God.' It means that at the heart of all true communion with God there lies this gripping truth: God takes the initiative. He is more inclined towards us than we are towards Him. We cannot earn His affection any more than we can earn a loving mother's affection. We have simply to receive it. Always the initiative is from God. When you originally came to Him you came because He drew you. The very faith by which you believe in Him is not of yourself; it is, as today's text tells us, 'the gift of God'. Nor is it only your salvation that is a free gift. Every step you make on your spiritual pilgrimage is possible simply because of God's grace. This teaching, I know, affronts people these days because they like to feel that they can 'work their passage to heaven', to use the words of one preacher. That is like someone in debt for a million pounds trying to get the one to whom he is indebted to accept his resources of a few pence as being sufficient to clear the debt. Listen again to Paul's words to the Ephesians and let them sink deep into your soul: 'For it is by grace you have been saved, through faith – and this not from yourselves, it is the gift of God.' Grace is a gift. You do not have to achieve, but simply receive.

O Father, once again my heart is moved as I realise it was not my merit but Your mercy, acting in grace, that drew You to me, and me to You. All honour and glory be to Your mighty and everlasting name. Amen.

Romans 3:19–31; Titus 3:3–7
1. What was the purpose of religious laws?
2. What could grace achieve that the law could not?

We've Won a Holiday

19 FEB

FOR READING AND MEDITATION – EPHESIANS 1:1–14

'In him we have… the forgiveness of sins,
in accordance with the riches of God's grace…' (v7)

What is it in the heart of most men and women that causes them to reject the idea of God's free and generous offer of salvation? It is pride. The playwright George Bernard Shaw said, 'Forgiveness is a beggar's refuge. We must pay our debts.' But we cannot pay our debts. As our spiritual predecessors saw so clearly, the only language we can use in the presence of a God who demands so much and whose demands we are unable to meet is this:

> *Just as I am, without one plea*
> *But that Thy blood was shed for me,*
> *And that Thou bidd'st me come to Thee,*
> *O Lamb of God, I come, I come.**

In response to our coming, the free unmerited favour of God flows down to us, cancels our debt, and imparts Christ's righteousness to us. How can Christ's righteousness be imparted to us? It's His righteousness, not ours. A simple illustration may help to explain this point. A little boy came home from school one day and said to his mother, 'We've won a holiday.' The truth was that another boy had come top in the examinations for that region, and the head teacher decided to mark the success by giving the whole school a holiday. Yet the little lad said, 'We've won a holiday.'

Grace is like that. God permits the righteousness of Jesus to cover us and then, as we open ourselves to it – to enter us. He did what was necessary to make us righteous, but we benefit from His work. Isn't grace really amazing?

O Father, as I contemplate still further the 'riches' of Your grace, once again I have to confess it's truly amazing. No wonder men and women use that term to describe Your grace. No other adjective will do! Amen.

Romans 5:1–11, 20–21; Galatians 3:21–25
1. What has Christ given us access to?
2. What have we been released from?

*Charlotte Elliott (1789–1871).

Scan to download today ▸

The God of All Grace — 20 FEB

FOR READING AND MEDITATION – 1 CORINTHIANS 15:1-11

'But by the grace of God I am what I am...' (v10)

Is it any wonder that throughout the history of the Christian Church men and women have found the thought of grace so overwhelmingly wonderful that they have absolutely revelled in it? Grace was the constant theme of their prayers, their preaching, their writings and their hymns. Take, for example, these lines written by Samuel Davies in the eighteenth century:

> *Great God of wonders! all Thy ways*
> *Display the attributes divine;*
> *But countless acts of pardoning grace*
> *Beyond Thine other wonders shine;*
> *Who is a pardoning God like Thee?*
> *Or who has grace so rich and free?*

Many have fought to uphold the truth of God's grace, accepting ridicule and loss of privilege as the price of their stand. Paul waged war against the legalists in the Galatian churches over the matter of 'grace', and the battle to uphold this great truth has gone on ever since. St Augustine fought it in the fourth and fifth centuries, as did the Reformers in the sixteenth century.

There are signs that the Church once again is in danger of losing out to legalism as more and more Christians get caught up with doing rather than being. Talk to people about what they are doing and they are with you at once; talk to them about being – who they really are – and their attitude is one of deferential blankness. The Church of Jesus Christ is in a sad state when it can't say with conviction and meaning, as did the apostle Paul, 'By the grace of God I am what I am.'

God of all grace, give me grace to feel my need of grace. And give me grace to ask for grace. Then give me grace to receive grace. And when grace is given to me, give me grace to use that grace. In Jesus' name I pray. Amen.

Galatians 3:1-14; 5:4
1. Why were the Galatians foolish?
2. How may we fall from grace?

God Knows All   21 FEB

FOR READING AND MEDITATION – EZEKIEL 11:1–15
'I know what is going through your mind.' (v5)

The final aspect of God's nature that we examine together is His knowledge and wisdom. I link these two characteristics together because really it is almost impossible to consider one without considering the other. This is true of many of God's attributes, but it is particularly true of the two we are now about to reflect on.

The difference between knowledge and wisdom has been described like this: 'Knowledge is what we know; wisdom is the right application of what we know.' God, of course, knows everything – everything possible, everything actual. He is perfectly acquainted with every detail in the life of every being in heaven, in earth, and in hell. Daniel said of Him, 'He knows what lies in darkness, and light dwells with him' (Dan. 2:22). Nothing escapes His notice, nothing can be hidden from Him, and nothing can be forgotten by Him. I am aware that many Christians, when referring to their conversion, say that God has forgotten their sins, but strictly speaking that is not so. God never forgets anything. What He promises to do with our sins is to 'remember [them] no more' (Jer. 31:34). There is a great difference between forgetting something and deciding not to remember it.

The realisation which we have that God knows everything ought to strengthen our faith and cause us to bow in adoration before Him. The hymnist put it effectively when he wrote:

> *My knowledge of that life is small,*
> *The eye of faith is dim,*
> *But 'tis enough that Christ knows all*
> *And I shall be with Him.**

O Father, what a comfort it is to realise that You know everything. How glad I am that I have put my trust in You, my Lord and my God. Amen.

Psalm 139:1–6; Isaiah 11:1–3
1. What does God know about us?
2. What would rest on the Messiah?

*Richard Baxter (1615–1691).

Reflection on Perfection

22 FEB

FOR READING AND MEDITATION - PSALM 145:1-20
'They speak of the glorious splendour of your majesty –
and I will meditate on your wonderful works.' (v5)

Yesterday we ended by saying that the fact God knows everything ought to strengthen our faith and cause us to bow in adoration before Him. Yet how little do we reflect on this divine perfection. Those who are rebelling against God hate this aspect of His Being and would do away with it if they could. They wish there might be no Witness to their sin, no Searcher of their hearts, no Judge of their deeds. How solemn are the words of the psalmist recorded in Psalm 90:8: 'You have set our iniquities before you, our secret sins in the light of your presence.'

To the believer, however, the truth of God's omniscience (His infinite knowledge) ought to bring us tremendous comfort and security. In times of perplexity we ought to be like Job and say, 'He knows the way that I take; when he has tested me, I shall come forth as gold' (Job 23:10). Even when things are happening in our lives that are profoundly mysterious to us and quite incomprehensible to those who are around us, we must never lose sight of the fact that 'He knows the way that [we] take'.

Throughout the ages God's people have consoled themselves with the fact that God knows everything about them. The psalmist, when seeking to stir his soul to confidence and hope, reminded himself in the midst of his weakness and weariness that 'He knows how we are formed, he remembers that we are dust' (Psa. 103:14). And Simon Peter's response to the question, 'Do you love me?', after his failure when Jesus was arrested had brought him close to the point of despair, was, 'Lord, you know all things; you know that I love you' (John 21:17).

Father, help me reflect on this fact that You know everything, for I see that the more I understand it the more secure I will feel in my soul. Teach me still more, dear Lord. In Jesus' name. Amen.

Psalm 139:7-16; Jeremiah 17:10
1. Where can we escape God's gaze?
2. What does God search?

The God Who Sees

23 FEB

FOR READING AND MEDITATION – GENESIS 16:1–16

'I have now seen the One who sees me.' (v13)

What matters most – that I know God or that God knows me? In a sense I think it is the latter. For my knowledge of God depends on Him knowing me. He is the One who takes the initiative. Just as the knowledge of His love for me causes the scales to fall from my eyes and turns my soul in His direction, so the realisation of how intimately He knows me does something similar. I am engraved on the palms of His hands (Isa. 49:16). I am never out of His thoughts. He knows me as a friend, and there is not a single moment when His eye is not upon me.

It was this that Hagar discovered when she was feeling utterly bereft and forgotten – that God saw her and knew everything there was to know about her. 'I have now seen the One who sees me,' she said. There is immense comfort in being aware that God knows all about us. I don't think we have quite got hold of this truth in these modern times as it is something that is rarely preached or written about. When I read biographies of the great Christians of the past, I see that they understood this great truth, and some of them even revelled in it.

I have referred before to Dietrich Bonhoeffer, the German pastor who was executed by the Nazis, and how during the days prior to his death the thing that brought him great solace was not so much that he knew God, but that God knew him. The poem he wrote in his prison cell entitled 'Who am I?' ends with the words 'Who am I? O Lord, Thou knowest I am Thine'. Realising how much he was known by God brought him great comfort and consolation. He knew that whatever happened to him, it would not happen without God's knowledge.

Gracious and loving Lord, thank You for reminding me that my knowledge of You depends on Your knowledge of me. Your knowing me stirs my soul to know more of You. You initiate – and gladly I respond. In Jesus' name. Amen.

Exodus 3:7–10; 2 Chronicles 16:9; Psalm 34:15; 139:17–18
1. How does God feel about what He sees?
2. How did the psalmist view God's knowledge of sin?

Fullness – Only in God

24 FEB

FOR READING AND MEDITATION – ROMANS 16:17-27

'To the only wise God be glory
for ever through Jesus Christ!' (v27)

The subject of God's knowledge, as we said earlier, must be linked to His wisdom, and it is this aspect of the divine nature that we consider now. What is the wisdom of which the Bible speaks? It is, as we have already noted, the ability to use knowledge to the best possible ends. And this ability is found in its fullness only in God. God is never other than wise in everything He does.

Knowledge without wisdom would be pathetic – a broken reed. Wisdom without knowledge would be inoperative and quite frightening. God's boundless knowledge and wisdom are perfect in every way, and it is this that makes Him utterly worthy of our trust.

But it must be said that one of the great difficulties we have in the Christian life is in trusting the divine wisdom. We can recognise wisdom only when we see the end to which it is moving. Yet God often calls us to trust Him when we can't see the end that He is pursuing, and at such times we have to ask ourselves: How much do I trust Him?

Once I spoke to a Christian youth group on the subject of God's wisdom, and before I began I asked if someone could offer a definition of the subject we were about to discuss. A young man said, 'God's wisdom is the ability to get us through scrapes and difficulties without getting hurt.' Though I gave the young man full marks for attempting a definition, I had to explain to him that that is not what divine wisdom is all about. God's wisdom is not, and never was, intended to get us through life without being hurt. The goal of divine wisdom, as we said, is to bring about the best possible results, which for us means making us holy. And sometimes pursuing that goal may involve us in considerable pain.

Father, here I am again – at the road less travelled. Help me tread the road ahead knowing that whatever pain You allow me to feel is for my good. I do not welcome it, but I do not run from it either, as long as You stay with me. Amen.

Romans 11:33-36; Colossians 2:2-4
1. Why is faith necessary to follow God?
2. Where is wisdom and knowledge hidden?

God's One Great Goal

25 FEB

FOR READING AND MEDITATION – ROMANS 8:28–39

'For those God foreknew he also predestined
to be conformed to the image of his Son...' (v29)

Those who think that God's wisdom is being directed towards getting them through life free from any personal discomfort or pain have no real understanding of this divine attribute. What is God's great goal in the universe to which His energies are devoted? We discover it in our text for today.

The paraphrase of this verse found in the Living Bible really helps us to grasp its message – a message I find tremendously exciting. This is what it says: 'For from the very beginning God decided that those who came to him—and all along he knew who would—should become like his Son, so that his Son would be the firstborn, with many brothers.' God's great energy and wisdom, working on behalf of all Christians, is directed to making us like His Son Jesus Christ. Of course, this purpose will only be fully realised in the world to come, but while we are here He is pursuing that selfsame purpose nevertheless.

Only when we comprehend this will we be able to understand the purpose that lies behind all our trials and difficulties. Romans 8:28 – 'And we know that all that happens to us is working for our good' (TLB) – must be read in connection with Romans 8:29. Because God is committed to making us like His Son, His wisdom will bring from every trial that comes our way something that will enrich our character and make us more like Jesus Christ. Infinite power is ruled by infinite wisdom. God could deliver us from difficult situations and make our lives comfortable, but in a fallen world that is not the best purpose. Understanding this is crucial if we are to live our lives in the way God desires.

Father, forgive me that so often my goals are the opposite of Yours. Help me to bring my goals in line with Your goals. And please enable me to become more and more like Jesus. Amen.

2 Corinthians 3:13-18; Ephesians 4:21-32
1. How can we become like Christ?
2. What are the marks of a Christ-like person?

Some Extra Practice 26 FEB

FOR READING AND MEDITATION – JAMES 1:1–18
'Consider it pure joy, my brothers and sisters, whenever you face trials of many kinds...' (v2)

The Bible contains countless instances of God's wisdom moving men and women through extremely difficult times to the most wonderful ends.

Take Abraham, for example. Although he is known in Scripture as 'God's friend' (Jas 2:23), he was capable at times of some shabby behaviour. Twice he actually passed his wife, Sarah, off as his sister (Gen. 12:10–20; 20:1–18), and while still childless he submitted to her pressure and fathered a child by Hagar, her maid (Gen. 16:1–16). Then, seeking to avoid Sarah's hysterical recriminations, he allowed her to drive Hagar away from their household (Gen. 21:8–21). Clearly, Abraham was not always a man of strong principle, and there were flaws in his character. But God, in wisdom, dealt with him, and brought him through some great trials until he was changed from a man of the world to a true man of God.

The same wisdom which ordered the course of Abraham's life orders your life and mine today. We should never be taken aback when unexpected things occur. Our first reaction should be not to exclaim in despair, 'Oh no, what's happening now?', but to recognise that no matter how hard the experience, God's power will be there to get us through, and God's wisdom will ensure that the benefit outweighs the cost. I like the almost tongue-in-cheek way in which Jim Packer describes what may be God's point of view when He permits us to go through trials: 'Perhaps He means to strengthen us in patience, good humour, compassion, humility, or meekness by giving us some extra practice in exercising these graces under specially difficult situations.' 'Some extra practice.' How much some of us need that practice.

Father, help me grasp this truth once and for all – the truth that Your wisdom ensures the trials I go through are worth far more than the cost. You are so committed to making me like Jesus. Even when this hurts, deep down may I be grateful. Amen.

Daniel 3:13–27; 1 Peter 1:6–7
1. What did the fire do to the three Jews?
2. What will fiery trials do for us?

Our Only Hope 27 FEB

FOR READING AND MEDITATION – JEREMIAH 9:17–24

'I am the Lord, who exercises kindness,
justice and righteousness on earth…' (v24)

In these last two days, let's look back at what we have said about God's character. We started by recognising that in today's Church we seem more interested in knowing about ourselves than in knowing God. We are more people-centred than God-centred, and we are paying the price in increased anxiety, depression, and a hundred other ills. Quietly we have worked our way through the Scriptures and have seen that the God who is there for us to know is the God who has revealed Himself in many different ways: as powerful, personal, plural, having holy love, a God of wrath, trustworthy, gracious, all-knowing, and all-wise.

It's interesting, isn't it, as today's text shows us, that when the Lord talks about Himself in the Scriptures it is often in terms of His attributes or character traits – kindness, justice, righteousness, and so on. And there is a clear and definite purpose in this: the more we know of God, the more established our lives will be here on earth. There is nothing more important, in my view, than gaining knowledge of God through contemplation of Him. And this knowledge is not mere intellectual knowledge. The knowledge of God that is acquired through contemplation of Him gives us the ability to see life from His perspective, through His eyes. When we know God we can look at life's circumstances through the lens of faith, bearing in mind His plan. We find it possible to accept that whatever is happening is allowed by God, and that everything comes under His personal surveillance. That kind of understanding of God and awareness of God is our only hope for coping with the problems of the twenty-first century.

Father, I am convinced. I see that when my knowledge of You has increased I can look at life through Your eyes. May I not just glance at You occasionally but gaze on You continually. Amen.

Psalm 46:10–11; Philippians 3:2–11
1. What was Paul's desire?
2. How can we know God more?

The Truth in a Nutshell   28 FEB

FOR READING AND MEDITATION - DANIEL 11:14-35

'The people who know their God will firmly resist him.' (v32)

What are the benefits of keeping our gaze continually focused on God? There are at least three. First, the more we discover about Him, the more we will want to become like Him. The most natural thing in the world when there is a good relationship between parents and their child is for that child to want to become like them. That is the way it is also with God our Father. The more we discover of His love, His holiness, His purity, His trustworthiness, His strength, His patience, the more we want to emulate Him.

Second, the more we study God, the better we will know ourselves. When Isaiah entered the Temple and was given a vision of God, he not only saw the glory of God, he also perceived the truth about himself. Things that were hidden deep within him came to light in the presence of the Eternal One. Third, the better we come to know God, the clearer will be our perspective on the world. When we understand that God is in charge we won't panic every time we open the newspaper or watch the news. We won't give up hope because of such evils as terrorism, earthquakes, disease, or murders. Naturally we will be saddened by these events, but we will not be devastated by them. We can only know God, of course, through Jesus Christ. But once we do know Him, instead of saying, 'Look what the world has come to,' we will be able to say, 'Look what has come to the world.'

The people who know their God will firmly resist the adversary, says Daniel. The Amplified Bible puts it well: 'The people who are spiritually mature and know their God will display strength and take action [to resist].' I can do no more than to say – there you have it in a nutshell: The more you know God, the stronger you will be.

My Father and my God, with Your truth as my compass, and Your Word as my chart, I now embark on this great adventure – getting to know You better. Please guide me day by day, I pray. In Jesus' name. Amen.

Job 19:25-27; 2 Timothy 1:1-12
1. Why did Job not fear death?
2. Why was Paul not devastated by suffering?

PRAY IT FORWARD ▶▶▶

Lord, thank You that You are faithful, gracious, and unchanging. As I grow in knowing who You are, help me to reflect Your character in my words and actions today. Shape me to be a living witness to Your goodness. Amen.

PAY IT FORWARD ▶▶▶

At Waverley Abbey, we long to help people discover the true character of God in their own lives through teaching, counselling, and resources that draw them closer to Him. Your gift makes this possible. **Will you help us continue to reveal His love and truth to others?**

Visit **waverleyabbey.org/donate-to-edwj** call **01252 784700** or scan the **QR code** ▶

MARCH & APRIL

EAT, PRAY, SHARE

INTRODUCTION

What do you call it in your church? 'The Sacrament', 'The Lord's Supper', 'The Lord's Table', 'The Eucharist', 'The Breaking of Bread'?

In these notes, Selwyn invites us to meditate on the Easter story, with a special focus on the service of Holy Communion. Recall or discover for the first time the deep significance of gathering as Christians to commemorate Jesus' sacrifice for us. In particular, we will explore: what we are remembering; the call to humility; the importance of being together; a continuous festival.

Let's allow the wonder of God's love to lead us to renewed thankfulness and commitment.

An Urgent Need   1 MAR

FOR READING AND MEDITATION – 1 CORINTHIANS 10:14–22
'You cannot have a part in both the Lord's table
and the table of demons.' (v21)

Our topic, 'Eat, Pray, Share', is one that I hope will draw us in thought and spirit towards the great sacrifice which Jesus made for us on the cross of Calvary. We will be considering the Communion table, a central feature of most Christian churches, at which is celebrated the event variously described as 'The Sacrament', 'Holy Communion', 'The Lord's Supper', 'The Lord's Table', 'The Eucharist', or 'The Breaking of Bread'.

Almost every Christian participates from time to time in a service of Communion, but how many of us, I wonder, understand the rich significance that lies behind the simple act of taking and sharing the bread and drinking the wine? Over the years I have inquired of many people of all denominations as to how they understand the act of 'Holy Communion' and, generally speaking, I have discovered only a superficial understanding. Why is it that an event which was intended by Jesus to be a source of continuous spiritual enrichment is, for many, nothing more than a ritual? *I am convinced myself that one of the most urgent needs of the contemporary Christian Church is to return meaning to the Communion.*

When we fail to appreciate the meaning of this deeply significant act, then our meeting together around the 'Lord's Table' will have little impact on our lives – individually or corporately. I believe that those who see it as nothing more than a sentimental forget-me-not service will, as a result, be spiritually poorer. Those who see it for what it is – a service of deep spiritual significance – will be continually enriched, enlightened, and satisfied.

My Father and my God, help me to see, as I begin these meditations, that whatever table I sit at, none is more sacred and special than Your table. Reveal to me more clearly than ever before its meaning and its purpose. In Christ's name I pray. Amen.

Luke 24:28–35; 1 Corinthians 11:23–32
1. When did the disciples recognise Jesus?
2. Why might some be weak?

The Law of First Occurrence

2 MAR

FOR READING AND MEDITATION – MATTHEW 26:17–30

'While they were eating, Jesus took bread, and when he had given thanks, he broke it and gave it to his disciples…' (v26)

Today we ask ourselves: if the Christian Church is greatly in need of returning meaning to the Communion, where do we start? There is a law of biblical interpretation known as 'the law of first occurrence' which states that whenever you wish to understand a truth of Scripture, you should examine in detail the first occasion when that truth is mentioned.

If we are to understand the deep meaning that lies in the commemorative act of Holy Communion, then our first task must be to focus our attention on the very first Communion service in history – the one conducted by Jesus that famous night in the Upper Room. When a jeweller wants to show off a diamond to its best advantage, he often puts it on a background of black velvet. There, as natural or artificial light strikes it, the diamond catches fire, whereupon its beauty and brilliance are greatly magnified and its value made more apparent.

The Lord's Supper is like that diamond. It needs to be prised from its traditional setting, where, by reason of endless controversy, it borders on becoming lack-lustre, and set against the velvet of the blackest night in history – the night before Jesus was crucified. It is only there, in its original setting, with the light of the Holy Spirit falling upon it, that it yields its true and proper meaning. And I say again – if we do not understand what happened at that very first Communion service, then we will not be able to understand what it means for us now – here in the twenty-first century.

O God, thank You that it is Your Holy Spirit who illuminates the truth. As a diamond catches the light, help me to understand the brilliance of the act of Holy Communion. Amen.

Luke 22:39–53
1. Identify Jesus' emotions on that night.
2. How did Jesus shine in the dark?

The Christ of the Unexpected   3 MAR

FOR READING AND MEDITATION – JOHN 2:13–25; 6:1–14

'At the Passover Festival, many people saw the signs
he was performing and believed in his name.' (2:23)

Before we begin a detailed examination of the first Communion service in history (which, as you know, was also Jesus' last collective event with His disciples), we refer briefly to the event that led to the institution of what we now call 'Holy Communion' – namely, the feast of the Passover. More will be said about this later, but the feast of the Passover was the annual celebration of the night when God passed over the land of Egypt and spared the firstborn of the children of Israel. It is still celebrated by many Jews today.

It is probable that Jesus and His disciples had shared together in the ceremony of the Passover on previous occasions, but we cannot be certain. According to John, we know, however, that the disciples had been with Him on two previous Passover festivals, and on both these occasions, something unexpected and unusual had taken place. On the first occasion, Jesus entered the Temple and in an act of righteous indignation, proceeded to empty it of the money changers who, He said, had turned His Father's house into 'a den of robbers' (Luke 19:46). On the second occasion, He performed the miracle of the feeding of the 5,000 (John 6:1–14).

I wonder, as once again the Passover approached, did the disciples think to themselves: what surprises will the Master have for us on this occasion? Will He once again do the unexpected and the unusual? It is only conjecture, of course, but if this thought did arise in their minds, they could have had no idea that they were about to be witnesses at the most central Passover of all time, and be observers of an event that would change the entire course of history.

O Father, help me never to forget that You are the God of the unusual and the unexpected. Show me that when I follow You and Your Son, there are surprises around every corner. Thank You, dear Father. Amen.

Deuteronomy 16:1–8; Luke 2:41–51
1. Why and how was Passover to be celebrated?
2. How did Jesus surprise people at Passover?

Believing the Master's Word

4 MAR

FOR READING AND MEDITATION – LUKE 22:7–13

'They left and found things just as Jesus had told them.' (v13)

If, as we said yesterday, the disciples were wondering whether Jesus might once again perform the unusual and unexpected at the Passover feast, we can see from our passage today that they were not left wondering for long. At the beginning of the Passover, the Master issues them with a set of very unusual and unexpected instructions. 'Go into the city', He tells them, 'and you will see a man carrying a pitcher of water; follow him and he will take you to a room where we will celebrate the Passover together.'

There can be little doubt that the knowledge Jesus had concerning the man and the room was supernatural, but there is another point to be noted here: that is, the complete and utter confidence the disciples had in the word and command of Jesus. No one remonstrated with Him and said, 'But, Master, men don't usually carry pitchers of water – that is normally a task that women perform.' Neither did they say, 'Lord, what will this man think of us when we attempt to follow him?' The disciples had obviously learned to trust the word of Jesus and to act without questioning His commands.

That is a lesson every one of us sorely needs to learn. How often things go wrong in our lives because we quibble over Jesus' words. I wonder, am I talking to someone at this very moment who is hesitating or drawing back from something the Master has shown you that He wants you to do? If so, then let me give you the word that Mary, Jesus' mother, once gave to a group of interested but hesitant people: 'Do whatever he tells you' (John 2:5).

O Father, how expertly You put Your finger on my need. I am often afraid to do what You ask me to do – afraid that it might not be in my best interests or that I might make a fool of myself. Help me see how foolish that is. Amen.

John 2:1–11; Hebrews 11:8–10,17–19
1. What was the result of obeying Jesus?
2. How are faith and obedience related?

The 'Pass-Over'

5 MAR

FOR READING AND MEDITATION – EXODUS 12:1–13

'The blood will be a sign for you... and when
I see the blood, I will pass over you.' (v13)

If we are to comprehend the real meaning of the Communion, then we must begin to understand what the feast of the Passover was all about, for it was out of that that the first Communion service emerged. During the time of Israel's bondage and slavery in Egypt, God spoke to Pharaoh through Moses and warned him that on a certain day, at the hour of midnight, He was going to pass through the land and strike down every firstborn. There was to be no discrimination between human beings and animals, or between different social classes – every firstborn would die.

God then devised a plan whereby the firstborn of His own people, the Israelites, would be protected. Each Israelite was to choose a lamb (a year-old male without defect) and kill it. They were then to take some of the lamb's blood, dip a branch of hyssop in it and sprinkle it on the lintel and side posts of their front door. They were not to go out of the house at all that night. Having shed and sprinkled the blood, they must shelter under it. At midnight God passed through the land, and in every house which did not have a blood-sprinkled door, the firstborn died. The God who passed *through* Egypt in judgment passed *over* every blood-marked dwelling place – hence the term, 'Pass-over'.

It is worth noting – if rubies or some other precious stones had gleamed like red flames from every door, it would not have saved the firstborn of the children of Israel. God had decreed that it was only by the shedding of blood that they were to be saved. If the Israelites had stumbled here, they would never have made it to this point in history.

My Father, I realise that this question of redemption by blood is of vital importance, even for us today. Help me to grasp the immensity of the sacrifice Jesus made in shedding His blood that I might be redeemed. For His name's sake. Amen.

Leviticus 4:27–35; 17:11; 1 Peter 1:18–21
1. What is special about blood?
2. What is special about Christ's blood?

The Meaning of Passover

6 MAR

FOR READING AND MEDITATION – EXODUS 12:14-28

'This is a day you are to commemorate; for the generations to come... celebrate it as a festival to the Lord...' (v14)

As an understanding of the feast of the Passover is a vital key to comprehending the meaning that lies behind the act of 'Holy Communion', we must spend another day exploring it further. On Passover night itself, the Israelites were bidden to feast on a roasted lamb, with bitter herbs and unleavened bread, and they were to do so with their cloak tucked into their belt, their sandals on their feet and their staff in their hand, ready to make a quick departure from the land of slavery.

The night of the Passover was so important that it marked the beginning of a new year for Israel – 'This month is to be... the first month of your year' (12:2). From that day to this, the Jewish religious new year begins with *Pesach* – the Hebrew word for 'Passover'. God gave the Israelites an instruction that this feast should be commemorated throughout the generations to come, and families should explain to their children what the whole ceremony meant: 'It is the Passover sacrifice to the Lord, who passed over the houses of the Israelites in Egypt and spared our homes when he struck down the Egyptians' (v27).

This celebration was to last seven days and was known as the Feast of Unleavened Bread, during which time the Israelites were to remind themselves that their deliverance from Egypt's bondage had been planned by Jehovah, purchased by blood, and implemented by divine power. Being a redeemed people, this meant that they belonged to the Almighty in a special way and were therefore to be consecrated to His service and be an illustration to the world of what redeemed people should be like.

Father, the implications of all this go deep into my soul as I reflect on whether I am an illustration to the world of what a redeemed person should be like. I take a step closer to You today. Make me what I ought to be. In Jesus' name. Amen.

Exodus 13:1-16; 2 Chronicles 30:21-27
1. How was Passover to be a 'passing on'?
2. How did the Israelites experience a double blessing?

The Passover Table

7 MAR

FOR READING AND MEDITATION – MARK 14:12–16

'So they prepared the Passover.' (v16)

Having seen what the feast of the Passover means and why it was to be celebrated annually, we return now to the details of the last Passover feast which Jesus commemorated with His disciples. Upon finding the room in which the Master purposed to celebrate the Passover, the disciples began at once to make the preparations for the feast.

Although every one of the four Gospels contains an account of the Last Supper, we are not given any details as to how the feast was prepared and what items were placed on the Passover table. We know from the instructions given by God in the Old Testament and tradition that certain items would be laid out on the table. There would have been a supply of bitter herbs – a reminder of the suffering that their forefathers went through in Egypt. Another item would have been a bowl of salt water to remind them of the tears that were shed during the years of bondage and slavery. A further item would have been grated apple mixed with nuts and made into a paste (called *charoseth*) which would resemble the colour of clay and thus remind them of the endless amount of bricks that were made in Egypt.

Yet another item would have been unleavened bread, the absence of yeast symbolising the haste of that unforgettable night and also the need to break with the leaven of evil. On the table, too, would have been an egg symbolising new life, candles to remind them of the worship that went on in the tabernacle, wine to symbolise the shedding of blood, and last but not least – a roasted lamb. All this had a supreme and important purpose – the event must be kept alive in the memory of Israel. For great events ought never to be forgotten.

Lord Jesus, help me see the value of keeping alive in my memory the great Passover act that You accomplished for me on Calvary. May the wonder of it reverberate within my being yet again this day. In Your dear name I ask it. Amen.

2 Chronicles 35:1–19; 1 Corinthians 5:6–8
1. What was special about Josiah?
2. How is Christ linked to Passover?

A Seeming Contradiction

8 MAR

FOR READING AND MEDITATION – PSALM 19:7–14

'The law of the Lord is perfect, refreshing the soul.
The statutes of the Lord are trustworthy...' (v7)

Before looking in detail at the Passover which Jesus shared with His disciples, we must pause to deal with a relevant but sometimes controversial issue. I refer to the fact that at first glance, there appears to be a contradiction in Scripture as to the actual date of that Passover. The difficulty can be seen when we compare two separate passages of Scripture, the first in Luke 22:15 and the second in John 18:28. The first reads, 'And he said to them, "I have eagerly desired to eat this Passover with you before I suffer."' The second says, 'Then the Jewish leaders took Jesus from Caiaphas to the palace of the Roman governor. By now it was early morning, and to avoid ceremonial uncleanness they did not enter the palace, because they wanted to be able to eat the Passover.'

The first passage shows Jesus eating the Passover with His disciples on Thursday, while the second shows the priests, early the next morning, refusing to go into the palace because the Passover had not yet been celebrated. Does that mean (as many have supposed) that what Jesus celebrated with His disciples was not the Passover but a simple family meal? No, for Jesus says, quite clearly, 'I have eagerly desired to eat *this* Passover with you...'

Tomorrow we will explore further these two passages, but it is important to keep in mind that God's Word is without contradiction. Some passages of the Bible may look, at first glance, to be contradictory, but we must remember that we may not have the key that reconciles the two apparently contradictory passages. The inspired Scriptures can be relied on, and we can ask God to help us gain deeper understanding.

Gracious and loving heavenly Father, help me to have confidence in Your Word, for I know that You are trustworthy. Give me a heart that longs to know more of Your truth, and guide me as I explore further. Amen.

Psalm 119:97–104; 2 Timothy 3:14–17; 2 Peter 1:16–21
1. What was the psalmist's testimony?
2. What is the origin of Scripture?

A Suggested Reconciliation

9 MAR

FOR READING AND MEDITATION – 1 CORINTHIANS 5:1–8
'For Christ, our Passover lamb, has been sacrificed.' (v7)

We continue looking at the two apparently contradictory passages which we brought up in our discussion yesterday. There have been many attempts to harmonise these passages, one view being that Jesus, anticipating the fact that He would die on the night the Passover would be celebrated (Friday) decided to celebrate it one day earlier with His disciples. Another view says that as John's statement contradicts the other three Gospel writers, he was obviously mistaken in what he wrote. Those who believe in the inspiration of Scripture (as I do) find these explanations unacceptable.

The best reconciliation I have read is that offered by Joachim Jeremias in his book, *The Eucharistic Words of Jesus*, in which he says that it was possible for the Passover to be eaten *officially* on two nights of the year. He claims that during this period of history, the Pharisees and Sadducees were using calendars which differed from each other by a day. One group celebrated it a day earlier than the other, and in the light of this, it was possible for Jesus to eat the Passover with those who followed the Pharisees (Thursday) and go to the cross on Friday at the time that the other group were beginning their Passover celebrations.

If this was so, then it adds a rich and wondrous meaning to the words of our text today: 'For Christ, our Passover lamb, has been sacrificed.' It would mean that Jesus actually died on the cross at the very time the ritualistic lambs were being slaughtered by the Sadducees at the Temple in Jerusalem.

O Father, help me to see that for every contradiction, there is a reconciliation. Teach me how to look for this reconciliation, not only in Your Word but in the seeming contradictions of my daily life. For Jesus' sake. Amen.

Isaiah 53:1–12; John 1:29–34
1. Why is Jesus likened to a lamb?
2. Why did Jesus endure suffering?

Great Enough to be Humble

10 MAR

FOR READING AND MEDITATION – JOHN 13:1–17

'He poured water into a basin and began to wash his disciples' feet...' (v5)

We move on now to focus our attention on the interesting and dramatic events that went on in the Upper Room in Jerusalem where Jesus observed the Passover feast with His disciples. Picture the scene with me. It is dusk, and Jesus and His disciples are reclining around a low table in an atmosphere that is heavy with unborn events. Outside a storm is brewing that will eventually engulf the Son of God and sweep Him towards the cross. Jesus had already seen the sun set for the last time. In less than eighteen hours, His limbs would be stretched on what one writer calls those 'grisly timbers of torture'; within twenty-four hours, He would be dead.

Evidently no servant was in attendance to wash the feet of those present – a usual courtesy of the day – so Jesus rises from the table, strips off His outer clothing and, taking a towel and a bowl of water, proceeds to wash the disciples' feet. We said earlier that the disciples would face many surprises at this last crucial Passover. This was another – in the form of the Saviour who stooped to wash their feet.

Isn't it interesting that *none* of the disciples volunteered for that lowly task? They were so unsure of themselves that they dared not be humble – such an action might have caused them to lose their frail sense of identity. Jesus, on the other hand, had such a clear sense of identity – knowing that He had come from God and was going to God – that He could choose to be humble. How sad that the disciples were willing to fight over a throne, but not over a towel. Things don't seem to have changed much in twenty-one centuries, do they?

Gracious and loving Father, forgive me that I too am more interested in a throne than a towel; more concerned about status than I am about serving. O Father, help me become more like Jesus. For His own dear name's sake. Amen.

Mark 10:35–45; Philippians 2:1–11
1. Contrast Jesus and the disciples.
2. How can we show the same attitude as Jesus?

Humility – a Choice

11 MAR

FOR READING AND MEDITATION – MATTHEW 20:17-28

'The Son of Man did not come to be served, but to serve,
and to give his life as a ransom for many.' (v28)

We said yesterday that Jesus was so conscious of greatness that He could afford to be humble. What does this really mean? Consider once again the account given by the apostle John: 'Jesus knew that the Father had put all things under his power, and that he had come from God and was returning to God; so he got up from the meal, took off his outer clothing, and wrapped a towel round his waist... he poured water into a basin and began to wash his disciples' feet' (John 13:3-5).

Notice how John, under the inspiration of the Holy Spirit, sees right into the mind of Jesus before He stoops down to wash the disciples' feet. And what does he see? He sees Jesus' consciousness of His own greatness – 'Jesus knew... that he had come from God and was returning to God...' The consciousness of greatness is the secret of humility. Those who do not have a high sense of their worth and value in God can never, in the true sense of the word, be humble. Their 'humility' borders more on self-belittlement. They do not *choose* to be humble, for more often than not, they are forced into situations which they can do very little about except say to themselves, 'Well, now that I am here, I will be humble.'

Humility is always a choice – a choice which arises out of a high sense of one's worth and value. Look at this phrase: 'Jesus knew that the Father had put all things under his power...' Everything was under His power! And what did He do with that power? He used it to take a towel, pour water into a bowl, and wash the disciples' feet. Knowing who He was made Him great – and humble. Great because humble, and humble because great.

O Father, if it is true that the consciousness of greatness is the secret of humility, then give me a vision today, not only of Your greatness, but of my greatness also – my greatness in You. In Christ's name I pray. Amen.

Luke 22:24-30; Galatians 5:13-14
1. How did Jesus describe His role?
2. Why should we serve others?

No, Not My Feet!

12 MAR

FOR READING AND MEDITATION – 1 PETER 5:1-11

'Clothe (apron) yourselves, all of you, with humility
[as the garb of a servant...]' (v5, AMPC)

We spend another day looking at that moving moment when Jesus began washing the disciples' feet. I can imagine that by the time Jesus got to Simon Peter, the arguing and small talk that had been going on among the disciples would have diminished. No doubt they began to realise how slow and insensitive they had been not to take the servant's role themselves. But as Jesus bends before Peter, the disciple almost shouts, 'No! Not my feet! You shall never wash my feet.'

Is that what humility is – refusing to let Jesus wash one's feet? Of course not. In fact, it sometimes takes more humility to be ministered to than it does to minister. You see, when we are always giving out to others, it is fairly easy to cover up our pride, but when we are put on the receiving end and others are ministering to us, then our pride has nowhere to hide. Jesus said some strong words to Peter at this point: 'Unless I wash you, you have no part with me' (John 13:8). This firm statement penetrated Peter's defences, but rather than face his pride, he found another way out – the way of over-reaction: 'Then, Lord... not just my feet but my hands and my head as well!' (v9).

After Jesus had brought about some balance in Peter's life and had finished washing the disciples' feet, He sat back at the table and gave them this instruction, 'Now that I, your Lord and Teacher, have washed your feet, you also should wash one another's feet' (v14). Notice the words – 'one another's feet'. Had He said, 'You should wash my feet', every disciple would have clamoured for the privilege. Who wouldn't stand in line to wash the Saviour's feet? But 'one another's feet' – ah, that's different. That puts obedience to its maximum test.

Lord Jesus Christ, You who stooped to wash the disciples' feet, put in my heart this very day that same spirit of humility and love. Make of me what You can, dear Lord. For Your own dear name's sake. Amen.

Colossians 3:22-24; 1 John 3:16-18
1. How should we serve others?
2. What is true love?

Judas the Betrayer

13 MAR

FOR READING AND MEDITATION – JOHN 13:18–30

'As soon as Judas had taken the bread,
he went out. And it was night.' (v30)

We look now at another scene from the great drama that was enacted in the Upper Room on that first Maundy Thursday – Jesus' confrontation with Judas. It must have come as a great surprise to Judas when the Master made the announcement that there was someone present who was about to betray Him. E.F. Kevan says, 'It was the custom at the Passover feast for the presiding father, if there was an especially honoured guest, to break off a large piece of bread and give it to him first. It was that large piece that Jesus gave to Judas.'

As soon as Judas received the bread from Jesus' hand, we read that 'Satan entered into him'. He then went out to put into action his plan of betrayal and the Scripture cryptically says, 'And it was night.' Night in Jerusalem, and night in his soul! How it must have hurt Jesus to have been betrayed by one of His own disciples. In this hard and cruel world, people expect to be shot at by their enemies, but no one, except a cynic, expects to be shot at by his friends.

Did you know that the origin of the superstition concerning the number thirteen stems from this scene in the Gospels? Thirteen sat down at the Last Supper, and one of them was a traitor. Superstitious people have dreaded the number thirteen ever since. Have you ever been betrayed? It's not easy to remain unembittered when someone who has stood at your side and claimed to be your friend lets you down. Jesus, despite the pain that the knowledge of Judas' betrayal caused Him, did not allow it to deter Him from ministering to the other disciples. Nor, too, must we.

Lord Jesus, I am thankful that You make it possible for me to go on even when I am in pain. And whenever I am next let down, help me to drink deeply of Your own determination – and keep on ministering to others. For Your name's sake. Amen.

Psalm 41:1–13; Hebrews 12:14–15

1. Identify the psalmist's emotions.
2. How can we remain unembittered?

Accountant Turned Embezzler   14 MAR

FOR READING AND MEDITATION – 1 TIMOTHY 6:3–19
'For the love of money is a root of all kinds of evil.' (v10)

Today we ask ourselves: who was Judas Iscariot and how do we explain his involvement in the betrayal of Jesus? It is believed by most Bible commentators that Judas was a Judean, and if this was true, then he would have been the only member of the apostolic band who was a southerner. Observe that, for it is not unimportant. Eleven of Christ's disciples were Galileans and only one came from the south. This would have meant that not only did Judas speak with a different accent, but also his views and outlook on things would have been quite different from the rest of the group. This might have put him a little bit on his own from the start. I am saying this, I hasten to add, not to excuse him, but to explain him.

It seems also that he was a man with a commercial mind, for he was appointed to be the treasurer of the party – the 'keeper of the money bag' (John 12:6). The little company, as it moved from place to place, needed someone to handle simple purchases, and as Judas possessed some business acumen, he was the one chosen for the task. But Judas was not just a man with a business mind: he was also a man with a covetous heart. We are told that he had been dipping into the money bag for a long time before he took the traitorous step of betraying Jesus.

With some natures, there is nothing so holy that money cannot besmirch it. Watch money – it is so terribly useful and yet so terribly dangerous. What is dangerous is not the money itself, but the way in which it can tempt us to become attached to it. When money becomes our god, then a susceptible personality is the price we pay for the worship of that god.

Gracious and loving heavenly Father, show me how to cut out of my nature that 'root of all kinds of evil' – the love of money. I want money to be my servant, not my master. Help me, dear Lord, in this quest. For Jesus' sake I pray. Amen.

Matthew 6:19–34; John 12:1–6
1. How can money be our master?
2. Describe Judas' character.

A Free Agent

15 MAR

FOR READING AND MEDITATION – PSALM 41:1–13

'Even my close friend, someone I trusted… has turned against me.' (v9)

We spend one more day discussing Judas and his involvement in the betrayal of Jesus. Some Christian writers have expressed great sympathy for Judas. They feel he had an unfair deal in his life and has suffered from a bad press ever since. 'After all,' they say, 'if Jesus had to die, somebody had to betray Him. So why blame Judas? He was but the tool of providence, the victim of predestination.'

The Bible certainly indicates that Jesus foreknew that He would be betrayed by him (see John 6:64), but foreknowledge is not the same thing as foreordination. I know the sun will rise tomorrow, but my knowing it does not make it rise. The foreknowledge that Jesus had concerning Judas did not compel him to act the way he did – he was a free agent in it all. Judas got involved in the act of betrayal by following the same method that every one of us follows when we commit sin – first we are tempted, then, instead of showing it the door, we bring it into our living room and entertain it. After that, the temptation is more difficult to resist and then it is just a step downward into sin.

However strong the various influences were around Judas, there must have been a time when he opened himself to them. Jesus clearly regarded him as a responsible agent, for even at the last minute in the Upper Room, He carefully worded His statement so that Judas had an opportunity to recant. So underhand was this action of Judas that throughout history, whenever Maundy Thursday comes around, the first thing that comes into our mind is this – it was the night on which our Saviour was betrayed.

Father, I ask one thing, not that I shall be preserved from being betrayed, but that I shall be preserved from betraying others. And above all – from betraying You. Make me a person who is not only trusting, but trustworthy. In Jesus' name. Amen.

1 Corinthians 10:1–13; James 1:12–15

1. What is our consolation when tempted?
2. Outline the process of temptation?

The Order of Service

16 MAR

FOR READING AND MEDITATION – EXODUS 13:1–10

'You must keep this ordinance at the appointed time year after year.' (v10)

We turn now from looking at some of the personalities who were present in the Upper Room when Jesus conducted the first Communion service to focus on the Master Himself. I wonder how Jesus felt as He realised that He was setting up His own memorial service? What were the things He emphasised as He celebrated this Passover of all Passovers? Where was the transition point when the Passover feast took on the nature of a new commemorative act? These are some of the questions we will come to grips with – but first let's reflect together on the way in which the Passover meal was conducted.

None of the four Gospel writers give exact and detailed accounts of the traditions that they followed during a Passover meal – they focused more on the highlights of that memorable evening – so we have to depend on sources outside of Scripture for information concerning this. I am drawing therefore on the writings of Jewish authors and the practice of many Jews today, as I describe to you the tradition of a Passover celebration.

Just after dusk on the night of the Passover, a Jewish family gather around a table on which has been laid out the various items I described for you a few days ago. The meal begins with the father holding up the first of the four cups that are on the table and praying over it, then all drink from it. This is called the 'Cup of Kiddush', meaning separation or sanctification. It was the cup that separated this meal from all other meals and marked it out as being different.

Loving Father, as I come to study the order in which the Passover feast is conducted, help me to see the ways in which it conceals Your great plan of eternal salvation. In Jesus' name I pray. Amen.

Leviticus 8:1–12; 2 Thessalonians 2:13–17
1. How were the priests consecrated or sanctified?
2. How are we sanctified?

The Meaning of the Four Cups 17 MAR

FOR READING AND MEDITATION – EXODUS 6:1–13
'I have heard the groaning of the Israelites...
and I have remembered my covenant.' (v5)

We continue looking at the manner in which the Passover meal was conducted during the time of Christ, and is still conducted by Jews today. We said yesterday that the meal commenced with the drinking of the first of four cups – the 'Cup of Kiddush'. The four cups were reminders of the four promises of Exodus 6:6–7: (1) I will bring you out from under the yoke of the Egyptians; (2) I will free you from being slaves to them; (3) I will redeem you with an outstretched arm and with mighty acts of judgment; (4) I will take you as my own people, and I will be your God.

After the drinking of the first cup, the host would take a bowl of water and a towel and pass them around the table so that all could wash their hands. He would then draw attention to the bitter herbs and the bowl of salt water that were on the table, which they would all be invited to taste – a reminder of the bitterness of slavery in Egypt and of the tears that had been shed so profusely by their forefathers.

Then the main course would be brought out, which consists of roast lamb, although it would not be eaten yet. The family would be reminded that it was through the shed blood of a lamb that their homes had been protected when the destroyer passed through Egypt. Their attention would be drawn, too, to the presence of the unleavened bread on the table and how they had to leave behind them all reminders of the culture when fleeing from Egypt, including the leaven for their bread. Then would come the second eating of bitter herbs, a further reminder of the bitterness of slavery. A further benediction was then offered in gratitude to God for His deliverance on that dark and fateful night.

O God, I sense that wondrous and miraculous though that first Passover night was, it was but a dress rehearsal for another and greater Passover – the deliverance wrought through our Lord's sacrifice on the cross. I am eternally grateful. Amen.

Matthew 6:1–5; Luke 12:1; 1 Corinthians 5:6–8
1. What was the yeast or leaven of the Pharisees?
2. What are we to leave behind?

The Eating of the Lamb　　18 MAR

FOR READING AND MEDITATION – EXODUS 15:1–19
'By the power of your arm they will be as still
as a stone – until your people pass by, Lord...' (v16)

We continue looking at the way in which the Passover meal was celebrated, as it is an important and necessary background to our understanding of the Lord's Supper. After the second eating of the bitter herbs would come the drinking of the second cup, which was called the 'Cup of Haggadah' or the 'Cup of Explanation'. The father would once again lead the family in the drinking of this cup.

At this point, the youngest son in the family would be prompted formally to ask a series of questions starting with, 'Why is this night different from all other nights?' The head of the household would then give a potted history of Israel right down to the deliverance of the Passover, explaining how this demonstrated God's everlasting power and mercy. Following this would begin the singing of the first part of what was called the Egyptian Hallel – the name given to the group of psalms of praise from Psalm 113 to Psalm 118, which were used for Passover. Designated here were just Psalms 113 and 114.

Next came a second act of hand washing. The host would wash his hands and then prepare a 'sop' – a piece of unleavened bread filled with lamb and dipped in the paste called the *charoseth*. He would give the sop to the honoured guest on his left, then to others sitting around the table. It was this 'sop' Jesus offered to Judas (in place of the honoured guest) who, at this point in the Last Supper, left to betray Him (John 13:26–30). Following this would come the eating of the meal, the roasted lamb, which by tradition had to be wholly eaten. Anything left over was to be destroyed and not used for a common meal.

Loving Father, as I follow these procedures, I see how painstaking You were in preparing Your people for that Passover of all Passovers. Understanding each part will help me gain more from each Lord's Supper I celebrate. Thank You. Amen.

Psalm 114:1–8; James 4:1–8
1. Why would the first part of the Hallel be relevant?
2. What should we do as well as wash our hands?

The Hallel

19 MAR

FOR READING AND MEDITATION – PSALM 136:1–26

'Give thanks to the Lord, for he is good. *His love endures for ever.*' (v1)

We spend one more day exploring the formalities of the Passover meal. Once the lamb had been eaten, then came the drinking of the third cup – called the 'Cup of Thanksgiving'. This cup was served with a piece of unleavened bread. Once the cup had been drunk, the host would then give thanks for the meal that they had eaten, after which would follow the singing of the rest of the Egyptian Hallel – Psalms 115 to 118. Then the fourth cup would be drunk, whereupon the family would sing what is known as 'The Hallel' – the psalm before us today. The singing of 'The Hallel' would bring the Passover meal to its conclusion.

We cannot be certain, of course, whether or not Jesus followed this precise pattern at the Passover feast He celebrated with His disciples, although I think we can safely assume that apart from those moments when He gave the Passover a new direction, He did. It's interesting to note that none of the Gospels go into detail about the exact location of the room, the position of the disciples around our Lord, or the number of artefacts upon the table – all these things seemed to be considered as relatively unimportant.

What was important – and every Gospel writer recorded it – was the stunning revelation that Jesus gave concerning a new commemorative act that would become the ultimate Passover feast. No wonder Jesus said, at the beginning of the meal, 'I have eagerly desired to eat this Passover with you before I suffer' (Luke 22:15). He longed to let them know that the story of His death had been hidden all the time within the Passover celebration – waiting to be revealed.

Blessed Lord Jesus, I bow in adoration and worship before You as I contemplate the eagerness with which You reached out to the cross. 'All this Thou didst for me – what can I now do for Thee?' Amen.

Psalm 118:1–29; Acts 4:10–12
1. How might Psalm 118 relate to Jesus?
2. What did Peter explain?

Born to Die

20 MAR

FOR READING AND MEDITATION – JOHN 12:20–36

'No, it was for this very reason I came to this hour.' (v27)

Now that we have familiarised ourselves with the traditional manner in which the feast of the Passover was conducted, we ask ourselves: what must have been going on in the heart and mind of the Master as He shared the Passover meal with His disciples? He was clearly aware of the fact that His death was imminent, for, as we saw yesterday, He had said, 'I have eagerly desired to eat this Passover with you before I suffer.'

The astonishing thing is that even though our Lord knew that within twenty-four hours He would be dead and buried, it was clear that He was thinking of His mission, not as something that was past, but as something that yet awaited Him. Normally, a person who has lived barely half the allotted span of life, when told that he is about to die, is plunged into deep depression. Kübler-Ross, the famous anthropologist, who made a special study of the reactions people go through when they know they are about to die, said that there are five clear stages through which a person passes when confronted by the news that death is imminent.

I watched my wife go through these five stages when her doctors informed her that her sickness was terminal. But I find nothing of this in the heart and mind of Jesus. He suffered intense grief in the Garden of Gethsemane but, as we shall see, this was not because He was unprepared or unwilling to die. The cross was not something our Lord ever tried to avoid: it was the reason why He came. He saw the cross, not as the end of His mission, but as the accomplishment of it – His lifelong goal.

Blessed Lamb of God, slain from the foundation of the world, give me an ever-increasing consciousness of the love that led You to leave the eternal throne and die on the cross for me. I am so deeply, deeply thankful. Amen.

John 18:36–37; 1 Timothy 1:12–17
1. What was Christ's great purpose?
2. How can Christ's purpose become ours?

Startling Vehemence

21 MAR

FOR READING AND MEDITATION – MATTHEW 16:21-28

'Jesus began to explain to his disciples that he must
go to Jerusalem and suffer many things...' (v21)

We said yesterday that Christ's death was not something He wanted to avoid: indeed it was the very reason why He came into the world. He was born to die.

Do you know that great painting by Holman Hunt entitled 'The Shadow of Death'? It depicts the inside of the carpenter's shop in Nazareth and shows Jesus, stripped to the waist, standing by a wooden trestle on which He has put down His awl. He is obviously a little tired and stretches both His arms towards heaven. As He does so, the evening sunlight, flooding in through the open door of the little carpenter's shop, casts a dark shadow in the form of a cross on the wall behind Him. In the foreground can be seen His mother, Mary, who, kneeling among the chips of wood, looks up and is obviously startled as she sees her Son's cross-like shadow on the wall.

Some regard this painting as sickly and sentimental, but the idea it contains is a scriptural one – the cross loomed large in the mind and perspective of Jesus, probably from His earliest days and certainly from the commencement of His ministry. The verse before us today is the first prediction of His passion. There had been passing allusions to it before, but here it is quite clear that Jesus knew He was destined for a cross. And so horrified was He by Peter's insistence that He put the thought away from Him that He addressed him with strange and uncharacteristic words, 'Out of my way, Satan!' (v23, J.B. Phillips). The vehemence was not aimed at Peter, but at the satanic ploy that was sounding through him. Nothing could deter Jesus from going to the cross – for He knew that this was the very reason why He had come.

My Lord and Saviour, I am grateful beyond words that You allowed nothing to deter You from going to Calvary. Help me show the same determination in the face of a lesser cross that may confront me. For Your own dear name's sake. Amen.

Matthew 20:17-19; 26:1-2; Luke 24:1-8
1. Why did Jesus speak so much of His death?
2. What was the message of the angels?

The Moment of Revelation   22 MAR

FOR READING AND MEDITATION – MATTHEW 26:26–30
'This is my blood of the covenant, which is poured out
for many for the forgiveness of sins.' (v28)

We come now to the question which has intrigued Christians in every century of the Christian Church: at what point in the evening did Jesus make clear to His disciples that He was instituting His own commemorative meal? We cannot be absolutely sure, but most commentators believe it was probably after the drinking of the third cup – 'The Cup of Thanksgiving'.

There are two reasons for this belief – one is that Paul, in his letter to the Corinthians, refers to the Communion cup as 'the cup of thanksgiving' (1 Cor. 10:16). The second is the fact that 'The Cup of Blessing' was served with a piece of unleavened bread, at which time the head of the household would say, 'This is the bread of affliction which our fathers had to eat as they came out of Egypt.' If this was the moment of revelation, then you can imagine how astonished the disciples must have been when Jesus said those tremendous and powerful words, 'This is my body given for you; do this in remembrance of me', and 'This cup is the new covenant in my blood, which is poured out for you' (Luke 22:19–20).

This is the impact of what He was saying – 'Never again need you keep as the central focus of your worship the memory of your forefathers' deliverance from Egypt, for I am about to go to my death as the true Passover sacrifice. From now on, I want you to remember regularly an even greater event – the giving of my own body and blood for your redemption.' In a few simple but powerful words, our Lord transformed an ancient ritual into the world's most wondrous revelation.

Lord Jesus, as You interpreted the real meaning of the Passover to those around You that day, help me to interpret the meaning of Your cross to those around me today. Amen.

John 6:48–59; 1 Corinthians 11:23–26
1. How do we feed on Jesus?
2. What part of Passover should we pass on?

God's Paschal Lamb

23 MAR

FOR READING AND MEDITATION – ISAIAH 53:1–12
'He was led like a lamb to the slaughter…' (v7)

We continue drinking in the wonder of that moment when Jesus revealed to His disciples that He was God's Paschal Lamb, His ultimate sacrificial lamb. In a play, a character standing in the wings with the lighting behind him will cast a long shadow across the stage and, by reason of this, will attract the audience's attention. But when the character himself steps on to the stage, whatever degree of interest the shadow aroused is surpassed by the wonder of seeing the character appear personally.

For centuries, Jesus stood in the wings of history, casting His shadow before Him. He can be seen on almost every page of the Old Testament – in the deliverance of Israel from Egypt, in the sacrifices, in the details of the tabernacle, in the ministry of the priesthood, and so on. Throughout the prophetic books, predictions concerning the coming Messiah give the shadow more detail. Finally, 400 years after the Old Testament times, John the Baptist made the declaration, 'Look, the Lamb of God, who takes away the sin of the world!' (John 1:29). At last, the shadow had substance.

Notice the words, 'the Lamb of God who takes away the *sin of the world*' (my emphasis). The Old Testament shows a progressive revelation as related to the offering of a lamb: first a lamb atoned for an individual, as in the case of Isaac; then for a family, as at the first Passover; then for a nation, as on the Day of Atonement. The world waited for the day when a lamb would come whose sacrifice would take away, not just the sins of an individual, a family, or even a nation, but the sins of the entire world. Now that day had arrived. And the sacrifice? None other than Jesus – God's Paschal Lamb.

Gracious Father, I am so thankful that before ever there was a man, there was a lamb. For Jesus, Your Son, is the Lamb who was slain from the foundation of the world. I am eternally grateful. Amen.

Revelation 5:1–14; 7:9–10
1. How does Jesus appear in heaven?
2. Why is He praised?

Where God Puts the Emphasis

24 MAR

FOR READING AND MEDITATION – HEBREWS 9:11-28

'He entered the Most Holy Place once for all by
his own blood, so obtaining eternal redemption.' (v12)

We must meditate a little further on that wondrous moment when Jesus revealed Himself to His disciples as the Paschal Lamb and gave them clear and definite instructions for His own memorial service. Reflect with me on the deep importance of what He was saying. His memorial was not to be a single occasion, like our modern-day memorial services – the final tribute of loved ones and friends – but it was to be a regular meal, or service, or both. He told them also that He desired this act of memorial to be repeated: 'Do this in remembrance of me.'

What were they to do? They were to follow His actions and use the words He Himself had used when He had broken the bread. I always feel myself that something is missing in a Communion service when there is any departure from the act of taking, breaking, blessing, identifying, and sharing the bread and the wine. But what do the bread and wine signify? The words Jesus spoke on that night make it crystal clear; of the bread, He said, 'This is my body given for you', and of the wine, 'This cup is the new covenant in my blood, which is poured out for you.'

John Stott said of this moment, 'The bread did not stand for His living body as He reclined with them at the table, but His body as it was shortly to be 'given' for them in death. Similarly, the wine did not stand for His blood as it flowed in His veins while He spoke to them, but His blood which was shortly to be poured out for them in death.' It is clear that it is not so much by His life, but by His death, that Jesus wishes to be remembered. His life is important, but much more His death. It has accomplished so much for us.

O God, help me ever to put the emphasis where You have put it, not so much on my Saviour's life, spotless and exemplary though it was, but on His sacrificial and atoning death. I ask this in and through His peerless and precious name. Amen.

Hebrews 10:1-23
1. Contrast Christ's sacrifice with that of bulls.
2. Why can we appear before God confidently?

The Centrality of the Cross   25 MAR

FOR READING AND MEDITATION – GALATIANS 6:1–15
'May I never boast except in the cross of our Lord Jesus Christ...' (v14)

We continue meditating on the fact that although the life of our Lord was supremely important, the place where God puts the highest emphasis is on His sacrificial and atoning death. Modern-day theologians who bypass the death of Christ and focus instead on such things as His exemplary life, His powerful words, His great miracles, and so on, have their priorities all wrong. The emphasis which Jesus placed on His own death shows quite clearly that He regarded this as central to His purpose in coming to the world. Not that His exemplary life and character have no purpose – they most certainly do – but had He not died on the cross, then we would never have known what it means to be 'saved'.

One commentator puts it like this: 'The Lord's Supper, which was instituted by Jesus, and which is the only regular commemorative act authorised by Him, dramatises neither His birth nor His life, neither His words nor His works, but only His death.' It was by His death that He wished above all else to be remembered. You see, then, how essential the cross is to Christianity. In a day and an age when religionists are attempting to turn the spotlight away from the cross and focus instead on the life and words of Jesus, we must do everything in our power to proclaim the centrality of the cross. No cross – no Christianity; it is as simple as that. I take my stand – and I pray that you do too – with the hymnist who said:

> *Forbid it, Lord, that I should boast*
> *Save in the death of Christ my Lord*
> *All the vain things that charm me most*
> *I sacrifice them to his blood.*
> *— Isaac Watts (1674–1748)*

O God my Father, I am so glad that even though I cannot fathom all the mystery of the cross, I can take hold of its saving power. It is sometimes darkness to my intellect, but sunshine to my heart. Thank You, Father. Amen.

Romans 1:16–17; 1 Corinthians 1:17–30
1. What is the power of the cross?
2. How do people regard the message of the cross?

Getting the 'Me' into Calvary 26 MAR

FOR READING AND MEDITATION – GALATIANS 2:15–21

'I live by faith in the Son of God,
who loved me and gave himself for me.' (v20)

Before we leave the Upper Room and go down with Jesus into Gethsemane, we draw one more concluding lesson from what went on in that memorable first Communion service. It concerns the need for each one of us personally to apply and appropriate the death of Christ for ourselves. If, as we have been saying, it was in the Upper Room that Jesus gave to His disciples an advance dramatisation of His death on the cross, it is important that we see further what this was designed to convey.

The celebration of that first Communion did not just involve Jesus, but it involved all the disciples also. Christ initiated it, but the others took part in it as well. They could hardly have failed to get the message that it was not enough for the bread to be broken and the cup of wine to be handed to them – they had to eat and drink and thus appropriate it for themselves. They were not spectators – they were participants.

What does all this say to us? It says that the death of Christ is the means by which we are saved, but we will not be saved until we receive and appropriate for ourselves the sacrifice He made for us on the cross. This is extremely important, for there are many this Easter who, when they are reminded of Christ's death on the cross, will think that because of that, they are automatically forgiven. That is not so. Unless we do as John Wesley said, and get the 'me' into the cross – Christ died for me – and personally receive His forgiveness by an appropriating act of faith, then the tragic situation is this – it will be as if He never died for us.

O Father, thank You for reminding me that it is only as I appropriate what Christ did for me on Calvary that I am saved. I have seen it – may millions more come to know it this Easter time. In Jesus' name I pray. Amen.

John 3:16–21,36; Romans 10:8–13
1. What happens to those who reject Christ?
2. Who can be saved?

The Agony in the Garden 27 MAR

FOR READING AND MEDITATION – EZEKIEL 23:32-34
'You will be filled with drunkenness and sorrow,
the cup of ruin and desolation...' (v33)

Supper is now over and, after singing, Jesus and His band of disciples make their way down into the Kidron Valley to a little olive orchard known as the Garden of Gethsemane. It was evidently a favourite retreat for Jesus, for John comments that He often met there with His disciples (John 18:2). Here something takes place which many have come to call 'the agony in the Garden'. It is clear from the record that Jesus is in great distress of soul, as on three separate occasions He prays a similar prayer: 'My Father, if it is possible, may this cup be taken from me. Yet not as I will, but as you will' (Matt. 26:39).

What is this 'cup' which Jesus is talking about here? Is He recoiling from the thought of the physical suffering He is about to endure – the awful torture and agony of the cross? Possibly so. This prospect would likely bring deep distress to the soul. In Luke 22:43-44, we read that an angel came to strengthen Jesus, and yet, even after this, He was still in anguish, and He prayed with increased fervour.

Perhaps also something deeper than the thought of physical or even mental suffering was striking deep into His soul. The cup from which He shrank symbolised not just the physical pain of being crucified and the mental distress of being humiliated and despised, but also the spiritual agony of bearing the sins of the world. As Jesus looked into that cup and saw the temporary spiritual break with His Father that would happen on the cross, His soul may have recoiled in horror. You see, it was not the fear of death that caused Him such agony, but the awful prospect of being separated from the One to whom He had been joined throughout all eternity.

Blessed Lord, as I contemplate Your suffering in the Garden of Gethsemane, I feel like bowing in the dust. If my sin brought such pain to You, then how can I ever sin again? Please give me the grace to live wholly for You. Amen.

Psalm 22:1-18; Luke 22:39-46
1. How did David foresee Christ's agony?
2. What happened after the angel strengthened Jesus?

He Drained the Cup

FOR READING AND MEDITATION – MATTHEW 26:36-46

'If it is not possible for this cup to be taken away
unless I drink it, may your will be done.' (v42)

We look once again at that lonely figure of our Lord in Gethsemane's Garden – sweating, prostrate, overwhelmed with grief, and asking His heavenly Father that, if possible, He be spared the drinking of the cup. Each of the three prayers He prayed began in a similar way: 'My Father, if it is possible…'

Although, in theory, everything is possible to God, this was something which Jesus recognised as being part of God's will. It was God's purpose to save us from sin, and to save us in a way that would impart to us His righteousness. But this would be impossible without the substitutionary death of the Saviour. No one else could have borne our sins. There have been many who would have been willing to die for the sins of the world, but no one who was worthy to die. As the hymn so beautifully puts it:

> *There was no other good enough*
> *To pay the price of sin*
> *He only could unlock the gate*
> *Of heaven and let us in.*
> *— Cecil F. Alexander (1818-1895)*

So despite Jesus' agonising prayer, the cup was not taken from Him. We have noted that each of His prayers began in a similar way: 'My Father, if it is possible…' Now we recognise that they each ended with submission to His Father's will. Personally, I am so grateful to Jesus – and so, I am sure, are you – that on that dark night long ago, He put that bitter cup to His lips *and drained it dry*.

My Saviour and my God, how can I sufficiently thank You for drinking that bitter cup of sin so that I could drink the better cup of salvation. My gratitude and appreciation just won't go into words. Amen.

Psalm 69:1-36; Matthew 27:34
1. Describe the psalmist's feelings.
2. How does the psalm foretell Jesus' experience?

Darkness at Noon   29 MAR

FOR READING AND MEDITATION – MATTHEW 27:45-54

'From noon until three in the afternoon darkness came over all the land.' (v45)

We turn from gazing on Jesus in the Garden to his agony on the cross. If the anticipation of bearing the wrath of God against sin was so terrible, then what must the reality have been like? We can only glimpse in some small way what Jesus passed through in that grim ordeal on Golgotha by examining the deeply suggestive text which is before us today: 'darkness came over all the land'.

A strange and eerie darkness swept over Jerusalem on that awful day when Jesus was crucified, which seems to have lasted for three hours – from noon to 3pm. What a contrast there was between our Saviour's birth and His death. As Douglas Webster puts it, 'At the birth of the Son of God, there was brightness at midnight; at the death of the Son of God, there was darkness at noon.'

What was the purpose of this strange phenomenon? I think myself it was the outward symbol of the spiritual darkness that was enveloping Jesus as '"He himself bore our sins" in his body on the cross' (1 Pet. 2:24). What is darkness, in biblical symbolism, but separation from God, who is light and in whom there is no darkness at all (1 John 1:5)? The term 'outer darkness' is an expression that Jesus once used to describe hell, since it is absolute and utter exclusion from the light of God's presence. Hold this thought in your mind as you go through the day – at Calvary our Lord, in some mysterious way, plunged into that 'outer darkness' and experienced, on our behalf, the awful terror of temporary separation from God.

Blessed Lord Jesus, as I stand before Your cross and see something more of what it meant for You, I see something more of what it means for me. And I bow myself down. Thank You, dear Saviour. Thank You! Amen.

1 John 1:5-9; 2:1-11
1. How does John contrast light and dark?
2. Why might we be in darkness?

The Cry of Dereliction

FOR READING AND MEDITATION – PSALM 22:1–31

'My God, my God, why have you forsaken me?' (v1)

Today, we spend another day meditating on the cross. When Jesus emerged from the darkness that enveloped Him, He made a strange and puzzling statement: 'My God, my God, why have you forsaken me?' These words have come to be called by many theologians and Bible students, 'the cry of dereliction'.

What is the explanation of these anguished words? Everyone agrees that Jesus was quoting Psalm 22, but not everyone agrees as to the purpose of the quotation. Some say it was a cry of unbelief and despair – He was disappointed that His Father had not rescued Him from the awful horror of the cross. Others say it was a cry of loneliness – He was not really forsaken by God, but He *felt* forsaken. Another school of thought sees the words as a cry of victory, saying that as the psalm ends in a spirit of triumph and conquest, Jesus had in mind the end and not just the beginning of the passage.

I prefer myself to accept the words as they stand and believe them to be indicative of the fact that, due to the need for Christ to taste the full penalty of sin, an actual and dreadful separation voluntarily accepted by both the Father and the Son took place between them at the cross. Jesus not only felt forsaken – He was forsaken. It had to be if the Son was to taste fully the final consequence of human sin. And what is that final consequence? Solemnly I say it – separation from God. Jesus quoted the scripture from Psalm 22 as He quoted other scriptures – not because He was bewildered, stunned or confused, but because He knew and believed He was fulfilling it.

O Jesus, my Lord and my God, I stand in awe at Your sacrificial love. I am on holy ground. There is nothing I can do to repay You for what You have done for me. My best offering is my life for Your service. Amen.

2 Chronicles 24:20; 2 Corinthians 5:17–21; Hebrews 13:5
1. What is the 'Divine Exchange'?
2. What can we say confidently?

I Am Alive! I Am Alive!

31 MAR

FOR READING AND MEDITATION – JOHN 20:1–18; REVELATION 1:18

> 'I am the Living One; I was dead, and now look,
> I am alive for ever and ever!' (Rev. 1:18)

On the third day after Christ had died on the cross, He was miraculously brought back to life again, and on Easter Day millions of Christians around the world joyfully celebrate. Historians tell us that at the Battle of Hastings in 1066, there was a joyous moment when the Norman invaders were about to be overcome. For long hours they had striven without success to storm Harold's stockades, and they were beginning to get weary and lose heart. A rumour began to spread among them which almost led to panic – a rumour which reported that their leader, William, had been slain. As soon as William heard it, he jumped on his horse and rode up and down among the ranks shouting, 'I am alive! I am alive! I am alive!'

What a graphic picture this is of Jesus on the first Easter Day. Many of Christ's followers who were not present at the cross would have heard the sad news that He had been crucified and His body laid in a tomb. The report of His death would have been carried miles beyond the city of Jerusalem, and doubtless those who had believed in Him would have been deeply saddened and distressed.

Jesus, however, did not allow the news of His death to discourage His disciples for too long as, a little while later, He flung back from His face the mask of death and announced, first to Mary and then to other chosen disciples, 'I am alive! I am alive! I am alive!' Come with me and peer into the tomb in which Jesus was laid. What do you see? Nothing? Ah – that, I am sure you will agree, is the most marvellous and most sensational 'nothing' the world has ever known.

Lord Jesus, thankful as I am for the empty tomb, that is not the only thing that convinces me You are alive. The greatest evidence is that You are alive within my heart – and for that I am eternally thankful. Amen.

Luke 24:1–12; John 20:24–31
1. How did the disciples initially respond?
2. How did Jesus settle their doubts?

Victory All the Way

1 APR

FOR READING AND MEDITATION – COLOSSIANS 2:1–15

'He made a public spectacle of them,
triumphing over them by the cross.' (v15)

We spend another day reflecting on the wonder of Jesus' resurrection. Let's pause to consider now how Christ's death and resurrection are connected, for many Christians have a sentimental but not a connected understanding of these two great and momentous events. It is popularly believed that the resurrection is the way by which God turned the defeat of Good Friday into a glorious victory. But that is a part truth. The death of Jesus on that first Good Friday was not a defeat but a victory, and the resurrection is that victory endorsed, demonstrated, and proclaimed.

The apostle Peter, in his sermon on the Day of Pentecost, said, 'It was impossible for death to keep its hold on him' (Acts 2:24). It was possible for Him to die, but not possible for Him to be held by death. Why? Because on the cross, death had already been defeated. The evil principalities and powers which had been conquered by His death on the cross were, at the moment of resurrection, put under His feet and made subject to Him (Eph. 1:20–23).

Some Christians present Christ as a living Lord, but place no emphasis on His atoning death, while others talk about His atoning death but fail to focus on His resurrection. The two events belong together and exclusion of one diminishes the other. Nothing would have been accomplished by Jesus' death if He had not been raised from it, and nothing would have been accomplished by His resurrection if He had not dealt with death and defeated it *on the cross*. Good Friday was as much a victory as Easter Sunday.

My Father and my God, help me not to separate what You have joined together. Deepen my understanding of the cross and resurrection so that I might experience even more dynamically their power in my life. In Jesus' name. Amen.

Acts 17:30–34; 1 Corinthians 15:1–23
1. What was the decisive point in Paul's message?
2. Why could our faith be futile and our belief be in vain?

A Continuous Practice 2 APR

FOR READING AND MEDITATION – ACTS 2:38–47
'They devoted themselves to the apostles' teaching
and to fellowship, to the breaking of bread...' (v42)

Today we ask ourselves: how faithfully, after the cross and resurrection, did the disciples practice Jesus' instructions concerning the regular celebration of Communion? The chapter before us today makes it clear that within weeks of the Last Supper, the disciples had taught the converts the importance of this event, for we read, 'They devoted themselves to the apostles' teaching and to fellowship, to *the breaking of bread* and to prayer'. Again we read in verse 46, 'Every day they continued to meet together in the temple courts. They *broke bread* in their homes and ate together with glad and sincere hearts' (my emphases).

It would appear from these verses that the actual practice of celebrating Communion was as part of a fellowship meal, but later the Church came to set aside a specific time in which they focused exclusively on remembering their Lord's sacrifice for them on Calvary: 'On the first day of the week we came together to break bread' (Acts 20:7). By the time the first letter to the Corinthians was written (around AD 55), it is clear that the celebration of Communion was a regular practice in the Corinthian community, as evidenced by the phrase, 'The cup of thanksgiving for which we give thanks... the bread that we break' (1 Cor. 10:16).

What the Church of the first century practised ought to be the practice of the Church of the twenty-first century. Jesus said, 'Do this in remembrance of me,' and so, until He returns to take us to be with Him, we are to obey His command and make this feast a continuous practice. Jesus' sacrifice is of too great importance not to be regularly brought to mind and celebrated.

O Father, I see that if the Church misses its step here then it will miss it all along the way. Help us to be faithful to Your commands, for they are there for our benefit and for Your glory. In Jesus' name we ask it. Amen.

Luke 24:13–35
1. What happened when the stranger broke bread?
2. How did it affect them?

Why Paul?

3 APR

FOR READING AND MEDITATION – 1 CORINTHIANS 11:23-26
'For I received from the Lord what I also passed on to you...' (v23)

We come today to the only passage in the epistles where the purpose and meaning of the Communion table is expounded and explained. At first, it seems a little strange that this task is given to the apostle Paul, especially when we remember that he was not present at Jesus' last meal with the disciples. Where did Paul get his deep understanding of Holy Communion? From one or more of the original band of disciples? No – he got it directly from Jesus Himself: '*I received from the Lord* what I also passed on to you' (my emphasis).

But why was Paul chosen to be the one to give the only exposition of the meaning of Communion in the whole of the epistles? Why not Simon Peter, or John? I believe myself that the reason for this is because Paul had been given a special commission to bring the gospel to the Gentiles (Rom. 15:16) and to him also had been given the revelation of the true nature of the Christian Church (Eph. 3:1-11).

Two things emerge from this – one, that Paul was specially gifted to make clear to the Gentiles the significance of Old Testament truths that could easily elude them, and two, the great apostle was able, more than any of the other New Testament writers, to expound the truths that related particularly to the Church. As Holy Communion was intended by Jesus to be a corporate and not an individual celebration – something done within the context of the Body of Christ – then who better to instruct and apply that truth than the great apostle to the Gentiles?

Gracious Father, I am so thankful that You gave Your servant Paul an inspired insight into the Communion. May the same Spirit who inspired him be in my heart as I ponder these insights over the next few days. Amen.

Acts 22:1-3; 1 Corinthians 9:19-23; Galatians 1:11-24
1. What was special about Paul's background and character?
2. What was special about Paul's understanding?

The Five C's of the Communion   4 APR

FOR READING AND MEDITATION – 1 CORINTHIANS 11:26–34

'For whenever you eat this bread and drink this cup,
you proclaim the Lord's death...' (v26)

We said yesterday that Paul's exposition of the meaning of Communion contained in 1 Corinthians 11:23–34 is the only passage in the whole of the epistles where the meaning of Holy Communion is unfolded and explained. For this reason I intend to put it under a spiritual microscope day by day and draw out of it the lessons we need to learn. Firstly, let me say that as this is a devotional study read by people of all denominations, I do not intend to enter into some of the more controversial issues, but to focus on those things on which all (or at least most) Christians can agree.

Five clear aspects are seen in the Lord's Supper, and keeping these in view whenever we sit or kneel before the 'holy table' will, I believe, enable us to enter more fully into the meaning of this precious and sacred act. Firstly, the service of Communion is a corporate act in which the whole Christian community is expected to participate. Secondly, it is a commemorative act in which we focus on remembering Jesus' sacrificial and atoning death. Thirdly, it is a service in which the concept of covenant is highlighted. Fourthly, it is an act of celebration entered into with joy and thanksgiving. And fifthly, it is an act of commitment in which we dedicate ourselves more fully to representing our Master in a hostile and often Christ-rejecting world.

These five aspects, when understood and kept in view as we come to the Lord's Table, will, I believe, help to turn what can be a routine monotonous event into a momentous one. We owe it to God and ourselves to draw out from the Communion all that Father God has put into it.

Jesus, my Lord and Master, help me understand that the Communion service is not just a ritual but something that is close to Your heart. You initiated it – teach me how to appreciate it. For Your own dear name's sake. Amen.

Genesis 14:11–20; Isaiah 55:1–7
1. How did Abram experience a type of communion?
2. What is God's invitation?

A 'Together' Fellowship

5 APR

FOR READING AND MEDITATION – ACTS 20:1–12

'On the first day of the week we came together to break bread.' (v7)

We said yesterday that at least five clear aspects can be seen in the Communion, and an understanding of these will help to enrich the times we spend together at the Lord's Table. The first thing we must understand about the Communion is that it is a corporate act. God never intended that we should partake of the Lord's Supper alone in the privacy of our own room. We 'come together' (1 Cor. 11:20) in order to celebrate it.

Scripture calls us to come together to observe the Lord's Supper. Sometimes you hear Christians using the word 'communion' to describe their times of private prayer and fellowship with the Lord, but the word 'communion', when applied to the Lord's Supper, means more than that – it means fellowship with other Christians also. If you want an interesting evening in your Bible, go through the Acts of the Apostles and observe the number of times the word 'together' or its synonyms occur. You will come to the conclusion that the Early Church was a very 'together' fellowship.

Of course, those who are ill in hospital or housebound are unable to attend Communion services. Community can be found, however, when another Christian visits with bread and wine, and Communion can be shared where they are. At the Communion table, we not only share in Christ, but we share in each other. As I have said on numerous occasions in these pages over the years – everyone who belongs to Christ belongs to everyone else who belongs to Christ. There is no such thing as a solitary Christian.

O God, teach me the value of sharing my life with You, but also with others – for this is truly living. May sharing in Communion with others be part of that. In Jesus' name. Amen.

Acts 2:42–47; Hebrews 10:23–25
1. What can we learn from the Early Church?
2. What should we not neglect?

Trouble at Corinth   6 APR

FOR READING AND MEDITATION – 1 CORINTHIANS 11:17–22

'When you come together, it is not the Lord's Supper you eat...' (v20)

We saw yesterday, that Scripture calls us to join together in order to observe the Lord's Supper. This means more than just the physical act of coming together – it involves a spiritual coming together also.

Paul's exposition of the Communion is preceded by strong words which he felt obliged to speak to the church because of certain irregularities that were allowed to go on in their midst. Apparently, in the church at Corinth, the act of remembering the Lord's death was preceded by a 'love feast' – a communal meal to which all would contribute. Somehow the meal had become degraded into an act whereby the rich would sit to one side and enjoy their sumptuous provisions, while the poor would find a separate place to eat their meagre fare. Then, immediately after the eating of this meal, came the celebration of the Lord's Supper.

Paul was concerned because the evident lack of love that was demonstrated at the 'love feast' spilled over into the act of Communion and thus the two things contradicted one another. What should have been an act of communion was really nothing more than an act of collaboration. They sat together, but their hearts did not belong to one another. They came together physically, but they did not come together spiritually.

The problem that existed in the Corinthian church is with us in some sections of Christ's Church today. Believers meet together to celebrate the Lord's Supper, but never experience true communion. Thus, sadly, it cannot be said of them as it was said of the church after Pentecost: 'the company of believers was of one heart and soul' (Acts 4:32, AMPC).

O God, sweep through Your Church by Your Holy Spirit so that we may experience true communion. Break down all barriers between us, so that we might come together with one heart and one soul. For the glory of Your precious Son. Amen.

James 2:1–17; Jude 1–16
1. What is necessary for true communion?
2. What blemishes did Jude highlight?

The *Koinonia*

FOR READING AND MEDITATION – 1 CORINTHIANS 1:1–9

'God is faithful, who has called you into fellowship [*koinonia*] with his Son, Jesus Christ our Lord.' (v9)

We ended yesterday with the thought that some churches come together to celebrate the Lord's Supper but never really experience communion. The best word to describe the rich spiritual relationships which Christ looks for between believers is the Greek word *koinonia* – literally 'fellowship'.

This fellowship, however, goes deeper than mere 'mateyness' or sociability. In the words of George Fox, 'The church experiences a relationship where they seek to know each other in that which is eternal.' Other relationships let us know each other in that which is temporal; the relationship we have with one another in Christ lets us know each other at our deepest depths and 'in that which is eternal'. This thought is expressed beautifully in these words:

Oh, without spoken words, low breathing stole
Of a diviner life from soul to soul
Baptising into one tender thought the whole.
— John Russell Hayes

Without this rich fellowship, the Church is no different to a fraternity or a club. One of the reasons why the Christians of the Early Church 'turned the world upside down' was because they had a clear understanding of their relationship with God and their relationship to one another. They had a true sense of community. As someone put it, 'Once, the church was an incendiary fellowship which changed and challenged the course of history.' The *koinonia* turned the world upside down; what difference do we make?

O Father, I see we are made for the *koinonia* and we are restless and unhappy until we find it. Let this homesickness of the soul drive us closer to You and to each other. In Jesus' name we pray. Amen.

Ruth 1:1–22
1. Describe Orpah's relationship with Naomi.
2. Contrast Ruth's relationship with Naomi.

Living Well Together... 8 APR

FOR READING AND MEDITATION – 1 JOHN 1:1–10

'If we walk in the light, as he is in the light,
we have fellowship with one another...' (v7)

Today we ask ourselves: where and how can this rich sense of fellowship and community (*koinonia*) be cultivated and developed? One place is at the Lord's Table. The regular celebration of Holy Communion greatly assists in heightening our sense of community. All gathering together, of course, contributes to a sense of community, but the Lord's Table plays a special part in producing that rich fellowship of which we spoke yesterday.

Gathered around the table on which stand the bread and wine, we are not only reminded of our oneness in Christ but the thought is borne in upon us that we are a community of the cross. The regular exposure of our minds and spirits to the sight of the emblems which Jesus chose to perpetuate the memory of His death brings home to us most vividly that, having been brought into being by the cross, we continue to live by and under the cross. All our perspectives and behaviour are to be governed by the cross.

Just as the cross enables us to enjoy and experience a new relationship with God, so it enables us to enjoy and experience a new relationship with one another. And if there is one place where we need to open our lives to the power of the cross, it is in the area of relationships. 'Christianity,' says Dr E. Stanley Jones, 'is the science of living well together with others according to Jesus Christ.' Many of our attempts to live together in harmony are haphazard; we often do not follow the principles that flow out of the cross. Let's commit ourselves to following God's ways, ways which we find represented in the cross and the Lord's Table.

O Father, help me so to live that just as I am not outside of Your fellowship, no one shall be outside of mine. You have made clear that this is Your will for me; teach me how to make it my will also. Amen.

Amos 3:3; 1 John 3:11–24
1. What basis do we have to walk together?
2. How can we know and practise true love?

Suffering Love

9 APR

FOR READING AND MEDITATION – 1 CORINTHIANS 13:1-13

'Love… takes no account of the evil done to it
[it pays no attention to a suffered wrong].' (v5, AMP)

We spend one more day on the thought that the Lord's Table is a vivid reminder of the fact that we are a community of people called to live by and under the cross. The bread and wine portray and symbolise not just our togetherness in Christ but that our lives are to be governed and regulated by the cross.

Some prefer to think of themselves as the community of the resurrection rather than the community of the cross, and although the former is true, it should be recognised that the table instituted by Jesus has upon it, not the symbols of the resurrection but the symbols of the cross. The resurrection, as we saw, is part of it – a glorious and integral part – but the main focus is on the cross.

We pause now to consider this pointed and personal question: are our relationships with one another governed and regulated by the cross? When we eat and drink together at the Lord's Table, are we together physically but poles apart spiritually? Each Christian we relate to has within him or her the possibility of giving us joy or pain. If we relate well together, then the result is joy; if we relate badly, then the result is pain.

It is at this point of pain, however, that a cross becomes inevitable. For what is a cross? It is the point at which love crimsons into suffering. Jesus loved us so much that He was willing to suffer for us. In a similar sense, that is what we must do for each other, for Calvary love is suffering love. It holds on to relationships, no matter how difficult they may be, and suffers when necessary the pain that is sometimes inevitable when people of a different upbringing or a different background meet together.

O Father, You know that sometimes it is not easy to relate to some of my brothers and sisters in the Church, but when pain comes in my relationships, help me to demonstrate the quality of suffering love. In Jesus' name I pray. Amen.

John 15:9-17; Ephesians 4:25-5:2
1. Where is love most greatly displayed?
2. How can we imitate God?

Commanded to Come?   10 APR

FOR READING AND MEDITATION – GALATIANS 5:1–15

'You were running a good race. Who cut in on you
and kept you from obeying the truth?' (v7)

Now that we have spent a few days clarifying that one of the aspects of Holy Communion is to emphasise the corporate nature of the Church, we move on to explore the second aspect – commemoration. We are commanded to come together in order to remember Him. Notice what I say – 'commanded to come'. Jesus does not just invite us to His table, but insists on us being there.

Does this sound harsh and demanding? Then keep in mind that when Jesus insists on something, you can be sure that there is a wise and loving purpose behind it. His demands are not like those of an autocrat – they are the demands of One who has our highest interests at heart. If you have difficulty with this, then remember, the One who commands you is the One who was crucified for you. Consider His words once again: 'Do this in remembrance of me.' Note, it says '*Do this*' – not 'I *suggest* you do this', or '*Try* to do this'. We are to commemorate His loving sacrifice.

Some believe that this command was intended to apply only to the original band of disciples and not to the continuing life of the Church. There are two strong arguments that can be brought against this view. Firstly, the word 'do' in the Greek suggests repetition – something to be done again and again and again. Secondly, the words 'I received from the Lord what I also pass on to you' (1 Cor. 11:23) show it to be a command from the Lord for the whole Church. So, in the light of these things and because of Jesus' loving sacrifice for us, let's obey the command and meet around His table to remember Him.

O Jesus, Your loving demands strike deep into our hearts. When we sense You calling us to obey You, help us not to resist, for we know that You have our best interests at heart. For Your own dear name's sake. Amen.

Matthew 7:24–29; Luke 22:14–20
1. What are the results of ignoring Jesus' words?
2. Why does Jesus insist on us taking communion?

Lest We Forget

11 APR

FOR READING AND MEDITATION – PSALM 103:1-22

'And forget not all his benefits...' (v2)

We continue reflecting on the fact that one of the purposes of Communion is to commemorate Jesus' atoning death on Calvary. Whenever I read the words, 'Do this in remembrance of me', my first thought is how sad it is that we who are redeemed should need a reminder at all. One would think that once we come to Christ and understand just what His death has procured for us, the fact would remain in our consciousness through every moment of the day. But, as we know, such is not the case – we tend to forget.

One man speaks bitterly of his memory as 'that traitor' while another refers to it as 'the thing he forgot with'. My mother would never admit that she had a poor memory, but referred to it as 'a good forgettory'. I heard of one man who was lent the same book on seven different occasions without realising that he had read it before. His comment was, 'An excellent book, but the author sometimes repeats himself.'

Of all the forms of forgetfulness, however, infinitely the worst is to forget Christ. To guard against this contingency, Jesus instituted the sacrament, for He knew how the simple ordinance would help to quicken our memory. We look at the bread and wine, and the sight of the emblems triggers our memories and Calvary comes clearly into focus. The infirmity of memory is a contributory factor to our frequent failure to focus on Jesus' death and its meaning for our lives, but the finest antidote to this is regular attendance at the Lord's Table. The feast banishes forgetfulness. We remember, because we are reminded.

O God, I am sad that I should ever need to be reminded of what You did for me on Calvary. But I am glad that You have anticipated my forgetfulness and provided in the bread and wine such an amazing visual aid. Thank You, Lord Jesus. Amen.

Deuteronomy 4:9-10; 8:1-20
1. How may things slip from our hearts?
2. Why may God's blessings cause a problem?

Christ's Invisibility

12 APR

FOR READING AND MEDITATION – 1 PETER 1:3–12

'Though you have not seen him, you love him...' (v8)

Yesterday we saw how the infirmity of memory is a contributory factor to our frequent failure to focus on Jesus' atoning death. Another reason why we can so easily forget our Lord and what He has done for us on the cross is because of His invisibility. We know that He is alive but our eyes never see Him. We do not even have a bust or photograph of Him. No canvas carries His portrait and the Gospels do not give so much as a hint concerning His physical appearance.

Because Jesus is for the present invisible to our gaze, it is sadly easy to overlook His reality. Ian Macpherson puts it thus: 'What we see seems real and what we cannot see, unreal. The visible impinges vividly upon our consciousness; the invisible inclines to recede into oblivion.'

The invisibility of Christ can be one reason why we occasionally forget Jesus – yet it need not be. The Table, with its simple emblems, stimulates the memory; the bread is graphically reminiscent of His flesh; the wine, of His blood. To the devout and reverent imagination, the precious and sacred emblems objectify the reality of the unseen Redeemer, and we recall His atoning death and sacrifice for us. We remember because we are reminded. And when we remember, we can look forward to the day when we will see Jesus face to face. In the words of the hymn:

Only faintly now, I see Him,
With the darkling veil between,
But a blessed day is coming,
When His glory shall be seen.
— Mrs Frank A. Break (1855–1934)

Lord Jesus, how can I sufficiently thank You for this simple feast that serves to banish all my forgetfulness. The broken bread and the poured-out wine become the hands that reach out and draw me to Yourself. I am eternally grateful. Amen.

2 Corinthians 4:16–5:7; Hebrews 11:1–3,23–29
1. Where did Paul fix his gaze?
2. What did Moses see?

This Feast of Memory

13 APR

FOR READING AND MEDITATION – LUKE 24:13–35

'Jesus was recognised by them when he broke the bread.' (v35)

Today we look at yet another reason why we can so easily forget Jesus' redemptive sacrifice for us on the cross – the constant pressure of the world around us. As Wordsworth put it, 'The world is too much with us.' The current population of the earth is somewhere in excess of eight billion inhabitants, but, as someone has put it, 'There is always One more who is never taken account of in any census – the living Christ Himself.'

The people who bustle around us every day of our lives – for some just a few, for others hundreds or thousands – have a great influence upon us. We carry within us, albeit subconsciously, their words, their laughter, their tears, and even their angry words, gestures, and blasphemies. We can see them, hear them, and touch them. But the One whom no census recognises is intangible and inaudible. It is natural, therefore, that the people we rub shoulders with day by day, because they are tangible and audible, tend to influence us more than the spiritual realities which we know exist, but which cannot be seen with our physical eyes or heard by our physical ears.

Jesus seems to have anticipated this problem when He appointed for us the Communion table – this wondrous 'feast of memory'. Knowing how the world would impinge upon us and how influential that would be, He ordained that in the life of the Church, there should be regular seasons of remembrance when, with the graphic symbols of His Presence before us, we would deliberately and with set purpose call Him to mind. I have been startled many times, and so I am sure have you, by how powerfully Jesus can make Himself known in the breaking of bread.

O Father, when I see how lovingly You have anticipated my needs and how carefully You have provided for my spiritual development, I am utterly amazed. Such love deserves my total response. I give it – gladly and willingly. Amen.

Leviticus 23:1–44
1. What were the seven feasts of the Lord?
2. What did they signify?

Jesus *is* the Atonement

14 APR

FOR READING AND MEDITATION – PHILIPPIANS 3:1–16

'I want to know Christ – yes, to know the power
of his resurrection and participation in his sufferings...' (v10)

We spend another day meditating on the truth that one of the great purposes of attending the Lord's Supper is to stimulate our memories in the remembrance of Jesus. Indeed, the prescribed actions with the bread and wine (taking, breaking, eating, and drinking) make the remembrance vivid and dramatic.

Notice, however, that Jesus does not ask us to remember the date or the place, but *Him*. He does not say, 'Do this in remembrance of my death', although, of course, the fact that He died a redemptive death can never be far from our minds as we eat the bread and drink the wine. I think that what He had in mind when He uttered these words could be paraphrased like this: 'Do this in remembrance of all that I am to you.' It is terribly important that we catch what Jesus intended here, for there are some who focus more on the fact than the Person. Remember, it is not this, that, or the other that saves – it is Christ who saves.

When Dr Edwards of Bala, the great Welsh theologian, was busy at his book on the atonement, a thought burst in on him that seemed to set his soul on fire. Jumping up from the desk at which he was sitting, he dashed out into the street, shouting excitedly, 'Jesus *is* the Atonement! Jesus *is* the Atonement!' Then, going back to his study, he wrote, 'This is the Atonement, not the sufferings and not the death, but the person of the Son of God in the sufferings and the death.' This must always be a central focus in our minds whenever we approach the Communion table – not just the time, the date, the deed, or the place – but *Him*.

Blessed Lord Jesus, help me not to be so caught up with the events that surround Your death at Calvary that I fail to be caught up with You. Help me to make You central – and all else marginal. For Your own dear name's sake. Amen.

1 Corinthians 1:30; Colossians 1:15–29
1. How has the concept of righteousness become a person?
2. What is Christ's place?

Triggering the Memory

15 APR

FOR READING AND MEDITATION – JOSHUA 4:1–24

'In the future, when your children ask you,
"What do these stones mean?" tell them…' (vv6–7)

We have been saying that great events must not be forgotten. Doubtless, it was because of this that God commanded the children of Israel to observe the feast of the Passover at the beginning of every new year. It seems remarkable, on the surface of it, that a commemorative event should really be necessary. You would have thought that with such an outstanding event as the deliverance from Egypt in their history, the generations of the children of Israel would have talked about it, not once a year but every day of their lives. Why should they need a visible and concrete reminder of the event in the form of a seven-day feast?

God gave them this instruction because He knew the terrible tendency of the human heart to forget. It is simply astonishing how easily we can blot out from our minds, not only the unpleasant things of the past, but the great and important ones as well. It was because of this that God instructed the children of Israel, after they had miraculously crossed over the Jordan, to build a monument of stones so that future generations would be prompted to ask, 'What do these stones mean?'

One of the most devastating effects of sin is the paralysis it brings to both mind and memory. Dr Martyn Lloyd-Jones said, 'We are so dull and stupid as the result of sin, that we might even forget the death of the Son of God for us, if the Lord Himself had not ordained and commanded that we should meet together and take bread and wine. It is the setting up of the stones in Gilgal once more.'

O Father, I am so grateful for the redemption You have provided through Your Son. And I am grateful, too, that You have planned, through the institution of Holy Communion, to help me never to forget to be grateful. Amen.

Deuteronomy 11:8–25; 2 Peter 1:3–9
1. How were memories to be triggered?
2. What was Peter's concern?

Memorial Stones

16 APR

FOR READING AND MEDITATION – EXODUS 28:1-14

'Fasten them on the shoulder pieces of the ephod as memorial stones for the sons of Israel.' (v12)

We must spend one more day meditating on the importance of commemorative acts that help to keep alive in our minds and memories the great events of the past. We suffer so much from the effects of the Fall that we need objective things and tangible reminders – something outside of ourselves – that will lead us, as we saw yesterday, to ask, 'What do these stones mean?'

There are many reasons that could be given for the benefit that comes from commemorating divine acts and events, but perhaps the biggest reason is this – it reminds us of facts. Our security as believers rests not on theories, ideas, or suppositions – but *facts*. I have heard some theologians say that we can dispense with the facts of our faith and simply hang on to the teaching that arises out of those facts. This is a subtle and dangerous suggestion and leads to great error. The Exodus of the children of Israel from Egypt was a fact. The daily supply of manna in the wilderness (except on the Sabbath) was a fact. The crossing of the Jordan was a fact.

They are all great and glorious facts – facts of God. The death and resurrection of Jesus Christ is also a fact – something that belongs solidly to history. When the future generations of Israel would ask, 'What do these stones mean?' the reply would be given – something miraculous and wonderful happened here. When, today, the question is asked of us, 'What do the bread and the wine on the Lord's table mean?' the same answer must be given – something miraculous and wonderful happened here.

My Lord and my God, I am so grateful that I am a partaker of the most miraculous and mighty event this planet ever saw – Jesus' death on Calvary. Help me, through my life and witness, to make the meaning of redemption a little clearer to someone today. In Jesus' name I ask it. Amen.

Luke 1:1-4; 1 Corinthians 15:1-8
1. Why did Luke write his Gospel?
2. What was of first importance to Paul?

A New Covenant

17 APR

FOR READING AND MEDITATION – HEBREWS 12:18–29

'To Jesus the mediator of a new covenant...' (v24)

We come now to the third aspect of the Communion – the aspect of covenant. I have met many Christians over the years who are turned off by the word 'covenant'. They feel it to be a word that describes the technicalities of the faith – something to be debated in places of theological education rather than discussed as part of everyday discipleship.

Let me say two things about this: firstly, the concept underlying the biblical word 'covenant' is something even the youngest Christian can grasp. Secondly, not to grasp it means you will miss out on the real depth of meaning that lies behind the Communion. In all four records given to us of the institution of the Lord's Supper, we find an allusion to covenant. Matthew says, 'This is my blood of the covenant' (Matt. 26:28). Mark uses identical words and Luke uses similar words. Paul says, 'This cup is the new covenant in my blood' (1 Cor. 11:25). Notice particularly Matthew's words: 'This is my blood... which is poured out for many *for the forgiveness of sins*' (my emphasis).

Just think of the fantastic truth that lies enshrined in these words – through the shedding of the Saviour's blood, God was taking the initiative to establish a new pact or 'covenant' with His people, out of which would come the blessing of forgiveness for sin. God, of course, had always been *willing* to forgive sin, but because of its heinous and serious nature, some kind of 'satisfaction' was necessary. The Old Testament sacrifices could never really take away sin – a new way had to be found. At the Last Supper, Jesus stood to break the news that a new way had been found. Hallelujah!

O God my Father, I am so grateful that You found a way not to ignore my sin, but to forgive it. And it was not a cheap forgiveness, but a costly one. It drew blood. All honour and praise to Your wonderful and mighty name. Amen.

Genesis 9:1–17; 17:1–14
1. Who initiates a covenant between man and God?
2. What part do we play in covenant with God?

Awaiting a Signature — 18 APR

FOR READING AND MEDITATION – JEREMIAH 31:31-37

'The days are coming… when I will make a new covenant with the people of Israel and with the people of Judah.' (v31)

Today we ask ourselves the question: what exactly is a covenant? The dictionary meaning of the word signifies a mutual undertaking or agreement between two or more parties, each binding himself to its full obligations. The Bible word for covenant (Greek: *diatheke*), however, does not in itself contain the idea of a joint obligation; it mostly signifies a promise or an undertaking given by a single person.

To understand the idea behind the 'covenant' which Jesus spoke about at the Last Supper, we must again take a brief look at Jewish history. Many centuries before Jesus came, God had entered into a covenant with Abraham, sealed by blood, in which He promised to bless him and bring him into a good and prosperous land (Gen. 15). Later God renewed that covenant with Abraham's descendants – the Israelites – after He had rescued them from slavery in Egypt (Exod. 24).

Hundreds of years after this, in the seventh century BC, when the people had forsaken God and broken His covenant many times, the Almighty gave to Jeremiah the promise we have read in our passage today. But there is something missing here. When the first covenant with Abraham was inaugurated, it was sealed by blood (Gen. 15:9-10). Such was the case also when the covenant was renewed at Sinai (Exod. 24:8). However, there is no mention of blood in Jeremiah's covenant. It is like a legal document which has been drawn up, but not signed or witnessed. When and how was it made valid? I think you will already know how that validation came, but we must wait until tomorrow to have the full legal details.

O Father, I am impressed as I follow the track of Your purposes through the flow of history. I see that nothing was left to chance. You planned my salvation down to the tiniest detail. Thank You, dear Father. In Jesus' name. Amen.

Genesis 21:22-34; 31:43-55
1. What were the terms of the covenant between Abraham and Abimelech?
2. What were the terms between Laban and Jacob?

A Great Moment in History

19 APR

FOR READING AND MEDITATION – HEBREWS 13:5–21

'The God of peace... through the blood of the eternal covenant brought back from the dead our Lord...' (v20)

We ended yesterday by looking at God's promise of a new covenant as given to the prophet Jeremiah – a covenant, we noted, which had no ratifying blood. We described it, you will remember, as being like a legal document awaiting a signature. We have to pass on a further six centuries to learn how that covenant was ratified when, after years of patient waiting and increasing expectancy, the Son of God stood in an upper room in Jerusalem and announced that the ratifying blood of God's new covenant would be none other than His own. Is it possible to exaggerate the staggering nature of that moment?

Picture the scene with me once again. Jesus takes up the bread which was normally used at this stage in the Passover service and dedicates it to a new purpose. The ancient Passover, celebrated in the same way for centuries, is now being given a new direction. Luke says, 'In the same way... he took the cup, saying, "This cup is the new covenant in my blood, which is poured out for you"' (Luke 22:20).

It was at this point that the Passover was transformed so that it became the Lord's Supper of the new covenant. Jesus was saying, in effect, 'The new covenant promised by Jeremiah has been waiting for centuries to be ratified and sealed. Now that hour has come, and the blood of sealing is the blood that will flow out of My own veins. This cup is the symbol of that. Drink it in remembrance of Me.' So every time you approach the Communion table, let your mind focus on the thrilling thought that Jesus died to bring us into a new covenant relationship with God.

O God my Father, when I see what initiating this new covenant meant for You and Your Son, I feel like bowing to worship You. You put everything You had into my redemption; help me put everything I have into making it known. In Jesus' name. Amen.

1 Samuel 18:1–4; 20:1–17; 2 Samuel 9:1–10
1. Why did Jonathan make a covenant with David?
2. How did David fulfil the covenant?

The Wonder of Grace

20 APR

FOR READING AND MEDITATION – HEBREWS 8:1–13

'The covenant of which he is mediator is superior to the old one, since the new covenant is established on better promises.' (v6)

Now that we have seen a little of what the covenant Jesus referred to is all about, we must spend some more time meditating on the implications of it. It is described as a 'new' covenant to distinguish it from the old covenant which was mediated mostly through obedience to law.

This is why some Christians refer to the Old Testament covenant as the covenant of law and the new covenant, announced through Jeremiah and ratified with Christ's blood, as the covenant of grace. The difference between the covenant of law and the covenant of grace is this: the law said, 'Do this and you shall live'; grace says, 'I will do it for you.' This is why the new covenant supersedes the old – Christ lives within us to provide the power to reach the standards God requires of us.

Another thing to be observed as we look at the nature of this new covenant is that it is utterly and entirely an undertaking of God. Normally, as we said, a covenant involves two parties, and the principle underlying it is this: if you will do your part, I will do mine. But the word *diatheke* suggests that it is a covenant ordained and laid down by an authority. It is not God and man making an equal contribution, but God taking on the full obligation. There is a human side to it, of course, but compared to God's input, it is as if it is all of Him. There need be no fear that because of human weakness and frailty it will break down, for, as one quaint preacher put it, 'God thought it, Christ bought it, the Holy Spirit wrought it, and though the devil fought it – thank God, I've got it.' And, may I add – got it for ever!

O Father, the more I contemplate the wonder of Your covenant love, the more I want to bow my knees in gratitude. But I know You want more than my gratitude – You want my obedience also. For it is obedience that opens the door to Your power. Amen.

Hebrews 9:1–28
1. What does the law require?
2. Why is the new covenant better?

Forgiven!

21 APR

FOR READING AND MEDITATION – EPHESIANS 1:3-14

'In him we have redemption through his blood,
the forgiveness of sins…' (v7)

We have touched on the fact that one of the exciting features of the new covenant was that it promised the remission of sins, but let us now bring that aspect into closer focus. Under the old covenant, sin could not be dealt with effectively: 'It is impossible for the blood of bulls and goats to take away sins' (Heb. 10:4). The Old Testament sacrifices served as a type or shadow, which meant that God did not overlook sin, but rather 'looked over' it to the coming sacrifice of His Son on Calvary.

I wonder if you are someone who struggles with the use of the word 'blood' in books or hymns about the Christian faith. If so, I would encourage you to look again at the phrase 'the blood of Christ', for it is one of the most sacred and significant phrases in Scripture. Rather than being a morbid phrase, it speaks of forgiveness, cleansing, redemption, life.

Blood flows everywhere in the Bible. The red river runs from Genesis to Revelation: cut the Bible anywhere and it bleeds. For you see, it is not just by the death of Christ that we are saved – it is through death *by the shedding of blood.* His blood is covenant blood. It is not merely blood poured out in affectionate self-giving. It is the blood of a covenant sacrifice in which God commits Himself to us in the most solemn way possible. The well-known hymn puts it beautifully:

> *His oath, His cov'nant and His blood*
> *Support me in the whelming flood*
> *When all around my soul gives way*
> *He then is all my hope and stay.*
> *— Edward Mote (1797-1874)*

O my Father, how can You be so gracious to the ungracious, so loving to the unloving, so considerate to the inconsiderate? Your love overwhelms my heart. I freely receive what You so freely bestow. Thank You, Father. Amen.

Hebrews 10:1-22
1. Why is it impossible for the blood of bulls to remove sin?
2. Why is it possible for Christ's blood to remove sin?

Give Thanks

22 APR

FOR READING AND MEDITATION – PSALM 95:1–11

'Let us come before him with thanksgiving...' (v2)

We come now to look at the fourth aspect of Communion – the aspect of celebration. One of the words that is becoming increasingly popular in Christian circles to describe the Lord's Supper is the word 'Eucharist'. It simply means, 'Thanksgiving'.

The Communion service ought not only to be a time in which we remind ourselves that we are a corporate body, meeting together to commemorate the death of our Lord and to remember the nature of the new covenant, but a time when we open up our hearts to God in joyful celebration and praise. Jesus, you will remember, prior to distributing the bread and wine at the Last Supper, 'gave thanks' (Matt. 26:26-27). And following the conclusion of the Passover, we read that He and His disciples sang a hymn (Matt. 26:30). A Communion service (so I believe), though focusing on very solemn and profound truths, ought not to be doleful.

I remember the Communion services I attended in the early days of my Christian experience, and I could never understand why the people in my church were so gloomy and sorrowful. When I questioned them about this they said, 'The sufferings of Christ on the cross ought to be responded to with sympathy and sorrow.' 'That is true,' I used to say. 'We must start there, but surely we must not stop there. After we remember His suffering and sacrifice for us, our hearts should respond in grateful worship and praise.' After many years as a Christian, I have seen no reason to change my thinking. So I say with increased conviction – at the Communion table, we not only remind ourselves of our Lord's redemptive sacrifice, we *rejoice* in it too.

O Lord Jesus, You who knew how to give thanks in everything, teach me how to catch this note anew and apply it to every part of my life. For Your own dear name's sake. Amen.

Psalm 98:1–9; 100:1–5
1. Why was the psalmist jubilant?
2. How do we enter God's presence?

Enjoying Him 23 APR

FOR READING AND MEDITATION – JOHN 6:22–40

'I am the bread of life. Whoever comes to me will never go hungry...' (v35)

We continue reflecting on the thought that the Communion service is to be a time of rejoicing and worshipful celebration. E.F. Kevan points out that the Lord's Supper is a meal and throughout time, 'meals have been the occasions of conviviality and of friendship'. He goes on to say, 'A feast is the method of expressing joy. When you have a birthday, you have a birthday party; when you get married, you have a wedding meal. When you want to express gladness in any matter, you have a common meal together, and this is one of the aspects that the Lord has taken up in His ordinance of the Lord's Supper.'

As we have not yet developed the thought that the Lord's Supper is a spiritual feast, this seems to be an appropriate moment to do so. Our text for today, although not having a direct reference to the Communion, is nevertheless a description of what happens when we meet together at the Lord's table – we *feed* on Him. Just as we *eat* the bread – not merely look at it – and just as we *drink* the wine, and not merely observe it, so in the Communion we partake of Christ and feed our souls on Him.

One critic of the Gospels has described the verse which says, 'Unless you eat the flesh of the Son of Man' as 'Christian cannibalism'. He evidently did not understand how the soul can draw strength and nourishment from regular contact with Christ. It is a mystery, but don't let the mystery of it hinder you from experiencing and enjoying it. I say 'enjoying it', for one can no more partake of Christ without enjoying Him than one can partake of a good meal and not experience a degree of pleasure.

Blessed Lord Jesus, the more I feed on You, the more I enjoy You. And the more I enjoy You, the more I want of You. Only You can truly satisfy. I am eternally grateful. Amen.

Psalm 104:1–35
1. Why did God provide bread and wine?
2. What was the psalmist's response?

Let's Celebrate! — 24 APR

FOR READING AND MEDITATION – 1 CORINTHIANS 5:6–11

'Christ, our Passover lamb, has been sacrificed.
Therefore let us keep the Festival...' (vv7–8)

In the verses before us today, Paul expresses the common sense of joy and exhilaration that we experience in Christ by alluding to the best known of all the Jewish feasts – the feast of Passover. We have said so much about the Passover in these meditations that there seems little else left to say, but actually there is. Although, strictly speaking, the Passover was the communal meal eaten during the evening of what the Jews call 'the fifteenth Nisan', it came to be applied also to the week-long Feast of Unleavened Bread which followed.

Both the Passover meal itself and the week that followed was, and is to this day, a time of great rejoicing for the nation of Israel. The basis of that rejoicing was their deliverance from the tyranny and bondage of Egypt. However, a greater exodus than that enjoyed by Israel has been effected in human history. It is the deliverance wrought by Jesus Christ on the cross of Calvary. Because He, the Paschal Lamb, has been slain and because by His blood we have been set free, we are exhorted to keep the feast.

What can Paul be meaning here? Is he saying that we ought to keep the ancient feast of the Passover just as the Jews do to this day? No, he is saying that the whole of the Christian life should be conceived of as a festival in which we continuously celebrate what God has done for us in Christ. But although the Christian life is a continuous festival, the Lord's Supper – the particular Christian equivalent to the Passover – is a powerful means of crystallising truth and bringing home to our hearts the need and reason for continuous celebration.

O Father, when I see how much joy ought to be pulsing through my life, forgive me that I do not always take hold of it. Your cup is upturned to give, help me to turn up my cup to receive. For Jesus' sake I ask it. Amen.

Nehemiah 8:9–12; Philippians 4:1–7
1. How do we gain strength?
2. How can we always be rejoicing?

Sinners Saved by Grace

25 APR

FOR READING AND MEDITATION – REVELATION 5:1–14

'Worthy is the Lamb… to receive power and wealth and wisdom and strength and honour and glory and praise!' (v12)

Although, as we said yesterday, the Christian life is in many ways an unending festival, the Communion helps us (as did the Passover for the Israelites) to keep in focus the reason that lies behind our rejoicing – namely, the sacrificial death of our Lord Jesus Christ, God's Paschal Lamb. The Lord's Supper, as we said, is the Christian equivalent of the Passover and just as the Passover was central to Israel's life and identity, so the Lord's Supper is central to the Church's life of celebration.

There are many reasons that lie behind the praise of God's people when they meet together, but the central reason is always to be gratitude for our deliverance from the bondage of sin as accomplished through our Saviour's atoning death on the cross. When we focus on the cross, we are caught up in the worship of heaven and join with the angels and archangels to acknowledge the worth of our Creator and our Redeemer. To focus on the cross and not want to burst forth in praise means that we do not really understand what it is all about.

We attend church for many reasons – to find answers to life's perplexing questions, to find comfort when times are hard, to offer encouragement to others, and these are all valid occupations. However, the foremost purpose for our meeting together is to offer God praise for His great salvation. Everything else flows out of this. Christians sometimes make the rafters ring with their praise. And why not? If angels sing of the cross and have never tasted of its power, then how much more we, who are sinners saved by grace?

O Lord Jesus, when I realise how Your nail-pierced hand has passed over my life and cleansed me from every sin, my feelings will just not go into words. Just saying 'Thank You' seems so very inadequate. Yet I mean it. Thank You. Amen.

Hebrews 13:11–15; Revelation 7:9–17
1. What is our offering to God?
2. Describe the atmosphere of heaven?

Table Fellowship

26 APR

FOR READING AND MEDITATION – OBADIAH 6–15

'Those who eat your bread will set a trap for you...' (v7)

We come now to the last of our five aspects of the Communion – the aspect of commitment. In ancient times, and in some parts of the world today, sitting and eating a meal at someone's table implied a certain degree of commitment. You may have heard the phrase, 'the salt of the covenant', which arises from eating salt with someone, or in other words, having a meal with them. It was expected of those who ate at someone's table that they would never do anything to violate the friendship that had been shown them.

This kind of 'table fellowship' is illustrated in the passage before us today, where we see that the sacred loyalties which had been worked out together were being violated. Note the words again: 'Those who eat your bread will set a trap for you...' Another verse that points out the sacredness of table fellowship is Psalm 41:9: 'Even my close friend, someone I trusted, one who shared my bread, has turned against me.'

The thing that troubled the psalmist was not so much that he had been wronged, but that he had been wronged by someone who had sat at his own table. It was this verse, you remember, which Jesus used in John 13:18 with reference to Judas. It is clear from Scripture that taking a meal with someone implies a trust and a pledge. It is not dissimilar to the table of Communion. Jesus expects that when we eat and drink at His table, we will not be party to anything that would injure His cause or violate His eternal principles. Dare we eat and drink with Him and then go out and bring dishonour to His name?

O Lord Jesus, I tremble inwardly when I realise just what is involved in coming to Your table. I don't want ever to let You down. Empower me so that I will be a faithful follower of You – all the days of my life. In Your dear name I pray. Amen.

Leviticus 2:11–13; Joshua 9:1–20
1. Why would God ban yeast and honey but approve salt?
2. How did the Israelites honour a tricky covenant?

Self-Examination   27 APR

FOR READING AND MEDITATION – 1 CORINTHIANS 10:14-22

> 'You cannot have a part in both the Lord's table
> and the table of demons.' (v21)

We saw yesterday the importance of 'table fellowship' – the principle that once you 'eat salt' with someone, there is an implied commitment that you will never violate the friendship. All this takes on a deeper significance when we remember God's warnings to His people not to partake in heathen feasts (see Exod. 34:15; Num. 25:2-3).

A similar point is made in the passage before us today in the context of the Lord's Supper: 'Consider the people of Israel: do not those who eat the sacrifices participate in the altar?' (v18). Paul is saying here that for an Israelite to eat of a heathen sacrifice was to associate himself with all that the altar signifies. In verse 20 he goes on to say, 'The sacrifices of pagans are offered to demons, not to God, and I do not want you to be participants with demons.'

The clear meaning of all this is that the table at which we eat is, whether we realise it or not, the place where our loyalty is pledged. We cannot eat of the Lord's table if we are at the same time eating at the table of demons. This is why we should always approach the Lord's table with a willingness to bring our habits, our motives, and our lifestyle under careful scrutiny, and be prepared to break with all those things that are dishonouring to Jesus.

Note also that self-examination should end in an act of commitment: 'Everyone ought to examine themselves before they eat of the bread and drink from the cup' (1 Cor. 11:28). The purpose of self-examination is not to beat ourselves over the head with a spiritual club and say, 'I am a terrible Christian', but to surrender our failures to Christ, receive His forgiveness, and move a little closer towards Him.

Loving Father, I am challenged – but I know that *Your* challenges lead to life. Reveal in me any hidden resentment or wrong attitudes, and help me to let go of these things. Forgive me and make me clean again. In Jesus' name. Amen.

Psalm 139:23-24; 2 Corinthians 13:5-7
1. What was the cry of the psalmist?
2. What exam should Christians take regularly?

A Spiritual Health Check

28 APR

FOR READING AND MEDITATION – 1 PETER 4:12–19

'For it is time for judgment to begin with God's household…' (v17)

Today we hit a solemn and serious note – but one we cannot and should not avoid. If we fail to examine ourselves when we come to the Communion table and surrender to the Lord those things that are wrong, then they will become the virus within us that will bring about spiritual ill-health.

The apostle Paul told the Corinthians, 'Whoever eats the bread or drinks the cup of the Lord in an unworthy manner will be guilty of sinning against the body and blood of the Lord' (1 Cor. 11:27). What did he mean? Eating and drinking unworthily suggests participating in the Communion in a factious, unloving, critical, and judgmental spirit. This is a sin, not just against the Body of Christ, the Church, but against the Person of Christ as symbolised in the elements.

Almost every local church has those in its midst who come to the Lord's table bent on examination – not of themselves, but of others. I have no hesitation in saying that this attitude produces spiritual disharmony. There were some in the Corinthian church who, because they failed to examine themselves at the Lord's table and thus maintained wrong attitudes and wrong motives, became weak and sickly – some even died.

You see, spiritual ill-health can soon turn to physical ill-health – even death. Dare I say it? I must – there are some in the Christian Church who are sicker than they should be, for they allow the virus of wrong attitudes to take root in their souls. If we approach the Lord's table in the right spirit, then we will be able to approach the whole of life in the right spirit – period.

O Father, I am so quick to find fault with others, but You call me to pay attention to the state of my own spiritual health. Again I ask that You would cleanse me and make me whole. In the name of Jesus. Amen.

Matthew 7:1-5; 2 Corinthians 6:16–7:1; Hebrews 12:14-29
1. What should we avoid?
2. What should we embrace?

A Divine Command

29 APR

FOR READING AND MEDITATION – 1 SAMUEL 15:10–26
'To obey is better than sacrifice...' (v22)

As we begin to draw our meditations to a close, we return to the sentiment I expressed at the beginning of these two months – that one of the greatest needs of the contemporary Christian Church is to return meaning to the Communion. In view of this, we need to ask ourselves a personal and searching question: have we allowed our familiarity with the act of 'Holy Communion' to breed within us a sense of complacency? I would argue that to a large extent we have.

Roy Peacock, in his book, *This Do Ye*, says, 'To many, the Communion service has taken the form of an abstract set of actions performed, as one would watch a stage play, with interested or perhaps uninterested detachment. No longer do we hear the voice of Jesus, saying, "Do this in remembrance of me". No more is there the revelation that amazes us, challenges us and changes us, for our ears have waxed heavy and our eyes have been shut by a complacency of satisfaction.' He is generalising, of course, but even if the charge of complacency does not apply to us, every one of us cannot help but benefit from the attempt to comprehend more deeply the meaning of the Communion.

We meet around many tables during the course of our lives, but no table is more significant and meaningful than the one on which we place the simple emblems of bread and wine and celebrate Jesus' vicarious death and victorious resurrection. And remember: the Communion service is not a matter of inclination – it is a matter of command. Jesus said, 'Do this in remembrance of me.' As we said earlier – Jesus' sacrifice is of too great importance not to be regularly brought to mind and celebrated.

O God my Father, help me to embrace the meaning of Your Communion service. Help me never to lose the sense of its significance. In Jesus' name I pray. Amen.

Numbers 9:1–5; 1 Corinthians 11:23–26
1. What did the Lord command?
2. What did Jesus command?

Until He Comes

30 APR

FOR READING AND MEDITATION – REVELATION 22:7–21

'Look, I am coming soon!' (v7)

We remind ourselves, on this our last day together on this topic, of what we described earlier as 'the five c's of Communion' – community, commemoration, covenant, celebration, and commitment. Most Christians, irrespective of denomination, will agree that whenever we approach the Lord's table, we must recognise that it is a corporate act in which we focus our attention on Christ's redemptive death on Calvary, remind ourselves of its covenant nature, rejoice in the great benefits of the atonement and pledge our loyalty to Him who loved us and gave Himself for us.

There is just one more word I have to say before we close – the Lord's Supper is a wonderful but only a temporary provision for the Christian Church. We shall not celebrate it in eternity, for there faith will be lost in sight – we do it only 'until He comes'. As we move away from the holy table, we carry with us the thrilling thought that just as Jesus came at His first advent, so will He come again at His second advent.

The Lord's Supper commands, therefore, a confident belief in Jesus' second coming; it is the token of our Master's return. Indeed, without that belief it cannot be said to be truly celebrated. So permit me to repeat it once again – the Lord's Supper is 'until He comes'. This compelling verse puts it still more powerfully:

> And thus that dark betrayal night
> With the last advent we unite
> By one blest chain of loving rite
> Until He come.
> — George Rawson (1807-1889)

O Father, what can I say? My heart cries out in eager anticipation, 'Come, Lord Jesus.' Amen.

Revelation 19:6–9; 21:1–7; 22:1–6
1. How will Communion be consummated?
2. Describe our heavenly hope.

PRAY IT FORWARD ▶▶▶

Jesus, thank You for inviting me to Your table, where I am nourished, forgiven, and united with others in Your body. Teach me to live with open hands and an open heart, sharing what I have, that others may know Your grace. Amen.

PAY IT FORWARD ▶▶▶

Every day, people come to Waverley Abbey hungry for spiritual renewal. Your support helps us create spaces - both physical and digital - where people can be transformed by Christ. **Could you give today to share this blessing with others?**

Visit **waverleyabbey.org/donate-to-edwj** call **01252 784700** or scan the **QR code** ▶

MAY & JUNE

GOD'S NEW SOCIETY

INTRODUCTION

For over 2,000 years, the Church of Jesus Christ has been changing lives and serving the world. But what are the defining characteristics of the Church that have kept it strong throughout the ages?

Following the resurrection and ascension of Jesus, God established on earth a new society.

Over these two months we revisit the Early Church in the book of Acts, and re-apply some timeless principles for a thriving spiritual community.

Back to the Future

1 MAY

FOR READING AND MEDITATION – EPHESIANS 3:1-13

'His intent was that now, through the church, the manifold wisdom of God should be made known...' (v10)

Today we begin a series of meditations on the nature and characteristics of the Christian Church – what John Stott called 'God's New Society'. One of the best ways to discover how Church life was established and lived out is to look at the Acts of the Apostles, and that is where we will be spending much of our time. But on this opening day I must give you a warning: be ready to be challenged. For many, church life today is so very different to the Church's beginning on the Day of Pentecost. One theologian who studied in depth the differences between the Church of the first century and that of today said: 'The more I study the Early Church, the more I am convinced that we are desperately in need of a return to first principles and the ethos of the Acts of the Apostles.'

This theologian was not the only one to have made that observation. In the late 1940s, when Billy Graham was working as a Youth for Christ evangelist, he hosted an outreach event in Los Angeles. Thousands came to Christ, including many Hollywood celebrities. When the event was over, a group of ministers wrote to a newspaper complaining, 'Billy Graham has set the Church in Los Angeles back a hundred years.' When Billy heard this he is reported to have commented, 'Oh dear, I am so sorry... I was really trying to set it back 2,000 years!'

It is my conviction that every local church would do well to study the Acts of the Apostles with a view to identifying first principles. One thing is certain: if the Church of the twenty-first century reflects the principles and purposes of the Church of the first century, then there is considerable hope for the future.

My Father and my God, open our eyes that we may see – really see – how we, Your people, can truly walk in Your plans and Your purposes. Begin with me, I pray. In Jesus' name. Amen.

Psalm 85:6; Habakkuk 3:1-19
1. What was Habakkuk's prayer?
2. What was his attitude?

The Great Contemporary

2 MAY

FOR READING AND MEDITATION – ACTS 1:1–5

'In my former book, Theophilus, I wrote about
all that Jesus began to do and to teach...' (v1)

There is little doubt that the author of Acts is Luke, who travelled with Paul (Col. 4:14) and dedicated both his Gospel and Acts to a man named Theophilus. In the first five verses of the opening chapter of Acts, Luke sums up what he had dealt with in the twenty-four chapters of his Gospel – the purpose of Christ's coming to this world, His suffering on the cross, His resurrection, His appearance and instructions to the apostles, His promise of the Holy Spirit, and His ascension to heaven.

One word in the opening sentence tells us what the book is all about: 'began'. What Jesus began in the Gospels is continued in Acts. The Saviour had not finished when He ascended on high and returned to the royal throne. Through the Holy Spirit, He continues ministering in the lives of those committed to Him. Luke's opening statement could be paraphrased in this way: 'In this second book I am dealing with the things Jesus continues to do even though He is not around to be seen. He died, rose again from the dead, ascended to the Father – but now He is back. And how!'

Make no mistake about it: it is the risen Christ we see at work in the Acts of the Apostles, moving in the hearts of men and women and bringing them into His Church. The ministry of Jesus may have had a beginning, but it will never have an ending. Someone has written of Jesus, 'You can never catch up with Him as He is always going before – the Great Contemporary.' This ever present and ever active ministry of Jesus through the Holy Spirit means we will never have a complete biography of our Lord Jesus Christ. How can there be of someone who forever lives?

Lord Jesus, I am so thankful that the ministry You began when You came to this earth continues still, and I long that people today should become as aware of You as were the men and women of that first century. Help us, dear Saviour. Amen.

Philippians 1:1–7; Hebrews 12:2
1. What was Paul's confidence?
2. Why should we fix our eyes on Jesus?

Why a Church At All?

3 MAY

FOR READING AND MEDITATION – MATTHEW 16:13–20

> 'On this rock I will build my church, and the gates of Hades will not overcome it.' (v18)

Before we start to go through the Acts of the Apostles, we pause to ask ourselves these important questions: what is the Church, and why does it exist?

Many people associate the Church with tall Gothic buildings, stained-glass windows, and robed clergy. However, a church building is just a structure in which the Church worships. The Church is comprised of a farmer ploughing in a field, somebody at the kitchen sink, a student in a classroom, a mechanic in a garage, a business person at their desk, and so on. Wherever there is a heart that is redeemed and beats in unison with the heart of Christ – there a part of the Church exists. The Church is people – people who share the love of Jesus.

But why is there a Church at all? We remember that Jesus commissioned it. Deliberately He said, 'On this rock I will build my church.' The Church was not the idea or invention of the disciples. After Christ's death they did not decide, 'Let's get together and form a movement called the Church.' It was founded by Jesus and is a divine institution and revelation. There are many reasons why the Church was established, including to be His Bride (Rev. 21:2), but one of the main reasons for the Church being on earth is, as we saw earlier, to continue the work which Christ began. This is the exciting thing about the book of Acts – it shows us that what Christ once did, the Church was now doing. In terms of increase and the number of miracles that were performed, greater things happened through Christ in His Church than through Christ in the flesh. Let's not forget it was Christ in His Church that turned the ancient world upside down (Acts 17:6, KJV)!

Father, forgive us that by our lack of faith and courage we, Your present-day Church, tie Your hands and limit Your power. You long for Your Church to be bold and adventurous. Revive us again and set our hearts on fire for You. Amen.

Matthew 18:15–20; Ephesians 5:22–33
1. What did Jesus declare about the assembly of His Church?
2. What relationship did Paul liken the Church to?

They're Drunk!

4 MAY

FOR READING AND MEDITATION – ACTS 2:1–13

'Some... made fun of them and said, "They have had too much wine."' (v13)

It is impossible for me to give you a verse-by-verse exposition of the Acts of the Apostles – this would have to be spread over several months of *Every Day with Jesus*. So what I would like to do is to focus on some of the distinctives that made the Early Church the influence it was. Then we shall compare the Early Church with the Church of the present day to explore the differences and any adjustments we may need to make.

The first of these distinctives is this: the empowering ministry of the Holy Spirit. Without doubt, the day on which the Holy Spirit came upon the waiting disciples – the Day of Pentecost – is one of the greatest days in the history of the Church. When the Holy Spirit fell, His coming produced a transformation in the lives of ordinary everyday people, who became extraordinary people doing extraordinary things in extraordinary ways. A little while after they had received the Holy Spirit, they stepped out into the street, speaking in languages they had never learned. This strange phenomenon, and perhaps also the flushed look on their faces, caused some to yell, 'They're all drunk!'

The two main accusations directed at the early Christians – 'They're drunk' and 'They're mad' – are rarely heard today. Most twenty-first-century Christians do not come under such suspicion, though that is hardly to our credit. What would happen if we opened ourselves up to the Spirit as eagerly and responsively as did the Early Church? People would say the same about us as they said about the first believers: they're drunk and they're mad. Maybe the fact that they don't ought to be a matter of the greatest concern.

Father God, forgive us when we lack the empowering of Your Spirit in our Christian walk. Revive and refresh us today and help us to show You to others by our conduct and our character. In Jesus' name. Amen.

Isaiah 29:13; Colossians 2:20; 2 Timothy 3:1–5
1. What did Paul have to write to the Colossians?
2. What did Paul warn Timothy of?

The True Euphoria   5 MAY

FOR READING AND MEDITATION – ACTS 2:14–21
'These people are not drunk, as you suppose.' (v15)

Yesterday we ended with the thought that if we lived nearer to the heart of our faith, and were in closer touch with the Holy Spirit, we too might need to answer the suspicion that we are either drunk or unhinged. Alcohol provides temporary relief from day to day. It picks you up but then lets you down. Not to mention the various long-term harmful effects. The Holy Spirit instils a true joy. He picks you up without letting you down.

Permit me to ask you two personal questions: does your contact with the Holy Spirit energise you? Does He produce in you feelings of contentment and joyfulness? Has anyone ever decided that because of your commitment to Jesus you are somewhat unhinged or drunk? Don't let anyone tell you that devotion and exuberance cannot go together. They can.

Peter stood up on the Day of Pentecost to explain to the crowd that what they were witnessing was not a euphoria produced by alcohol; rather, he and the others were all under the influence of God's Holy Spirit. As he proceeded to unpack the truth about Jesus – His death, resurrection and ascension, and the outpoured Spirit – people suddenly cried out, 'What shall we do?' (v37). Within a short time 3,000 souls were added to the Church.

One talk, anointed by the Spirit, was responsible for bringing 3,000 people to the foot of the cross. 'Nowadays,' as someone has wryly remarked, 'in some places we might have to preach 3,000 sermons to bring one person to the foot of the cross.' Why the difference – especially since we in the twenty-first century have the same Holy Spirit? Perhaps this is the answer: it's one thing to have the Holy Spirit; it's another thing for the Holy Spirit to have us!

Lord God, drive out every fear that hinders my willingness to be fully empowered by You. Whet my appetite for You and Your Spirit. I long to be alive to You, intoxicated by You, filled with Your Spirit. In Jesus' name. Amen.

Matthew 3:1–11; Luke 11:13; 24:49
1. What did John the Baptist prophesy?
2. What did Jesus promise?

Three Thousand Resurrections!   6 MAY

FOR READING AND MEDITATION – ACTS 2:22–41

'When the people heard this, they were cut to the heart and said… "Brothers, what shall we do?"' (v37)

Today we continue thinking about the impact of the Spirit on the Church during the Day of Pentecost – page one of Church history! One interesting thing about the book of Acts – the only reliable account of the beginning of the Christian Church – is that on almost every page the Holy Spirit can be seen at work. It has often been said that if you removed the Holy Spirit from the book of Acts you would have nothing left.

Look at the deep conviction of the Spirit shown in today's text: 'When the people heard this, they were cut to the heart…' The scene in the second chapter of Acts is so different from that which we see in many churches today. We may be accustomed to hearing evangelists call people to be saved, but here the people are calling out to the evangelist, 'What must we do to be saved?' Such is the power of the Holy Spirit's conviction that they are 'cut to the heart'. How we long to see that same kind of empowering flowing through the Church today.

This raises a question: suppose there had been no Holy Spirit given on the Day of Pentecost, just what form would Christianity have taken? There would have been the message of the four Gospels without the life and power imparted on that day. The good news would have ended with the truth of the resurrection. But great though the resurrection was, and necessary in the divine scheme of things, clearly something else was needed to move people to cry out, 'What must we do to be saved?' That 'something else' was, of course, the Holy Spirit. At Pentecost, the same power that raised Christ from the dead (the Holy Spirit) raised 3,000 from the dead – that's 3,000 sinners who were dead in trespasses and sins!

Father, can it be that though the Holy Spirit is available to us in just the same way that He was to the Early Church, we do not allow Him the same freedom? If so, forgive us. And help us. In Jesus' name. Amen.

John 14:15–31; 16:5–16
1. What did Jesus say the Holy Spirit would do?
2. What would He convict the world of?

An Ideal Christian Meeting

7 MAY

FOR READING AND MEDITATION – ACTS 10:9–48

'They have received the Holy Spirit just as we have.' (v47)

We continue reflecting on the truth that one of the great distinctives of the first-century Church was the empowering ministry of the Spirit. Look with me now as we explore how the Holy Spirit worked to bring Gentiles into the Church, which up to this moment was mainly Jewish.

When Cornelius, a Roman centurion, had been instructed by an angel to send for Peter, Peter receives a vision of a sheet let down from heaven containing all manner of beasts, reptiles, and birds, some of which Jews were forbidden to eat (Lev. 11). A voice tells him: 'Get up, Peter. Kill and eat' (v13). Peter refuses because it goes against his Jewish customs and belief. After the sheet has been lowered and raised three times, he sees the full significance of the words: not only is the distinction between clean and unclean food being abolished; so too is the distinction between 'clean' and 'unclean' people.

When Peter arrives at Cornelius' house, he finds himself in what has been described as an 'ideal Christian meeting'. First, it had an ideal chairman. Cornelius did not prevaricate but gave the kind of introduction every preacher would like to have: 'Now we are all here in the presence of God to listen to everything the Lord has commanded you to tell us' (v33). It had an ideal preacher also. Peter began 'announcing the good news of peace through Jesus Christ' (v36). And it had, too, an ideal congregation who were eager and expectant, and as Peter spoke the Spirit came on them (v44). This perhaps highlights that if the Spirit is not at work in your church, don't necessarily look to the leader; it may be because the people are not expectant.

Holy God, I see how easy it is to paralyse a meeting of the Church simply by the lack of expectancy. When I gather with other believers may my spirit always be expectant, I pray. In Jesus' name. Amen.

Romans 2:25–29; 1 Corinthians 12:13; Galatians 3:26–29; Colossians 2:11–12
1. How does circumcision of the heart take place?
2. What is the result?

Refined Ineffectuality

8 MAY

FOR READING AND MEDITATION – ACTS 19:1–7

'[Paul] asked them, "Did you receive the Holy Spirit when you believed?" They answered, "No…"' (v2)

Two days ago we said that if Christianity had ended with the Gospels, it would have been a gospel without life and power – not a gospel that would conquer the world. The significance of the events recorded in the four Gospels had to be understood by Jesus' followers and conveyed to others in the power of the Holy Spirit.

In today's passage we see a Holy Spirit-less religion – good on facts and rules but lacking empowerment. When Paul arrived in Ephesus he sensed this lack in one group of disciples, and so his first question was, 'Did you receive the Holy Spirit when you believed?' They answered, 'No, we have not even heard that there is a Holy Spirit.' There were twelve in that group, and without the Holy Spirit what were they doing? Very little, it seems. They were just holding their own.

Apollos, when he came to Ephesus, was in a similar situation. Until instructed by Aquila and Priscilla, he was the picture of a present-day highly trained pastor who was eloquent and well-versed in Scripture (18:24–25). The result of theological training without the Holy Spirit is to produce what someone has termed 'refined ineffectuality'. Sadly, today there are pulpits occupied by people who have behind them years of training but no experience or dependence on the Spirit. The result? Refined ineffectuality and cultured emptiness.

What a difference between the 'twelve' at Ephesus and the other 'Twelve' – the twelve apostles. The other 'Twelve' were turning the world upside down; this 'twelve' were barely holding on. Training and refinement may be good but they are no substitute for the Holy Spirit and a God-dependent life.

Dear God, save us from this refined emptiness that makes Christianity a culture without conversion. Give us men and women who will stand in the pulpit and preach empowered by Your Spirit. In Jesus' name. Amen.

Ezekiel 36:26–30; John 14:17; Romans 8:9; 1 Corinthians 3:16
1. What had Ezekiel prophesied?
2. What did Jesus promise concerning the Holy Spirit?

This is What I Am Like

9 MAY

FOR READING AND MEDITATION – ACTS 17:1–9

'These men who have caused trouble all over
the world have now come here...' (v6)

Even a casual reader of Acts cannot help but be struck by the fact that Jesus Christ seems bigger and greater in the book of Acts (in terms of His miraculous and transforming power) than He does in the Gospels. Jesus on earth had great power, but Jesus in His Church is even more powerful. Jesus, working through the Holy Spirit, has enabled and empowered His people, as we see from today's text, to 'turn the world upside down' (v6, KJV).

It is clear that, in many countries of the world, congregations are going back to the book of Acts for a fresh vision of the Church. One correspondent said, 'Our church has just gone through the Acts of the Apostles once again, and all our hearts are ashamed as we see how far we have drifted from the original pattern.' Is the Spirit leading His people back to His blueprint, we wonder? I cannot help but believe it. God is concerned that in every age He should have people on earth who show the world what He is really like. He longs to indwell us and empower us in this century in the same way that He empowered the Early Church. A Holy Spirit-less Christianity does nothing for anyone; nothing for the Church and nothing for the world.

Perhaps the question we should ask ourselves is: are we as open to the energising and empowering ministry of the Spirit as were our brothers and sisters of the first century? Dr Harry Ironside, a pastor, said: 'In the Early Church the Holy Spirit was the pulse beat of all they did – the Life of their living. In the Church of [our] century sometimes it is difficult to find a pulse at all.'

Lord God, help us not to settle for anything less than the kind of power that energised Your Church in the Acts of the Apostles. Revive us, dear Lord, and bring us back to where You want us to be. In Jesus' name. Amen.

John 15:16; Acts 1:8; 4:1–13
1. What did the observers take note of?
2. What did Jesus say would happen when the Holy Spirit came on the disciples?

Feeding the Mind

10 MAY

FOR READING AND MEDITATION – ACTS 2:42–47
'They devoted themselves to the apostles' teaching…' (v42)

Now we move on to explore another distinctive of the Early Church: their devotion to divine truth. In fact, several distinctives of the Early Church can be identified in the passage before us today. We shall look at the others later, but first we focus on the words 'They devoted themselves to the apostles' teaching…' Notice: they *devoted* themselves to it, which means that they gave it their undivided attention.

The first community of Christians was a learning and listening one. Clearly, the 3,000 new converts that came into the Church on the Day of Pentecost, plus the many others who were daily added to their number, gave themselves to listening to the apostles as they unfolded the truths concerning Jesus Christ, the Lord. They didn't gather to listen (as some may do today) with an attitude that says: 'I hope they won't go on too long this morning. I have quite a number of things I want to do before the start of next week.' And they did not become so taken up with the manifestations of the Spirit that they resented understanding the truth underpinning the miraculous. The Early Church, it seems, did not put intellectualism on a pedestal, but they were not anti-intellectual either.

One leader tells how he asked a man why he didn't go to church. In response the man said: 'Because every time I go to church I feel I have no need of anything above my collar. I might as well unscrew my head and put it under the seat!' That man, I think, would have been very comfortable in the Early Church. In my opinion he would have found not only inspiration for his heart but also food for his mind.

Father, You have given me a mind with which to think through the great issues of life, and I am deeply grateful for it. Help me become as devoted to divine truth as were those first disciples. In Jesus' name. Amen.

John 5:31–40; Acts 17:10–12; Romans 15:4
1. What was Jesus' indictment of the Jews?
2. What was the example of the Bereans?

The Only Reliable Doctrine

11 MAY

FOR READING AND MEDITATION – 1 JOHN 2:18-27

'The anointing you received from him remains in you,
and you do not need anyone to teach you.' (v27)

Today we digress slightly to look at a verse outside of the Acts of the Apostles; one which has a bearing on this matter of devotion to divine truth. One of the saddest things I know is to hear a Christian who has experienced a deep work of the Holy Spirit say something like this: 'Now that I am filled with the Spirit, He is the only teacher I need. I can dispense with all other teachers. The Spirit alone is my guide.' The text Christians sometimes use to support this position is the one before us today.

In this verse, John is not ruling out human teachers but is drawing attention to the problem caused by a group known as the Gnostics, or 'Knowing Ones', who influenced some of the Early Church. This sect propounded the idea that the teaching of the apostles was to be supplemented with the 'higher knowledge' they claimed to possess. John was saying that what the Christians had been taught under the Spirit's ministry through the apostles was not only adequate, but was also the only reliable doctrine. They needed nothing more than that they had received through the Spirit's unfolding of the apostles' teaching.

The teaching that has come down to us in the New Testament is the teaching of the apostles. When the canon (rule of faith) came to be fixed in the second, third, and fourth centuries, the test of canonicity was whether a book had been written by the apostles or came with the authority of the apostles. Those who claim to be part of the Church but ignore or tamper with the apostles' doctrines are in error – plain and simple. Today's true followers will be like the Early Christians – 'devoted... to the apostles' teaching' (Acts 2:42).

God our Father, how can we sufficiently thank You for inspiring the first apostles to lay down for us the truths by which we, Your Church, are to operate? Help us not merely to believe them but to obey them. In Jesus' name. Amen.

Psalm 71:17; John 6:41-51; Acts 18:24-25; Ephesians 4:21-24
1. Who is the supreme Teacher?
2. What is said of Apollos?

At the Apostles' Feet

12 MAY

FOR READING AND MEDITATION – ACTS 5:12–16

'And all the believers used to meet together in Solomon's Colonnade.' (v12)

In order to get a feel of how important teaching was in the life of the Early Church, permit me to take you on an imaginary trip into that first Christian community.

We begin in one of the crowded homes in Jerusalem – crowded because many who were converted at Pentecost were visitors to the city, and a number stayed on in the homes of other Christians so that they might be grounded in the faith. Sometime after breakfast, everyone made their way to Solomon's Colonnade in the Temple. When they arrived, they sat on the floor with countless other believers to worship God and to understand the teaching of the apostles. There was no set schedule – just uninhibited worship, prayer, and teaching, which probably lasted several hours.

Imagine how they would have felt as they heard Peter or Matthew or John describe all the things they had seen Jesus do and explain the words that He had said, and picture their faces as they listened spellbound to the amazing truths these men unfolded. One moment they might have rocked with laughter as one of the apostles said something humorous, and the next they might have wept as they heard again the grim details of Christ's death on the cross. Their time would probably have ended in quiet contemplation as they considered the consequences of their new-found faith. Then they would return to their homes to continue in fellowship and discussion.

This portrayal may give us an idea of Church life in the beginning. However, we can still sit at the apostles' feet as we open the inspired Word they have left us.

God my Father, give me an ever-growing appetite for divine truth, I pray, for I know that without it I cannot develop as a Christian. The entrance of Your Word gives light – and also life. I am deeply grateful. Amen.

1 Corinthians 5:4; Ephesians 5:15–21; Hebrews 10:19–25

1. What did the writer of Hebrews exhort?
2. How are we to speak to one another?

The Best Training Ground   13 MAY

FOR READING AND MEDITATION – ACTS 7:1-16
'Brothers and fathers, listen to me!' (v2)

Today's reading shows that Stephen, who was a deacon, was obviously a gifted teacher too. He was chosen for his spiritual qualities (6:1-6), and his knowledge and grasp of Scripture as demonstrated in his sermon to the Sanhedrin is quite astonishing. Where did he get that knowledge and understanding? He got it, I imagine, first by studying the Scriptures for himself, but also by sitting at the apostles' feet, listening to their teaching.

Let's take another imaginary trip back to the days of the Early Church. Once again, picture yourself sitting in the large congregation that met in Solomon's Colonnade. Look around – who do you see? There's Stephen, Philip, Simeon, and over there is Agabus and an enthusiastic young convert named Silas. You will definitely be hearing from these men in the future, but not for a while. Despite the fact that it is a power-packed church, no one is going anywhere just yet – not even the apostles. In truth, it will be several years before the names I have mentioned come into prominence. They will one day have responsibility – great responsibility – but their main task right now is to experience daily the life of Christ as it is being worked out in His Church.

Men and women of God are often best prepared for future service by being involved in church life. Bible colleges are both helpful and important, but they are no substitute for serving Christ in the community of the Church. When you meet the people mentioned above a few years ahead, they will be towering spiritual giants. They were shaped by true Christian community – the best training ground there is.

Father, I must ask myself how willing I am to be shaped by the community in which You have put me. Give me a teachable and responsive spirit, I pray. In Jesus' name. Amen.

Colossians 2:6-7; 2 Timothy 2:1-15; Titus 1:9
1. What did Paul exhort Timothy to do?
2. What is one of the qualifications of an elder?

The Glorious Ascension 14 MAY

FOR READING AND MEDITATION – ACTS 1:6–11

'He was taken up before their very eyes,
and a cloud hid him from their sight.' (v9)

We pause in our meditations for a couple of days to consider Jesus' ascension. Although the Christian Church has celebrated Ascension Day (the sixth Thursday after Easter) for many centuries, there are those (sceptics and liberals) who regard the ascension of Jesus to heaven as nothing more than a graphic myth or a triumphalist parable. Accepting as I do the full authority and veracity of Scripture, I believe that what we read about in today's passage – the ascension of our Lord to glory – is a definite fact and one of the great cardinal truths of the Christian faith.

Ian Macpherson said that the New Testament represents the ascension as a sublime drama in three acts: secession, procession, and accession. By secession he means the withdrawal of Christ from the earth. Jesus not only had to leave the earth, He had to be seen to leave it. If Jesus had walked over the Mount of Olives and disappeared from sight, the disciples might have expected Him to reappear as He had during the previous forty days. His ascension from the Mount of Olives made it clear that He would not do so. A wider and greater ministry awaited Him.

The ascension, however, involved not only a secession but also a procession. Listen to this: 'When he ascended on high, he took many captives and gave gifts to his people' (Eph. 4:8). Jesus, when He passed into heaven, had behind Him a train of defeated adversaries – probably the spiritual enemies who were overcome at the cross.

Then to secession and procession we must add accession. Jesus remember, ascended to a throne and sits there now at the right hand of God – King of kings and Lord of lords.

Risen, exalted and glorified Lord, I see that Your ascension meant that You went from the here to the everywhere – although out of our sight, nearer to our hearts. Thank You, dear Saviour. Amen.

Mark 16:19; Luke 24:51; Hebrews 4:14; 9:23–28
1. How did the writer of Hebrews describe the ascension?
2. Why is Christ's ascension so crucial?

In the year this book went to print, Ascension Day fell on 14th May.
When your reading coincides with Ascension Day, you may find it helpful to read both today's and tomorrow's entries together.

Scan to download today ▸

A Ten-Day Prayer Meeting

15 MAY

FOR READING AND MEDITATION – ACTS 1:12–26
'They all joined together constantly in prayer…' (v14)

After Jesus had been taken up to heaven, the apostles returned to Jerusalem to await the 'promise of the Father' (v4, RSV). All the apostles were there except Judas, who by this time had gone to where he belonged (v25). The selection of an apostle to fill the vacancy left by Judas took place by lot (v26), and there has been much debate over the years as to whether or not this was the correct move. Some theologians think the disciples were rather hasty in choosing Matthias and should have waited a little longer. Had they done so they would have been able to include the apostle Paul as the twelfth member of the group. Those who counter this view suggest that the fact that Peter quoted from the book of Psalms suggests that he could not have been wrong in his understanding of the situation.

Important though the selection of a new apostle was, a matter of equal significance is recorded in this passage: the apostles, together with over a hundred of Christ's followers, 'joined together constantly in prayer'. We in the Christian Church tend to make much of the Day of Pentecost (and rightly so), but often we overlook what happened in the ten days between the ascension and Pentecost. This, remember, was the first time the 'believers' had met together after Jesus had returned to heaven – and they met together to pray. Mary the mother of Jesus was there, we are told (v14). Isn't it interesting that the last glimpse we have of the mother of Jesus is at a prayer meeting! She who had carried the Saviour in her womb – her gift to the world – was now waiting to be filled with the Spirit – His gift to her.

Father, I know that all great movements begin in prayer. But are things not being brought to birth because we, Your people, lack both persistence and power in prayer? Help us to pray more earnestly, dear Father. In Jesus' name. Amen.

Acts 4:23–31; 12:5,11–12; 16:13–15; 21:5
1. What was the pattern of the Early Church?
2. What were some of the results?

Slow But Sure   16 MAY

FOR READING AND MEDITATION – ACTS 7:17–43
'[Moses] received living words to pass on to us.' (v38)

We continue reading through Stephen's sermon to the Sanhedrin in order to grasp something of the depth of his biblical knowledge and understanding. What a powerful sermon it was. Stephen, Philip, Simeon, Agabus, and many others – who were not apostles – grew to great spiritual stature by experiencing and serving Jesus in His Church. Before these people were given any responsibility in the Church they, like us all, went through the stages of just-new-to-the-faith life, rejoicing in their salvation, fellowshipping with other believers, and sitting at the feet of the apostles in order to understand more fully God's purpose for their lives. Though we made this point yesterday, it bears repeating: you simply cannot find anything more effective for producing top-quality servants of God than ordinary church life – being the people of God in community.

It concerns me when I see organisations pick out promising young believers from a church and, after only a few weeks in the Christian life, thrust them into frontline activity. I fear they don't fully understand what they are doing. They are potentially robbing them of the joy of slow spiritual growth and maturity. The idea some Christians have is that everything in the book of Acts happened in the space of about two years. Stephen probably preached his famous sermon to the Sanhedrin about three years after Pentecost, and the first missionary journey took place about seventeen years after that great event! The Jerusalem believers were gradually, over time, equipped to live as God desired for them. They grew organically, steadily – the best way to grow.

Father, in an age when everything has to be 'instant', thank You for showing me the importance of slow growth. I want my life to be proven in the midst of church life. May this happen, I pray. In Jesus' name. Amen.

Colossians 1:3–11; 2 Thessalonians 1:3
1. What did Paul pray for the Colossians?
2. What did he give thanks for in relation to the Thessalonians?

Another Urgent Need   17 MAY

FOR READING AND MEDITATION – ACTS 5:17–25

'Look! The men you put in jail are standing
in the temple courts teaching the people.' (v25)

The Early Church, as we are seeing, was a Church devoted to the apostles' teaching. Those first Christians were eager to learn and gave themselves wholeheartedly to the task of assimilating the truth and principles expounded by the apostles.

The apostles' teaching has come down to us in its definitive form into what we now call the New Testament. These days, when there are so many different opinions and views being promoted in our churches, one of the most urgent needs is to recover an understanding of the authority of the apostles. When the apostles taught in the early years of the Church, they knew that Jesus had given them a unique authority, and the Church that existed in the period immediately after the apostles knew it also. Ignatius, bishop of the church at Antioch who was martyred about AD 110 had, according to tradition, heard the apostles and may have been ordained by Peter or Paul. However, he wrote: 'I do not issue you with commands like Peter or Paul for I am not an apostle.' He was a bishop, but not an apostle, and he knew that he did not have the authority to issue commands as did the apostles.

What is tragic about some sections of today's Church is that they have lost a sense of biblical authority. Consequently, no clear message flows out from many modern pulpits. A true New Testament church is a biblical church – a church that believes the Bible, understands the Bible, teaches the Bible, and lives according to the Bible. Where the Bible is not opened, the Church speaks with a stutter. It may express opinions, but really, without the authority of the Bible, it adds little to life today.

Lord God, bring Your Church back once again to Your Word. Show us that without the Scriptures we have no real authority. Save us from stuttering and help us to speak with a clear voice. Indeed, with one voice. In Jesus' name we pray. Amen.

Romans 10:1–13; 2 Corinthians 4:1–6; 2 Timothy 4:2
1. What did Paul proclaim?
2. What was Paul's charge to Timothy?

Real Community 18 MAY

FOR READING AND MEDITATION – 1 JOHN 1:1–10

'But if we walk in the light, as he is in the light,
we have fellowship with one another' (v7)

Now we move on to think about another distinctive of the Early Church: a rich sense of community and fellowship. Immediately after Pentecost we read, 'They devoted themselves to the apostles' teaching *and to fellowship*' (Acts 2:42, emphasis added).

As you may already know, the Greek word for 'fellowship' is *koinonia* (pronounced 'coinownia'). This word can also be translated 'community' – and implies living together as one family in deep, rich, and authentic relationships, and having things in common. The coming of the Holy Spirit produced in the lives of the early Christians a spirit of oneness and unity that was quite remarkable. Prior to Pentecost there was no real identifiable sense of fellowship among God's people. There was friendship, consideration, even love, but no deep sense of unity and oneness. As the Holy Spirit was living in them they were drawn together into the kind of fellowship that cannot be achieved in any other way. Once we belong to Jesus, we belong to everyone else who belongs to Jesus.

Perhaps we do not have the same concept of fellowship as did the Early Church. Today, generally speaking, the word 'fellowship' is used to describe a genial get-together of Christians, followed by coffee and biscuits. Have you ever wondered how the Early Church managed to do so much without coffee and biscuits? Please don't think I am opposing life groups or socialising. I am simply saying that *koinonia* goes far beyond that and is much deeper and much richer. May the Lord help us to redeem the word and, in our churches, live in true fellowship just as the Early Church did.

Father, help me to understand that without *koinonia* the Church is not at its best. We live well only when we are in fellowship – fellowship with You and with each other. Make us participants in true *koinonia*. For Jesus' sake we pray. Amen.

1 John 2:7–11; 3:11–24
1. What is the basis of our fellowship together?
2. What is the demonstration of it?

In Constant Review 19 MAY

FOR READING AND MEDITATION – GALATIANS 2:1–10

'James, Cephas and John… gave me and Barnabas
the right hand of fellowship…' (v9)

Yesterday we commented that sadly some church communities lack the rich, deep fellowship experienced by the first-century Christians. Anyone who reads the Acts of the Apostles will almost instantly realise that there is a world of difference between the way the Early Church lived and the way we live today. 'It is the depravity of institutions,' observes one author, 'that given in the beginning to express life, they often end in throttling that very life. Therefore they need constant review, perpetual criticism, a continuous bringing back to the original purpose and spirit.' You may feel, as you read day by day through these current meditations, that they are unnecessarily harsh but, believe me, behind them is much tenderness and sadness that we aren't living in the good of all that God desires, according to the original blueprint for His Church and His children. In attempting to live in Christian community, in its original purpose and spirit, we as His ambassadors and representatives need to be able to continually and honestly review our relationship and daily walk with God and each other.

A minister once told me about a group of Christian students at a particular university who carried out a survey of what their fellow students thought about Christ and the Church. The students were first asked to give an opinion on how they viewed Christ, and then on how they viewed the Church. Afterwards, when they analysed the survey, the Christian students got a shock. They found that only 5% of those questioned were for the Church, yet 85% said they were for Christ. Let's pray that Jesus will be free to reign in His Church.

Father, help us to be honest with You and each other. Help us see that one of the reasons why Jesus died was so that His followers could enjoy true fellowship and communion. Please enable us to understand this. In Jesus' name. Amen.

Acts 2:22–47; 1 Corinthians 2:2; 9:16; 2 Corinthians 4:5
1. What did Peter present?
2. What happened as a result?

Sharing in and Sharing Out

20 MAY

FOR READING AND MEDITATION – PHILIPPIANS 2:1–18

'If you have any encouragement from being united with Christ…
if any common sharing in the Spirit' (v1)

Today we continue focusing on the word *koinonia* in order to try to understand more of its meaning. *Koinonia*, as we said, means partnership or fellowship, and it is a fellowship in which all are equal. C.H. Dodd, a Greek scholar, explains: 'The noun *Koinonia* means fellowship, *Koinonos* (another noun) means partner, and the verb *Koinoneo* means to share.' From this we can see that those who partake in the *koinonia* share in a common concern. But what is it that we share?

First, we share in the same inheritance – rescued from the kingdom of darkness and brought into the kingdom of light, receiving a restored relationship with our heavenly Father, redeemed by the blood of the same Son, and indwelt by the presence of the same Holy Spirit. The same God who lives in me lives in you. The same blood that saved me also saved you. The same Spirit who empowers my life is also in you. This makes us one family.

Koinonia is something we share in together, but it is also something we share out. *Koinonia* has to do not only with what we possess, but what we do with what we possess. So what do we share with one another? We share everything God wants us to share. In the days immediately following Pentecost, Christians in Jerusalem were called to share their possessions with one another and to have everything in common. There were particular circumstances that required this; for example, the vast number of pilgrims who came to Christ at Pentecost who made their home in Jerusalem. Although God may not call us to do the same thing today, this question remains: are we willing and if He did, would we?

Father, help me in all honesty to answer this question. If self-interest has a strong hold on me then dissolve it by the power of Your love I pray. In Jesus' name. Amen.

Acts 10:34–35; Galatians 3:28; James 2:1–17
1. What does it mean to show favouritism?
2. How is this overcome by true fellowship?

God-Dependency

21 MAY

FOR READING AND MEDITATION – EPHESIANS 4:1–16

'Until we all reach unity in the faith and
in the knowledge of the Son of God…' (v13)

As we read Acts we can see that the Early Church enjoyed a degree of community and relationship that was greater than anything ever known before. At least four aspects of this unity can be observed in the Church that was established on the Day of Pentecost.

The first unity, of course, was unity with God. If there is no unity with God then disharmony spreads itself all down the line of human relationships. The first Christians were so God-dependent that they took on the significance of the one on whom they were dependent. The consciousness that God is working in and through you, thinking in and through you, is one of the greatest annulments of inferiority and fear that I know. 'In Him who strengthens me, I am able for anything,' said Paul (Phil. 4:13, Mof). God-dependence is a humbling experience, but it is also a Hallelujah experience.

A second unity was unity among themselves. Doubtless there were many strong personalities in the Early Church who were well able to express themselves, but in the atmosphere of the Spirit, self-centredness gives way to other-centredness. No one was more given to individualistic self-expression than Peter. That's why I love the verse that says, 'Then Peter stood up with the Eleven' (Acts 2:14). Previously he had often stood against the Eleven, but now he was with them and alongside them. When he spoke, the Eleven spoke in him and through him. They were one with each other and spoke with one voice. A 'good Christian' was once described as 'one who gets along well with others according to Jesus Christ'. How many of us, I wonder (myself included), can be described this way?

Father, help me understand that unity is not something I create; You have already created it through Christ and the Holy Spirit. Help us to stop trying to make unity, and simply surrender to it. In Jesus' name. Amen.

1 Corinthians 1:9; Ephesians 4:1–32; 1 John 1:7
1. What causes disunity?
2. How can we grow up together?

The Results of Unity

22 MAY

FOR READING AND MEDITATION – PSALM 133:1–3

'How good and pleasant it is when God's people live together in unity!' (v1)

Yesterday we thought about two aspects of the unity created by the Holy Spirit which became so clear in the Early Church after Pentecost. A third unity was one we have already touched upon: unity in their attitude to material possessions. 'All the believers were together and had everything in common' (Acts 2:44). The unity of the Spirit resulted in a unity of economic interests and goods. Today some Christians attempt to create the *koinonia* by getting together in a community and voluntarily sharing their possessions. But sharing possessions was not the cause of *koinonia* – it was the result of it. I do not doubt that God does call some people to live in community, but whether or not He calls you to do this, every one of us needs to be open to His prompting to share what we have with others.

A fourth unity was a unity of all people, regardless of race or culture. Admittedly, at first the Early Church revealed its prejudice – it took a vision from heaven to get Peter to go to the Gentiles – but eventually the Spirit prevailed. Look at this: 'In the church at Antioch there were prophets and teachers: Barnabas, Simeon called Niger...' (13:1). Simeon is widely thought to be an African Gentile and held an important position and ministry gifts which he exercised in the church at Antioch. Along with others, he laid his hands on Barnabas and Paul to send them out to preach the gospel (13:3). Gentile, Jew, African, Asian, rich or poor, whole or broken, God has opened the gates of His kingdom wide for all to enter and He has made His Church the welcome committee. Our prejudice and preferences have been superseded by God's heart of love for all.

Lord God, show us how we can restore this fourfold unity to the Church of the twenty-first century. You are not withholding Your Spirit – but are we withholding ours? If we are, please forgive us and help us. In Jesus' name. Amen.

Acts 20:32–38; 2 Corinthians 9:6; Galatians 6:10
1. What were Paul's farewell words to the Ephesian elders?
2. What did he remind the Corinthians of?

The Church as Bread

23 MAY

FOR READING AND MEDITATION – 1 CORINTHIANS 10:14–33

'Because there is one loaf, we, who are many, are one body…' (v17)

While considering the *koinonia* of the Early Church, we ought to acknowledge another phrase found in Acts 2:42: 'They devoted themselves to the apostles' teaching… to fellowship, *to the breaking of bread…*'

The term 'breaking of bread' is almost certainly a reference to what we now call the Lord's Supper or Holy Communion. At first the believers would celebrate their oneness in Christ over a meal, and at the same time remember the cause of that oneness – Jesus' death at Calvary. They would break open a loaf and pass it to each other, giving thanks to God as they did so for their unity in Christ. We know from Paul's first letter to the Corinthians that within a short period of time some Christians became more interested in eating than in celebrating their unity in Christ (1 Cor. 11:17–34). This prompted the apostle to lay down new guidelines for celebrating the Lord's Supper. The breaking of one loaf, practised by the Early Church, was meant to underline their unity as one Body.

A loaf of bread is a fitting figure of the unity of the Church for at least four reasons. First, bread is a unity made up of many units. Second, it is the product of both earth and heaven. Earth produces the grain, but it needs rain from heaven to water it. Third, bread, like the Church, is not a luxury, but a necessity. We can manage without cake, but bread is a staple food. Fourth, bread can only fulfil its function through fraction. It is made to be broken. The Church, like bread, is to be broken in God's hands if it is to be of service to the world. All this, and more, was caught up in the simple but sacred act of the breaking of bread.

Father, I am grateful for all that I receive when I draw near to the communion table, but may the wonder of the unity of Your body come home to me, too, when I draw near to my own dining table. In Jesus' name I ask it. Amen.

Matthew 5:23–24; 26:26; 1 Corinthians 11:17–34
1. What happens when we disregard the Lord's table?
2. How does 'examination' relate to 'unity'?

The Greatest of All Rooms

24 MAY

FOR READING AND MEDITATION – ACTS 2:1

'When the day of Pentecost came, they were all together in one place.' (v1)

Today we pause in our meditations on the distinctives of the Early Church to celebrate Pentecost Sunday. The disciples' experience at Pentecost was the catalyst for all that followed in the Acts of the Apostles and throughout history down to this very day.

An article appeared in an American magazine some time ago, which had these words as its title: 'Little rooms where new worlds were made'. It talked about some of the great rooms of history and the new worlds created from them. There was the chamber in Philadelphia where the Declaration of Independence was signed. There was also the room in London where Karl Marx wrote his communist classic *Das Kapital*. Then there was the room in the English seaside town of St Leonards on Sea where John Logie Baird succeeded in producing television. The article spoke of many other rooms, but by far the greatest of all rooms was that in which 120 disciples of Christ met in the days leading up to the Day of Pentecost (see Acts 1:13). From that room came the beginnings of a new society – the Church. This is the only society which is of any ultimate consequence.

Let me encourage you on this Pentecost Sunday to open your heart to all that God has for you. Has the fire in your heart died down? Are you just coasting in your Christian life rather than walking side by side with Jesus through every hour of every day? Are you conscious that your spiritual life is becoming mundane? Then confess your fears and desires to God right now and ask Him to touch your life once again and set your heart on fire. Pray this prayer with me:

God, on this Pentecost Sunday breathe Your fire once again into my life. I confess my fears and desires and ask that You will touch me afresh. Holy Spirit, come and fill me to overflowing. In Christ's precious name I ask it. Amen.

1 Chronicles 21:26; 2 Chronicles 5:12–14; Malachi 3:1–4

1. What is the link between prayer, praise, offerings, and God's fire?
2. What did the fire do and how might that relate to us?

In the year this book went to print, the Day of Pentecost fell on 24th May.

Is Church Life Dangerous?

25 MAY

FOR READING AND MEDITATION – 1 CORINTHIANS 11:17–22

'I have no praise for you, for your meetings do more harm than good.' (v17)

Having seen something of the deep sense of community and fellowship that existed in the Early Church, we must now ask the question: to what extent is first church *koinonia* reflected in the Church today? Generally speaking, possibly because twenty-first-century life is difficult to compare with the Early Church situation, it's a difficult question to answer. While there is love, friendliness, and sharing in Christian churches, when measured against the *koinonia* of the New Testament – the commitment to share each other's lives in the deepest way possible – today's Church seems a little lacklustre.

Please note that I am generalising, for there will be many exceptions to what I am saying here. However, as a first-hand observer of church life for many years, I am compelled to say that when it comes to true *koinonia*, many churches fall short of the ideal. 'Going to some churches,' says one writer, 'can be dangerous to your health.' He continues: 'I have the scars to prove it. But you can't see them at the front. They're all at the back!' Another disillusioned Christian said, 'I found more understanding and compassion in the world than I did in the Church.'

While we thank God for those churches where true *koinonia* functions, there are far too many where backbiting, gossip, cliquishness, and lack of consideration for others rules the day. How sad it is that in so many places God is worshipped and the Word of God is preached but *koinonia* is conspicuous by its absence. There is no doubt in my mind that the nearest thing to heaven on earth is a fellowship of Christians who are living in true community and relating to one another in the Spirit of Jesus Christ.

God my Father, help us, Your present-day Church, into a living fellowship which transcends all race and class, and to know a unity that the Church enjoyed in its beginnings. Amen.

Proverbs 11:30; Matthew 4:19; 1 Corinthians 9:1–27
1. How did Paul seek to win people?
2. How does this demonstrate *koinonia*?

Praying and Shaking

26 MAY

FOR READING AND MEDITATION – ACTS 4:23–31

'They raised their voices together in prayer to God.' (v24)

Moving on, we now look at another distinctive of the Early Church: the practice of persevering, faithful prayer. The book of Acts contains many accounts of how believers turned to prayer when they found themselves in difficulty. But their prayers were not just limited to times of emergency only; often they prayed for a long time just for the joy of developing their relationship with their loving heavenly Father.

This latter aspect of prayer – praying for the sheer pleasure of communicating with heaven – is, I believe, what is being conveyed in Acts 2:42: 'They devoted themselves to the apostles' teaching and to fellowship, to the breaking of bread *and to prayer*' (emphasis added). We should never forget that the Church was born in a prayer meeting, and I am convinced that to those early believers it was unthinkable that they could ever grow spiritually without recourse to prayer.

Look again at today's reading: Peter and John had been before the Sanhedrin and had been commanded not to speak any more in the name of Jesus (v18). So when they are released what do they do? They go back to their fellow Christians, report the facts – and pray. What might we have prayed for under the same circumstances? That the minds of the members of the Sanhedrin might be changed? But listen to their request: 'Enable your servants to speak your word with great boldness' (v29). How did God answer their prayer? We read, 'the place where they were meeting was shaken' (v31). It was as if God was saying, 'Don't be afraid; let me show you how much power is at my disposal.' It certainly worked, for we then read, 'they were all filled with the Holy Spirit and spoke the word of God boldly' (v31).

Dear God, wake us up to the power that is available to us through persevering faithful prayer. We know this in theory, but we are so reluctant to give ourselves unreservedly to such prayer. Forgive us and help us. In Jesus' name we ask it. Amen.

John 17:1–26; Acts 10:1–4
1. How did Jesus model prayer?
2. What is said of Cornelius?

He is Praying — 27 MAY

FOR READING AND MEDITATION – ACTS 9:1–19

'Ask for a man from Tarsus named Saul, for he is praying.' (v11)

We continue looking at this important aspect of prayer in the Early Church. One of the great characters of Acts is the apostle Paul. Above everything else he was a praying man, and the way in which his prayer life began is quite intriguing.

Paul (or Saul as he was known at first) was struck down and blinded when Jesus appeared to him on the Damascus Road. He who had laid many low was now himself laid low. 'For three days he was blind,' says the record, 'and did not eat or drink anything' (v9). What did he do during those three sightless days? He prayed. The fact that Saul, who had been bent on destroying the Church, was now praying to the one whose purposes he had tried to frustrate is surely incredible. But amazing as it may be to us, imagine how astonished Ananias must have been when God told him to go and lay hands of healing on the very man who had been coming to lay hands of destruction on him. Yet he obeys. Saul of Tarsus had lost his physical vision, but he gained a new spiritual vision. As he wrote in Ephesians 1:18, the eyes of his heart were gloriously opened.

Paul, who without doubt became one of the greatest prayer warriors of all time, instinctively prayed from his conversion. Granted, his conversion was powerful and dramatic, but it's important to emphasise that one of the very best things that those new to faith can do is develop their new relationship with God, and that is the primary purpose of prayer. Where and how we learn to pray is not important; what is important is that we do it, for without prayer there is only a stuttering and stilted march of progress in the Christian life.

My Father and my God, let this note go ringing through my soul today: my prayer moments are my greatest moments. Help me to remember that prayer is the Christian's vital breath. In Jesus' name. Amen.

Romans 1:9–10; Ephesians 1:15–23; Philippians 1:9–11; Colossians 1:9–14
1. What is a hallmark of Paul's letters?
2. What are some of the things he prays for?

Locked in and Locked Out

28 MAY

FOR READING AND MEDITATION – ACTS 12:1-19

'[Rhoda] exclaimed, "Peter is at the door!"
"You're out of your mind," they told her.' (vv14-15)

Today we look in on one of the great prayer meetings of history – a prayer meeting that brought about the deliverance of Peter from prison.

Herod had already put James to death (v2), and now no doubt it was his intention to do the same to Peter also. When some of the Christians in Jerusalem heard that Peter had been imprisoned, they immediately went to the house of Mary, the mother of Mark, and began to pray. Their prayer was sincere, earnest and 'without ceasing' (v5, KJV) and God answered by sending an angel into the prison to expedite Peter's escape. Imagine Peter's surprise when a light shines into his cell, the chains fall off his wrists, and the angel says to him: 'Quick, get up!... Put on your clothes and sandals... and follow me' (vv7-8). They reach the main gate of the prison, which opens up of its own accord – just like an automatic door. When Peter is well outside the prison and is able to manage on his own, the angel leaves him.

Immediately he makes his way to the house of Mary and knocks at the outer door. Rhoda, the servant girl who answers, recognises Peter's voice, but she is so excited that she runs back into the house, forgetting to open the door! Peter has to knock repeatedly before he is finally let in. The apostle seemed to have more trouble getting into the prayer meeting than he did in getting out of prison! It's not unusual that when Christians gather together to pray they are surprised to find that God actually answers our prayers. Unusual, and yet quite usual! I'm extremely glad God hears and answers those prayers that so often are mixed with unexpectancy and doubt.

Father, I am so grateful that You answer my prayers even when You know that I am going to react with amazement and surprise when Your answer comes. Thank You for Your steadfast love and faithfulness. Where would I be without it? Amen.

Isaiah 58:9; 65:17-25; Jeremiah 33:3; Romans 10:12
1. What had God promised?
2. How do we know these promises are for all who believe?

The Church Goes 'Catholic'

29 MAY

FOR READING AND MEDITATION – ACTS 13:1–12

'And when they had fasted and prayed,
and laid their hands on them, they sent them away.' (v3)

Another amazing moment in Acts that is surrounded by an atmosphere of faithful prayer is the commissioning of Barnabas and Saul for the work of the ministry. The whole history of Western civilisation was redirected in that hour, for out of that hour went two men who gave the gospel to Europe – and to us. This is the section of Acts that tells us how the Church became catholic, and by 'catholic' I mean 'universal'; for everyone without distinction.

Five men in the church at Antioch – Barnabas, Simeon, Lucius, Manaen and Saul (Paul) – met together to fast and worship God. As they did so, the Holy Spirit spoke to them, indicating that He had a special work to do through Barnabas and Saul. A good deal of discussion has taken place down the centuries on just how the Holy Spirit got His message across to these five praying men. Some say it must have come through the voice of one of the prophets; others say one of the teachers would have conveyed it. Still others believe it would have come as a distinct impression to all five of them at the same time. Scripture is silent on the issue, but what is clear is this: once the Spirit had made known His will, they continued to fast and pray.

How committed these early disciples were to be waiting before God in patient prayer. If this same situation occurred in today's Church, upon hearing the Spirit's voice we would no doubt rise to take immediate action. These believers, however, sensed that Barnabas and Saul were about to enter a historic moment, and they needed to be sure everything they did was in tune with the will of God. We would do well to remember that sometimes hasty action is worse than no action.

Father, teach me how to take every step in the atmosphere of patient prayer. And save me from doing everything in a rush. Slow me down, dear Lord, that I might keep pace with Your purposes. In Jesus' name. Amen.

Luke 11:1–10; Acts 16:1–10
1. How was Jesus' promise fulfilled?
2. What was the result?

Power Breaks Through

30 MAY

FOR READING AND MEDITATION – ROMANS 12:9–21
'Be… faithful in prayer.' (v12)

Over the past few days we have been seeing how important the practice of persistent, faithful prayer was to the Early Church. The Church, we said at the beginning of these meditations, was born in a prayer meeting, and on almost every page of the Acts of the Apostles, both individually and corporately, believers are seen to be at prayer.

It would not be true to say that the twenty-first-century Church has stopped believing in the power of prayer, but it could be true to say that we are not as good as the Early Church at practising it. Many churches report that the least attended meeting in the church programme is the prayer meeting. It might sound a simplistic observation to some, but in my opinion the main reason why some churches today do not experience the same degree of empowering in their life as did the Early Church is because it does not give the same amount of time to prayer.

Over the years I have asked myself this question many times: at what point does the power of God break through into the life of the Church? The only conclusion I can come to is this: it breaks through at the point of prayer. God's empowering surges like a mighty ocean just waiting to find a point at which it can break through into the life of every Christian community. But the only point where it can break through is the point of prayer. When we pray a little then a little of God's power breaks through; when we pray a lot then a lot of His power breaks through. It is as simple as that. One preacher put it like this: 'It is not that prayer has been tried and found wanting. It is rather that it has not really been tried.'

Lord God, show me again that the reason why You want Your Church to pray is not to bring Your purposes in line with ours, but to bring our purposes in line with Yours. Forgive us that we so easily forget that. In Jesus' name. Amen.

1 Chronicles 16:11; Matthew 26:41; Luke 18:1–8; John 16:24
1. What is Jesus' teaching in this parable?
2. How did Jesus chide the disciples?

The Key Doctrine   31 MAY

FOR READING AND MEDITATION – ACTS 2:22–41
'God has made this Jesus, whom you crucified,
both Lord and Messiah.' (v36)

Yet another distinctive of the Early Church that we discover in the Acts of the Apostles is the emphasis which the believers placed on the lordship of Christ. Did you know that there are over a hundred references in the book of Acts to the lordship of Jesus Christ? The prominence given to this theme indicates that this is an issue of tremendous spiritual importance. John Stott, in a sermon he gave one year at the Keswick Convention, said: 'If I were to ask you what is the master key doctrine in the Scriptures, I wonder what you would answer? The sovereignty of God? The cross? The fullness of the Spirit? I would argue that the master key is… the lordship of Christ.' I agree.

Peter's sermon to the crowd gathered on the Day of Pentecost is punctuated with references to the lordship of Christ, and this is the point he highlights in today's text: 'God has made this Jesus, whom you crucified, both Lord and Messiah.' You see, no one can become a disciple of Christ, or continue to be a disciple of Christ, unless they give themselves to Christ's lordship. There are some who claim that it is possible for us to take Jesus as Saviour at the moment of our conversion and then receive Him as Lord at a later stage when we decide to give to Him our all. This is not biblical teaching. The recognition that Jesus Christ is God (and therefore Lord of all) is the one and only door into salvation. We could never have been saved by the intervention of a created being, such as an angel. It took God to save us. And without this admission – that Jesus is the Lord – there is simply no way into the kingdom of God.

Lord God, thank You for finding a way to restore our broken relationship. Once again I give my life to You. Be Lord in my life. May Your will be done and Your kingdom come in me today. In Jesus' name. Amen.

Romans 14:9; 1 Corinthians 8:1–6; 12:3; 1 Peter 3:21–22
1. What does the Holy Spirit enable us to declare?
2. How does Peter describe Christ's lordship?

A Shock to the System

1 JUN

FOR READING AND MEDITATION – ACTS 22:1–16

'"Who are you, Lord?" I asked. "I am Jesus of Nazareth, whom you are persecuting," he replied.' (v8)

Focusing still on the theme of the lordship of Jesus, we look once again at the conversion of Saul of Tarsus. Ponder this question: what was it that put Saul off his food for three days and overturned his theology?

I am slightly amused at the different ways in which great thinkers and philosophers over the years have tried to explain the reason for Saul's discomfiture on the Damascus Road. One suggests that he had an epileptic seizure. This is what he says: 'Saul, who later became Paul, was an epileptic visionary who used his physical problems to spiritual ends.' Well, all I can say in response is that Saul, the 'epileptic visionary', has enabled more clarity and wholeness to a greater number of people than any man who ever lived – save only Jesus. One theologian suggests that what unsettled him was a lightning flash which he mistook for a revelation from heaven. 'We all know what happens to people when struck by lightning,' he says. 'They are disoriented for days.' I feel both sad and angry when I hear so-called scholars trivialising the conversion of the great apostle Paul. He who has been instrumental in converting multitudes – was his conversion unreal?

The thing, so I believe, that had such a profound effect upon Saul of Tarsus was not the blinding light but the illumination that came to his soul concerning Jesus of Nazareth. Previously he thought that Jesus was just a carpenter from Nazareth; now he saw that He was none other than the Lord of the universe. It was a shock to both his spiritual and physical systems. But he came through it to be the greatest advocate of Christ's lordship that the world has ever seen.

Father, I am so thankful for the way You brought Paul into Your kingdom and for the fact that his blazing heart has set others on fire. Set me on fire also so that I too can kindle a flame of love for You in others. Amen.

John 10:4; 18:37; Acts 9:1–19; Revelation 1:15
1. Who was Paul persecuting?
2. What impact did the voice of Christ have?

Jesus – Saviour and Lord

2 JUN

FOR READING AND MEDITATION – ACTS 16:16–40

'Believe in the Lord Jesus, and you will
be saved – you and your household.' (v31)

When the slave girl who followed Paul and Silas was delivered from an evil spirit – a spirit of clairvoyance – it immediately affected the pockets of her owners. They had used her to make money for themselves by fortune-telling, and when the evil spirit had gone, their profits plummeted. In their anger they brought Paul and Silas before the magistrates, who ordered them to be beaten and thrown into prison.

Paul and Silas were probably unable to sleep because of the painful welts on their back, but remarkably they sing hymns of praise to God. Suddenly an earthquake shakes the prison, the doors swing open and everyone's chains are loosed. The jailer, awakened by the shock, sees the prison doors open and, thinking everyone has fled, is deeply disturbed. Since their security was the guarantee of his life, he decides to kill himself. But Paul cries out, 'Don't harm yourself! We are all here!' (v28). When the jailer sees that the prisoners have not fled, he asks Paul, 'What must I do to be saved?' (v30). Paul replies, 'Believe in the Lord Jesus, and you will be saved – you and your household.'

Look at Paul's words again: 'Believe in the Lord Jesus'. In the days of Paul and the other apostles, new believers were introduced immediately to the truth of Christ's lordship. There was no suggestion, as we said three days ago, that they could accept Jesus as Saviour and then, at some point in the future, commit themselves to Him as Lord. The Early Church spoke with one voice when it gave converts this message: if you want to be saved then you recognise Jesus' lordship over the whole of your life. There is no other way of salvation.

Lord God, again I pray that You will help Your Church not to fudge this issue in an effort to make it easy for people to be saved. Let Your Spirit be at work, highlighting truth and helping us stay close to Scripture. In Jesus' name. Amen.

Psalm 24:1–10; Acts 10:36; 1 Corinthians 8:5–6
1. What did Peter declare?
2. What did Paul say?

Biblical Evangelism

3 JUN

FOR READING AND MEDITATION – ACTS 28:17–31

'He proclaimed the kingdom of God and
taught about the Lord Jesus Christ...' (v31)

Today we continue reflecting on the thought that one of the great distinctives of the Early Church was the emphasis on the lordship of Jesus. It's always been a matter of great interest to me that the final verse of Acts contains these words: 'the Lord Jesus Christ'. We should not be surprised, for the words provide a fitting conclusion to a book that has made so much of His lordship. There is only one Jesus Christ; He is our Lord and Saviour Jesus Christ. And response to Jesus is response to the totality of His Person – He is both Saviour and Lord.

In Romans 14:9 Paul writes, 'For this very reason, Christ died and returned to life so that he might be...' What? When I start to quote that verse to people and ask them to fill in the blank, do you know what most say? 'Saviour.' When I ask, 'Why do you say that?' they reply, 'That is the reason why Christ died and returned to life... to be our Saviour.' But that is not what Paul said. Listen to his words: 'For this very reason, Christ died and returned to life so that he might be the *Lord* of both the dead and the living.'

It's a half truth when, in our enthusiasm to reach out to those around us, we present the gospel in a way that suggests the important thing is finding forgiveness for one's sin. The real issue, the greater issue, is committing oneself to the living Lord. Forgiveness of sins is necessary before one can live in harmony with Christ, but important though the forgiveness of sins is – and let no one minimise it – what is of even greater importance is the commitment to Christ as Lord. Evangelism that does not make this clear is not worthy of the name.

Lord God, deliver us from any confusion on this matter. Show us that You cannot be our Saviour unless we are willing to acknowledge You as our Lord. And help us as Your Church to make this clear to everyone. In Jesus' name we pray. Amen.

Isaiah 9:6–7; John 3:22–31; Ephesians 1:22
1. What did John declare of Jesus?
2. What had Isaiah prophesied?

Mutiny in the Ranks? 4 JUN

FOR READING AND MEDITATION – LUKE 6:43–49

'Why do you call me, "Lord, Lord," and do not do what I say?' (v46)

We started this section by asking the question raised by John Stott: 'What is the master key doctrine in the Scriptures?' The answer is this: the lordship of Christ. When we acknowledge that Jesus is not only Saviour but also Lord, then we have the integrating point for our faith and our behaviour. This is a truth which I believe needs to be stressed more clearly.

'But we do believe in the lordship of Christ,' I hear you say. 'Fine,' I answer, 'but are you willing to look at the words of our text and apply them to yourself – without hesitation and argument?' The Living Bible paraphrases Jesus' words like this: 'So why do you call me "Lord" when you won't obey me?' The issue of obedience to Christ as Lord is a challenge to us as today's Church. Let's ask: who is calling the final shots? Is it the Commander or the troops? The soldiers or the General? When we 'do our own thing' it creates confusion and distraction from our great commission (Matt. 28:18–20). For example, when people come up against a scriptural truth that they don't like or that exposes their sinful lifestyle, they say: 'Some biblical principles are very difficult to follow these days. We try our best to live up to them, but it isn't possible to practise them all.' That is a self-dependent life, trying to make life work ourselves. It is not the God-dependent life we have been called to.

If we say we believe Jesus Christ is Lord but do not rely on Him to enable us to do what He calls us to do, then we are merely paying Him lip service. Let me remind you of an often-used statement: if we do not crown Him Lord of all, we do not crown Him Lord at all.

Father, I don't want to live as a self-dependent member of Your Church. Yet that is what I am when I merely pay lip service to the truth of Your lordship. Help me put my words into action. In Jesus' name I ask it. Amen.

Matthew 7:24–29; John 14:23; Hebrews 2:3
1. What was Jesus' conclusion at the end of the Sermon on the Mount?
2. What question did the writer of Hebrews ask?

A Sense of the Numinous

5 JUN

FOR READING AND MEDITATION – ACTS 4:32–36

'With great power the apostles continued to testify
to the resurrection of the Lord Jesus' (v33)

Before we examine further distinctives of the Early Church, let's once again remind ourselves why we are exploring this line of study. It is because when we see clearly how God established the Church in the very beginning, what energised it, and what its vital elements were, then we are in a better position to build and develop and grow as the Church today. When we compare the Church today with the Church of the first century there are differences. Naturally there are great cultural differences between the Church of the New Testament and the Church of today (particularly in the West), but it is not the cultural differences we are seeking to identify – it is the spiritual ones.

Another distinctive of the Early Church that made it such a spiritual force and power was this: it had a strong and pervading sense of the numinous. The word 'numinous' doesn't appear very much in evangelical writings, but it was a favourite word of men such as C.S. Lewis, George MacDonald and Rudolph Otto. My dictionary defines it as 'sensing the presence of divinity; awe-inspiring'. It is a word that conveys the holy fear we experience when we become aware of our creaturehood, and realise that we stand in the presence of a holy God.

When John the apostle, banished to the island of Patmos, caught a vision of the glorified Christ, he 'fell at his feet as though dead' (Rev. 1:17). When Daniel became conscious that he was in God's presence, he said, 'I had no strength left, my face turned deathly pale' (Dan. 10:8). There can be no real complete knowledge of God unless there is some sense of the numinous. The Early Church experienced it.

Gracious and loving Father, You made the Early Church the standard by which all future growth could be measured. Forgive us that we miss the mark, and reveal this day our next steps. Restore us we pray. In Jesus' name. Amen.

Daniel 10:4–18; Revelation 1:9–20
1. What did the pre-incarnate Christ say to Daniel?
2. What did the glorified Christ say to John?

Two Out of Fellowship 6 JUN

FOR READING AND MEDITATION – ACTS 5:1–11

'Great fear seized the whole church and
all who heard about these events.' (v11)

Now we look at an incident which took place in the Early Church that, perhaps more than any other happening, contributed to a powerful sense of the numinous.

Prior to the incident with Ananias and his wife Sapphira, there had been large accessions to the Church – 3,000 on the Day of Pentecost, hundreds more as a result of the healing of the crippled man at the Beautiful Gate of the Temple, as well as those being converted day by day. But the judgment that fell upon Ananias and Sapphira temporarily stopped the rush because it created in the whole community a deep sense of godly reverence and fear. Ananias and Sapphira produced a serious fracture in the *koinonia* because they thought more about themselves than they did about the fellowship. Their sin was not that they sold the land and kept back some of the money for themselves, but that they lied about the transaction and pretended they got a price for it which differed from the amount they actually received. They were quite free to give their money to the Church or keep it for themselves – but they were not free to lie. Their root sin was hypocrisy, and it swiftly brought upon them the judgment of God.

But why was the penalty so severe? Because God wanted to show His people that His *koinonia* was not to be taken lightly. However slow to come to judgment God would appear in later times, this first sin against the Body (the Church) could not go unrecognised. If you ever need to be reminded of what God really thinks about hypocrisy in His Church then turn to Acts 5.

My Father and my God, in these days when You seem slower to come to judgment than You used to be, help me see that Your abhorrence of sin, like Your nature, is the same 'yesterday, today and for ever'. Keep this truth ever before me. Amen.

Jeremiah 9:5; 17:1–9; Galatians 6:7
1. What was Jeremiah's conclusion concerning the human condition?
2. What solemn word did Paul bring to the Galatians?

Overcoming Power

7 JUN

FOR READING AND MEDITATION – ACTS 19:8-20

'They were all seized with fear, and the name
of the Lord Jesus was held in high honour.' (v17)

The incident we are looking at today not only increased the sense of the numinous in the believers but it had a profound effect upon the non-Christian community as well. The fame of Paul's ability to work miracles seems to have spread so widely that there was an attempt to imitate his power. Some itinerant exorcists undertook to pronounce the name of Jesus over those who had evil spirits. While the seven sons of Sceva (a Jewish priest) were doing this, an evil spirit recognised that the exorcists were using the name of Christ without His authority. This evil spirit then caused the man possessed by him to jump on those attempting to perform the exorcism and beat them.

To understand this unusual event we have to understand Ephesus. It was the seat of magic, of exorcism, and of belief in the powers of darkness. Paul worked extraordinary miracles there in order to demonstrate that the Jesus he proclaimed was greater than the prince of the powers of darkness. Against this background, Paul's letter to the Ephesians takes on a new perspective. (Look, for example, at Ephesians 1:19-23; 3:20; 5:11-12; 6:11-12.)

As a result of what happened to the sons of Sceva, who used Jesus' name without His authority, the whole community was seized with fear, and a great spiritual move took place. Believers confessed their former, and apparently their continued, performance of magical practices. The evidence that God's power was at work in the Early Church, overcoming every power set against Him, clearly contributed to a sense of the numinous. How we need that same power to be at work in our churches today.

Lord God, help us, Your community, to live as You originally intended. We have come too far to turn back now. Remain with us, dear Lord, so that we see Pentecostal days again. Amen.

Genesis 35:5; Joshua 2:1-13; 2 Chronicles 17:9-11
1. What did Rahab say to the spies?
2. What happened when the Book of the Law of the Lord was taught?

A Developing Trend   8 JUN

FOR READING AND MEDITATION – ACTS 17:16–34

'He himself gives everyone life and breath and everything else.' (v25)

We continue reflecting on the truth that the Early Church lived with a deep sense of the numinous. The first Christians were in awe of God and experienced His continuous holy presence. When we lose a sense of reverence for God it will not be long before we find ourselves rationalising our relationship, adapting His words to suit ourselves, and cauterising our consciences.

I have written before of my concern about the way in which God is often trivialised, packaged for entertainment, seen as a formula for success, or treated like a celestial slot machine. Some years ago, when in the United States on a speaking engagement, I watched a singing group perform. I say 'perform' because they hindered any opportunity to sing along with them by telling the congregation, 'We'll do the singing, you do the worship.' Like me, no doubt most in the congregation wanted to sing as we worshipped. Later the song leader said, 'Close your eyes now while I talk to the man upstairs and ask Him to bless you.' I shuddered as he said that and thought to myself: how impoverished all this is, how trite when compared to the experiences of the men and women of Scripture, especially those in the Early Church.

There is, I know, a fine line between being God's friend and being too much in awe of Him, but we need to be careful that over familiarity does not minimise the reality of God. It saddens and distresses me when God is referred to in 'chummy' ways. Personally, I do not know how it is possible to talk meaningfully about a God before whose glory we have not first trembled.

God, help me always to be in awe of You. Your own Son knew You better than anyone, yet called You 'Holy Father'. May this same sense of awe and reverence pervade my relationship with You too. In Jesus' name. Amen.

Exodus 15:11; 1 Samuel 6:20; Isaiah 6:1–13
1. What element of God's character is underlined?
2. What three elements of God's character did the seraphs focus on?

The Way to Worship

9 JUN

FOR READING AND MEDITATION – HEBREWS 12:14-29

'Worship God acceptably with reverence and awe,
for our "God is a consuming fire."' (vv28-29)

How deep or widespread is the sense of the numinous in today's Church? In an age when God is viewed as someone who is becoming therapeutic rather than transcendent, not only by those who might be described as liberals, but by many evangelicals also, I fear we are making God too small. From the pulpits of traditional churches, and the unplanned pulpits of house groups, the Church is being subjected to references to God that reduce Him.

I am not arguing that we should lose the sense of familiarity that flows from the relationship we have as a son or daughter with our loving Father (God forbid!). However, we must be careful we do not allow that to lead us to an overfamiliarity which causes us to lose the sense of the numinous. Christians will always pay a price when they become overfamiliar with God. A right balance must be maintained. We draw near to a Heart that is filled with indescribable love, and yet as we draw near we are in awe. But why should we be afraid of someone we love? Doesn't the Bible tell us, 'There is no fear in love,' and that 'perfect love drives out fear' (1 John 4:18)? Yes, it does, but it is talking about a kind of fear that is different to the one I have been describing over these past few days. The fear I am talking about is a godly fear – a healthy reverence and respect for the authority and power of the Almighty.

Is it not a tragedy that for all our biblical understanding, and all our claims about our experience of the Spirit's power, in our churches we still present a God who is small enough to fit inside our tiny brains? To truly know God we must learn to know Him as He really is, and not conjure up our own caricatures.

Lord God, help us achieve the right balance, so that we draw close to You in love yet maintain a respect and an awe for You that recognises how awesome You really are. In Jesus' name we pray. Amen.

Job 28:28; Proverbs 1:1-7; Revelation 15:4
1. What is the beginning of wisdom?
2. What did the victorious sing?

Dangerous Criticism   10 JUN

FOR READING AND MEDITATION – ACTS 6:1–7

'The Hellenistic Jews… complained against the Hebraic Jews because their widows were being overlooked…' (v1)

Another distinctive of the Early Church was this: the ability to reconcile or hold together in unbroken fellowship strong people who differed. The passage before us today informs us that as the Early Church increased in numbers, the Hellenistic, or Grecian, Jews began to complain that their widows were being overlooked in the daily distribution of food. The Living Bible puts it like this: 'But with the believers multiplying rapidly, there were rumblings of discontent.' The Greek word for 'rumblings' is *gongusmos*, meaning 'a complaint expressed in subdued tones'. In other words, murmuring and grumbling.

Now there is nothing wrong with criticism, providing it is presented openly and honestly. Criticism is dangerous, however, when it is expressed in murmurings and not brought out into the open. Fellowship is based on confidence and trust; unaddressed grumbling breaks that confidence. Once the apostles heard what was happening, they took immediate action to resolve the issue. Though they were novices in the art of church management, they knew, nevertheless, that matters such as injustice, inequality, and dissension needed to be addressed directly and not simply prayed about.

How different matters would be today if the causes of dissension were faced and dealt with instead of being swept under the carpet in an atmosphere of superspirituality. The apostles acted promptly and resolved the situation. Churches have been split because the leaders decided to pray and not to act. It's not that prayer is unimportant; it's that some things need action. Nothing can be allowed to mar the unity of the Body. Nothing.

Father, please give the leaders of Your Church the courage and confidence they need to face and deal with every issue that threatens the unity of Your Body. In Christ's name I pray. Amen.

Proverbs 10:12; 15:18; 16:28; 28:25; 29:22; Matthew 18:15–20
1. What sort of person stirs up dissension?
2. What principles did Jesus lay down?

No Place for Prejudice   11 JUN

FOR READING AND MEDITATION – ACTS 11:1–18

'They… praised God, saying, "So then, even to Gentiles God has granted repentance that leads to life."' (v18)

At present we are examining the ability of the Early Church to reconcile, or hold together in unbroken fellowship, strong people who differed. Today's passage shows us that the news of Peter's visit to the house of Cornelius reached Jerusalem before he did. This allowed the 'circumcision party' – the group who believed salvation was for Jews only – a little time to marshal their forces for an attack on Peter. When they met with him they asked quite directly, 'Why did you go to uncircumcised men and eat with them?' (v3, RSV). Peter replied by recounting the events we looked at earlier. The very fact that Luke repeats so much of what took place in Peter's own words is an indication that he regarded the incident as being of great importance. Peter recounted first the vision he received and the divine command to 'have no hesitation about going' (v12). Then he told how, as he was speaking, the Holy Spirit fell on everyone in Cornelius' house 'as he had come on us at the beginning' (v15). As they listened to Peter, they could not help but be moved, and concluded with him that even to Gentiles 'God has granted repentance that leads to life'.

It wasn't easy for Peter to go to the home of Cornelius, a Gentile, and it wasn't easy for the Jewish Christians to admit Gentiles. The fact that they did is a tremendous testimony to their openness and responsiveness to the work of the Holy Spirit, who was moving in their midst. Any personal prejudice at this critical moment in the life of the Early Church could have brought it to a halt. How wonderful it would be if prejudice or preconceptions were dealt with as easily in the modern-day Church as they were in this.

Our Father, give us such an experience of the Holy Spirit, and such a love for Christ, that we, in the Church of today, will have the ability the Early Church had to hold together strong people who differ. In Christ's name we ask it. Amen.

Leviticus 19:15; Job 13:10; 1 Timothy 5:21; James 2:1–13
1. What did Paul urge Timothy to do?
2. What was James' indictment?

You Need Grace!

12 JUN

FOR READING AND MEDITATION – ACTS 15:36–41

'They had such a sharp disagreement that they parted company.' (v39)

After Paul and Barnabas had returned to Antioch from their missionary tour of Asia, Paul wanted to visit the churches again. Barnabas agreed, but was eager to take John Mark with them. But Paul resisted this, and a paraphrase of his remarks might read: 'John Mark let us down when he deserted us on our missionary tour. We can't afford to take someone unreliable. Let's forget him.'

After a while the disagreement got more heated, and the two men became so irritated with one another that they decided to part company. *The Message* paraphrases today's verse like this: 'Tempers flared, and they ended up going their separate ways…' This split could easily have led to the start of two denominations – the Paulites, who believed the Church should be for fully committed and reliable believers, and the Barnabites, who believed people should be given another chance. Holders of both views might well have felt justified in starting a different denomination, but thankfully this did not happen. Who was right and who was wrong? In my opinion, Paul was right in saying that John Mark ought not to have left them, but perhaps wrong in not giving him a second chance.

The church at Antioch was well aware of the strong differences between the two men and was no doubt deeply concerned for them. It's interesting that when Paul and Silas – the man Paul chose to replace Barnabas – departed on their journey, they were 'commended by the believers to the grace of the Lord' (v40). I wonder if they did it with a twinkle in their eye and said inwardly, 'Paul and Silas, you need it!' For it's only grace that can keep strong men pulling together.

Father, even now, as I pray, somewhere in Your Church strong spiritual men and women will be differing – and may even be in danger of parting company. Let Your grace flow in and prevail, I pray. In Jesus' name. Amen.

Colossians 4:1–10; 2 Timothy 4:9–11; Philemon 23–24
1. What is clear about Paul's relationship to John Mark?
2. Is there anyone to whom you need to be reconciled?

A Grand Christian

13 JUN

FOR READING AND MEDITATION - 2 TIMOTHY 4:1-18

'Get Mark and bring him with you,
because he is helpful to me in my ministry.' (v11)

We continue reflecting on the sharp division that arose between Barnabas and Paul. Luke, as we saw yesterday, honestly reported the scenario: 'They had such a sharp disagreement that they parted company,' he said (Acts 15:39). *Paroxusmos*, or 'paroxysm', is the word Luke actually used, and although in his day it may not have conveyed such violent emotion as it does today, the word still indicates that there was an angry dispute.

But sharp though the disagreement was, good came out of it. If Paul and Barnabas had travelled together, they would have gone to Cyprus and Galatia. One commentator explains that this would have consumed all their energy. However, by going separately, Paul finished his visitation of the churches in Galatia with enough strength left to look for new worlds to win for Christ.

Another point to be noted is that John Mark was reclaimed for the work of Christ, and there is little doubt that Barnabas had much to do with it. One writer suggests that when Paul sat down in later years to write the words in today's text, the scribe might have looked up with a quizzical smile as if to say, 'You really mean that? Mark, helpful in your ministry?' Whereupon Paul possibly replied, 'Yes, he is – and Barnabas had much to do with that. Barnabas was a better man than me. He was always taking up with people whom others might find difficult to associate with. He pleaded my cause when nobody believed in me. A great man, Barnabas.' Perhaps a tear then trickled down his cheek. Whatever had gone wrong in the past, it was now forgiven and forgotten.

Father, how good it is when sharp divisions between Christians are forgiven and forgotten. Reconciliation has the marks of the cross upon it – marks of love and restoration. Please help me restore any broken relationships. Amen.

1 Corinthians 9:6; Galatians 2:1-10
1. What is clear from Paul's account of events at Jerusalem?
2. Besides himself, who is Paul arguing the case for?

Disagreeing Agreeably

14 JUN

FOR READING AND MEDITATION – 2 CORINTHIANS 5:11–21

'God… has committed to us the message of reconciliation.' (v19)

For one more day we consider the need for reconciliation between strong personalities who differ sharply with one another. Before I became a Christian I had the idea that there were no disputes between Christians in the first century; such things, I thought, happened only among Christians of today. After I became a Christian I began to make a special study of the Acts of the Apostles, and at once I saw that the men and women of the first century were exactly the same kind of people as we are. If the Early Church had not been so taken up with Jesus, so filled with the Spirit, and so committed to reconciliation, it might not have survived.

Today's Church does not always appear to be as successful at reconciling differences as were the early Christians. Huge divisions split our churches. And the difficulty is not so much that Christians disagree – but that they disagree so disagreeably. It ought to be possible for those who are 'in Christ' to maintain a loving spirit even though they see things from different points of view.

I wrote that last sentence tongue-in-cheek for, as I look back, I am aware there have been times in my own life when I have failed in this respect. However, I don't think there has ever been an occasion when, after a short period of time, I have not sought reconciliation. Strong people will differ, and sometimes differ sharply, but the Church must always point them to the way of reconciliation. Any church that does not do that is not following the example set by the Church of the New Testament. Reconciliation is the heart of the gospel; all else is subsidiary.

Lord God, please bring Your Church to the place where it is a redeeming and a reconciling community. For how can we preach reconciliation to a lost world when we ourselves remain unreconciled? Help us, dear Father. In Jesus' name. Amen.

John 13:34–35; Romans 5:1–10; 2 Corinthians 5:18–20; Colossians 1:22
1. What is the heart of the gospel message?
2. How can we demonstrate this to a broken world?

The First Christian Martyr

15 JUN

FOR READING AND MEDITATION – ACTS 7:51–60

'While they were stoning him, Stephen prayed,
"Lord Jesus, receive my spirit."' (v59)

A further distinctive of the Early Church was this: there was no distinction between what we refer to as laity and clergy. Although Luke's book is called 'The Acts of the Apostles', it records some significant things which were done by people who were not apostles – such as the man we have read about today. We looked at Stephen earlier, but now we examine his life from a different perspective.

Stephen was one of those who were chosen to 'wait on tables' (6:2). He was a man of the ranks – a layman. We are told he was 'full of faith and of the Holy Spirit' (6:5), and 'full of God's grace and power' (6:8). People with these characteristics can often stir up strong reactions in others, although it does not usually produce the kind of consequence that fell upon Stephen. Some members of the synagogue tried to debate with Stephen, but his wisdom and knowledge of Scripture was too much for them (6:9–10). So, feeling grieved that they had lost the debate, they embarked upon a course of deceit and cunning that led to him becoming the first Christian martyr.

Stephen lost his life under a shower of stones. Did the godless win? Apparently, but only apparently, for look at the sequel. Standing in the crowd, 'holding the coats', was Saul of Tarsus. I don't think he ever forgot Stephen's prayer as the stones pounded the life out of him. I have no doubt that occasion was one of many events that led to his conversion. The stones are still there somewhere, now trodden underfoot, but the Spirit of Christ which was in Stephen marches deathless through the ages. Stone it and you simply scatter it throughout the earth.

Father, drive deep within me the truth that Your truth, will, and purposes always prevail. In You I have hold of something that nothing can hold back. And for that I am eternally grateful. Amen.

Acts 6:3–15; 8:2; 11:19; 22:20–21
1. How did the group describe Stephen and respond to his death?
2. What was the result of the persecution of Stephen?

Philip the Evangelist

16 JUN

FOR READING AND MEDITATION – ACTS 8:4-13,26-40

'Philip went down to a city in Samaria
and proclaimed the Messiah there.' (v5)

Today we think about another significant member of the laity – Philip. He too was one of 'the Seven' chosen to 'wait on tables' (6:2-4). But the reach of Philip's ministry went beyond the reach of his hand; he wanted to distribute the gospel as well as distribute goods. Philip was a man whose evangelistic gifting went beyond his role. He is an inspiration to all those ordinary men and women who want to serve Jesus.

Philip went down to a city in Samaria and preached Christ to crowds of people there – and many became Christians as a result. Soon the Jerusalem Church sent Peter and John to lay hands on the converts so they might receive the Holy Spirit. The Samaritans, you remember, were the people who would not receive Jesus 'because his face was set toward Jerusalem' (Luke 9:53, RSV). Two disciples had wanted to call fire down from heaven on them (Luke 9:54). Now two apostles were calling down upon them, not the fire of judgment but the fire of the Spirit!

Right in the middle of this amazing mission, Philip is sent to meet someone in the desert. Fancy being sent into a desert! Yet Philip doesn't hesitate to follow this guidance and move from a place where he was ministering to thousands to a congregation of one – the Ethiopian eunuch.

Philip was not a theologian like Peter or Paul, but he knew enough about the gospel to lead a soul to Christ. To have a firm hold on the basic truths of the gospel, and to feel responsibility for sharing it with others, is to stand in the splendid tradition of this great layman who, over the years, has earned the distinction of being known as 'Philip the Evangelist'.

Lord, this is indeed the greatest work in the world – introducing others to You. No matter what my role in life, help me to see that You can use me to share Jesus. Someone shared Him with me; may I be used to share Him with others. Amen.

John 1:43-50; 12:20-22; Acts 21:8-9
1. Who did Philip the apostle bring to Christ?
2. What is said of Philip the Evangelist's household?

Son of Encouragement 17 JUN

FOR READING AND MEDITATION – ACTS 9:19–31

'When he came to Jerusalem, he tried to join
the disciples, but they were all afraid of him…' (v26)

Another great layman who comes to prominence in the book of Acts is Barnabas – a man on whom we have already focused a little. He pops up in so many different places in the book that we have to move around to get a full portrait of him.

The first appearance of Barnabas is in Acts 4:36–37, where we see him selling his land and bringing the money to lay at the apostles' feet. He appears next in 9:26–27, where we observe him befriending Saul of Tarsus and introducing him to the apostles in Jerusalem. Then, in 11:25–26, we see him seeking out Paul to be his co-worker. He is described as 'a good man, full of the Holy Spirit and faith' (11:24). Barnabas, whose name means 'Son of Encouragement' (4:36), was a man who had a large heart and a magnanimous spirit, especially where people in need of help were concerned.

Today's passage brings out this point most sharply. Saul of Tarsus came down from Damascus to Jerusalem to share his testimony with the apostles, but we read, 'they were all afraid of him, not believing that he really was a disciple' (v26). Look, though, at the next verse: 'But Barnabas took him and brought him to the apostles. He told them how Saul on his journey had seen the Lord'. Here, in the presence of the sceptical disciples, Barnabas demonstrated that he was a person who would not hold a new convert at arm's length and would not doubt his conversion because of the great harm that he had previously done the Church.

Barnabas welcomed a man who needed acceptance and couldn't get it. It's sad when Christian disciples are so orthodox in their theology but so hardened in their sympathy.

Father, help me never to be like that – keep me orthodox in my theology and tender-hearted, I pray. May I, by accepting Your forgiveness, mirror Your forgiveness. In Jesus' name. Amen.

1 Thessalonians 4:18; Hebrews 3:12–13; 10:25
1. What are we to do daily?
2. Is there someone you can be a Barnabas to today?

A Place For Everyone   18 JUN

FOR READING AND MEDITATION – 1 CORINTHIANS 12:12–31

'Now you are the body of Christ, and each one of you is a part of it.' (v27)

Over the past few days we have looked at three laymen whose ministry in some ways matched that of the apostles. They show us that Jesus, the Head of the Church, has a purpose for every one of us in His Body.

During the Reformation, set in motion by Martin Luther, the principle of the priesthood of all believers was taught. However, it's a pity that the Reformers failed to make it even more clear that the laity (as they are referred to) are as truly and as fully the servants of Christ in the Church, and as responsible for its functioning, as those who have been ordained. A phrase which encapsulates this is: 'the apostolate of the laity'. The word 'laity' comes from the Greek word *laos*, and simply means 'people'. 'Apostle' comes from a word that means 'sent'. The Church here in the twenty-first century needs to take note that when Jesus said to the disciples, 'As the Father has sent me, I am sending you [or apostling you]' (John 20:21), He was commissioning the whole Church.

A papal encyclical issued by Pope Pius X in 1906, entitled *Vehementer Nos*, said, 'As for the masses, they have no other right than that of letting themselves be led and of following their pastors as a docile flock.' That, of course, is a view with which many Catholic theologians disagree today, but there are still people in some sections of the Church who think that the ministers who operate from the front of the church are the only ones who should do the work of Christ. Once, while ministering in Malaysia, the church notice sheet had on it these words: 'Ministers – the entire congregation.' I smiled to myself as I thought, 'You've got it.'

Father, help me find my place in Your Body, for I see that if I don't then I am like a square peg in a round hole. Show me, Lord, just what You want me to do, and where You want me to be. In Christ's name I pray. Amen.

Romans 12:1–8; Ephesians 1:23; Colossians 1:24; 2:19
1. What does Paul teach the Romans?
2. How is the Church described?

Church Growth

19 JUN

FOR READING AND MEDITATION – ACTS 4:1–12

'But many who heard the message believed; so the number of men who believed grew to about five thousand.' (v4)

Now we come to the penultimate section of our meditations on the distinctives of the Early Church. The theme we are going to focus on over the next few days is this: the first Church was a growing Church to which converts were added in ever increasing numbers.

    The first influx of people took place on the Day of Pentecost when Peter, using the keys of the kingdom of heaven previously promised to him by Christ (Matt. 16:19), opened up the doors of the Church – and 3,000 souls streamed in (2:41). Add to that the 120 who had already started to follow Christ before Pentecost (1:15), and the many hundreds to whom He appeared in the days following the resurrection (on one occasion He appeared to 500 of His disciples at once – see 1 Cor. 15:6). There must have been at least 4,000 of Jesus' followers now in and around Jerusalem in the first few days after Pentecost. From then on, souls were added to the Church daily (2:47). As someone has put it: 'He did not save them without adding them to the Church, and He did not add them to the Church without saving them.'

    Then, following the miracle performed on the crippled man at the Beautiful Gate of the Temple (3:1–9), we read today that the number of men grew to 5,000. Please notice that the figure given here is only for the men, and we can assume that about the same number of women also became committed followers of the Christ. In Acts 5:14 and 6:7 still more growth is recorded. Some Church historians reckon that just four weeks after Pentecost there must have been around 12,000 to 15,000 converts in the Early Church. Now that's Church growth! And there was more to follow.

Father, as I reflect on the wave after wave of new believers who streamed into the Early Church, and how today in some churches we do not see much growth from one year to another, my heart cries out: do it again, dear Lord, do it again. Amen.

Hosea 2:23; Mark 4:30–34; Acts 13:48; Ephesians 3:6
1. To what did Jesus liken the kingdom of God?
2. What had Hosea prophesied?

God Has No Energy Crisis

20 JUN

FOR READING AND MEDITATION – ACTS 4:23–30
'Stretch out your hand to heal and perform signs and wonders...' (v30)

Yesterday we saw how in the first few weeks after Pentecost the Church grew from 120 to approximately 12,000 to 15,000 people. This brings us to an intriguing question: what particular method did the Church employ in order to bring people to a place of faith and trust in the recently crucified Jesus? It might be helpful if we looked a little at how the Early Church grew, and what caused its phenomenal expansion.

First, the Jerusalem Church reached the size it did because of the empowering ministry of the Holy Spirit and miracles. There were, for example, the amazing events at Pentecost – people speaking in languages they had never learned. It is true that it was Peter's clear message that finally convinced the crowd, but it was the miracles that first got their attention. Notice also that supernatural things did not stop happening after Pentecost. The post-Pentecost period is filled with accounts of wonderful events, such as outstanding healings (some were even healed when standing in Peter's shadow, 5:15), a building being shaken by the power of God (4:31), prison doors opening of their own accord (5:19; 12:10), two people being struck down dead because of their deception (5:1–10), and so on.

There can be little doubt that the Holy Spirit in the Early Church had a tremendous pulling power on the hearts of the people. But can we expect similar manifestations today? It must be acknowledged that different convictions are held within the Church about these things, but I believe we can. God doesn't have an energy crisis. His Spirit still works in great power in some parts of the world today. Why not where we are?

Yes Father – why not? Can it be that we are more problem-conscious than power-conscious? Although we do not hanker after miracles alone, surely they are still part of Your purposes. Visit us today, dear Lord. In Jesus' name. Amen.

John 3:1–2; 10:34–42; Acts 8:1–8
1. What did Nicodemus declare?
2. Why did the crowds pay close attention to what Philip said?

No Place for the Spurious

21 JUN

FOR READING AND MEDITATION – JOHN 14:1–15

'Whoever believes in me will do the works I have been doing, and they will do even greater things than these...' (v12)

The matter of the miraculous is such a contentious issue in the Church all around the world that we spend another day considering it. We should discern and consider the miraculous and ask: can we really expect miracles and supernatural events to take place today in the way they did in the Early Church? Wasn't the miraculous merely an element that was necessary to get the Church going, but now it is established, aren't we supposed to be walking by faith?

The idea that God withdrew the supernatural and the miraculous from the Church a few decades after Pentecost, I believe, is scripturally untenable. Dr Martyn Lloyd-Jones, in true expository manner, has laid that idea to rest in a number of his books. It is my personal belief that God intends the supernatural and the miraculous to be as much part of today's Church as it was of the Early Church.

However, having said that, I must add that I deplore the fact that where there is no evidence of the supernatural and the truly miraculous, people try to create it by psychological means. In the New Testament it wasn't the apostles or evangelists who made a fuss about healing, but the people who were healed! Think, for instance, of the lame man at the Beautiful Gate (Acts 3:8–10). I have longed to see the miraculous power of God at work in His Church today – just as it was in Bible days, but I loathe what is spurious. And perhaps it's the spurious that is stopping the reality coming through.

Lord God, if it is the spurious that is holding back the pure stream of Your Spirit then flush it out we pray. Give us once again the pure stream of Pentecost – the power that nothing can gainsay. In Jesus' name we ask it. Amen.

Acts 3:1–16; 5:16; 9:34; 14:8–18
1. How did Peter and John react to the crowd's response?
2. How did Paul and Barnabas react to the crowd's response?

The Peril of Second Best

22 JUN

FOR READING AND MEDITATION – ACTS 6:1–7

'So the word of God spread... and a large number of priests became obedient to the faith.' (v7)

A second factor that contributed to the amazing growth of the Early Church was the release of the apostles for the work of the ministry. Consider this issue carefully with me, for there is more to it than at first appears.

When 'the Seven' had taken over the administrative tasks, the apostles had the opportunity to concentrate entirely on doing what they did best – teaching and preaching. There can be little doubt that transferring the administrative tasks to 'the Seven' marked a turning point in the life of that first Christian community. It is interesting that once this was done we read 'a large number of priests became obedient to the faith'. We can only assume that this was a direct result of the apostles being able to focus entirely on prayer and the work of making known the truths concerning Christ and the Church. The apostles were led by the Spirit to differentiate between the good and the best. What they were doing in administration was good, but it was not the best. The best was to give themselves to God in prayer and concentrate on presenting the Word in a clear and effective way.

One of the devil's favourite devices is to get the Church engaged in doing things that are second best, thus robbing them of their real cutting edge. How many modern churches, I wonder, have fallen into the trap of expecting their spiritual leaders to be estate agents, transport managers, financial advisers, and so on, rather than ministers of the Word? The present-day Church, like the Church of the first century, needs to realise the importance of the division of labour so that people can fulfil their God-given roles and avoid the peril of second best.

Lord God, how desperately we need the wisdom of the Spirit, for sometimes it is very difficult to differentiate between the good and the best. Baptise us afresh with heavenly wisdom that we might see – really see. In Jesus' name. Amen.

Luke 10:38–42; 2 Timothy 2:1–7
1. What did Jesus say of Mary?
2. What did Paul say to Timothy about civilian affairs?

A Domestic Context

23 JUN

FOR READING AND MEDITATION – ACTS 5:29-42

'Day after day… they never stopped teaching
and proclaiming the good news…' (v42)

Another factor that contributed to the phenomenal growth of the Early Church was the way in which the disciples shared with each other in small groups. In addition to meeting together as a large congregation in Solomon's Colonnade, they continued that fellowship in smaller groups in their homes. Listen to the way in which the Amplified Bible words Acts 2:46: 'And day after day they regularly assembled in the temple with united purpose, and in their homes they broke bread [including the Lord's Supper].' They supplemented the large services with more informal gatherings in their homes.

Even though the Scriptures do not say so precisely, I think it highly likely that many came to faith in people's homes. Today's text tells us that from house to house the teaching concerning the crucified and resurrected Jesus continued and was a constant theme. Nothing held back the apostles from teaching and sharing, both in the Temple and in the people's homes. But this was not the only form of Christian witness. As friends and families went in and out of the homes where believers were present, I feel sure they would have been drawn to the Christian faith by what they observed.

Vital as it is for the health of a local church to meet together corporately, it is also valuable to meet in smaller more informal gatherings. Those who practice this, and invite along those who are not yet Christians, say that people are often more ready to receive Christ in a home than in a formal church setting. Amazing ministry can come out of a home where Christ is the head, and where the doors are open to those who do not yet know Him.

My Father and my God, I know You are as much at home in a cottage as You are in a church, for You see Your Church not as a brick building but as a living Body. Help me to see it in the same way. In Jesus' name I pray. Amen.

Matthew 9:10; Mark 14:3; Luke 10:38; 19:7; John 12:1-8
1. Which home did Jesus often visit?
2. How often do you share Jesus with someone in your home?

Original-Style Evangelism 24 JUN

FOR READING AND MEDITATION – ACTS 8:1–8

'When the crowds heard Philip and saw the signs he performed, they all paid close attention to what he said.' (v6)

The Early Church, we have been seeing, expanded in the way it did for three primary reasons: the presence of the Holy Spirit, the powerful teaching of the apostles, and the daily witness of the believers in their homes.

One of the main ministries of the Church in this early period was establishing those who became believers and modelling for all time what can happen when the people of God dwell together in unity. And this went on in spite of the problems the Church faced, which included strong opposition from the Jewish authorities (4:1; 5:17), and complaints concerning the treatment of the poor (6:1). Then there was the death of Stephen – an event that must have been a severe blow to the Early Church. But during the persecution that followed his death many of Jesus' followers were scattered throughout Judea and Samaria.

Philip, one of those who served with Stephen (6:5), conducted mass evangelism in Samaria, during which crowds came to listen to what he said. Here we see why perhaps God allowed persecution to hit the Church in Jerusalem. It was not because the believers were failing to extend the Church there but because the message now needed to be heard 'in all Judea and Samaria, and to the ends of the earth' (1:8).

Psalm 133 says that when God's people live together in unity, then it is there the Lord imparts His blessing. And it seems that both history and experience have shown us that the most powerful and successful evangelistic efforts are those made by a church that knows true *koinonia* and real spiritual unity. That kind of evangelism rarely fails.

Father, help us understand that we cannot be evangelical without being evangelistic. And show us also that evangelism which is practised by a church in unity is evangelism according to Your pattern. In Jesus' name we pray. Amen.

Matthew 5:12; 10:17–20; 2 Timothy 2:10–12
1. How are we to respond to persecution?
2. What did Paul promise Timothy?

Another King

25 JUN

FOR READING AND MEDITATION – ACTS 5:25–32

'Peter and the other apostles replied: "We must obey God rather than human beings!"' (v29)

Now we come to the last on our list of the Early Church's distinctives: their unswerving allegiance to Christ and His eternal kingdom. The first Christians, while maintaining respect for the civil authorities that were over them, saw that their primary allegiance was to the laws and principles of the kingdom of God. They never planned or even thought to overthrow the ruling authorities, but sought only to live their lives in harmony with the truths being taught by the apostles.

The passage we have read today brings out this thought most clearly. The high priest and his associates ordered the arrest of the apostles and put them in jail, but during the night an angel of the Lord opened the doors of the jail and set them free. Before leaving them, however, the angel gave them a command that was contrary to the wishes of the high priest: 'Go, stand in the temple courts… and tell the people all about this new life' (v20).

An issue that puzzles many Christians is the matter of obedience to authority. They ponder such scriptures as Romans 13:1, where we are told 'Let everyone be subject to the governing authorities', and then consider today's passage where the apostles' actions differed to wishes of the spiritual authority of the high priest – and wonder how can these two forms of behaviour be reconciled. The answer is this: we are expected to live in obedience to earthly authorities unless they are contrary to God's design for living. The apostles were not out to overthrow the systems of their day; they simply understood that Jesus had first call on their lives and relationships.

Our Father and our God, we come to You once again to ask that You will help us understand Your priorities. May we always remember that while we have a responsibility to be good citizens in this world, we live first for You. Amen.

Daniel 3:13–30; John 18:28–36
1. What assertion did the Hebrew young men make?
2. What did Jesus reply to Pilate?

A Right Response

26 JUN

FOR READING AND MEDITATION – ACTS 23:1–11

'Paul replied, "Brothers, I did not realise that he was the high priest…"' (v5)

We continue considering the thought that the early believers, while respecting the authorities that were over them, gave themselves first to Jesus and His will. Some commentators claim that the Early Church, being 'God's new society', completely disregarded the old systems of authority and government. However, the passage before us highlights that viewpoint to be false.

When the apostle Paul was brought before the Sanhedrin, Ananias, the high priest, commanded those who were close to Paul to strike him on the mouth. Paul, understanding that the order implied he was a liar, reacted to this and, in condemning Ananias, called the high priest a 'whitewashed wall' (v3). When it was made clear to Paul that it was the high priest he was addressing, he immediately apologised, and brought himself under the authority of Scripture by saying, 'I did not realise that he was the high priest; for it is written: "Do not speak evil about the ruler of your people" [Exod. 22:28]' (v5). Paul was clearly offended by the command of the high priest, but when he discovered that he was talking to a man with spiritual authority, he knew that he should show respect.

But how could Paul respect a man who had just ordered him to be hit across the mouth? By focusing not so much on the person but on his position. When we respect the position of those over us in authority because we have a high regard for the principle of authority, then it helps to transform our view of the situation. It may not stop the person over us continuing to be difficult, but because of our biblical response it will make God's grace available to us.

Lord God, I see that a right response to authority is one of our supreme responsibilities. May we not be confused over this matter. Help us to respect those that You have given authority over us. For the sake of Your dear Son. Amen.

Romans 13:1–7; 1 Peter 2:17
1. What do we do when we rebel against authority?
2. How does Paul describe rulers in authority?

In Tune With Heaven   27 JUN

FOR READING AND MEDITATION – ROMANS 12:1–8

'Do not conform any longer to the pattern of this world…' (v2)

If there is one thing that is becoming clear as we examine this last distinctive of the Early Church, it is this: the believers of that day not only followed the laws and principles of the society in which they lived, but ultimately the principles and practices of God's kingdom.

The Church of the first century marched through the world to the beat of a different drum. I'd like to borrow the words of the American essayist, Thoreau, who said: 'If a man does not keep pace with his companions, perhaps it's because he hears a different drummer. Let him step to the music he hears, however measured or far away.' The beat the early Christians listened to came not from around, but from above. Their spiritual ears were tuned in to the music of heaven, and they tried to keep in step with that, even though it brought them into direct conflict with the world.

Earlier we saw that following the death of Ananias and Sapphira, 'No-one else dared join them, even though they were highly regarded by the people' (5:13). Yet the next verse says, 'Nevertheless, more and more men and women believed in the Lord and were added to their number.' The two verses appear to be contradictory, but really they are not. The death of Ananias and Sapphira (as we saw) produced in the community a sense that the Church was a society in which a remarkable power and presence was at work. This produced a sense of awe in people that to become a Christian meant coming under the lordship of Christ, and involved personal cost because of belonging to a community that shared sacrificially with others. How different things would be if this were the case today.

Father, help Your Church today to march to the beat of heaven's music and not to be influenced by the ideas of the world. May we seek first the kingdom of God and let all other things become secondary. In Christ's name we ask it. Amen.

Ephesians 4:17–24; Philippians 3:15–20; Colossians 3:1–2
1. What did Paul point out to the Ephesians?
2. What did he exhort the Colossians to do?

True Non-Conformity

28 JUN

FOR READING AND MEDITATION – ACTS 8:18-24

'Peter answered: "May your money perish with you, because you thought you could buy the gift of God with money!"' (v20)

Yesterday we commented that if those who belonged to the Early Church did not keep in step with the rest of society it was because they marched to the beat of a different drum. Our challenge in the Church of today is to pick up that beat and make a determined choice to follow it.

In today's reading we find the apostle Peter turning down Simon's offer of money for the power to be able to lay hands on people and see them receive the Holy Spirit. Was Peter tempted to respond to Simon's offer of financial reward? I doubt it. This man, who at one time was like a reed blown in the wind, is now as steady as a rock. His only concern is to serve the interests of Jesus and His people.

As I thought of Simon Peter, and others in the Early Church who stood out against the trends and ideas of their day because they marched to the beat of heaven's music, I called to mind the writer and broadcaster Malcolm Muggeridge who, in the latter years of his life, openly confessed to being a follower of Jesus. During his time as rector of Edinburgh University, he expressed concern over a decision by the authorities that he felt conflicted with his Christian principles. Unable to support the university's decision, he resigned. His farewell address was widely reported. Malcolm Muggeridge concluded his speech from the pulpit of St Giles' Cathedral in Edinburgh with these powerful words: 'The reason why I resign from my duties today is because I cannot go along with this. I belong to another kingdom and to another King – one Jesus.'

Father God, if ever I am placed in a situation where I have to choose between Your ways and the ways of the world, may I have the courage to go Your way. In Jesus' name I pray. Amen.

Mark 8:27-30; John 6:60-70
1. How did Peter respond to the question Jesus put?
2. What conclusion did he come to?

Picking Up the Beat

29 JUN

FOR READING AND MEDITATION – 1 PETER 1:3–25

'As obedient children, do not conform to the evil desires
you had when you lived in ignorance.' (v14)

Having thought for the last two days about how the first-century Church marched to the beat of a different drum, we must now ask ourselves this searching question: who are we, the Church of the twenty-first century, in step with? The world around, or the world without end? Society today mostly disregards the Church, frequently see it as source of comedy, and few really understand its outworking and calling, and so live, they believe, as good a life as their church-attending neighbours. The Church is made up of individuals. And it's sad when we miss the greatest evangelistic impact highlighted for us by Jesus in John 13:34–35: 'Let me give you a new command: Love one another. In the same way I loved you, you love one another. This is how everyone will recognize that you are my disciples—when they see the love you have for each other' (*The Message*).

The Church in Acts was 'highly regarded by the people' (Acts 5:13); but can we claim that such high regard is paid to the Church from all sections of society today?

There is no doubt that today's Church is contributing and giving considerably to the wider community. However, I wonder, if we are really to be more like the Early Church and be effective in this generation, then we must stop trying to be like the world and rediscover the original design. The Church is not misunderstood by the world because it is like Jesus; it is misunderstood because it is not like Him. When we stop trying to keep in step with the music of the world and march to the beat of a different drum, we will make a far more powerful impression. Again I say: the greatest challenge of our time is to pick up heaven's beat – and follow it.

Father, again we pray, help us – we who form today's Christian community – not to conform to the patterns of the world, but to march to the beat of heaven's drum. For that beat, we know, is the right beat. In Jesus' name we ask it. Amen.

Psalm 51:10; 85:1–6; Isaiah 40:31
1. What was the psalmist's prayer?
2. Make it your prayer today.

The Return

30 JUN

FOR READING AND MEDITATION – JEREMIAH 6:9–20

'This is what the Lord says: "Stand at the crossroads and look; ask for the ancient paths…"' (v16)

On this, the last day of these meditations in which we have been taking a look at the Church – 'God's new society' – what are our conclusions? The first is this: when we put the Church of today alongside the Church of the first century, we cannot help but see that there are major differences. Naturally, we must be balanced about this, for there are so many things for which we are thankful, but nevertheless the truth remains – we have not arrived, there is much to learn and much to live out in our daily lives together in our communities.

Second, as we think about the future and how we can live and apply the new truths we may have discovered, we also consider how we can return to the old paths – to the sincerity, eagerness, and enthusiasm of those first-century Christians. When we see how the original Church practised everyday life, we can more easily spot the differences. There are cultural variances between now and then of course, but we cannot use the cultural differences as an excuse for failing to see the spiritual differences.

Third, although challenging, it's important to go often to the book of Acts and take whatever steps are necessary to make our fellowships a living illustration of what community life in Jesus is like. In every hamlet, village, town, and city the local church needs to ask itself: are we reflecting to the world around us that we are citizens of heaven? If we fail to do this, says one commentator, then it may well be that in the twenty-first century the Church could be 'a conscious minority surrounded by an arrogant militant paganism'. Let's give ourselves afresh to God, and make sure this observation has no place today.

Gracious and loving heavenly Father, having seen how Your Church can live life, my prayer and deepest longing is this: give us another Pentecost. In Jesus' name we pray. Amen.

Joshua 24:14–24; Matthew 12:30; Mark 9:40; Luke 16:13
1. What was the challenge of Joshua's day?
2. What is the challenge we face?

PRAY IT FORWARD ▶▶▶

Lord, thank You for calling me into Your church, a people shaped by Your Spirit. Help me to live in unity, generosity, and boldness, just as the early believers did, so that others may see You at work in us. Amen.

PAY IT FORWARD ▶▶▶

At Waverley Abbey, we're committed to equipping the church of today to live like the church in Acts. **Your gift helps train leaders, resource communities, and strengthen the church.**

Visit **waverleyabbey.org/donate-to-edwj** call **01252 784700** or scan the **QR code** ▶

JULY & AUGUST

ARMOUR OF GOD

INTRODUCTION

The Christian life is not a playground; it is a battleground. In The Armour of God, we explore what it means to stand firm in the face of spiritual warfare.

Every believer, whether aware or not, is engaged in an invisible but very real conflict between the kingdom of God and the kingdom of darkness. Selwyn Hughes guides us into a deep, practical understanding of the spiritual protection that God provides – His divine armour – so that we may withstand the enemy's assaults and remain steadfast in our faith.

These devotions will not only awaken us to the reality of the battle but also equip us to fight victoriously, clothed in truth, righteousness, faith, and the power of God's Word.

A Call to Arms

1 JUL

FOR READING AND MEDITATION – EPHESIANS 6:10–13

'For we do not wrestle against flesh and blood…' (v12, NKJV)

Today, we begin a focused study on the spiritual protection available to every Christian as they navigate the realities of spiritual conflict. Every believer in Jesus Christ should be aware that there are two opposing realms at work in the world: the kingdom of God and the forces of darkness. These two are locked in ongoing struggle, and as followers of Christ, we find ourselves drawn directly into the heart of that conflict.

While many Christians may embrace pacifism in earthly matters of war, when it comes to spiritual battles, neutrality is not an option. Once we commit to God's service, we are called to prepare ourselves for both offensive and defensive aspects of spiritual warfare. Throughout the Christian life, there will be moments when we face intense, close-quarters struggles with the powers of darkness – and if we are unprepared, we risk being overwhelmed.

Scripture teaches us that the forces opposed to God are fiercely committed to resisting His purposes. Unable to challenge God directly, they focus their opposition on those who belong to Him – on you and me. If you noticed in the passage we studied today, the word 'against' appears repeatedly – six times in fact – highlighting the reality that choosing to stand with Christ inevitably means standing against the powers that oppose Him. There can be no middle ground; to be for God is to stand firmly against anything that would seek to undermine His work.

Gracious and loving Father, help me get my perspectives clear. Train me in the art of spiritual warfare so that I will be able to resist every onslaught of the devil and come through every conflict victoriously. In Jesus' name. Amen.

2 Corinthians 10:1–5; 1 Timothy 1:18, 6:12
1. What was Paul's charge to Timothy?
2. What does Paul say about our weapons of warfare?

Is There a Personal Devil?

2 JUL

FOR READING AND MEDITATION – JOHN 8:36–44
'He was a murderer from the beginning...' (v44)

Before we begin to unpack God's resources for spiritual battle, we will spend a few days looking at what the Bible teaches about our enemy. Some Christians are unsure about the concept of a personal being that represents evil. A modern-day theologian writes: 'Let us put to sleep this idea of a personal devil who walks about with a pitchfork seeking to tumble people into hell. Evil is not a personality but an influence – it is just the darkness where the light ought to be.'

While I agree that the picture of a personal devil walking about with a pitchfork and with horns and a tail is not to be found anywhere in Scripture, the concept of a personal devil is found everywhere in Scripture. One evidence of this is the fact that many of the names given to him denote personality: Satan, deceiver, liar, murderer, accuser, tempter, prince of the power of the air, and so on. Listen to what someone has written on this subject:

> Men don't believe in the devil now, as their fathers used to do
> They reject one creed because it's old, for another because it's new
> But who dogs the steps of the toiling saint,
> who spreads the net for his feet,
> Who sows the tares in the world's broad fields
> where the Saviour sows His wheat,
> They may say the devil has never lived,
> they may say the devil has gone,
> But simple people would like to know – who carries his business on?

Take it from me, whether or not you believe in the devil, he most certainly believes in you.

Father, help me see that it is to Satan's advantage for me not to believe in him. Then he can do his evil work unresisted. Over these coming weeks, unfold to me the strategies I need to overcome him. In Christ's name I ask it. Amen.

2 Corinthians 11:1–14; 1 Thessalonians 3:5; 1 Peter 5:8; Revelation 12:10
1. What are some of the guises in which Satan comes to us?
2. How does Peter describe him?

Satan – an Influence or an Intelligence? 3 JUL

FOR READING AND MEDITATION – MATTHEW 4:1–11
'Then Jesus said to him, "Away with you, Satan!
For it is written…"' (v10, NKJV)

We said yesterday that some of the names given to the devil in Scripture – deceiver, liar, murderer, and so on – show him to be a real personality. But if more proof is required, then consider the passage that is before us today. Jesus is seen here in direct confrontation with the devil, even engaging in conversation with him. Some theologians explain this in these terms – Christ (so they say) was having a conversation with the dark thoughts that arose from within His nature, so any 'devil' that was present was subjective, not objective.

If we allow that Christ had dark thoughts within His nature, then the whole scheme of redemption tumbles like a pack of cards, for a saviour who is not perfect could never fully atone for our sins. As Dr Handley Moule puts it: 'A saviour who is not perfect is like a bridge broken at one end and is not a reliable passage of access.' Once we try to get around Scripture, we create endless difficulties for ourselves and finish up looking foolish. Far better to accept the Bible as it stands and believe its testimony on everything.

Actually, as we said yesterday, it is to Satan's advantage to get us to believe that he is not a personal being, for if there is no personal devil, there can be no personal resistance. Don't allow yourself to be deceived into thinking that the term 'devil' is a synonym for the evil influence that is in the world. The devil is more than an evil influence; he is an evil intelligence. Only when we recognise this fact will we be motivated to take steps to effectively resist him.

Father, help me see that the first step in spiritual warfare is to 'know the enemy'. For until I know and understand my enemy, I will not be able to defeat him. Deepen my knowledge of these important truths, I pray. In Jesus' name. Amen.

1 John 3:1–8; Hebrews 2:14; John 12:30–31
1. Why was Jesus made manifest?
2. What did He declare?

Who Cleft the Devil's Foot?   4 JUL

FOR READING AND MEDITATION – ISAIAH 14:9–15; EZEKIEL 28:11–19

> 'For you have said in your heart... "I will be
> like the Most High."' (Isa. 14:13–14, NKJV)

The question is often asked, especially by new Christians: just who is the devil, and where did he come from? The seventeenth-century poet John Donne wrote that there were two things he could not fathom: 'Where all the past years are, and who cleft the devil's foot". The origin, existence, and activities of the devil have always been among man's most puzzling problems. The books of Isaiah and Ezekiel give us a very clear picture, however, of what someone has called "The Rise and Fall of the Satanic Empire'.

Jesus, while He was here on earth, said one day to His disciples: 'I saw Satan falling from heaven as a flash of lightning!" (Luke 10:18, TLB). Before he was known as the devil, Satan was called Lucifer and was created as a perfect angelic being. The passages before us today show him to have been a beautiful and morally perfect being. 'You were the perfection of wisdom and beauty' (Ezek. 28:12, TLB). 'You were perfect in all you did from the day you were created' (Ezek. 28:15, TLB).

Upright, beautiful, brilliant, and with an enormous capacity for achievement, God entrusted Lucifer with the highest of all the offices in the interstellar universe: 'I appointed you to be the anointed Guardian Angel. You had access to the holy mountain of God...' (Ezek. 28:14, TLB). In his heart, however, arose a rebellious thought: 'I will... be like the Most High' (Isa. 14:14, TLB). Five times that phrase 'I will' is used in this passage. Those two little words 'I will', reveal what lies behind the awful blight of sin – a created will coming into conflict with the will of the Creator.

O Father, now that I see the real issue that lies behind sin – a created will colliding with the will of the Creator – help me constantly to align my will with Your will. In Jesus' name I ask it. Amen.

Proverbs 16:1–18; 26:12; 3:7
1. What comes before a fall?
2. What attitude should we guard against?

The Strength of Satanic Forces

5 JUL

FOR READING AND MEDITATION – JUDE VERSES 1–13

'The angels who did not keep their positions of authority…
these he has kept in darkness, bound with everlasting chains…' (v6)

We continue with the question: just who is the devil and where did he come from? We saw yesterday that the devil was created as a wise and morally perfect being (then known as Lucifer) who aspired to take over the throne of God and thus usurp the position of his Creator. Once that happened, Lucifer was expelled from heaven, together with the other angels who had sensed and shared his rebellious attitude. This is the fall from heaven that Jesus told His disciples He had witnessed.

Since his fall from heaven, Satan, apparently losing little of his administrative skill, has marshalled these fallen angels (now known as demons) into a hostile force to work against God and His creation. We do not know just how many angels fell with Satan, but doubtless it must have been a colossal number. Once when Jesus asked a demonic, 'What is your name?" (Luke 8:30), the demons answered: "Legion.' If they were telling the truth, the man was controlled by thousands of demons. A Roman legion contained 6,000 men!

It is little wonder, then, that the apostle Paul warned the Ephesians that they were involved in a tremendous spiritual conflict: 'We are not fighting against people made of flesh and blood, but against persons without bodies—the evil rulers of the unseen world, those mighty satanic beings and great evil princes of darkness who rule this world… (Eph. 6:12, TLB). Is it any wonder our world is in the mess it is today? One of America's founding fathers said: "If men will not be governed by God, then they will be ruled by tyrants.' How sad that men and women actually choose to be governed by Satan rather than by God.

O God my Father, I am so thankful that I have left the tyranny and rule of Satan to come under the sway of Your eternal and everlasting kingdom. May I come more and more under its sway hour by hour and day by day. In Jesus' name I pray. Amen.

Luke 10:1–19; Psalm 44:5; Romans 8:31
1. What event did Jesus witness?
2. What power did He give to His disciples?

The Second Coming of Satan

6 JUL

FOR READING AND MEDITATION – 1 TIMOTHY 4:1–16

'The Spirit clearly says that in later times some will abandon the faith and follow deceiving spirits and things taught by demons.' (v1)

If we are to be effective in the art of spiritual warfare, then we must see that mankind's fiercest foe is not death or disease, but the diabolical deceiver we know as the devil. He is behind all our individual woes and international wars. He is the one who instigates all our crime and violence. He writes the script for human sorrow, sickness, and death. That is not to say that humankind does not bear some responsibility for the things I mention, but the motivation for these things springs directly from the devil. And there are signs that the devil's mission is hotting up – just as our text for today predicted it would.

I think it is safe to say that during the twentieth and into the twenty-first centuries, the devil has received more exposure than he has had in any previous generation since the beginning of recorded time. On its release in 1973, *The Exorcist* broke all box office records, grossing over 150 million dollars. It was followed by a spate of films on the subject of the paranormal – *The Omen*, *The Antichrist,* and many others – so much so that someone described this age as the Second Coming of Satan.

In songs, in art, in the theatre, Satan is making his presence felt in new and powerful ways. The so-called science of parapsychology has given him admittance to the halls of academia. How sad that some colleges and universities present accredited courses on Satanism but bar any reference to the teachings of Jesus Christ. Make no mistake about it, the devil is on the march. But don't let that thought trouble you too deeply, for the Scripture shows it to be a march to oblivion (Rev. 20:10).

O God, I am so grateful for the assurances of Scripture. They come to me at the moment I most need them and hold me fast when the strongest currents threaten to sweep me away from my spiritual moorings. Thank You, dear Father. Amen.

Job 1, 2 & 42
1. Who was the source of Job's troubles?
2. What was the final outcome?

Danger – the Devil at Work

7 JUL

FOR READING AND MEDITATION – 1 PETER 5:1–11

'Your enemy the devil prowls around like a roaring lion...' (v8)

We said yesterday that the spiritual battle between Satan and God is hotting up. When I made a similar statement in a meeting at which I spoke some time ago, a woman came up to me and said: 'I think you are giving too much credit to the devil. He is such an insignificant person compared to God that we ought not even mention his name.' In one way I can sympathise with this view, for when you listen to some Christians talk, you get the impression that they have a small God and a big devil.

However, it would be unrealistic to think that we can go through life without coming into direct contact with Satan and his forces. And what is more unrealistic is to think that many (not all) of the problems which confront us day by day have no devilish strategy behind them. Satan is responsible for more of our troubles and difficulties than we may believe. The late Dr Martyn Lloyd-Jones said: 'I am certain that one of the main causes of the ill state of the church today is the fact that the devil is being forgotten... we have become so psychological in our attitude and thinking. We are ignorant of this great objective fact – the being, the existence of the devil, the adversary, the accuser and his 'fiery darts'.'

Does the thought of doing battle with the devil frighten you? Then heed the words of Corrie ten Boom who said: 'The fear of the devil is most likely from the devil himself.' God has given us all the protection we need to defend ourselves against the attacks of Satan, and when we know how to avail ourselves of this protection, we will no longer be afraid of the devil – rather, he will be afraid of us.

O God, as I go deeper into this subject, I am becoming increasingly aware of the intensity of the spiritual battle in which I am engaged. Dispel every fear that may arise in me and show me the way to power and victory. In Jesus' name I pray. Amen.

2 Corinthians 2:1–11; 11:3; 2 Thessalonians 2:9
1. What did Paul say about his knowledge of the devil?
2. What was his reason?

God's Armour – Our Only Protection

8 JUL

FOR READING AND MEDITATION – EPHESIANS 6:11–18

'Put on the full armour of God, so that you can take your stand against the devil's schemes.' (v11)

We come now to focus our attention on the six separate sections of the spiritual armour which God has provided for us in Christ, but before we do we must pause to make clear a couple of important points. One, the armour of God is our only protection against the wiles of Satan, and two, it will do us no good unless we avail ourselves of it in its entirety.

Today we concentrate on the first of these two vital issues. We must constantly keep before us the fact that such is the might and power of Satan that nothing apart from the armour of God will protect us from his onslaughts. Mark that and mark it well, for there are many Christians who have tried to stand against Satan in their own strength and have found themselves not victors, but victims. One of the 'wiles' or schemes of Satan is to get us to believe that we can resist him in our own strength, but when we think that – we are finished.

In my time I have seen many believers lulled by Satan into thinking that their long experience in the faith and their understanding of Christian doctrine were all they needed to protect them from satanic attack, but they found to their cost that this was inadequate and insufficient. We never live more dangerously than when we depend on our spiritual experience and understanding to protect us from the fiery darts of the enemy. One thing and one thing only can protect us from the attacks of Satan and that is the spiritual armour which God has provided. You see, in the devil we are dealing with a foe that is inferior in power only to the Almighty Himself. Therefore, nothing less than the protection that God provides is adequate for our need.

O Father, I need to get this matter straight, for I see that if my dependence is on anything other than You, then I am sunk. Drive this truth deep into my spirit this day. In Jesus' name. Amen.

Romans 13:1–12; 1 Thessalonians 5:8; 2 Timothy 2:4
1. What are we to put aside?
2. What are we to put on?

How Not to be a 'Wobbly Christian'   9 JUL

FOR READING AND MEDITATION - ROMANS 13:8-14

'So let us put aside the deeds of darkness
and put on the armour of light.' (v12)

Now we are clear that only the armour of God can give us the protection we need against the wiles of Satan, we must remind ourselves also that it will not do us any good unless it is worn in its entirety. We are exhorted to put on the whole armour of God – not just a few of the pieces we think are most suitable for us.

This again is something of crucial importance. It means we are not to pick and choose in this matter. If we are to be steadfast soldiers in the Lord's army, if we are to avoid becoming what John Stott calls 'wobbly Christians who have no firm foothold in Christ", then we must put on the entire equipment which God provides for us. We cannot, we dare not, select parts of the armour and say, 'I don't really like the helmet of salvation, but I don't mind wearing the breastplate of righteousness.' The moment you say, "I need the breastplate, but I don't need the helmet' – you are defeated. You need it all – the whole armour of God.

You see, our understanding of what is involved in spiritual defence against evil is extremely inadequate – we just don't have sufficient knowledge of what is involved. It is God alone who knows our enemy and it is God alone who knows exactly how to protect us so that we remain firm and steadfast when Satan and his forces hurl themselves against us. So learn this lesson now before going any farther – every single piece of God's armour is essential, and to select some and leave the others is to take the route to failure and defeat.

O God, deliver me from the attitude of pride that seeks to put my ideas ahead of Your ideas. You know more about what I need to protect me from the enemy than I do. Help me ever to trust Your judgment. In Jesus' name I ask it. Amen.

2 Corinthians 6:1-10; Philippians 1:27; 1 Peter 5:9
1. What did Paul include as a necessary requirement for his ministry?
2. What are we called to do?

The Belt of Truth

10 JUL

FOR READING AND MEDITATION – PSALM 119:145–160

'You are near, Lord, and all your commands are true.' (v151)

Paul, in listing the six main pieces of a soldier's equipment, does so in order to illustrate the six main ways by which we can defend ourselves against the power of Satan – truth, righteousness, steadfastness, faith, salvation, and the Word of God. Most commentators believe that the reason why Paul selected these six pieces of a soldier's armour to illustrate the Christian's protective system against attack was because he was chained to one as he wrote the letter (Eph. 6:20). And although it is unlikely that the soldier would have worn the full armour of an infantryman on the battlefield, the sight of him would have kindled Paul's imagination.

The list begins with the belt of truth. Why, we ask ourselves, does the apostle start with such a seemingly insignificant item? Why did he not begin with one of the bigger and more important pieces of equipment, such as the breastplate, the shield, or the sword of the Spirit? The order in which these pieces are given to us is an inspired order, and if we change the order we make our position extremely perilous. For example, the reason why many Christians fail to wield the sword of the Spirit effectively is because they have not first girded their waist with truth. If we reverse the order, we succeed only in weakening our spiritual defence.

It is very important that we grasp this. Girding our waist with truth is always the place to start whenever we are under attack. If you don't start right, then you will not finish right. So let this thought take hold of you: you cannot do battle with the devil until you first gird your waist with truth.

Gracious and loving Father, help me to absorb this thought into my inner being this day so that it will stay with me for the rest of my life: I cannot do battle with the devil until I first gird my waist with truth. Amen.

2 Peter 1:1–12; Proverbs 23:23; 3 John:1–4

1. In what are we to be established?
2. In what did John rejoice?

The Power and Importance of Truth   11 JUL

FOR READING AND MEDITATION – PSALM 51:1–17
'You desire truth in the inward parts...' (v6, NKJV)

We ended yesterday by saying that we cannot do battle with the devil until we have girded our waist with truth. Girding the waist was always a symbol of readiness to fight. That is why this comes first. The officers in the Roman army wore short skirts, very much like a Scottish kilt. Over this they had a cloak or tunic which was secured at the waist with a girdle. When they were about to enter into battle, they would tuck the tunic up under the girdle so as to leave their legs free and unencumbered for the fight.

We must now ask ourselves: what does Paul's phrase, 'gird your waist with truth' really mean? What significance or application does it have for us right here in the twenty-first century? The word 'truth' can be looked at in two ways: one, objective truth, as it is to be found in Jesus Christ, and two, subjective truth as it is to be found in the qualities of honesty and sincerity. The Puritan, William Gurnall, points out that whether the word implies truth of doctrine or truth of heart, one will not do without the other.

I personally believe that in Ephesians 6, Paul is emphasising subjective truth – truth in the inner being. You see, when we are deceitful or hypocritical, or resort to intrigue and scheming, we are playing the devil's game. And believe me, you will never be able to beat the devil at his own game! What Satan despises and dislikes is transparent truth – he flees from it as quickly as darkness runs from the dawn. Having our waist girded with truth, then, means being possessed with truth, guided by truth and controlled by truth. No truth – no power over Satan. It is as simple as that.

O Father, I see that You have set standards by which I rise or fall. When I fulfil them I rise, when I break them I fall. Give me the strength I need to fulfil all Your laws, especially the law of truth. In Jesus' name. Amen.

John 8:34–45; Colossians 3:9; Proverbs 12:22
1. What did Jesus declare about the devil?
2. What delights the Lord?

Under the Searchlight of Truth — 12 JUL

FOR READING AND MEDITATION – PSALM 139:1–24

'Search me, God, and know my heart;
test me and know my anxious thoughts.' (v23)

We remind ourselves of what we said yesterday – that to have our 'waist girded with truth' means to be possessed by truth, to be willing for truth to govern and regulate every part of our lives. If we are to defend ourselves effectively against the attacks of Satan, then truth and honesty are vital necessities.

The mental health experts tell us that being willing to face the truth about ourselves is an important part of our growth towards maturity; the same is true in the realm of the spiritual. How easy it is to hide from the truth and imagine ourselves to be truthful when really we are not. Whatever his personal idiosyncrasies and his rebellious attitude towards Christianity, Sigmund Freud made an interesting contribution to our understanding of human personality when he documented with true genius the incredibly subtle ways in which we lie to ourselves. Psychologists call them 'defence mechanisms', but a more biblical view of them would be 'lying mechanisms'.

We would all much prefer to be called defensive than dishonest. But whenever we allow ourselves to be self-deceived, we not only impede our spiritual growth – we also lower our defences. The enemy thrives on deception, and if he can push us towards self-deception, he maintains a definite advantage over us. Many of us might react with horror to the suggestion that we may be dishonest, for we would not dream of doing or saying anything that was not according to the truth. Yet it is possible to be open and honest on the outside and yet hide from truth on the inside. All of us, even mature and experienced Christians, are capable of hiding from truth.

O Father, I see that if I am to overcome Satan, then I must know truth inwardly as well as outwardly. Search my heart today, dear Lord, and bring to the surface the things within me that are untrue. In Jesus' name I ask it. Amen.

2 Chronicles 7:1–14; Isaiah 44:20; James 1:22
1. What are God's people to turn from?
2. What does James warn against?

Three Forms of Dishonesty

13 JUL

FOR READING AND MEDITATION – 1 JOHN 1:1–10

'If we claim to be without sin, we deceive ourselves and the truth is not in us.' (v8)

The suggestion I made yesterday, that even experienced and mature Christians can inwardly resist truth, might surprise and shock some, but the real issue is this – is it true? Let me identify three of the most popular defences we use to resist truth, ones that almost all of us use from time to time. The first is projection. This where we are to blame for something, but we project the blame on to someone else so that we can feel more comfortable about ourselves. It may sound a simple thing, but all dishonesty deprives – even simple dishonesty.

Then take the defence of denial. How many times do we refuse to face the fact that we may be angry about something, and when someone says: 'Why are you angry?' we reply with bristling hostility: 'I'm not angry!' We fail to recognise what others can plainly see. And denial, no matter how one looks at it, is a form of inner deceit and dishonesty.

Another dishonest defence is rationalisation. We do this whenever we persuade ourselves that something is what it is not. C.S. Lewis points out in his writings that when our neighbour does something wrong, it is obviously because he or she is 'bad', while if we do something wrong it is only because we did not get enough sleep, or someone gave us a rough time, or our blood chemistry is at fault, and so on.

All defence mechanisms deprive us of inner honesty, and apart from hindering our spiritual growth (as we said) they lower our defences against Satan. This is why over and over again in Scripture we are bidden to open up to honesty. The more honest we can be, the more spiritually powerful and effective we can be.

Lord Jesus, help me to open up to honesty. For I see that the more honest I am, the more authority I can wield over Satan. I want to be able to say, as You said: 'The prince of this world is coming. He has no hold over me...' For Your own dear Name's sake. Amen.

Revelation 3:14–22; James 1:26; Galatians 6:3
1. How did the Laodiceans see themselves?
2. How did God see them?

Without Truth – We Get Nowhere

14 JUL

FOR READING AND MEDITATION – HOSEA 10:12

'It is time to seek the Lord...' (v12)

The phrase 'gird your waist with truth' clearly suggests that this is something we must do and not expect God to do for us. Clinton McLemore says: 'Whenever any one of us embodies and promotes personal honesty, we are knowingly or unknowingly doing God's work.' So ask yourself right now: 'Am I an honest person?' If there are areas of your life where you are not sure, then spend some time before God in prayer today asking Him to help you root out all dishonesty and insincerity. For honesty is our first line of defence against evil. If we are not honest, or not willing to be honest, then the devil will soon disable us.

We live in an age which, generally speaking, evades the truth. We seem to take it for granted that advertisements distort, contracts contain fine print that no one draws our attention to, and professionals conceal one another's malpractice. There are few domains of life that are uncompromised, few social structures that are not tainted, few relationships that retain any semblance of honesty and wholesomeness.

The Christian Church is not without blame either. Consider the endless and often angular manoeuvrings of some church boards and committees. God put the Church in the world but somehow the devil has put the world in the Church. Our text for today sums up the present church situation: 'It is time to seek the Lord.' Am I speaking too strongly? I think not. If we don't get things straightened out at the start, then how can we hope to be victorious in the war against the enemy? Always remember that sin, at its root, is a stubborn refusal to deal with truth.

O God, forgive us that we, Your redeemed people, sometimes pursue our own interests and allow truth to be dragged in the gutter. Help us, dear Lord. For without truth we have no power. In Jesus' name we ask it. Amen.

1 Peter 4:12–19; Romans 12:17; Jeremiah 17:9
1. What is the natural condition of the heart?
2. Where must things be put right first?

The Breastplate of Righteousness   15 JUL

FOR READING AND MEDITATION – PSALM 132:1–18

'May your priests be clothed with righteousness;
may your faithful people sing for joy.' (v9)

We look now at the second piece of armour with which we are to defend ourselves against the wiles of the devil – the breastplate of righteousness. A soldier's breastplate generally extended from the base of the neck to the upper part of the thighs, so it would cover many important parts of the body, in particular the heart.

Some commentators are of the opinion that the word 'breastplate' suggests that this piece of equipment covered only the front of the chest and thus no protection was provided for the soldier's back. They deduce from this that a Christian should face the devil and never turn his back on him or otherwise he will expose a part that is unguarded. It is an interesting idea but it must not be given too much credence, for the soldier's breastplate often covered his back as well as his front.

What spiritual lesson and application can we draw from the 'breastplate of righteousness'? Most commentators believe that because a soldier's breastplate covered mainly his heart, the spiritual application of this is that in Christ we have all the protection we need against negative or desolating feelings – the heart being seen as the focal point of the emotions. What an exciting thought is presented by this – by putting on the breastplate of righteousness, we have the resources to deal with all those debilitating feelings that tend to bring us down into depression and despair – unworthiness, inadequacy, fear, and so on. When I once mentioned this to a friend who asked me what I thought the breastplate of righteousness was for, he said: 'It sounds too good to be true.' I replied: 'It's too good not to be true.'

Gracious Lord and Master, how can I sufficiently thank You for providing a defence against this most difficult of problems – emotional distress. Show me how to apply Your truth to this part of my personality. In Jesus' name. Amen.

Matthew 15:10–20; Mark 7:21; Proverbs 4:23; 28:9
1. What comes out of the heart?
2. How are we to guard our hearts?

Nothing Wrong with Christ

16 JUL

FOR READING AND MEDITATION – ROMANS 8:31–39

'Who then will condemn us? Will Christ? *No!*
For he is the one who died for us...' (v34, TLB)

Today we face the question: when Paul talks about the 'breastplate of righteousness', is he talking about our righteousness or Christ's righteousness? I believe he is talking about Christ's righteousness. That is not to say, of course, that our own righteousness (or moral uprightness) is unimportant, for as Paul points out in 2 Corinthians 6:7, our personal righteousness can be a definite defence against the enemy. In Ephesians 6, however, the emphasis is not on our righteousness in Christ, but Christ's righteousness in us.

So how does putting on the breastplate of righteousness act as a spiritual defence against the wiles of the devil? Take, for example, those people who have definitely surrendered their lives to Christ but who are afflicted with a feeling that they are not good enough to be saved. Why do they have such feeling? The answer is simple – they have taken their eyes off Christ and His righteousness and have focused on themselves and their righteousness. And in doing that, they play right into the devil's hands.

You see, the devil can find all kinds of flaws and blemishes in your righteousness, but he can find nothing wrong with the righteousness of Christ. The way to withstand an attack like this is to put on the breastplate of righteousness. In other words, remind yourself and the enemy that you stand, not on your own merits but on Christ's. This may sound simple, even simplistic to some, but I have lived long enough to see people latch on to it and come from the depths of emotional distress to the heights of spiritual exaltation.

Lord Jesus, help me to latch on to it too. Make it crystal clear to my spirit that although the devil can find many flaws in my righteousness, he cannot find a single flaw in Yours. I rest my case – on You. Thank You, dear Lord. Amen.

1 Corinthians 1:19–31; Isaiah 64:6; Philippians 3:9

1. What is our righteousness like?
2. What was Paul's declaration?

The Tyranny of the Oughts

17 JUL

FOR READING AND MEDITATION – ROMANS 5:1–11

'Therefore, since we have been justified through faith,
we have peace with God through our Lord Jesus Christ...' (v1)

We looked yesterday at how the breastplate of righteousness protects us from the feeling that we are not good enough to be saved. Today we look at another feeling which can whip up in the heart of a Christian – the feeling that we are only accepted by God when we are doing everything perfectly. It is this feeling which gives rise to the condition known as perfectionism – a condition which afflicts multitudes of Christians.

The chief characteristic of perfectionism is a constant overall feeling of never doing enough to be thought well of by God. Karen Horney describes it as 'the tyranny of the oughts'. Here are some typical statements of those who are afflicted in this way: 'I ought to do better', 'I ought to have done better', 'I ought to be able to do better'. There is nothing wrong with wanting to do better, but in the distorted thinking of a perfectionist, he or she believes that because they could or ought to have done better, they will not be accepted or thought well of by God. They come to believe that their acceptance by God depends on their performance; they constantly try to develop a righteousness of their own rather than resting in the righteousness which Christ has provided for them.

If you suffer from this condition, then it's time to put on your spiritual breastplate. You need to remind yourself that the way you came into the Christian life is the way you go on in it – by depending on Christ and His righteousness, not on yourself and your righteousness. You are not working to be saved; you are working because you are saved.

Lord Jesus, I see that when I stand in Your righteousness, I stand in God's smile. But when I stand in my own righteousness, I stand in God's frown. Help me move over from frown to smile. In Your dear Name. Amen.

Galatians 3; Genesis 15:6; Acts 13:39
1. What was the purpose of the law?
2. What does it mean to be 'justified'?

Paul's Breastplate in Place

18 JUL

FOR READING AND MEDITATION – 1 CORINTHIANS 15:1–11
'But by the grace of God I am what I am...' (v10)

Another feeling which can arise in a heart that is unprotected by a spiritual breastplate is that of discouragement. I am thinking here not so much of the discouragement which comes directly, but a more subtle form of attack in which the devil draws our attention to what other Christians may be saying or thinking about us.

The apostle Paul particularly struggled in this respect, but see how he used the breastplate of righteousness as his spiritual defence. Paul's background was anti-Christian and he could never get completely away from that. He had been the most hostile and brutal persecutor of the Church. Some might even have doubted his claim to be an apostle. We can't be sure about that, of course, but some commentators claim that in 1 Corinthians 15:9, he was replying to such an accusation.

How does Paul react to the criticism? Does he succumb to discouragement? Does he say: 'What's the use of working my fingers to the bone for these unappreciative people? They don't do anything but hurl recriminations in my face!' This is what the devil would have liked him to do. But look at what he does. He says: 'By the grace of God I am what I am.' Can you see what he is doing? He is using the breastplate of righteousness. He is saying, in other words: 'I don't need to do anything to protect myself; what I am is what Christ has made me. I am not standing in my own righteousness, I am standing in His.' What a lesson in how to use the spiritual breastplate. You and I need to learn this lesson too.

O God, day by day I am catching little glimpses of what You are trying to teach me – that the more I depend on Your righteousness and the less I depend on my own, the better off I will be. Help me to learn it – and learn it completely. Amen.

Psalm 73:1–28; 2 Corinthians 5:7–21
1. What brought discouragement to the psalmist?
2. How did Paul encourage the Corinthians?

How to Handle Confusion

19 JUL

FOR READING AND MEDITATION – ROMANS 8:29-39

'Nothing will ever be able to separate us from the love of God demonstrated by our Lord Jesus Christ...' (v39, TLB)

We look at yet another feeling which can arise in a heart that is unprotected by a spiritual breastplate – the feeling of confusion. None of us likes confusion because it erodes our sense of competence. Satan, knowing this, steps in whenever he can to take full advantage of it. Deep in the centre of our being is a compulsive demand to be in control, and to satisfy that demand, we have to live in a predictable, understandable world. Confusion presents a serious challenge to our desire for control and is the enemy of those who like to have clear answers for everything.

Whenever the enemy sees that we are not wearing our spiritual breastplate, he comes to us and says something like this: 'Look at the great problems that are all around you – earthquakes, famines, violence, cruelty to children... how can you believe in a God of love when these things are going on in the world?' Sometimes he presses home these arguments with such power and force that you scarcely know where you are or how to answer. You cannot make sense of it, you cannot understand and you have no clear answers.

There is only one clear answer against such assaults; it is to put on the 'breastplate of righteousness'. You cannot understand particular happenings, you cannot give any explanation, but you do know that the God who clothed you with His righteousness and saved you from a lost eternity must have your highest interests and those of His universe at heart. When you hold on to that, your heart is protected from despair, even though your mind struggles to comprehend what is happening. You can live in peace even though you do not know all the answers.

Father God, I see that I can experience security in my heart even when my mind cannot understand Your ways. Hidden in Christ and His righteousness, I am safe. I am so thankful. Amen.

2 Timothy 1:1-7; 1 Corinthians 14:33; Isaiah 26:3
1. Where does our peace stem from?
2. Where does confusion come from?

Satan as an Angel of Light   20 JUL

FOR READING AND MEDITATION – PHILIPPIANS 1:1–11
'He who began a good work in you will carry it on to completion…' (v6)

Yet another feeling which the devil delights to arouse in an unprotected and unguarded heart is the feeling that God does not love us. He times his attack to coincide with those moments when everything is going wrong and we are beset by all kinds of difficulties and problems. Then he moves alongside and whispers in our ear: 'Do you still believe that God is love?' And when you respond by saying that you do, he transforms himself into an angel of light and tries another tactic: 'Well', he says, 'you may not be able to deny that God is love, but it is obvious that He does not love you, for if He did then He would not allow you to go through these difficult situations you are experiencing at the moment.'

Again, there is only one protection against such an assault; it is to put firmly in place the 'breastplate of righteousness'. Nothing else will avail at this point. You must point him to the truth of Romans 8:28 – 'We know that in all things God works for the good of those who love him'. Notice, Paul does not say, 'we understand', but 'we know that in all things God works for the good of those who love him, who have been called according to his purpose'.

This brings you directly to the theme of justification by faith, which is in fact the righteousness of Christ. You rest on that, and that is all you need. You must say to yourself: 'He would never have clothed me with His righteousness if He had not set His love upon me and saved me. I will have courage. I do not know what is happening to me now. I cannot fathom it. But if He has begun His work in me, then I know He will go on to complete it.'

O God, what wondrous power there is in Your Word. I can feel it doing me good even as I read and ponder it. Give me a greater knowledge of Your Word, for only through that can I maintain an advantage over the devil. In Jesus' name. Amen.

Jeremiah 31:1–3; Ephesians 2:1–7; 3:16–19; Romans 5:8
1. How has God demonstrated His love?
2. What was Paul's desire for the Ephesians?

What Happens When We Sin?

21 JUL

FOR READING AND MEDITATION – 1 JOHN 1:5–10; 2:1–2

'If we confess our sins, he is faithful and just and will forgive us our sins and purify us from all unrighteousness.' (1:9)

We look finally at another feeling which arises in an unguarded and unprotected heart – the feeling that when we have committed a sin, we will be rejected by God and have to forfeit our salvation. You are probably aware that the Hebrew name 'Satan' means 'adversary' and the Greek name for 'devil' means 'slanderer'. This gives us a pretty good idea of the nature of the Evil One – he is never happier than when he is engaged in pointing the finger of scorn and accusation at us whenever we have sinned or failed.

It is part of the doctrine of the Church that a Christian may sometimes fall into sin. We are saved, but we are still fallible. God forbid that we should fall into sin, but when we do, we must remember that we have 'an advocate with the Father, Jesus Christ the righteous'. You can be sure, however, that when you fall into sin, the devil will come to you and say: 'You were forgiven when you became a Christian because you sinned in ignorance, but now that you are a Christian you have sinned against the light. There can be no forgiveness for you now. You are lost – and lost for ever.'

The answer to this, as with all of Satan's accusations, is to put on the 'breastplate of righteousness'. You must remind him that God's righteousness not only covers us at our salvation but continues to cover us for time and eternity. Never allow the devil to use a particular sin to call into question your whole standing before God. That is something that has been settled in heaven, not in the debating chamber of the devil.

My Father and my God, my heart overflows at the revelation of Your full and free forgiveness. Help me not to take it for granted but to take it with gratitude. In Jesus' name I pray. Amen.

Isaiah 55:1–7; 43:25; Ephesians 1:7–8; Acts 13:38
1. What does God do when He blots out our sin?
2. How does the Lord respond when we return to Him?

The Shoes of Peace   22 JUL

FOR READING AND MEDITATION – PHILIPPIANS 1:12–30

> 'Stand firm in the one Spirit, striving together
> as one for the faith of the gospel…' (v27)

We come now to the third piece of armour – having our feet shod 'with the the readiness that comes from the gospel of peace' (Eph. 6:15). Shoes are absolutely essential to a soldier. Imagine an infantryman clad in armour but with no shoes on – a barefoot soldier. The rough ground would tear his feet to pieces and would soon render him unfit for duty. But with a stout pair of shoes, he would be ready to face anything that came.

Markus Barth, a Bible commentator, says that the shoes which a Roman soldier would have worn in Paul's day were not so much a shoe as a sandal. They were known as *caligae* (half boots) which consisted of 'heavy studded leather soles and were tied to the ankles or shins with more or less ornamental straps'. These equipped the soldier for a solid stance and prevented his feet from slipping or sliding.

What is the spiritual application of all this? What did the apostle Paul have in mind when he penned the words: 'Stand firm then… with your feet fitted with the readiness that comes from the gospel of peace'? The New English Bible brings home the point of the passage in a most effective way when it translates it thus: 'Let the shoes on your feet be the gospel of peace, to give you firm footing' (REB). The shoes we are to put on are the gospel of peace – the tried and tested truths of the gospel – and their purpose is to prevent us from slipping and sliding when we do battle with our wily and nimble adversary, the devil. What are you like when under attack? Firm and resolute – or unsteady and unsure?

O Father, I see that if I am to stand firm and resolute when under enemy attack, my feet must be securely shod. Show me what is expected of me, dear Lord – and help me apply it. In Jesus' name I pray. Amen.

Psalm 40:1–5; 1 Samuel 2:9; Isaiah 52:1–7
1. What was the psalmist's testimony?
2. Is that your testimony?

Don't Miss the Point

23 JUL

FOR READING AND MEDITATION – 2 TIMOTHY 2:1–15

'Do your best to present yourself to God as one approved,
a worker who does not need to be ashamed and
who correctly handles the word of truth.' (v15)

One interpretation of having our 'feet fitted with the readiness that comes from the gospel of peace' means that we should always be eager and ready to carry the gospel to others. That interpretation certainly fits in with Romans 10:15, which says: 'How beautiful are the feet of those who bring good news!', but it is not, in my opinion, what Paul had in mind when he wrote the words in Ephesians 6:15.

We must keep constantly before us as we ponder the verses in Ephesians 6 that the apostle here is dealing with one thing, and one thing only – the Christian's engagement with the devil. 'For our struggle is not against flesh and blood, but against the rulers, against the authorities, against the powers of this dark world...' (v12). His whole point and purpose is to show us how to stand against the 'wiles' of the devil. Although Paul was an evangelist and had a strong evangelistic spirit, he was not thinking here of evangelising, vital and important though that is. He was rather picturing a Christian who is under attack and warning us that unless our feet are firmly shod, we can easily be knocked down and disabled.

Those who claim that the phrase 'the readiness that comes from the gospel of peace' relates to evangelism miss the point of his exposition. No one would deny the importance of always being ready to share Christ with others, but the readiness Paul is referring to here is the readiness to stand firm on the truths of the gospel. In other words, he is saying: don't get into a fight with the devil in your bare feet. Make sure you are well shod, for if you are not, he will most certainly get the better of you.

O Father, I am so grateful that You breathed into Your servant Paul to write these illuminating words. They are inspired, for they inspire me. Continue to teach me, dear Lord. I am hungry for more and more of Your truth. Amen.

Psalm 119:97–105; Isaiah 40:8; 1 Peter 1:23–25
1. How did the psalmist view God's word?
2. Why is God's word a sure foundation?

Nothing To Hold On To

24 JUL

FOR READING AND MEDITATION – 1 CORINTHIANS 16:1–18

'Be on your guard; stand firm in the faith;
be courageous; be strong.' (v13)

The point we made yesterday, that having our 'feet fitted with the readiness that comes from the gospel of peace' means being ready to stand firm on the truths of the gospel, is brought out also in the text before us today.

One of the great tragedies that is evident in many church circles at the moment is that large numbers of Christians do not have their feet fitted with the readiness that come from the gospel of peace. They are slipping and sliding in all directions because they do not know what to believe or what to hold on to. Once I met a few Christians from the area in South Wales where I was brought up, Christians who at one time were on fire for God and had a solid confidence in Scripture. As I talked with them, however, I saw that they no longer thought of the Bible in the way they once did, for their conversation about Christ and His Word was filled with doubts and denials. How sad.

If my correspondence is anything to go by, as well as my conversations with Christians in all denominations, there are signs that large numbers of men and women are no longer standing for the truths of the gospel – they no longer know what to believe or what to hold on to. How the devil must rejoice as he sees Christians slipping and sliding in their faith. Here in Britain we see evidence of it, not just in ordinary believers but in some of our notable theologians and bishops. Do you know what you believe? Do you stand firm on the truths of the gospel? Remember, if you don't stand for anything, then you will fall for anything.

Dear Father, help me to keep close to the words of Scripture, for they take me beyond the words to You, the Living Word. Strengthen me so that I might hold fast to the truths of the gospel, for without them I cannot help but stumble and fall. Amen.

Psalm 17:1–15; Philippians 4:1; 1 Thessalonians 3:8
1. What was the psalmist's prayer?
2. What was Paul's exhortation to the Philippians?

The Irreducible Minimum　　　　25 JUL

FOR READING AND MEDITATION – 2 CORINTHIANS 1:12-24

'For no matter how many promises God has made, they are 'Yes' in Christ.' (v20)

Do you believe the Bible is the Word of God, divinely and uniquely inspired and reliable in all it affirms? Do you believe that Jesus Christ is the Son of God, born of a virgin, and the only way to God? Do you believe that He was crucified for your sins, raised again on the third day, and is now sitting on the right hand of God?

I could go on raising more and more questions but the ones I have mentioned are what I consider to be the irreducible minimum of Christianity. In other words, these are the basic truths of the gospel and if you don't take your stand on these truths, then you cannot call yourself a Christian. This is what is meant by having your feet fitted with the readiness that comes from the gospel of peace – you are ready to stand for the authority of Scripture, the deity of Christ, His substitutionary death, His resurrection from the dead, and His return to earth in power and glory.

Do you know where you stand on these matters? Are you sure of your spiritual position? How can you fight the enemy if you do not know what you believe? All over the world, there is a call for church leaders to give a spiritual lead. But many of our leaders do not have a high view of Scripture. How can they give a lead when they don't know where they are going? They don't know where they stand and no one else knows either.

O Father, Your Word promises to be a lamp to our feet and a light for our path. Bring those whose feet are slipping and sliding in the faith back to an unshakeable confidence in the gospel. In Jesus' name I ask it. Amen.

2 Peter 1; Colossians 2:7; 1 Corinthians 3:11
1. Why are we given so many great and precious promises?
2. What should our foundation be?

A Word to New Christians

26 JUL

FOR READING AND MEDITATION – 2 THESSALONIANS 2:13–27

'Stand firm and hold to the teachings we passed on to you...' (v15)

There can be little doubt that the great need of the hour is for Christians to stand with their feet fitted with the readiness that comes from the gospel of peace. The moment we begin to compromise on the Word of God and the great truths of the gospel, we shall not only slip and slide in the understanding of our faith but also in its practice.

Permit me to say a word to those who have been in the Christian life for just a short time. Now that you are a Christian, take your stand unflinchingly on the Lord's side. When you meet your old friends, those you used to hang around with in the days before you came to know the Lord, and they propose that you go on doing the things you used to do which you know are not in harmony with God's Word, then be resolute and refuse. Take a firm stand in the matter and watch that you do not slip or slide towards them. Have your feet fitted with the readiness that comes from the gospel of peace.

The first thing that strikes everyone who comes into the Christian life is that it is entirely different from one's former life. You must determine to take your stand with Jesus Christ and when others tempt you, say: 'I cannot betray my Lord. I am bound to Him for all eternity. My feet are shod and I am not moving.' You have to know what you believe and be resolute and determined to stand for it, come what may. If I had not done this in the days following my conversion, then I would have forfeited an adventure that has taken me deeper and deeper into God.

O God, how can I have faith in You unless I have faith in the words You have spoken to me in the Bible? Help me stand firm in the faith – today and every day. In Jesus' name. Amen.

Galatians 5:1–13; Philippians 1:27; 1 Peter 5:7–11
1. What did Paul say to the Galatians?
2. How should we conduct ourselves?

A Spiritual Adventure

27 JUL

FOR READING AND MEDITATION – JUDGES 7:1–22

'The LORD said to Gideon, "With the three
hundred men that lapped I will save you…"' (v7)

I have selected this passage today because it illustrates the point I have been making over the past few days, namely that God is looking for people who will 'stand'. When the hosts of Midian came against the Israelites, Gideon gathered together a large army of 32,000 men. Then God reduced them to a mere handful. Of the 32,000, there were only 300 whom God could trust. He saw that they were men who would stand and never quit, so He dismissed the rest and with just a small army of 300 proceeded to discomfit and rout the Midianites.

God has always done His greatest work in and through a comparatively small number of people. When it comes to spiritual victories, forget the idea of numbers – what God wants is men and women who are prepared to 'stand', whose feet are 'fitted with the readiness that comes from the gospel of peace'. He will not entrust great responsibility to people whom He knows will not 'stand', for that would be an exercise in fruitlessness.

Are you standing for God – in your place of work, your home or the environment in which God has put you? Let me put the question another way – are you ready to stand? You see, you cannot stand until you are prepared to stand. It begins with a firm and resolute attitude which then issues in firm and resolute action. As in Gideon's day, the Lord is looking for men and women who will take their stand on His Word, come what may, and commit themselves to doing what He asks even though they may not feel like it or see the sense of it. Are you such a one? If you are, then I predict that ahead of you is an exciting spiritual adventure.

O God, help me not to miss the highest because of my spiritual unpreparedness. Help me to be ready for all that You have for me – even before I see it. In Jesus' name I pray. Amen.

Galatians 6:1–9; 1 Corinthians 15:58; Ephesians 4:15
1. What is the result of remaining steadfast?
2. What can hinder our spiritual success?

Peace That Does Not Go to Pieces 28 JUL

FOR READING AND MEDITATION – COLOSSIANS 3:1–17
'Let the peace of Christ rule in your hearts...' (v15)

Over the past few days we have been building up a picture of what it means to have our 'feet fitted with the readiness that comes from the gospel of peace'. One question remains – why the phrase 'the gospel of peace'? Well, the gospel is first and foremost a message about peace. First we experience peace with God, and then we experience the peace of God.

A soldier in battle has to be certain about a number of things or else he will be distracted and become an easy prey for the enemy. He needs to be certain that he is fighting in a just war, that his commander is a wise strategist and that he has the constant support of those under whose authority he fights. He needs to know also that his loved ones are being cared for and that they are being protected by a defence force. It is the same with a Christian soldier. He too has to be certain about a number of things – his relationship with God, the truth and reliability of the Bible, the resources that are available to him, and so on. How can his heart be at peace if he is not assured of these things?

It is precisely at this point that we Christians have an advantage over every other soldier, for not only are we led by the wisest military strategist in the universe, but we have inside information on how the battle will end – we win! We would never be able to stand against the 'wiles' of the devil unless we enjoyed peace with God and the peace of God. Even in the midst of the hottest conflict, we know that although the devil may win some of the battles, he will most definitely lose the war. If you have peace about the outcome, then you have peace all the way – period.

O Father, I see so clearly that if I have doubts about You or about my salvation, then I will not be able to fight the enemy. I shall have to spend the whole time struggling with myself. But there are no doubts. I have peace with You and peace within. I am so thankful. Amen.

Philippians 4:1–7; Psalm 29:11; John 16:33; Romans 14:17
1. What keeps our hearts and minds?
2. How does this relate to battle?

The Shield of Faith — 29 JUL

FOR READING AND MEDITATION – 1 JOHN 5:1–12

'This is the victory that has overcome the world, even our faith.' (v4)

We come now to the fourth piece of equipment in the Christian soldier's armoury – the shield of faith: 'Above all,' says the apostle, 'taking the shield of faith with which you will be able to quench all the fiery darts of the wicked one' (Eph. 6:16, NKJV).

Note two important facts, the first being Paul's use of the expression 'above all'. Some take this to mean, 'above everything else in importance' and from this, they go on to argue that the last three pieces of armour are more important than the first three. But the phrase really means 'in addition to these', and should not be seen as comparing one section of the armour with another. It is a transition phrase designed to introduce us to a section of the armour which has a different point and purpose.

The second fact is this – the six pieces of armour fall clearly into two main groups, the first consisting of the belt of truth, the breastplate of righteousness and the shoes of the readiness of the gospel of peace. The second group comprises the shield of faith, the helmet of salvation and the sword of the Spirit. The first three pieces of armour were fixed to the body by a special fastening, and hence, to a certain degree, immovable. But with the next three, there is a difference. The shield was not fixed to the body; it was something quite separate. The same applies to the helmet; that, too, was something that could be put on or taken off quite easily. And obviously the same was true of the sword of the Spirit. The lesson, quite clearly, is this – the first three pieces of equipment should be worn at all times, while the other three are to be taken up when and where necessary.

Gracious and loving heavenly Father, I am so thankful for the care and design that has gone into providing for me a sure defence against Satan. I have learned much, yet I see there is still much more to learn. Teach me, my Father. Amen.

1 Timothy 1:12–20; 6:12; 1 Thessalonians 5:8
1. What had some rejected?
2. What was the result?

'Having' and 'Taking'

30 JUL

FOR READING AND MEDITATION – HEBREWS 11:1-16

'Without faith it is impossible to please God...' (v6)

We ended yesterday with the thought that the first three pieces of the Christian armour should be worn at all times, while the last three should be taken up and used when and where it is necessary. Evidence for this can be seen when we look at Paul's use of the words 'having' and 'taking'.

Listen again to the passage: 'Stand therefore, having girded your waist with truth, having put on the breastplate of righteousness, and having shod your feet with the preparation of the gospel of peace...' Then, in the second section, the word changes: 'Above all, taking the shield of faith... And take the helmet of salvation, and the sword of the Spirit'. The difference between the first three pieces of equipment and the last three is the difference between 'having' and 'taking'.

The 'shield' referred to in Ephesians 6 was an extremely large object, something like four feet in length and about two and a half feet wide, and designed to give as much protection as possible to the front of the body. More important, the front surface was covered with a sheet of fireproof metal so that the fiery darts of the enemy would have little or no effect.

Clearly, the thought Paul would have had in mind when referring to this piece of equipment was that in addition to the three items we have already considered, a further defence was needed to protect us from the devil's preliminary attacks. When we consider the lengths to which God has gone in order to give us the protection we need against attack, one wonders why we ever allow ourselves to be defeated by the devil.

O Father, once again I want to record my gratitude for the way in which You have provided for my defence against satanic attack. Help me to see, however, that it will do me no good just to appreciate it; I must use it. In Christ's name I will use it. Amen.

Hebrews 11:17-40; Romans 10:17; Philippians 3:8-9
1. How does faith come?
2. List some of the things accomplished through faith.

Fiery Darts

31 JUL

FOR READING AND MEDITATION – 2 TIMOTHY 4:1–18

'The Lord stood at my side and gave me strength...
And I was delivered from the lion's mouth.' (v17)

The main purpose of the shield in Roman times was to protect the soldiers from the fiery darts that would be thrown at them by the enemy. These fiery darts, made either of wood or metal, were covered with inflammable material and set alight immediately before being thrown. Enemies would throw these at each other in great numbers and from all directions so as to produce confusion and distraction. When attacked in this way, a soldier would hold up the shield in front of him, allowing the fiery darts to land on the fireproof metal surface, from which they would drop away harmlessly.

The apostle says that we Christians, too, need a shield – a 'shield of faith' – in order 'to quench all the fiery darts of the wicked one'. An understanding of what these 'fiery darts' are is essential if we are to stand firm against the adversary. Have you ever gone to bed at night feeling perfectly happy and content, only to wake in a sad and melancholy mood? If there was no obvious physical or psychological reason for that, the chances are that you have experienced one of Satan's 'fiery darts'.

Sometimes they come as evil thoughts, even blasphemous thoughts, which intrude suddenly into our thinking, often at the most incongruous times. We may be reading the Bible, we may be kneeling in prayer, when all of a sudden some impure or inappropriate thought flashes into our mind. It is an example of a 'fiery dart' from the devil. The point you must see is this – they do not come from inside us but from outside us. They strike us. Some thoughts arise from within our carnal nature but these come from without – from Satan. And we are foolish if we do not recognise this and deal with them in this light.

O Father, help me to be alert and able to recognise the 'fiery darts' of Satan when they are hurled at me. For I see that it is only when I recognise them that I can deal effectively with them. Give me insight and understanding. In Jesus' name. Amen.

James 1:1–22; 1 Corinthians 10:13; 2 Corinthians 11:3
1. What is the progression in temptation?
2. What was Paul's concern?

The Satanic Strategy

1 AUG

FOR READING AND MEDITATION – JOHN 13:1–11

'The devil had already prompted Judas,
the son of Simon Iscariot, to betray Jesus.' (v2)

We are seeing that the 'fiery darts' of the devil are quite different from the thoughts that are generated by our carnal nature. They come at us, rather than from within us. A satanic attack can usually be differentiated from something that arises from within by the strength and force with which the thought hits us. Thoughts that arise out of the carnal nature are unpleasant and offensive, but the thoughts that come as 'fiery darts' from the devil burn and sting and inflame.

Many Christians have told me that they often experience these attacks when they sit down to read their Bibles or get on their knees to pray. When they read a newspaper nothing seems to happen, but when they turn their attention to something spiritual, they find it almost impossible to concentrate by reason of the shameful thoughts that occupy their minds.

The other thing one notices about these attacks is that they seem to come in cycles. They are not there permanently but they come at certain times and seasons. I once counselled a man for one hour a week over a period of a whole year and got him to write down in his diary the times and dates when he felt under satanic attack. When we looked through his diary together at the end of the year we discovered an amazing thing – every single attack took place immediately prior to him doing something special for the Lord, like leading a Bible study, conducting a service, visiting the sick, or giving a public testimony. I shall never forget the expression on his face as he looked at me and said: 'Who says that Satan isn't a strategist?'

My Father and my God, I realise that even though Satan is a strategist, he is no match for You. You know how to out-manoeuvre his every move. Help me to stay close to You that I might experience Your strategy and not His. Amen.

Genesis 3; Matthew 4:1–10
1. How did Satan seek to penetrate Eve's mind?
2. How does this correlate with the temptation of Christ?

Blasphemous Thoughts

2 AUG

FOR READING AND MEDITATION – 2 CORINTHIANS 2:1–11
'For we are not unaware of his schemes.' (v11)

Today we begin by looking at a form of attack which is probably the most difficult of all to endure. I refer to the matter of blasphemous thoughts. Dr Martyn Lloyd-Jones said on this matter: 'The devil has often plagued some of the noblest saints with blasphemous thoughts – blasphemous thoughts about God, blasphemous thoughts about the Lord Jesus Christ, and blasphemous thoughts about the Holy Spirit.'

How horrible and terrifying such thoughts can be. Sometimes the devil hurls the most awful words and phrases into the mind, but again, it is important to see that these do not arise from within the heart of the believer – they come from the devil, who is trying to confuse and demoralise you. How grateful we should be to the saints down the ages who have recorded these attacks, for otherwise we would be tempted when experiencing them to believe that they have never happened to anyone else. Many masters of the spiritual life have described these satanic attacks in great detail – John Bunyan and Martin Luther being the two best examples.

But how do we deal with these 'fiery darts'? What action must we take to repel these devilish attacks? There is only one answer – we must take and use the shield of faith. Faith alone enables you to meet and overcome this particular type of attack. What you must not do is expose your chest and expect the breastplate of righteousness to deal with this problem. Each piece of the equipment is designed to deal with a particular attack. And the answer here is – faith.

Heavenly Father, I understand the problem – now show me how to apply the answer. The answer, I see, is faith. But how does it work? How can I apply it? Teach me more. In Jesus' name. Amen.

2 Corinthians 10:1–5; Matthew 22:37–38; Ephesians 1:22–23; James 4:7–8

1. In what ways does Satan attack the mind?
2. What is the Scriptural antidote?

Prompt Action   3 AUG

FOR READING AND MEDITATION – ROMANS 10:1–18

'Faith comes by hearing, and hearing by the word of God.' (v17, NKJV)

We ended yesterday with a prayer for God to help us understand how to use the shield of faith when we need to defend ourselves against the fiery darts of the devil. Prayerfully, then, we ask ourselves the question – how does faith act as a protective shield?

First of all, we must understand what faith is and how the word is being used by Paul in Ephesians 6:16. A little boy, when asked to give a definition of faith, said: 'Faith is believing something you know isn't true.' Well, that is precisely what faith is not. Faith is believing what you know to be true. But it is even more than that – it is acting on what you know to be true. Some people see faith as something vague and mysterious, but faith is one of the most practical commodities in the Christian faith. Take this verse, for example: 'Faith without deeds is dead' (Jas 2:26). There is always the element of activity in faith; it always prompts us to action. 'Faith is confidence in what we hope for and assurance about what we do not see' (Heb. 11:1).

Taking the shield of faith, then, is responding to the things the enemy hurls at us by the quick application of what we believe about God and His Word, the Bible. When Satan sends his 'fiery darts' in our direction, we can either stand and lament the fact that we are being attacked, or quickly raise the shield of faith and remind ourselves that the devil is a liar from the very beginning, and because we are redeemed by the blood of Christ, he has no legal or moral right to taunt us. But believing that is not enough; it must be acted on – and acted on quickly.

Father, I see that when Satan throws his 'fiery darts' at me I must act, and act quickly. Help my faith to be so strong that it will not need a 'jump start' to get it going. This I ask in Jesus' name. Amen.

James 2:14–26; Hebrews 11:1; 1 John 5:4
1. How are we justified?
2. Write out your definition of faith.

I Am Your Shield   4 AUG

FOR READING AND MEDITATION – GENESIS 14:18–24; 15:1–6

'Abram believed the Lord, and he
credited it to him as righteousness.' (15:6)

We spend one more day focusing on how faith acts as a shield against the 'fiery darts' of the devil. You see, it is no good saying you believe God is stronger and more powerful than the devil if you do not act on that belief. Faith not only believes that, but acts on it by quickly and defiantly standing up to the devil and saying something similar to what David said when he stood before Goliath: 'You come against me with sword and spear and javelin, but I come against you in the name of the Lord Almighty...' (1 Sam. 17:45). You must never forget that God is much more powerful than the devil. Hold on to that and quickly raise your shield whenever you experience an attack of 'fiery darts'.

Our passage today focuses on an incident in Abraham's life which took place when he was tired and exhausted after making a great stand, and I have no doubt that Satan would have attacked him with thoughts like this: 'What is the point of all this action of God on your behalf when you do not have an heir to carry on your line. What is the use of all these great promises when you do not have a son? God doesn't seem to have as much power as it would appear.'

Abraham was fearful at this point until the Lord came to him and gave him these glorious words: 'Do not be afraid, Abram. I am your shield, your very great reward' (15:1). 'I am your shield.' Hold on to that great truth, my friend, and when under attack, quickly lift it up and remind the devil that you belong to One whose power is endless and eternal. His promises are ever sure. That is what it means to hold up the shield of faith.

O God, how grateful I am for the sureness and certainty of Your Word. Once again I feel it entering into the core of my being. Help me to put these truths into practice the very moment I come under satanic attack. In Jesus' name I pray. Amen.

Proverbs 30:1-5; Deuteronomy 33:29; Psalm 33:20; 59:11; 84:9
1. Why was Israel blessed?
2. What was the psalmist's continual testimony?

The Helmet of Salvation

FOR READING AND MEDITATION – 2 CORINTHIANS 11:1–15

> 'I am afraid that just as Eve was deceived by the snake's cunning, your minds may somehow be led astray...' (v3)

We come now to the second piece of armour which is not tied or fixed to the body but which a Christian soldier has to take up and put on – 'the helmet of salvation' (Eph. 6:17). The helmet worn by a Roman soldier was usually made of bronze or iron with an inside lining of felt or sponge. In some cases, a hinged visor added frontal protection. When a Roman soldier saw an enemy coming, he would take hold of his shield, put on his helmet, take his sword in hand, and stand alert and ready to do battle.

The figure of a helmet immediately suggests to us that this is something designed to protect the mind, the intelligence, the ability to think and reason. Just as the breastplate of righteousness protects us from emotional distress, so the helmet of salvation protects us from mental distress. This helmet can help us keep our thinking straight and preserve us from mental confusion and darkness.

As you look out at the world, has there ever been a time when we needed something to keep our thinking straight more than we do now? Politicians vacillate and oscillate between despairing pessimism and unrealistic optimism. Just think of the staggering complexities of the issues we face in our generation – global pandemics, violence, culture wars, international tension, economic collapse, poverty, displacement, and so on. The intelligentsia of our day confess to being utterly baffled in dealing with the problems with which human society is confronted. Where can we turn to ease the pressure on our minds? The only answer is God – and in the helmet of salvation which He provides.

O Father, I am so grateful that You have provided freedom from that most terrifying of human problems – mental distress. Teach me all I need to know in applying Your truth to the important area of my mind. In Jesus' name. Amen.

Ephesians 4:1–17; Proverbs 23:7; Romans 8:7; Colossians 1:21
1. How were the Ephesians not to live?
2. How powerful is the influence of the mind?

The Tenses of Salvation   6 AUG

FOR READING AND MEDITATION – 1 THESSALONIANS 5:1-11

'Let us be sober, putting on faith and love as a breastplate, and the hope of salvation as a helmet.' (v8)

We said yesterday that never has there been a time when we need to keep our thinking straight more than we do now. You can be sure that the enemy will take advantage of every situation that comes his way to disable a Christian and he will not hesitate to use chaotic world conditions and problems to oppose the mind. God's answer to this is the helmet of salvation.

It is important to realise that Paul is not talking here about the salvation of the soul. He is not referring to salvation as regeneration or conversion. This is the mistake that many make when attempting to interpret this verse. They say: 'Whenever the devil attacks your mind and seeks to oppress it, remind yourself that you have been saved.' Well, there is nothing wrong with that, of course, and this explanation is mistaken, not because it is untrue, but because it does not go far enough.

The best way to interpret a verse of Scripture is with another verse of Scripture. Thus the text before us today throws a shaft of light on Paul's statement in Ephesians 6:17, for it shows salvation, not just as something in the past but something that is also future. He uses the word in the same way in Romans when he says: 'Our salvation is nearer now than when we first believed' (Rom. 13:11).

In the Bible, the word 'salvation' has three distinct tenses – past, present, and future. At conversion, we are saved from the penalty of sin. Now, day by day, we are being saved from the power of sin. And one day in the future, we will be saved from the presence of sin. And it is to the future Paul is looking when he invites us to put on the helmet of salvation.

O Father, thank You for reminding me of the tenses of salvation. I see that in order to live effectively, I must view the present tense by the future tense. Help me lay hold on this. In Jesus' name. Amen.

Psalm 27:1-14; 37:39; Isaiah 12:2; 25:9
1. What was the psalmist's conviction?
2. What is the prophet proclaiming?

An Atheist Who Lost His Faith

7 AUG

FOR READING AND MEDITATION – ROMANS 8:18-30

'For in this hope we were saved.' (v24)

Our passage today shows even more clearly what we were discussing yesterday – salvation in the future tense. What is Paul talking about in these verses? He is talking about the time when Christ will return, when the kingdom of God will be established and when creation will be delivered from its bondage. The helmet of salvation, therefore, is the recognition that all human schemes, all human disorder, and all human chaos will one day be ended, and when that happens, the whole universe will see that God has been quietly working out His purposes in and through everything.

That truth, when understood and embraced, is the one thing above all others that will enable us to keep our thinking straight in a world that is full of confusion and darkness. Why is it that some of the most thoughtful minds in literature and philosophy were and are so bewildered by what they see in the world? It is because they pin their hopes on unreliable and unrealistic resources. As the Dean of Melbourne wrote about H.G. Wells: 'He hailed science as a panacea for all ills and the goddess of knowledge and power.'

But what were H.G. Wells' conclusions about the world before he died? He wrote this: 'The science to which I pinned my faith is bankrupt. Its counsels, which should have established the millennium, led instead directly to the suicide of Europe. I believed them once. In their name I helped destroy the faith of millions of worshippers in the temples of a thousand creeds. And now they look at me and witness the great tragedy of an atheist who has lost his faith.' There is no protection in the world for the mind.

Something, my Father, is being burned into my consciousness – there is just no hope outside of You. If I break with You I break with sanity. Help me to walk closely with You so that Your mind becomes my mind. In Jesus' name. Amen.

Titus 2; Proverbs 14:32; Acts 24:15; Colossians 1:5
1. How should we live?
2. What are we to look for?

Everything is Under Control   8 AUG

FOR READING AND MEDITATION – EPHESIANS 1:3–14

'According to the plan of him who works out everything in conformity with the purpose of his will...' (v11)

We are seeing that the salvation spoken of in the phrase, 'the helmet of salvation', is not so much the salvation we are enjoying at the present but the salvation we are going to enjoy when God works out His eternal purposes. The Christian has a hope for the future; he has an understanding that God is working out His purposes in history and therefore we need not be disturbed when human programmes appear to be going wrong. We hear about 'new deals' and 'fair deals' and 'better deals', yet they end up in disappointment for all concerned.

The Christian expects the world to get worse and worse, for that is what the Bible tells us will happen. He expects false teachings and false philosophies to abound. He expects the world's systems to fail, for anything that is not built on Christ has no guarantee of success. The Christian knows that wars and international tension are unavoidable, even though every effort is made to avoid them. The world is in such a state and such a condition that the more attention we give it, the more weary our minds become.

What is a Christian to do in such a world as ours? How are we to react when the devil takes advantage of our sensitivity to world conditions and focuses our thoughts upon them? Shall we give up? Shall we withdraw from life? No, we put on the helmet of salvation and remind ourselves that in the face of everything that appears contrary, God is working out His eternal plan and purpose. History is His-story. The Almighty God is at work in the very events that appear to be filled with darkness and confusion.

O God, help me see that although You are apart from the events of history, You are also in the events of history. Ultimately all things are going to glorify You. Thank You, Father. Amen.

Hebrews 6; 1 Peter 1:3; 1 John 3:3
1. What does this hope provide for us?
2. How does Peter describe our hope?

Not a Private Fight

9 AUG

FOR READING AND MEDITATION – 2 CHRONICLES 20:4–26

'Do not be afraid or discouraged...
For the battle is not yours, but God's.' (v15)

At the risk of being repetitive, let me spell out once again what I believe is the spiritual application of the helmet of salvation. It is not so much the enjoyment of our present salvation (though it includes that) but the assurance that a certain, sure salvation is coming and is even now at work.

You see, this is what we need to know if we are to prevent the devil from bringing us into a state of mental distress – not merely that things will finally end right but that God's plan is being worked out now. 'History,' writes Ray Stedman, an American Bible teacher, 'is not a meaningless jumble but a controlled pattern, and the Lord Jesus Christ is the one who is directing these events.' The attack of Satan on the mind proceeds along this line. He says: 'Just look around you at the state of the world. God seems powerless to put things right. He has given lots of promises that things will one day get better, but none of those promises has come to pass. Hadn't you better give up this foolish idea that it's all going to work out right?'

If you were to let your mind dwell on that kind of argument, you would soon find yourself in distress. The answer is to put on the helmet, the hope of salvation. You must remind yourself that things are not as they appear. The battle is not ours, but the Lord's. This is not a private fight we are engaged in. We may be individual soldiers fighting in the army of God, but the ultimate cause is sure and the end is certain. We need not be unduly troubled by what is happening in the world – our commander is not just winning; He has already won.

Lord Jesus, I am grateful that the cross is the guarantee that neither sin nor Satan will ever defeat You. Your victory at Calvary has settled for ever the question of who has the final word in the universe. I am so deeply, deeply thankful. Amen.

Luke 21:10–28; John 14:1–4; 16:33
1. How did Jesus describe the world?
2. What did He say to His disciples?

We See Jesus

10 AUG

FOR READING AND MEDITATION – HEBREWS 2:1–15

'We do not see everything subject to them. But we do see Jesus…' (vv8–9)

Are you troubled as you look out at the situation in the world? Well, according to the Bible things are going to get worse; as Jesus said, 'People will faint from terror, apprehensive of what is coming on the world…' (Luke 21:26).

How are Christians going to stand when the darkness deepens and things get very much worse? What will we do when international tension increases, making it difficult for nation to communicate with nation? Christians have a glorious hope – the hope of salvation. It is this, and this alone, which enables believers to live out their lives free from mental distress. I am sure you have already discovered that after reading the morning news, you move into the day feeling somewhat jaded and depressed. Why is this? This is largely due to the fact that our newsfeeds are filled almost daily with reports of violence, economic hardship, abuse, and other deeply troubling events. And our conscience, which through conversion has been sensitised to the moral laws of God, begins to reverberate as it comes up against the reports of things we know are contrary to the divine principles.

The enemy, seeing our concern, attempts to exploit it to his own ends. 'Things are getting worse, aren't they?' he says. 'Why don't you just admit that God has lost control of His world?' If we do not have the helmet of salvation to put on at such a moment, we would finish up with the same attitude as H.G. Wells, who, after the Second World War, wrote: 'The spectacle of evil in the world has come near to breaking my spirit.' Again I say, there is no protection in the world for the mind.

My Father and my God, where would I be if I could not cling to a text such as that in my reading for today? My spirit too would be near to breaking. I am so thankful that in You there is hope – hope with a capital H. Amen.

John 17; Romans 8:35–37; 1 John 5:4
1. What did Jesus pray for His disciples?
2. What was Paul's conviction?

The Way to an Undisturbed Mind **11** AUG

FOR READING AND MEDITATION – COLOSSIANS 1:9–28
'Christ in you, the hope of glory.' (v27)

Here in the British Isles, we are relatively shielded from many of the challenges that trouble others around the world. While we face our own sorrows, we also have much to be thankful for. We can still preach the gospel freely in our churches and enjoy the right to speak openly. But I'm aware that some will be reading these words in parts of the world where such freedoms do not exist – where faith must be hidden, and where even open worship of Satan can occur.

What do Christians living in these places do to prevent themselves from becoming wearied by their adverse conditions and circumstances? There is only one thing they can do – they must put on the helmet of the hope of salvation. This, more than anything, will help keep their thinking straight. But no matter where in the world we live, those of us who have enlisted in the army of God must do the same. We must not succumb to the popular delusion that the working out of all human problems lies just around the corner through the application of humanistic ideas and philosophies.

How long has the world grasped at this futile dream? Almost from the dawn of history, men and women have been grasping after the elusive hope that something can be worked out here. But God has never said that. Consistently throughout the Scriptures, He has said that humans in their fallen condition are totally unable to work out their problems. We know, however, that He has reserved a day of salvation when all wrongs will be righted, and it is only in the strength of the hope of that day of salvation that our hearts and minds can be kept undisturbed.

O Father, how can I ever be grateful enough that I am caught up in an eternal purpose. I live in the present, yet I draw also from the certainties of the future. Nourish this hope within me until it drives out every fear. In Jesus' name. Amen.

Galatians 2; John 14:20; 1 John 3:24
1. How did Paul describe his Christian walk?
2. How would you describe your Christian walk?

The Sword of the Spirit 12 AUG

FOR READING AND MEDITATION – JAMES 4:1–10
'Resist the devil, and he will flee from you.' (v7)

We come now to the last of the six pieces in the Christian soldier's armour – 'the sword of the Spirit, which is the word of God' (Eph. 6:17). John Stott points out that 'of all the six pieces of armour or weaponry listed, the sword is the only one which can clearly be used for attack as well as defence'. And the kind of attack envisaged here is one that involves a close encounter, for the word used for sword is *machaira*, meaning a short sword or dagger.

As soon as we begin talking about the sword as being a weapon of attack, we see that there is much more to spiritual warfare than standing up to the devil – we have, according to our text today, the potential to make him 'flee'. The word 'flee' is a very strong word in the original Greek. It means much more than a strategic withdrawal; it means beating a swift and hasty retreat. What an amazing truth! It is possible for a Christian so to resist the devil that he races away as fast as he can.

This truth must not be seen in any way as limiting the devil's power, for he is a strong and determined foe. It means rather that although he has great power and strength, a Christian able to wield the sword of the Spirit can ensure that he is overpowered and discomfited. We are right when we develop a healthy respect for the devil's wiles and ingenuity, but we are wrong when we allow him to terrorise and frighten us. We must have the assurance, given everywhere in the New Testament, that to engage in conflict with the devil is not a hopeless task. We are not to indulge in over-confidence but, at the same time, we are not to be terrorised or frightened by him.

O Father, the thought that I, a sinner saved by grace, am able to send Satan into retreat almost overwhelms me. Yet I must believe it, for Your Word tells me so. Help me understand even more clearly the authority I have in Christ. In His Name I ask it. Amen.

Luke 10:1–20; Acts 3:6–8; 16:16–18; 1 Peter 5:8–9
1. How much authority over Satan have we been given?
2. How did the Early Church exercise this authority?

The Power of Precise Scripture

13 AUG

FOR READING AND MEDITATION – MATTHEW 4:1–11

'It is written... It is also written...' (vv4,7)

We must now focus on what is meant by the phrase – 'the sword of the Spirit, which is the word of God'. Some interpret it to mean that the Holy Spirit is the word of God. But nowhere in the Bible is the Holy Spirit described as the word of God. That description is confined solely to our Lord Jesus Christ. Well, if the Spirit is not the sword – what is? The sword is the Word of God, the Bible, the inspired Scriptures.

In the passage before us today we see a perfect illustration of how Jesus used the sword of the Spirit when rebutting the temptations of the devil. Notice how, prior to the temptation, Jesus was anointed by the Holy Spirit (Matt. 3:13–17). Next we are informed that Jesus was 'led by the Spirit into the wilderness to be tempted by the devil' (v1). During the temptation our Lord, filled with the Spirit, resisted every one of the devil's statements by using the precise words of Scripture. Follow me closely, for this is extremely important: Christ did not merely utter a newly formed statement or something that came to Him on the spur of the moment, but quoted a text which had already been given by God and written down. The weapon used by our Lord was the Word of God, the Scriptures.

Can you see the point I am making? Satan is not rebuffed by clever phrases that are made up on the spur of the moment and may sound theologically sophisticated and refined; he is defeated only when we quote to him the precise words of Scripture. If this was the strategy Jesus had to use, then how much more you and I? Nothing defeats Satan more thoroughly and effectively than the sword of the Spirit, which is the Word of God.

O God, open my eyes that I might see more clearly than ever the power and authority that lies in Your sacred Word, the Bible. Help me to know it better. For Your own dear Name's sake. Amen.

1 Peter 1:13–25; Psalm 119:89,103; Jeremiah 15:16
1. What did Jeremiah do with God's word?
2. How did the psalmist describe it?

The Bible – an Inspired Book   14 AUG

FOR READING AND MEDITATION – JOHN 16:1–15

'When he, the Spirit of truth, comes,
he will guide you into all the truth.' (v13)

Today we ask ourselves: why are the Scriptures described as a sword provided by the Holy Spirit? It means, quite simply, that it is the Holy Spirit who has given us the Scriptures. They come altogether from Him. It was the Holy Spirit who inspired men to write them: 'Prophets, though human, spoke from God as they were carried along by the Holy Spirit' (2 Peter 1:21). Again in 2 Timothy 3:16 we read: 'All Scripture is God-breathed' – a statement which assures us that the Scriptures come from the Holy Spirit.

The Bible is not a mere human document, the product of the mind of man. The Holy Spirit breathed into men and inspired them to write the way they did. This does not mean that the people who wrote the Scriptures did so mechanically, in the way that someone would dictate into a dictation machine. The Holy Spirit used their natural way of expression but gave them an additional ability to write without error. It is vital, if you are to win the battle against Satan, that you not only see this but believe it. When you consider how strong and powerful the enemy is, then you need something that is even more strong and powerful. And the Bible, the inspired Word of God, is your strength.

We must, however, go one step further – only the Holy Spirit can enable us truly to understand God's Word: 'What we have received is not the spirit of the world, but the Spirit who is from God, so that we may understand what God has freely given us' (1 Cor. 2:12). Without the Holy Spirit, we would be no more able to understand the Scriptures than a blind man could judge a beauty contest.

Gracious Holy Spirit, just as You breathed into the Bible to give it its life and power, breathe also into my heart today so that I might know and understand its truth. I ask this in Jesus' name. Amen.

Colossians 3:1–16; Deuteronomy 6:6; 11:18; Hebrews 10:15–16
1. What does the word 'dwell' mean?
2. Where must God's word be written?

Divide and Conquer

15 AUG

FOR READING AND MEDITATION – 1 CORINTHIANS 2:1–16

'The things that come from the Spirit of God...
are discerned only through the Spirit.' (v14)

We ended yesterday with the thought that only the Holy Spirit can help us to understand the Word of God. I will go further and say that only the Holy Spirit can help us properly to interpret it. A person may have a fine mind, a good seminary training, even a theological degree, but that is not a sufficient foundation on which to attempt to interpret the Word of God. Truth, as our text for today tells us, is 'discerned only through the Spirit'.

But there is one more thing we need to understand – only the Holy Spirit can show us how to use it aright. Doubtless this was the consideration in the mind of the apostle when he penned the statement we are considering: 'the sword of the Spirit, which is the word of God'. It is one thing to know the contents of Scripture; it is another thing to know how to use those contents in a way that defeats and overcomes the devil. Only the Holy Spirit can enable us to do this.

The relationship between the Holy Spirit and the Word of God is an important one. Some tend to put the emphasis on one side or the other. But the moment we separate the Spirit and the Word, we are in trouble. The late Donald Gee once said: 'All Spirit and no Word, you blow up. All Word and no Spirit, you dry up. Word and Spirit, you grow up.' Without the Spirit, the Word is a dead letter; with the Spirit, it is a living and powerful force. The devil has a policy of 'divide and conquer', and if he can get us to separate the Word from the Spirit, then he has us just where he wants us.

My Father, I see that when I separate the Spirit from the Word and the Word from the Spirit, I am in trouble. Help me to be as open to the Spirit as I am to the Bible, and as open to the Bible as I am to the Spirit. In Jesus' name. Amen.

2 Corinthians 3:1–6; John 6:63 (KJV); 1 Peter 3:18
1. What does the word 'quickened' mean?
2. What made Paul an able minister of truth?

The Divine Design   16 AUG

FOR READING AND MEDITATION – JOHN 14:15-27

'The Advocate, the Holy Spirit… will teach you all things and will remind you of everything I have said to you.' (v26)

We said yesterday that only the Holy Spirit can enable us to use the contents of Scripture in a way that helps us to overcome and defeat the enemy. How does this work out in practice? When we come to God's Word, laying aside all preconceived ideas and depending entirely on the Holy Spirit to reveal its truth to us, we put ourselves in a position where the Holy Spirit can impress the truth of the Scriptures into our innermost being. There it takes root within us, and whenever we stand in need of a word with which to rebut the devil, the Holy Spirit brings it to our remembrance.

And here's the most wonderful thing – the Word of God on our lips will have the same effect upon the devil as if he was hearing it from the lips of Jesus Himself! Every time we open the Bible, we must be careful to pray for the help and illumination of the Spirit so that we don't finish up making the Bible mean what we want it to mean. When we do that, we are following the divine design – letting the Spirit bring home to our hearts the truth and meaning of His own Word.

This attitude of humility and receptivity gives the Holy Spirit the opportunity He needs to build the truth of the Word of God into our spirits. Approaching the Bible in this way, said the late J. B, Phillips, 'is like rewiring a house where the electricity has not been turned off'. You touch something that lets you know there is a current of power flowing through its pages that was not put there by any human. The Holy Spirit has gone into it, so is it any wonder that the Holy Spirit comes out of it?

My Father and my God, I know the Spirit dwells in Your Word. I come now to ask that He might dwell also in me, to open up my whole being to the truth and power that lies in its inspired pages. In Jesus' name I ask it. Amen.

John 15:18-27; Luke 12:11-12; Romans 8:14
1. What did Jesus declare about the Holy Spirit's ministry?
2. What promise did Jesus give to His disciples?

The Coal Miner and the PhD   17 AUG

FOR READING AND MEDITATION – HEBREWS 4:1–13

'For the word of God is alive and active.
Sharper than any double-edged sword...' (v12)

Not everyone has had the opportunity for a broad or formal education, and many may feel unacquainted with subjects such as science, philosophy, or the arts. Yet the encouraging truth is this: such knowledge is not what determines victory over Satan. What truly matters is faith and dependence on God's power.

I remember being present some years ago in a church in South Wales when a debate was held between a university professor and an ordinary coal miner. The subject was: 'Is the Bible true?' The university professor presented his arguments in a clear and cogent fashion and I remember feeling quite sorry for the miner as I envisaged some of the difficulties he might have when making his reply. After the professor had finished, the miner stood to his feet and for over an hour I witnessed one of the most amazing demonstrations of the Holy Spirit at work that I have ever seen in my life.

The miner began by asking everyone to bow their heads as he prayed a prayer which went something like this: 'Lord, I have not had much education, but You know that I love Your Word and have spent my life searching its pages. Help me now to say something that will convince my friends here that Your Word is true.' He then proceeded to demolish the arguments of the professor simply by quoting appropriate scriptures without making even a simple comment. When he finished, there was thunderous applause. The professor's highly intellectual arguments had been torn to pieces by the sharp edges of the sword of the Spirit – by that, and by that alone.

O Father, the more I hear, the more I want to hear. For I was created by Your Word, designed according to Your Word, and I can never remain content until I am indwelt with Your Word. Teach me even more. In Jesus' name. Amen.

Jeremiah 5:1–14; 23:29; Psalm 119:105,130
1. What was God's word in Jeremiah's mouth?
2. What was it to the psalmist?

Scan to download today ▸

Go Still Deeper

18 AUG

FOR READING AND MEDITATION – JOHN 17:1-19
'Your word is truth.' (v17)

Christians who do not accept the authority of the Scriptures undermine the very foundation they need to stand on when coming into conflict with the devil and all his forces. Without an authoritative Bible, we have no effective weapon with which to overcome. It is as simple as that. If you are not certain that the Bible is the Word of God, if you do not believe that it is without error in all that it affirms, then you are like a soldier with a broken sword in his hand.

To use the sword of the Spirit effectively, we need to have as wide a knowledge of the Bible as possible. Let me take you back to Christ's encounter in the wilderness of temptation once again. When Satan advanced, Jesus took up the sword of the Spirit and knew exactly what Scriptures to use. There were three different temptations and Jesus selected three different parts of Scripture. He knew exactly the right words to select to rebut each temptation of the devil.

If we are to conquer the enemy in the same way that Jesus conquered him, then we must know the Bible in its entirety. It is no good saying, 'The verse I want to use against you is somewhere in the Bible.' You must quote it to him and quote it precisely. I hope you do not think that *Every Day with Jesus* will do this for you, because it won't. These daily readings will help you start the day, but you need a deeper and more intensive programme of study if you are to become proficient in the use of the Scriptures against Satan. Decide right now to commit yourself to exploring the Bible more deeply and thoroughly than you have ever done before.

O Father, I see that the more I know of Your Word, the more effective I will be in resisting Satan. Show me how to go more deeply into the Scriptures than I have ever done before. In Jesus' name I pray. Amen.

Ezekiel 37:1-10; Acts 17:11; Romans 10:8
1. What was the result of the spoken word through Ezekiel?
2. What did Paul say of the Bereans?

A Final Exhortation

19 AUG

FOR READING AND MEDITATION – LUKE 21:20–36

'Be always on the watch, and pray...' (v36)

One might think that, having examined in detail the six pieces of the armour of God, this would be a natural place to end our discussion, but there is one more verse to consider: 'And pray in the Spirit on all occasions with all kinds of prayers and requests. With this in mind, be alert and always keep on praying for all the Lord's people' (Eph. 6:18).

What is the meaning of this further and final exhortation? Well, it is not, as so many Christians believe, an additional but unnamed piece of armour. One commentator writes: 'Paul is giving us in this verse the final piece of armour for the Christian who is in conflict with the devil: praying always with all prayer...'. This surely cannot be so, for Paul's reference to 'praying always with all prayer', or praying 'on all occasions with all kinds of prayers', although closely related to the six pieces of armour, is quite different from it and does not fall within the bounds of the careful and close analogy that he has been making.

What then does he mean when he includes this further intriguing statement? He is saying (so I believe) that 'praying in the Spirit' is something that ought to pervade all our spiritual warfare and is something we have to do and keep on doing if we are to win the battle against Satan and his forces. Paul is saying, 'Put on the whole armour of God, every single piece, and in the proper order; but in addition to that, at all times and in all places, keep on praying.' In other words, the armour which is provided for us by God cannot be used effectively unless it is worn by a praying Christian.

O Father, thank You for inspiring Your servant Paul to give us this insight, for we see that without it we would be defeated by the devil. Help me become a watchful and praying Christian. In Jesus' name. Amen.

Luke 18:1–8; 1 Chronicles 16:11; Colossians 4:2; 1 Thessalonians 5:17
1. What was Jesus teaching in this parable?
2. How did Paul exhort the Colossians?

Not a Postscript — 20 AUG

FOR READING AND MEDITATION – COLOSSIANS 1:1–12

'We always thank God, the Father of our
Lord Jesus Christ, when we pray for you...' (v3)

We saw yesterday that we must not think, when Paul finishes his description of the Christian's armour in verse 17 of Ephesians 6, that he has ended his exhortation. In fact, if we were to stop there we would miss the whole meaning of the apostle's thought, for the six pieces of armour only provide us with adequate defence against the devil when worn by a praying Christian. Ephesians 6:18, therefore, is not a postscript but a culmination of all that the apostle has been saying before. 'And pray in the Spirit', cries the great apostle, 'on all occasions with all kinds of prayers and requests'.

The danger facing us is that we can feel, once we have our spiritual armour on, that we are safe, we can relax, all is well, that the armour will protect us. But that is the height of folly and something Satan would love to get us to believe. And if we do believe it, then it means we are already defeated. The armour of God and its spiritual application must always be thought of in terms of our relationship and fellowship with God. If there is no communion with Him, then the six pieces of armour will be ineffective. The armour of God is not something that is magical or mechanical; it functions as a spiritual defence only when worn with prayer. One of the great hymns of our faith expresses the thought most beautifully when it says:

> *To keep your armour bright*
> *Attend with constant care*
> *Still walking in our Captain's sight*
> *And watching unto prayer.*
> *— Charles Wesley (1707–1788)*

Father, I see that with all I have learned about defending myself against the devil, I must still go a step further. Help me to understand this step, for it is vital that I am not just protected against Satan, but fully protected. Amen.

John 15:1–7; Jeremiah 29:13; Matthew 26:41; Mark 11:24
1. Why can we pray with confidence?
2. What must accompany prayer?

And Yet...

FOR READING AND MEDITATION – 1 THESSALONIANS 5:11–24

'Be unceasing in prayer [praying perseveringly]...' (v17, AMPC)

We continue meditating on the truth that the armour of God must be put on in an attitude of believing prayer. John Stott, in his commentary on Ephesians, says: 'Equipping ourselves with God's armour is not a mechanical operation; it is in itself an expression of our dependence upon God.'

Note the phrase, 'is not a mechanical operation'. Some Christians like to begin each day by going through the motions of dressing themselves in the armour of God. In their minds they put on the belt of truth, the breastplate of righteousness, the shoes of the preparation of the gospel of peace, and so on. I have no objection to this myself, but I do see a danger that it can become merely a mechanical operation in which they look just to the armour to protect them from the wiles of the devil, and think that nothing more needs to be done. Let me remind you again – every single piece of armour, excellent and valuable though it is in itself, will not work for us unless always, and at all times, we are in a close, prayerful relationship with God.

Cast your mind back once again over the six pieces of the Christian soldier's equipment: the belt of truth, the breastplate of righteousness, the shoes of peace, the shield of faith, the helmet of salvation and the sword of the Spirit. What strong protection our Lord has provided for us in this conflict against Satan and his forces. And yet, having all this great and wonderful equipment available, we can still suffer defeat if we do not stand in the strength and power which God provides. And that power can flow only along the channel of fervent, believing prayer.

Father, day by day it is becoming increasingly clear that unless I am continually linked to Your resources through believing prayer, the armour You have provided for me gives me only a limited defence. Help me never to forget this. Amen.

Colossians 1:1–12; Philippians 4:13; Ephesians 3:16; 1 Peter 5:10
1. What was Paul's prayer for the Colossians?
2. Where does our strength come from?

Standard Operating Procedure

22 AUG

FOR READING AND MEDITATION – 1 TIMOTHY 2:1–10

'I want the men everywhere to pray, lifting up holy hands, without anger or disputing.' (v8)

We must spend another day considering the fact that we can carefully and meticulously put on every single piece of God's armour and yet suffer defeat at the hands of the devil if we do not go on to consider the injunction – 'pray in the Spirit on all occasions with all kinds of prayers'. Dr Martyn Lloyd-Jones says on this point: 'I have known Christians who have been well acquainted with the theology of the Bible and known it in an extraordinary manner, but who did not believe in prayer meetings, who did not seem to see the utter and absolute necessity of 'praying always' in the way that is indicated here by the apostle.'

You see, it is possible to be orthodox in your doctrine and still, as far as spiritual warfare is concerned, be a defeated Christian. You cannot fight the devil, even with orthodoxy, if you know nothing of a vital, day-by-day relationship with God through prayer. I know people, and I am sure you do too, who have a wonderful understanding of Scripture and are experts at pointing out the errors in other people's teaching, but because they do not have a close relationship with God in prayer, they fall easy prey to the devil.

A whole church or community of Christian people can experience the same problem; they can have a good, sound knowledge of the Bible, yet know nothing of a strong corporate ministry of prayer in their midst. Such a church can be easily paralysed by the devil. It may seem that I am labouring the point, but it is absolutely imperative we understand that our effectiveness in spiritual warfare depends not on the armour alone, but on our ability to maintain a close and intimate relationship with God through prayer.

Father, I think I have it now – no prayer, and everything else fails to work the way You designed it to. Drive this truth so deeply into my spirit that for the rest of my life, it will be standard operating procedure. Amen.

Luke 11:1–13; 6:12; Mark 1:35; 6:46–47
1. What was the disciples' request?
2. What was Jesus' pattern?

The Four 'Alls'

23 AUG

FOR READING AND MEDITATION – MATTHEW 14:22–23

'He went up on a mountainside by himself to pray...' (v23)

If, as we have seen, the effectiveness of our spiritual warfare depends not just on wearing the six pieces of armour, but also on constant believing prayer, then we must ask ourselves: what can we do to make our prayer lives more contributive?

The place given to prayer in both the Old and New Testaments is remarkable. All the great saints of the Old Testament knew how to pray – Abraham, David, Daniel, Jeremiah, Isaiah, to mention just a few. The same prowess in prayer can be seen also in the New Testament saints. But of course the greatest pray-er was none other than our Lord Jesus Christ. Although He possessed great knowledge and wisdom, He found it essential to turn aside time and time again to pray. On certain occasions He would spend whole nights in prayer or rise long before dawn in order to pray and maintain His communion with God. Is it surprising, therefore, that being so dependent on prayer, He should have told His disciples, 'Men ought always to pray, and not to faint' (Luke 18:1, KJV)? Praying is the only alternative to fainting – we must pray or else we faint.

Paul's teaching with regard to prayer in Ephesians 6:18 revolves around four 'alls'. We are to pray at all times, with all prayer, with all perseverance, and for all the saints. Most Christians, however, pray at some times, with some prayer, and some degree of perseverance for some of God's saints. When we replace 'some' by 'all' in these expressions, we are on our way to effective praying.

My Father and my God, I see that through prayer, You offer me the most breathtaking power. Help me humbly to take it and use it wisely. In Jesus' name I pray. Amen.

1 Samuel 7:1–10; 1:27; Exodus 15:24–25; 1 Kings 18:37–38
1. List some prayers God answered.
2. List some answers to prayer you have received.

The Various Forms of Prayer   24 AUG

FOR READING AND MEDITATION – COLOSSIANS 4:1–12
'Devote yourselves to prayer, being watchful and thankful.' (v2)

Today we ask ourselves: what does it mean to 'pray always with all prayer and supplication'? The phrase 'praying always' presents no difficulty, for that, quite clearly, means praying as often as possible, regularly and constantly, but what does it mean to pray 'with all prayer and supplication'? Paul means, I believe, that we should pray with all forms or kinds of prayer.

You see, there are many different forms of prayer that are available to us. Firstly, there is verbal prayer when we present our prayer to God in carefully chosen words and phrases. Secondly, there is silent prayer, when no words cross our lips but prayer flows directly from our hearts. Thirdly, there are those brief, spontaneous prayers – often expressed not in words, but through heartfelt sounds like sighs or groans – as we pour out our spirit before God. Then there is public prayer, common prayer or 'praying together' – or, as some prefer to call it, 'praying in concert'. So praying with all prayer means using every form of prayer available to us and praying in every way and manner that we can. We are to be at it always, and in endless ways.

But there is a certain form of prayer to which the apostle refers which deserves closer examination – the prayer of supplication. This refers to that aspect of prayer which we sometimes describe as 'petition', when we pray with regard to special requests and needs. We must not overlook this, for it is so easy to be caught up in adoration and praise that we neglect to focus our prayers on the various needs that arise from time to time, not only in our own lives, but also in the lives of others.

Father, help me to see the senselessness of trying to muddle through life in my own strength when You have made Your power and resources available to me through prayer. Help me grow in prayer. In Jesus' name. Amen.

Matthew 7:1–12; Acts 1:14; 4:24; 12:12; 21:5
1. What is evident about the Early Church?
2. How does Jesus relate fatherhood to prayer?

Praying in the Spirit

FOR READING AND MEDITATION – ROMANS 8:18–30

'We do not know what prayer to offer nor how to offer it worthily...
but the Spirit Himself... pleads in our behalf...' (v26, AMPC)

Having looked yesterday at the phrase 'praying always with all prayer and supplication', we turn now to focus on the words 'in the Spirit'. What does it mean to pray 'in the Spirit'? Here again, there is a good deal of misunderstanding among Christians as to the true meaning of this phrase.

Some claim the words 'in the Spirit' mean praying with the emotions – or feeling greatly moved as one prays. There are times when one feels deeply affected emotionally as one prays, but this is not the meaning of the phrase 'praying in the Spirit'. It has no relationship to the emotions that we feel in prayer. I am not saying that feelings are unimportant in prayer; I am simply saying that I do not believe this is what Paul had in mind when he used the phrase 'praying in the Spirit'. The 'spirit' spoken of here is not the human spirit, but the Holy Spirit. Some believe that 'praying in the Spirit' takes place when we pray in other tongues, and although it can include that, I believe it is much more than that.

Prayer that is 'in the Spirit' is prayer that is prompted and guided by the Spirit. One commentator puts it this way: 'It means that the Holy Spirit directs the prayer, creates the prayer within us, and empowers us to offer it and to pray it.' Dr Martyn Lloyd-Jones calls praying in the Spirit 'the secret of true prayer' and goes on to say: 'If we do not pray in the Spirit, we do not really pray.' I would hesitate to make such a sweeping statement myself, but I would go so far as to say that if we do not know what it means to pray in the Spirit, our prayers will have little impact upon Satan and his forces.

Dear Father, I have so much to learn about prayer that unless You take my hand and guide me, I can soon lose my way. Teach me how to enter the deeper levels of prayer. In Jesus' name. Amen.

Romans 8:1–17; Luke 11:13; 24:49
1. To what does the Spirit bear witness?
2. What was Christ's promise to His disciples?

Spirit-Aided Praying

26 AUG

FOR READING AND MEDITATION – JOHN 6:56-69
'The Spirit gives life...' (v63)

We continue with the question we looked at yesterday: what does it mean to pray 'in the Spirit'? The more I consider this phrase, the more convinced I am that the majority of Christians do not know what it means to pray in this particular way. Many are content to recite prayers and know nothing of the thrill of entering a dimension of prayer in which the Holy Spirit has full control.

Not that there is anything wrong with liturgical or written prayers – they can be a wonderful primer for one's spiritual pump. Many people tell me that the prayers I frame at the bottom of each page of *Every Day with Jesus* have sometimes helped them more than the actual notes I have written. Using written prayers can be helpful, but we must heed the apostle's exhortation to move on into that dimension which he calls 'praying in the Spirit'. The best description of 'praying in the Spirit' I have ever heard is that given by some of the old Welsh preachers, like Daniel Rowlands, Christmas Evans, and others. They describe it as 'praying with unusual liberty and freedom'.

There is hardly anything more wonderful in the Christian life than to experience liberty and freedom in prayer. I can remember the minister and elders of the church in which I was converted in South Wales saying after a prayer meeting in which there had been great liberty and power: 'Tonight we have prayed in the Spirit.' Have you not experienced moments when, after struggling and halting in prayer, you were suddenly taken out of yourself and words just poured out of you? At that moment, you were 'praying in the Spirit'.

O Father, forgive me that I try to do so much in my own strength instead of learning how to let You do it in me. Teach me how to let go and let You take over in everything – particularly my praying. In Jesus' name. Amen.

2 Corinthians 3:6-18; Matthew 6:7-8; 1 Corinthians 14:15; Jude 20
1. What does the Spirit of the Lord bring?
2. What are we to avoid when we pray?

First Principles

27 AUG

FOR READING AND MEDITATION – LUKE 5:1-11
'Launch out into the deep…' (v4, NKJV)

I find myself compelled to spend another day discussing Paul's pregnant phrase 'praying in the Spirit'. We said yesterday that we enter this realm whenever we find ourselves praying with unusual liberty and freedom.

There are times in my own life, as I am sure there are in yours, when I struggle in prayer and find it difficult to concentrate, only to discover that suddenly I am taken out of myself and given a fluency and freedom that transforms my prayer time from that point on. When that happens, I know I have been praying in the Spirit. This is the kind of thing about which the apostle Paul is exhorting us in Ephesians 6:18. Formal prayer is fine and has its place, but oh, how we need to experience more and more times of praying in the Spirit.

But how do we attain these times? Is it the Spirit's responsibility to bring us there or do we have some responsibility in the matter too? I believe we can learn to pray in the Spirit. Some first principles are these: (1) Come to God in an attitude of dependence. This means recognising that your greatest need in prayer is not an ability to put words together or form fine phrases, but the Holy Spirit's empowerment. (2) Yield yourself totally to the Spirit for Him to guide and direct your praying. Be continually aware that He wants to have the bigger part in your prayer life. Start with these two principles, and learn to depend less and less on your own experience or ability, and more and more on the Spirit's enabling. Once you experience what it means to 'pray in the Spirit', you will long to experience it more and more.

O Father, my appetite is being whetted. Help me 'launch out into the deep' and give myself to You in the way that You are willing to give Yourself to me. In Christ's name I ask it. Amen.

John 3:22-27; 2 Chronicles 20:12; 2 Corinthians 3:3-5
1. What was John's declaration?
2. How did Paul express his dependence on God?

Not Some... But All

28 AUG

FOR READING AND MEDITATION – EPHESIANS 4:17-32

'For we are all members of one body.' (v25)

We have two more phrases to consider before we bring to a close our meditations on Ephesians 6:10-20: (1) 'Keep alert with all perseverance' and (2) 'making supplication for all the saints' (Eph. 6:18, RSV)

The first phrase draws our attention to the fact that we should never allow ourselves to become indolent and lethargic in relation to the matter of prayer, but always eager and ready to make our requests and petitions known to Him. But what is the purpose of this spiritual alertness and watchfulness? This question brings us to the second phrase: 'Making supplication for all the saints'. Our watchfulness and concern must not be only on our own behalf, but on behalf of all other Christians also.

Why does Paul exhort us to pray for all rather than some Christians – those, for example, whom we know are enduring a particular attack of Satan? The answer is because all Christians need praying for. Every believer is under attack; no one is exempted. The letter of Jude tells us that we are partakers of a 'common salvation'. But not only do we enjoy a common salvation: we are fighting a common enemy, and in our encounter with this common enemy we experience common difficulties – hence the need to be intensely aware of each other's needs. We cannot, of course, take the armour of God and put it on another Christian, but we can pray for one another and thus call in spiritual reinforcements. We can pray that their eyes might be opened to the danger they are in and that they might be able to equip themselves to stand against Satan and his powerful forces.

O Father, forgive me, I pray, that sometimes I am so taken up with my own spiritual struggles that I forget my brothers and sisters face the same difficulties also. Save me from my self-centredness, dear Lord. In Jesus Name I pray. Amen.

Genesis 18:23-33; Matthew 15:21-28; Acts 12:5
1. How did Abraham intercede?
2. How did the Canaanite woman demonstrate persistence?

Satan's Pincer Movement

29 AUG

FOR READING AND MEDITATION – LUKE 22:24–34

'I have prayed for you, Simon, that your faith may not fail.' (v32)

Another reason why the apostle Paul bids us pray for one another is because the failure of any one of us is going to have some effect upon the spiritual campaign which, through the Church, God is waging against the devil. Think back to what we said on the first day of our meditations: all those who have committed themselves to Jesus Christ know (or should know) that there are two orders and two kingdoms in existence, the forces of which are locked together in mortal combat. One is the kingdom of God and the other is the kingdom of the devil. And Christians, whether they like it or not, are thrust right on to the cutting edge of that conflict.

The battle line between the forces of God and the forces of evil is the Church – and that means you and me. What is the enemy's best tactic in attempting to bring about the Church's spiritual defeat? He probes at every point he can, looking for the weakest part. When he finds a weak Christian (or a group of weak Christians), he calls for reinforcements and in what military strategists call 'a pincer movement', he attempts to break through at that point. And when one Christian fails, all of us to some extent are affected, for we are all part of the one line of defence.

How the devil rejoices when an individual Christian falls – especially a church leader; he will make sure there is a witness around to pick up on the story. We are called to a ministry of prayer, not just for ourselves but for one another also, that we might stand perfect and complete in the will of God and that our faith will not fail when under attack by the devil.

Father, I am encouraged as I think that today, millions of Christians around the world will be praying for me. Help me never to fail in my responsibility to pray for them. In Christ's peerless and precious Name. Amen.

Galatians 6:1–10; 1 Corinthians 9:27; Philippians 3:12; James 5:16
1. What are we to carry in prayer?
2. Of what was Paul conscious?

Pray For Me That...

30 AUG

FOR READING AND MEDITATION – ROMANS 12:1-13

'Be transformed by the renewing of your mind.
Then you will be able to test and approve what
God's will is – his good, pleasing and perfect will.' (v2)

The apostle ends his section on spiritual warfare (Eph. 6:10-20) on the following personal note: 'Pray also for me, that whenever I speak, words may be given me so that I will fearlessly make known the mystery of the gospel... Pray that I may declare it fearlessly, as I should' (vv19-20).

Paul was wise enough to know his own need of supernatural strength if he was to stand against the enemy, and was humble enough to ask his brothers and sisters to pray for him in this matter. Imagine this great apostle, probably the most powerful and effective disciple of Christ the world has ever seen, asking his friends to pray for him. And why not? The greater a Christian is, the more he realises his dependence on the prayers of others. Paul knew full well the power that was against him and he does not hesitate to ask for the prayers of the church in Ephesus.

Notice that his request for prayer is clear and specific – 'that whenever I speak, words may be given me so that I will fearlessly make known the mystery of the gospel'. Whenever you ask someone to pray for you, be equally specific. Don't just say, 'Pray for me', but 'Pray for me that...' Note, too, that Paul's request was not that he might be delivered from prison, but that through his testimony in prison the gospel of Christ might be advanced. He knew that the most important thing at the moment was not to triumph over prison but to triumph in it. He knew he was where God wanted him for that time, and he would allow no self-interest to interfere with the divine schedule.

O Father, teach me, as You taught Your servant Paul, to know Your will and purpose so clearly that I might know just how and what to pray for. I ask this in and through the strong and mighty Name of Jesus. Amen.

2 Thessalonians 3; 1 Thessalonians 5:25; Hebrews 13:18-19
1. What was Paul's request?
2. Who are you praying for regularly?

The Final Word

31 AUG

FOR READING AND MEDITATION – EPHESIANS 3:8-21

'His intent was that now, through the church,
the manifold wisdom of God should be made known
to the rulers and authorities in the heavenly realms...' (v10)

Today, we gather up what we have been saying on this important theme of 'The Armour of God'. Once we become Christians, we said, we are involved in a fight – a fight against Satan and his forces. God, however, has given us a defence against Satan and his wiles, which consists of six separate pieces of spiritual equipment.

Firstly, He has given us the belt of truth – a willingness to let God's truth govern and regulate every part of our lives. Secondly, the breastplate of righteousness – seeing clearly that we are not saved by our own righteousness but Christ's. Thirdly, we must have our feet fitted with the readiness that comes from the gospel of peace – our determination to stand firmly in the faith.

Fourthly, we must raise the shield of faith – the quick action by which we act upon God's truth and refuse Satan's lies. Fifthly, we must put on the helmet of salvation – the glorious hope that, one day, God will right all wrongs and establish His eternal kingdom. And sixthly, we must take up the sword of the Spirit, the Word of God, and wield the written scriptures in the same way that our Lord did in His wilderness temptations.

Yet we noted also that having done all this, it is still possible that we could be defeated by the devil unless we know how to pray in the power of the Spirit. And we must pray, not just now and again, not simply when we are in trouble, not only when things go wrong, but continuously, fervently, powerfully, and perseveringly. Our prayers must catch alight and burst into flame. Against such praying, the principalities and powers are helpless.

My Father, now that I have seen the resources that are available to me in Christ, I realise that my responsibility to avail myself of those resources is greater than ever. Help me to put everything I have learned into action. For Your own dear Name's sake. Amen.

Psalm 18:1–50; 65:6; Habakkuk 3:19; Isaiah 41:10
1. With what was David armed?
2. Have you put on your armour today?

Scan to download today ▸

PRAY IT FORWARD ▶▶▶

Lord, clothe me in Your armour today - the belt of truth, the shield of faith, the sword of the Spirit. Help me to stand firm against all that would draw me away from You, and to fight not with fear but with courage rooted in Christ. Amen.

PAY IT FORWARD ▶▶▶

Life brings many battles, and Waverley Abbey walks alongside people as they put on God's armour. Through training in pastoral care, counselling, and discipleship, we equip others to stand firm. **Will you partner with us so more people can be trained and equipped?**

Visit **waverleyabbey.org/donate-to-edwj** call **01252 784700** or scan the **QR code** ▶

SEPTEMBER & OCTOBER

PERFECT BALANCE

INTRODUCTION

In a world that often pushes us toward extremes, the call to spiritual maturity is a call to balance. In this theme, Perfect Balance, Selwyn Hughes reflects on the profound insight that our greatest strengths can become weaknesses when not held in tension with other virtues.

Drawing inspiration from thinkers like Blaise Pascal and Martin Luther, these devotions will help us examine areas of imbalance in our character – where determination may slide into stubbornness, or enthusiasm into fanaticism.

With honesty and grace, we are invited to bring our uneven growth before God and seek His help in shaping a well-rounded, Christlike life. For just as imbalance weakens us, so godly balance makes us strong.

Don't Lose Your Balance

1 SEP

FOR READING AND MEDITATION – PHILIPPIANS 1:1–18

'That your love may abound… in knowledge and depth
of insight, so that you may be able to discern…' (vv9–10)

The theme we set out to explore these next two months was suggested to me when I came across this statement made by the great French Christian and philosopher, Blaise Pascal: 'No one is strong unless he or she bears within their character antitheses strongly marked.' In other words, in order to be a fully developed person, one's virtues must be held in tension. For it is in that very tension – the tension between virtues – that strength is to be found.

Take, for example, the virtue of determination. In some people determination can quickly become stubbornness, and when it does, the virtue is dangerously close to becoming a vice. I use the word 'vice' in the sense of something bad – a fault. Take again a virtue – the virtue of enthusiasm. It is easy for enthusiasm to turn into fanaticism – a vice. One writer puts it like this: 'Zeal can often degenerate into hysteria, integrity become hard and unforgiving, and thrift pass over into stinginess. The art of living is to find the balance.'

Human nature being what it is, we seem to find it difficult to retain a balance. Most of us, if we are honest, would admit that although we are growing spiritually, our growth is often lopsided. Our virtues are unbalanced. John Stott says: 'It seems there is no pastime the devil enjoys more than tipping Christians off balance.' Martin Luther put it even more graphically when he said: 'Some Christians are like a drunk man getting on a horse; he pulls himself up on one side and falls off the other.' What can we do about this imbalance in our virtues? We can bring the whole issue to God and with His help seek to correct it. God loves balance as much as the devil hates it.

My Father and my God, give me the grace to face the fact that my virtues may be out of balance. I don't want my growth as a Christian to be lopsided. Instead I want to be beautifully balanced. In Jesus' name. Amen.

1 Peter 2:2; 2 Peter 1:1–11
1. What have we already received?
2. What do we still need to acquire?

God's Perfect Poem

2 SEP

FOR READING AND MEDITATION – EPHESIANS 2:1–10

'For we are God's handiwork, created
in Christ Jesus to do good works...' (v10)

The verse before us now could justifiably be translated, 'You are God's poem' (the Greek word translated 'handiwork' is *poiema*, from which we get our English word 'poem'). I am a great lover of poetry as well as prose, and although I am not an expert in the structure of poetry, I know that traditional poetry must be rhythmical, each part balanced against the other. It is the same with life. A medical doctor says, 'There is a rhythm of the body. If this rhythm is disturbed there is a functional disturbance that leads to a structural disturbance.'

As there is a rhythm in our bodies, so there is a rhythm in our souls. If this rhythm is upset by some virtues being over-emphasised and others being underemphasised, our spiritual growth will be lopsided. It might sound irreverent to refer to Jesus as 'God's Poem', but that is what He was. In Him all virtues were perfectly blended. If the statement I referred to yesterday is true – 'No one is strong unless he or she bears within their character antitheses strongly marked' – then no one was stronger in His personality than Jesus. He was world-renouncing and world-embracing, tender and terrible, a Man of prayer and a Man of action, self-renouncing and self-asserting.

A missionary to India whom I heard speak said that many of the deities who are revered have qualities missing, so people invent other deities whose supposed qualities compensate for those which are lacking. We can be thankful that the Saviour we worship was the most balanced character ever seen on our planet. He was God's perfect Poem, with each one of His qualities perfectly balanced against the other.

O God, I must ask myself: Is there anything poetic about my life? Are my virtues rhythmic and balanced? Do they express the beauty of the divine Poet? I want to become Your perfect poem, dear Lord. In Jesus' name. Amen.

1 Peter 2:21–25; Hebrews 4:14–5:10
1. What was the one thing absent in Jesus?
2. What weakness did Jesus overcome?

Show Me Your Gods

3 SEP

FOR READING AND MEDITATION – HEBREWS 12:1–13

'Let us run... fixing our eyes on Jesus,
the pioneer and perfecter of faith.' (v2)

We continue with the thought that our Lord was the most balanced Person this world has ever seen. I once read that in China there is a leaning tower built by a ruler who saw in a dream the deity he worshipped as being lame. His deity was lopsided, so the tower he built to honour him was also lopsided. 'We always make our earth in the image of what we see in the sky,' stated one philosopher. And he went on to say: 'Show me your gods and I will show you your men.' We tend to become like that we worship. If our god is unbalanced we become unbalanced. How thankful we should be that the God we worship is not unbalanced.

Look with me in more detail at how Jesus' virtues were so perfectly balanced. Take, for example, a few of the qualities we mentioned yesterday. First, world-renouncing and world-embracing. He said on one occasion, 'I am not of the world' (John 17:16), yet He lived out His life in touch with people and died on a cross because humanity declared independence. Then take again the qualities of assertiveness and meekness. He was filled with righteous anger at the moneychangers who were defiling His Father's house, and drove them out. Yet, without resistance He allowed Himself to be hammered to the cross. Then what about prayer and action? The two were perfectly blended in Him. He spent whole nights in prayer, yet we are also told He went about doing good and healing all who were oppressed by the devil.

We can see the antitheses so strongly marked in Jesus. Each one of His virtues was balanced by its opposite. How wonderful it would be if the same balance could be found in us.

My Father and my God, can all my virtues be as balanced as they were in Jesus? Am I reaching for the impossible? I dare to believe. Show me the way. I will follow. In Jesus' name I ask it. Amen.

1 Kings 20:22–30; John 8:1–11
1. What was wrong with the Arameans' thinking?
2. What balance in His character did Jesus show to the woman?

Growing, Not Groaning 4 SEP

FOR READING AND MEDITATION – 2 PETER 3:8-18

'But grow in the grace and knowledge
of our Lord and Saviour Jesus Christ.' (v18)

Yesterday we ended by wondering whether the balance found in Jesus can be found in us. I believe it can. It may not be found as perfectly, but close. It depends on a number of things – our willingness to understand how sin has marred our personalities, our readiness to admit to our spiritual lameness, and a firm resolve to surrender to Christ so that He might make us in His image. We also said that all of Christ's virtues were perfectly balanced and held in tension. And that tension makes a growing point. If we are honest, we would admit that for most of us the tension is a groaning point rather than a growing point. But it need not be so.

For many years now in this daily devotional, I have encouraged readers to grow spiritually and to identify those things that endanger that growth. I consider unbalanced virtues, the subject we are presently discussing, an impediment to spiritual growth. The other day I came across this by Dr E. Stanley Jones: 'When a man's right leg is too long – longer than the other – then he is lame. When one good quality is long in proportion to others then we are spiritually lame.'

Most would classify strong conviction as a virtue, but if we are not careful, strong conviction can make a man or woman blind to other people's points of view and prevent them from seeing any flaws in their own convictions. A Scottish theologian said, 'God grant that I may be always right, for I will never change.' One must admire a person who has strong convictions, but we must be sure they are convictions and not just opinions. The person who thinks he is always right and will never change is always wrong.

O Father, by Your Spirit make me into the image of Jesus. Help me understand that You can only do a perfect job as I remain steady and do not pull away. In Jesus' name I ask it. Amen.

Romans 8:25-29; Colossians 1:9-14
1. What has God planned for us?
2. List different aspects of spiritual growth.

Synthesis

5 SEP

FOR READING AND MEDITATION – GALATIANS 5:16–26

'But the fruit of the Spirit is love, joy, peace, forbearance, kindness, goodness...' (v22)

Yesterday we talked about the danger of allowing strong convictions to stand in the way of our seeing other people's points of view. Before we go on to consider in detail a number of 'opposite' virtues, we spend one more day introducing the subject of perfect balance.

Two centuries ago a German philosopher by the name of Hegel developed the theory of thesis and antithesis. First you lay down something, then you look at its opposite. This dialectic (form of argument) has been used by many teachers, including some in the Christian Church. However, as Hegel said, the eventual resolution of the thesis and antithesis leads to a richer synthesis. There is a tendency among some Christians to think that when we exhibit one of an opposite pair of virtues then we don't need to concern ourselves about the other. This is quite wrong.

A man once told me, 'My strength is confronting people with the reality of what they are doing or how they are living, and I do so without prevarication, letting the chips fly where they will.' He was good at exposing – he could cut right to the heart of issues – but he was seriously lacking in love. His strength became a weakness because it was not balanced by the Christian grace of kindness. When I pointed this out to him he said, 'But we are all gifted in different ways. What I lack in the gift of kindness can be made up by someone else.' I explained that virtues are quite different from gifts. Gifts are what we are given, virtues are an integral part of us. No one has all the gifts; they are distributed in different measure to God's people. But graces are different. All can be evident in us all.

Father, thank You for reminding me of the difference between gifts and graces. I may have some of the gifts but I can have all of the graces. Grant that it may be so. In Jesus' name. Amen.

John 15:1–17; 2 Thessalonians 1:3
1. Is love a gift, a fruit, or a command?
2. How can love increase?

Words and Deeds

6 SEP

FOR READING AND MEDITATION – ACTS 7:17–36

'Moses... was powerful in speech and action.' (v22)

In the coming weeks, we shall consider a number of opposite virtues and qualities, but the first pair I want to draw your attention to is words and actions. Some are good at *talking* but don't *do* much good. They are long on words but short on actions.

It was said of Jesus that He was 'a prophet, powerful in word *and* deed before God' (Luke 24:19, my emphasis). Compare that with our text for today that tells us Moses 'was educated in all the wisdom of the Egyptians and was powerful in speech *and* action' (Acts 7:22, my emphasis). Both prophets were strong in two things – words and action. It's interesting to note that at the beginning of Moses' career he was better at actions than words. When told by God at the burning bush that he was called to be Israel's deliverer he complained, 'I am slow of speech and tongue' (Exod. 4:10). Once he got started, however, he made a speech that covered most of the book of Deuteronomy. Not bad for someone who said he was not good at talking!

In some of us, these two things – words and actions – have got out of balance. We talk more than we act, and very often the talking substitutes for the doing. We are building a crooked tower leaning 'wordward'. Then, on the other hand, there are those who are strong on action but not on words. They cover up their unwillingness to talk about their faith by saying, 'It's my life that counts.' Of course our lives count, but we are called to represent Christ not only with our lives but also with our lips. Our fallen human nature seems to enjoy inhabiting one or other of the polar regions of truth. Jesus was able to bridge both camps. So also must we.

Father, forgive us that in many ways we lack biblical balance. So often we remain at one pole of virtue and neglect the other completely. Help us, dear Lord, for without You we are sunk. Amen.

Luke 9:10–17; 24:19
1. How did Jesus combine words and deeds?
2. What was said of both Moses and Jesus?

I Can't Hear What You Say

7 SEP

FOR READING AND MEDITATION – TITUS 2:1–15

'To show that they can be fully trusted, so that…
they will make the teaching about God… attractive.' (v10)

Deeds and words were the alternate beats of Jesus' heart, and they should be the alternate beats of our hearts too. With Jesus the content of His words went into His actions. This is how it must be with us also. We need to talk, and we need to act out our talking in good deeds. Some talk more than they act, and others act more than they talk. Our talking and our actions must go hand in hand.

Let's think of those who are good at talking about the gospel but whose lives do not match up with what they say. The story has often been told of the man who was constantly talking about his faith but whose life lacked holiness. Eventually someone said to him, 'I am sorry, but your life is speaking so loudly I can't hear what you say.' In the village where I was brought up in South Wales, there lived a man who was always ready to speak at an open-air meeting. People would listen respectfully to those who witnessed to their faith, but when it was this man's turn they would shake their heads and walk away. Why? Because they knew that his life did not match his words. He was as ready as they were to steal such things as electric wiring, nails, and small tools from the local colliery. His words sounded hollow because they were not backed up by a righteous life.

You don't have to tell a non-Christian that words and actions must go hand in hand. They know instinctively that a life which purports to be committed to God but is short on actions is shallow. Many have been deterred from responding to the gospel by those who say they are Christians but do not show the fruit of it in their lives.

Father, I must search my own heart today and ask myself: do my actions match my words? Am I as good at doing as I am at talking? Forgive me if I veer in one direction, and help me be a more balanced Christian. In Jesus' name. Amen.

Isaiah 58:1–14; James 2:14–26
1. Why would God not respond to prayer?
2. How are faith and action linked?

Word Become Flesh   8 SEP

FOR READING AND MEDITATION – ACTS 10:23-48
'They have received the Holy Spirit just as we have.' (v47)

One of the tragedies of our time,' said a fine elderly Christian to me just a few hours before he died, 'is that the word has not become flesh.' I pondered what he meant for a few days and struggled to understand. Finally, during his committal service, the sense of what he had said dawned on me, and I referred to it in my funeral address. What he had in mind, I think, was this: If we do not back up our words by actions then the word remains word. We begin with words and end with words. But when we put the word into action, then the word becomes flesh.

The word remains word, for example, when we talk about racial and cultural equality but do nothing practical to advance it. The passage before us today shows how one of the deepest and ugliest chasms that separates people was bridged – the chasm of racial prejudice. The early Christians could have proclaimed the doctrine of all men and women being equal, but it would have had little effect on the prejudiced hearts of many of that day. Preaching against racism would have been word remaining word. But an amazing thing happened: the Gentiles received the gift of the Holy Spirit on exactly the same basis as the Jews. Peter used a word that became the funnel through which God could pour the Holy Spirit. He said, '… everyone who believes in him receives forgiveness of sins…' (v43). *Everyone.*

As soon as Peter used that word, 'everyone', the Holy Spirit fell on all who were in Cornelius' house. 'Everyone' was Peter's invitation. The Holy Spirit coming 'on all' was God's reply. That day the great gulf between racial groups was bridged – bridged not by a word, but by a word become flesh.

O God, forgive us again that prejudices and circumstances press us to say 'some' when Jesus presses us to say 'everyone'. Grant that my faith shall not end in words, but in words become flesh. In Jesus' name. Amen.

Luke 3:7-14; John 1:1-14
1. What accompanies genuine repentance?
2. In what sense is Christianity an international faith?

Walking Your Talking

9 SEP

FOR READING AND MEDITATION – ACTS 18:9–17
'But since it involves questions about words and names and your own law – settle the matter yourselves.' (v15)

We saw yesterday how one of the greatest chasms between people – the chasm of racial prejudice – was bridged by a simple thing – the word of equality became flesh. Would that have happened if Peter had not responded to God's challenge and gone personally to the house of Cornelius? I doubt it. It was not the custom to sit down with Gentiles – but he did so anyway. And what followed was one of the most powerful and breathtaking events recorded in the Acts of the Apostles. Racial prejudice melted before this tender act of God's acceptance of the Gentiles.

I once heard about the captain of a British ship who, visiting Cape Town during the time of apartheid, picked up a baby from its mother's arms and gently cradled the child. Many white onlookers were horrified and said, 'This isn't done in South Africa, you know.' That simple act revealed a division: some clung to the racist conventions of the day, while the captain pointed toward a different future. In him, the word of equality became flesh.

In our reading today we see a proud Roman official fed up with the bandying of words and legal wrangles. With a wave of his hand he dismissed what he thought was another philosophy – another instance of the word ending in word. But history has not been able to dismiss Christianity so glibly, because multitudes have proved beyond any shadow of doubt that their commitment to Christ meant more than just spouting words. They 'walked their talk' as one old preacher quaintly put it. 'Faith without deeds is dead,' said James (Jas 2:26). It is. When we back up our words by actions, the gospel leads not to a comment, but conversion.

O God, forgive us if our words just end in words. Help us to 'walk our talk', for we may be the first and only Bible some people will ever read. May we be doers of the Word and not hearers only. In Christ's name. Amen.

Matthew 5:13–16; Acts 9:36–42; 1 Peter 2:11–12
1. Exactly how can we be salt and light in our communities?
2. How may unbelievers come to know God?

The Word of Coffee...   10 SEP

FOR READING AND MEDITATION – 1 TIMOTHY 4:1–16
'Watch your life and doctrine closely. Persevere in them...' (v16)

'The interest of men and women in the world,' said one missionary, 'is to see the Word become flesh.' He told of sitting with a group in a restaurant when a waitress came to the table empty-handed and asked, 'Anyone want more coffee?' 'No, thank you,' they all replied. A few minutes later another waitress appeared with a steaming coffee pot in her hand and said, 'Anyone want more coffee?' 'Yes, please,' they all responded. The difference? The first waitress presented the word of coffee remaining word; the second, the word of coffee become flesh. Sometimes we have to see reality before we seek it.

Paul stressed this when talking to the young Timothy. In our reading today he tells him, 'Watch your life and doctrine closely.' It's easy to become preoccupied with doctrine and forget the need to match it with action. While I was in Malaysia once, a young minister told me this: 'I have spent three years in a theological college, but I have never done an act of love for someone in need in all that time. When you referred to the verse '... do good to all people, especially to those who belong to the family of believers' (Gal. 6:10), I was struck by the fact that I didn't know that verse. I went down by the river and saw a beautiful young family who were obviously very poor. I took all the money I had in my possession, put it into an envelope and handed it to them, then walked away.' The word had become flesh.

If all we have to give to the world are words, that is likely to make people feel inferior. But if we put actions to our words, that gives added weight to what we say. Words *and* actions make for balanced Christian living.

Father, help me if I am building a crooked tower that leans 'wordward'. From now on I want deed and word to be the alternate beats of my heart. In Jesus' name I pray. Amen.

Galatians 6:1–10; 1 John 3:11–20
1. How can we fulfil the law of Christ?
2. How should we love people?

Be Prepared

11 SEP

FOR READING AND MEDITATION – 1 PETER 3:8-22

'Always be prepared to give an answer to everyone who asks you to give the reason for the hope that you have.' (v15)

In some of us, the two things we have been referring to have got out of balance. We talk more than we act. And very often the talking substitutes for the doing. But on the other hand, there are those who are strong on deeds and weak on words. They cover up their unwillingness to share the Christian faith by substituting deeds. Someone has defined piety as 'the art of right growing'. But if that growing is to be 'right', it must be balanced. Every Christian must not simply know the faith but learn to share it also. This doesn't mean that we must all become preachers, but we must all be ready, as the apostle tells us, 'to give an answer to everyone who asks… for the hope that you have'.

What I don't want to do is to lay a guilt trip on those who find it difficult to share their faith in Christ – and neither would the apostle Peter. Read again what he says: 'Always be prepared to give an answer to everyone who asks you…' Note: *everyone who asks you.* We are not expected to buttonhole people in the street and ask them if they know Jesus Christ (though some are especially gifted to do this and to do it in an inoffensive manner). However, all of us are expected to be able to give an explanation, when asked, of what we believe.

If someone asked you today to explain why you are a Christian, do you know what you would say? If you don't, may I suggest that you take a blank sheet of paper and write down at least three reasons why you are a Christian. Then memorise them. If you prepare yourself, God will lead someone to you. He will not send fish towards unprepared nets.

O Father, forgive me if I hide my reticence to share my faith by relying on good deeds. Help me become a prepared witness – one who, without losing spontaneity, can give clear reasons for their commitment to You. Amen.

John 3:16; 15:26-27; Acts 4:8-12; Ephesians 2:1-10
1. What help do we have to explain our faith?
2. Identify and list the key elements of the gospel?

The Fear of Rejection

12 SEP

FOR READING AND MEDITATION – 1 JOHN 4:7–21

'But perfect love drives out fear…' (v18)

We looked yesterday at the text, 'Always be prepared to give an answer to everyone who asks you… for the hope that you have'. A few weeks after my conversion, I heard my pastor preach on that same text, and when he had finished I went up to him and said, 'Why is it that people don't often ask me if I am a Christian?' His reply was devastating: 'Perhaps they don't see much difference between the way you used to live and the way you live now.' I examined my life and found he was right. When I gave up the habits that were clearly non-Christian, people soon started saying, 'What's happened to you?' The quality of our lives should provoke people to ask us, 'What's different about you?' And when they do we should be ready to tell them.

Does that mean we should wait for someone to question us about our faith before we share it? No. We can be ready at all times to put in a good word for Jesus and to tell others about our faith in Him. I have little time for the aggressive kind of personal evangelism that buttonholes strangers in the street and demands, 'Do you realise you are going to hell?', though I have known instances where people have been converted through such an approach. It ought, however, to be more the exception than the rule.

Behind a reluctance to share one's faith lie many reasons, but the biggest one I have found is the fear of rejection. Overcome that, and sharing your faith becomes a lot easier. And how is the fear of rejection overcome? The answer is given by our text today: fear is expelled by the invasion of love. When love flows in, fear flows out. Love for God is the key.

Father, I have to ask myself: is my love for You stronger than my fear of being rejected? I open my heart to be invaded by Your love today. Open Your reservoirs and flood me out. In Jesus' name. Amen.

1 Corinthians 9:16–23; 2 Corinthians 5:11–21
1. What did Paul fear?
2. Describe the role and responsibilities of an ambassador of Christ.

Time for a Check-Up

13 SEP

FOR READING AND MEDITATION – LAMENTATIONS 3:25–42

'Let us examine our ways and test them,
and let us return to the Lord.' (v40)

Having looked over the past week at words and actions, and seen how easy it is to get them out of balance, we must now ask ourselves these questions: How balanced is my life in relation to this matter? Do I use words as a substitute for doing? Or do I expect my deeds to speak for themselves and absolve me from any responsibility to share my faith verbally? Some of us may be living polarised lives. Like Abraham and Lot, we separate from one another.

Why not take a few moments following today's reading and, before going any further, stop and look at your life as a whole. Just what kind of life is emerging? Are you an unbalanced person? Have you grown lopsided? What impression do you make on people? When people think of you, what do they think of: balance or imbalance? After looking at your life overall, go over it minutely. Invite the Holy Spirit to join you. Ask Him to help you be objective. Go over your qualities one by one and see if they are still virtues, or if they have become vices. Have you pushed them to an extreme? Has your strength become stubbornness, your meekness become weakness, your righteousness become rigid and rutted?

Let God render the verdict on each one. He can see things you cannot. You may come out of the assessment better than you expected. Don't be defensive. Surrender yourself afresh into His hands and look away from yourself to Jesus Christ. Don't end up trying to be balanced by using your own strength. Fix your eyes on Jesus. He has all the virtues perfectly blended in Him. Become Christ-centred, not self-centred, even in the balancing of your virtues.

Lord Jesus, how I long to be like You – perfectly mature and perfectly balanced. But I can't become like You through self-effort. I give You my heart that You might work afresh in me. Amen.

Psalm 139:23–24; 2 Corinthians 13:5–9
1. Why should we ask God to examine us?
2. Why should we examine ourselves?

On Being a Whole Person

14 SEP

FOR READING AND MEDITATION – COLOSSIANS 3:1–17

'And whatever you do… do it all in the name of the Lord Jesus…' (v17)

We begin now to consider another pair of 'opposites': the mental and the emotional. Christian discipleship involves every part of our personalities. Our minds are to be renewed (Rom. 12:2), our emotions purified (Eph. 4:26), our consciences kept clear (Acts 24:16), and our wills surrendered to God's will. All we are as persons is to be committed to all we know of God. Yet of the various parts of the personality mentioned in Scripture, the mind and the emotions are by far the most often referred to. Some have trained the mind to the neglect of the emotions; some indulge their emotions to the neglect of the mind.

Our reading talks about letting the Word of Christ dwell in us richly as we teach and admonish one another (v16). Here is the awakening of the mind so that it is enriched with divine wisdom. Then the verse goes on to say, 'and as you sing psalms, hymns and spiritual songs with gratitude in your hearts to God'. Here is the awakening of the emotions, giving vent in joyful song. Both are necessary to our growth in Christ – the awakening and enriching of the mind and the awakening and enjoyment of the emotions.

One man I know is a wonderful Bible teacher but is often referred to as 'a dry old stick'. When I asked him why he never seemed to appear passionate about what he taught he said, 'I have been like this all my life. I have never had much feeling.' He is wrong. He has a lot of feeling but it is all repressed. Any imbalance in the personality is a cause for concern, but none more than the mental and the emotional.

O Father, stimulate my personality so that there is a more perfect balance between my mind and my emotions. I don't want one to take precedence over the other. Help me, my Father. Amen.

Psalm 119:1–16; Matthew 23:23; 2 Corinthians 3:6
1. How did the psalmist combine the mental and the emotional?
2. Why did Jesus criticise the Pharisees?

I Don't Need My Head

15 SEP

FOR READING AND MEDITATION – MARK 12:28–34

'Love the Lord your God with all your heart and
with all your soul and with all your mind...' (v30)

Let's think now about those whose emotions are ahead of their thinking. Contemporary culture, I am afraid, tends to understand truth by how one feels about it rather than the other way round. A university student I sat next to on a plane told me that something had to *feel* true before he believed it. This is a perilous position to adopt, but many do so. Over the years I have had discussions with several Christians who have come into the Church with the attitude 'But I can't believe something simply because it is written in the Bible. I can only believe it if it authenticates itself to me in my feelings.'

A danger in some charismatic churches (not all) is the continual emphasis on emotion and experience to the exclusion of the mind. One man commented, 'When I go to my church I might as well unscrew my head and put it under the seat, for you can be sure it won't be needed.' Now that is not just sad; it is tragic. It is assimilating the spirit of the age and that, says one writer, is nothing but worldliness. For worldliness is adopting uncritically the attitudes of the world.

In our reading today, a teacher comes to Jesus and asks Him which is the greatest commandment. Jesus quotes from Deuteronomy 6:4-5 but He adds something to that statement. He says, 'Love the Lord your God with... all your *mind*'. The phrase 'with all your mind' was not in the verse in Deuteronomy. I know it can be argued that the mind is part of the heart or soul but, to my way of thinking, it is interesting, to say the least, that Jesus inserts the word *mind*.

Jesus would encourage us to use our minds, to think. He would awaken us mentally as well as emotionally.

O God, forgive me if I have focused on the development of my emotions to the detriment of my mind. Help me stand against a world that would try to squeeze me into its own mould. In Christ's name. Amen

Hebrews 8:10-12; Romans 14:5-23
1. Where would God put His laws?
2. Why are our minds important?

I Don't Have a Good Mind

16 SEP

FOR READING AND MEDITATION – 1 CORINTHIANS 14:1-25

'Brothers, stop thinking like children. In regard to evil
be infants, but in your thinking be adults.' (v20)

'To be perfectly frank, I'm getting exasperated with your childish thinking. How long before you grow up and use your head—your *adult* head?' That's the way Eugene Peterson paraphrases our text for today in *The Message*. Jesus told us that we must be like children in many ways – our willingness to trust, for example. But in relation to the use of our minds, we are to be mature and adult.

I heard a Christian leader tell a story about two women chatting in a supermarket check-out line. One remarked to the other: 'What's the matter with you? You look so worried.' 'I am,' responded her friend, 'I keep thinking about the world situation.' 'Well,' said the first lady, 'you want to take things more philosophically, and stop thinking.' God thinks, and He has made us with the ability to think also. When we *think*, we glorify God. A scientist has been defined as 'someone who thinks God's thoughts after Him'. Now I know some will say, 'But I don't have a very good mind. I didn't do well at school and thinking doesn't come easily to me.' I can sympathise, for I didn't do well at school either. But then I took Jesus into my life and He awakened my mind in a way that no earthly teacher could.

Ephesians 1:3 tells us that God has blessed us with every spiritual blessing in Christ. *Every* spiritual blessing. Does that mean He can bless us mentally? Well, He did that for me and I am sure He can do the same for you. Listen to this: '… by his power he may bring to fruition your every desire for goodness and your every deed prompted by faith' (2 Thess. 1:11). *Desire* to think better and more clearly and ask God to help you achieve this aim. He will.

My Father, I turn my mind over to You so that You can come in and think in me. I may not know a lot but I know this: my mind works better when You are in it. In Jesus' name I pray. Amen.

Psalm 119:97-104; Isaiah 55:8-9; Romans 12:1-8
1. How can we think God's thoughts?
2. How are our minds renewed?

The Mind Matters

17 SEP

FOR READING AND MEDITATION – PHILIPPIANS 4:1–9

'Brothers and sisters, whatever is true,
whatever is noble… think about such things.' (v8)

Think! That's Paul's admonition in our reading today. And that has been the admonition of all the great Christian leaders of the past.

The other day I was looking at what some of the notable Christians in history had to say about faith. This is how Dr Martyn Lloyd-Jones defined faith when commenting on the Sermon on the Mount: 'Faith… is primarily thinking… and the whole trouble with a man of little faith is that he does not think. He allows circumstances to bludgeon him. The way to avoid that, according to our Lord, is to think. Christian faith is essentially thinking. Look at the birds, says Jesus, think about them and draw your deductions. Look at the grass, look at the lilies of the field, consider them. The trouble with most people, however, is they will not think. Instead of doing this they sit down and ask, what is going to happen to me? What can I do? That is the absence of thought; it is surrender, it is defeat. We are entitled to define 'little faith' as being a failure to think, of allowing life to master our thoughts instead of thinking clearly about it.'* Powerful words.

Drawing on my time in the counselling room, I can tell you this: the people who experience extreme stress and anxiety are those whose thoughts are not under control. They don't think. Well, strictly they do think, but not in the way the Bible instructs and invites us to. They fail to think about what God says and think instead about what the devil is telling them. Their thinking is not according to Scripture and, therefore, they feel overwhelmed. There are many remedies on offer for worry, but really there is only one successful way. It is to think – to think with God.

Father, often my problems arise because I don't think in the way I should. Help me develop the mind You have given me so that my thinking is in line with Your thinking. In Jesus' name. Amen.

Numbers 13:17–14:4; Luke 12:27–28

1. How is thinking linked with faith?
2. What should we think about?

*Dr Martyn Lloyd-Jones, *Studies in the Sermon on the Mount* (Grand Rapids: Eerdmans, 1996).

Blunted Sensibilities

18 SEP

FOR READING AND MEDITATION – MARK 14:32–42
'He began to be deeply distressed and troubled.' (v33)

Now that we have seen the importance of the mental aspect of life, we move on to consider the importance of the opposite end of the spectrum – the emotional. Some, it has to be said, are all head and no heart. I have heard such people described as tadpoles – a tadpole is a creature with a huge head and not much else beside! The mind has to be developed but so do the emotions if we are to be thoroughly integrated people.

A psychologist claims that killers who murder for gain or gratification are almost always lacking in affect, that is, the capacity for entering into the feelings of others. Pamela Jonson in her book *On Iniquity* says of our present generation, 'We are in danger of creating an *affectless* society in which nobody cares for anyone but himself or herself, or for anything except instant gratification. We demand sex without love, violence for 'kicks'... we are encouraging the blunting of sensibility.'

People can be emotionally flat for many reasons. Sometimes the problem stems from the developmental years. Some were never encouraged to show emotion as children, or have been taught to suppress their emotions. Others have a fear of emotion. They are afraid to feel emotions that arise because they are not sure how to handle them. And some believe God is incapable of emotion. This doctrine is known as the *impassibility of God*. This view is held despite the fact that we can be certain His Son was capable of emotions. All through the Bible we see God touching the whole gamut of emotion, from joy to sadness, from deep inner peace to the turmoil of soul that our text for today talks about. To be fully human and fully alive one must *feel*.

Father, You have made me to be a feeling being, yet some emotions scare me. Teach me how to feel without being frightened, how to experience my emotions without being intimidated by them. In Jesus' name I pray. Amen.

Genesis 6:5–6; Mark 3:1–6; 10:21; John 11:35; 15:11
1. List God's emotions.
2. Why would God allow Himself to feel pain?

Four Ways

19 SEP

FOR READING AND MEDITATION – EPHESIANS 4:17–32

'In your anger do not sin...' (v26)

We continue thinking about the emotions. The four most common ways of managing our emotions are as follows. First, we can *repress* them – we can push them deep into the unconscious and forget all about them. Second, we can *suppress* them – we can push them into the subconscious, where they are not entirely forgotten, but temporarily submerged. Third, we can *express* them – we can laugh, cry, stamp our feet, get angry, shout, and so on. Fourth, we can *confess* them – admit to our feelings but control the expression of them so that it is in accord with biblical principles.

It is always right to feel an emotion but it is not always right to express it. Take anger, for example. Some say that because the Bible teaches us not to be angry we should never feel anger, so whenever these people feel anger swelling up within them they pretend they are not feeling it. That is dishonest. Integrity requires that whatever is true must be recognised. We go wrong not when we feel anger but when we express it in a manner that is inconsistent with biblical teaching.

'In your anger do not sin...' tells us that we can admit to feeling angry, but by an act of self-control (a fruit of the Spirit) we must ensure that our anger is not dumped on to someone in a way that hurts them. But what if they have hurt us? '"It is mine to avenge; I will repay," says the Lord' (Rom. 12:19). You ask, 'Lord, can I help You a little bit with the avenging?' He answers, 'No, that part is Mine. I can do it better than you, and My method will be constructive, not destructive.' Always be willing to feel your emotions, but be careful about how you express them.

Father, You have me cornered. No argument I can present justifies the uncontrolled expression of my anger. Your Spirit gives me self-control. May I yield more to Your Spirit than to my own spirit. In Christ's name. Amen.

Psalm 43:1–5; 1 Peter 2:21–23
1. What emotions did the psalmist express?
2. How did Jesus deal with unfair treatment?

The Soul's Tambourine 20 SEP

FOR READING AND MEDITATION – LUKE 24:13–35
'Were not our hearts burning within us
while he… opened the Scriptures to us?' (v32)

We have been seeing that emotional awareness is a rich part of living. But isn't there some way to avoid feeling negative emotions and just feel the good ones? The short answer is: No. As C.S. Lewis pointed out, if we are not willing to feel negative emotions, we will not experience the richness of our positive emotions. You can't have one without the other.

I can imagine someone saying, 'But what about me? My problem is that I feel dead on the inside.' If you have been hurt, bring that hurt to God right now and ask Him to heal you. But remember, there will be no healing until there is forgiveness on your part towards the one (or ones) who hurt you. You counter, 'But I can't forgive.' Change the word 'can't' to 'won't' and you are closer to the truth. You *can* forgive. Christ says so (see Luke 6:37).

If your emotional constriction is due to years of mishandling, of never being taught how to express your emotions, then do this. Read through the Psalms – the book where almost every conceivable emotion is registered – and meditate on the passages where the psalmist expresses a particular emotion. Linger over those verses and ask God to help you feel what the psalmist felt. Many emotionally constricted people have practised this simple technique and discovered through it an expansion of their emotional spectrum. One woman summed up her experience like this: 'I learned to feel my way into the sadness of the psalmists and also into their joy. Unafraid to feel the dark side I discovered I could feel more of the joy. I never felt joy before, not as deeply anyway. Nothing is more wonderful than when my soul takes its tambourine and dances with delight.'

O Father, give me a cool head and a warm heart. Help me experience my emotions without being overemotional. Move me further along the road to being a well-balanced personality. In Christ's name I pray. Amen.

Psalm 73:1–28
1. Why did the psalmist feel negative?
2. What changed his perspective?

Was Jesus Assertive?

21 SEP

FOR READING AND MEDITATION – JOHN 7:14-24

'Stop judging by mere appearances, but instead judge correctly.' (v24)

We move on now to consider another pair of opposites: assertiveness and yieldedness. I have often heard people say, 'My problem is to know when to be assertive and when to give in. Am I to be someone's doormat or am I to stand up for my rights?' A translation of the text 'Let your moderation be known unto all men' (Phil. 4:5, KJV) suggested by the commentator Handley Moule reads, 'Let your yieldingness be known to all men'. But total yieldedness would make us everybody's doormat (not necessarily a good thing), and total assertiveness would make us everybody's thorn in the flesh. We must possess both qualities and occupy both camps.

My dictionary defines assertiveness as 'insistence on a right or opinion; declaring yourself, making a positive statement'. Keep in mind that assertiveness is not aggressiveness. Sometimes the two words are used interchangeably, but their sense is quite different. The word 'aggressive' carries the meaning of being hostile, offensive, disposed to attack. Christians should not be aggressive, but at times need to be assertive. The challenge we face is to know when to be assertive and when to yield.

Was Jesus an assertive Person? Of course He was. The passage before us today gives us just one glimpse of Him in this role. He was strong without being overbearing and forthright without being obnoxious. But His assertiveness was balanced by a spirit of yieldedness. He was at one and the same time the most assertive and yielded Person the planet has ever seen. As with all His other qualities, He was perfectly balanced. Happy is the man or woman who knows when to be assertive and when to yield.

Blessed Lord Jesus, You who were so openly and positively assertive, help me to function in this way too. Teach me to be as balanced as You were. For Your own dear name's sake. Amen.

John 2:13-17; 18:1-13,33-40
1. What was Jesus' main concern?
2. How was Jesus both assertive and yielded to the soldiers?

Are You Non-Assertive?

FOR READING AND MEDITATION – 1 SAMUEL 15:10–26

'I was afraid of the men and so I gave in to them.' (v24)

We continue considering the virtues of assertiveness and yieldedness but focus first on those who are non-assertive. Are you someone who says 'Yes' when you want to say 'No'? Do you eat a lukewarm bowl of soup rather than mention it to the waiter? If you have to return something to a shop when there is good reason to do so, are you beset with anxiety? Is it difficult for you to express your opinion to a group of friends and be direct in what you say? Then you are probably more yielding than assertive.

Many Christians I have met explain their non-assertive attitude as evidence of meekness and yieldedness. But more often than not this is an excuse rather than an explanation. What underlies non-assertiveness? A common cause is a fear of displeasing others. You tell yourself that you need the approval of others in order to function and therefore you can't stand their disapproval. This could mean you are dependent on others for the energy to drive your life rather than dependent on God. Whenever you elevate someone to the position where their interaction with you, or their approval of you, is necessary to you to function as an individual, that person is your life. The Bible has a word for it – idolatry. It is putting another person in the place of God.

King Saul was a people-pleaser, as can be seen from the passage before us today, especially today's text. What a non-assertive individual really fears is that the other person will withdraw his affection, or end the relationship, or use his power to get back at them. How sad that so much of our life is driven by fear when it ought to be under the control of our Saviour's love.

My Father and my God, forgive me that often I am more dependent on people than I am on You. If my sin is idolatry – putting people in Your place – then I repent of it now. In Jesus' name. Amen.

Mark 15:1–15; Galatians 1:10; 2:11–16
1. Why did Pilate convict an innocent man?
2. Contrast Peter and Paul.

Let Your 'Yes' be 'Yes'

23 SEP

FOR READING AND MEDITATION – MATTHEW 21:1–17

'It is written… "My house will be called a house of prayer,"
but you are making it a "den of robbers."' (v13)

Someone might be saying at this stage, 'But is assertiveness right for a Christian? Aren't we supposed to turn the other cheek and go the second mile?' There are times when it is appropriate to yield, but there are times also when it is right to stand up for an issue and not back down.

Another underlying cause of non-assertiveness is a mistaken sense of responsibility. We wrongly hold ourselves responsible for others' hurt feelings even when what we have said is right and was put across in a gentle and gracious manner. In such a situation we may need to remind ourselves that their feelings are not our responsibility. Sometimes assertiveness does cause hurt to people, although no hurt is intended. The thing to ask yourself is this: did *you* hurt the other person or did that other person simply *feel* hurt? If you made a snide remark, ridiculed the other person or knowingly violated their rights, then you have hurt that person, and you need to hold yourself accountable. On the other hand, if you have simply refused for a valid reason to do something the other person wanted you to do, your assertiveness was not in itself hurtful even though the person may have *felt* hurt.

Non-assertive people often wait until their anger builds up before passing on their opinion about something, and then what they say comes across as hostile. One person admitted, 'When I say 'Yes' to someone even though really I want to say 'No' – but am afraid to – then after a while anger builds up inside me and my feelings of hostility explode like a volcano.' That type of situation can only be avoided when a person learns not to say 'Yes' when they mean 'No'.

Gracious and loving heavenly Father, help me to be a person whose 'Yes' means 'Yes' and whose 'No' means 'No'. Deliver me from a mistaken sense of responsibility. In Christ's name. Amen.

Matthew 5:33–37; John 21:15–17
1. Why did Jesus advise against taking oaths?
2. Why was Peter hurt?

Take the First Step

FOR READING AND MEDITATION – JAMES 4:1–17

'You do not have because you do not ask God.' (v2)

There are some who think the role of a Christian is to be a doormat. Well, let me tell you something: you are not meant to be a doormat; you are someone made in God's image, with rights and responsibilities. A group of non-assertive people started an organisation called the 'Dependent Order Of Really Meek And Timid Souls'. Look at the first letter of every word and what does it spell? DOORMATS. Their motto was: The Meek Shall Inherit the Earth – if that's OK with everyone else.

How can those who feel non-assertive start to act more appropriately? The first step is to talk to God about the issue. I am astonished at the number of Christians who, when they have told me they have problems and I have asked them if they have talked to God about them, have looked blank, shaken their heads and said, 'No.' Why are we sometimes more ready to talk to a counsellor about our problems than to God?

The verse before us today tells us that a reason why we don't have is because we don't ask. So talk with God in prayer about the matter and ask Him to help you and guide you towards being a more assertive person. If God is not in your life, and not the centre, then you can never be a truly secure person. If the centre is not secure, you are not secure. Make sure you are surrendered to Him. Next get hold of good resources on the subject of assertiveness. Check that what you read is based on Christian teaching, for much of what the world teaches (not all) is designed to make you aggressive rather than assertive.

O Father, forgive me if I am more ready to talk to others about my problems than to You. Help me and guide me in this matter of being assertive, for I want to live life in a balanced way. In Jesus' name. Amen.

Jeremiah 1:4–10; Luke 11:1–13; Hebrews 11:6
1. How was Jeremiah's lack of confidence overcome?
2. What is promised to those who seek God?

Big – Yet Small   25 SEP

FOR READING AND MEDITATION – TITUS 3:1–11
'Be peaceable and considerate,
and always ... be gentle towards everyone.' (v2)

Now that we have looked at assertiveness we will focus on its opposite – yieldedness. Many are assertive but their assertiveness is not balanced by yieldedness. They are polarised. These people ought to follow the suggestion given to me by my pastor when I was a young man: 'Be ready to give way in small things that do not involve principles.' He also said, 'The bigness of a person can be measured by the size of the things on which he or she takes a stand.'

As I was writing these notes I read about a night watchman responsible for looking after the equipment belonging to a building contractor. Every night he would walk around the large yard where the tools were kept and in the morning faithfully give account for everything. He tended, however, to concentrate on guarding the smaller items, such as shovels and picks. One morning his boss came in and found that although all the smaller items were accounted for, a fork-lift truck had gone – stolen! The watchman gave his time to the little and missed the big. That story reminded me of another I have heard concerning an English cricket player who, running to catch a ball, lost his cap, turned back to grab it, and missed what appeared to be an easy catch. He made an issue of the little – the cap – and missed the big – the catch.

I know a man – an assertive individual – whose life is a failure on the whole because he doesn't know how to yield. He gets tangled up over little issues and misses the large ones. He makes molehills into mountains and mountains into molehills. He thinks he is big and influential, but his acquaintances consider him to be petty.

O God, help me not to be big when it comes to small issues, nor small in connection with big issues. Teach me to maintain the right balance between all of life's issues, particularly the things I am considering now. Amen.

Luke 6:1–11,41–42; 10:38–42
1. What was the Pharisees' problem?
2. What was Martha's problem?

Be Sure of the Big

26 SEP

FOR READING AND MEDITATION – MATTHEW 23:1–25

'You give a tenth of your spices... But you have
neglected the more important matters of the law...' (v23)

If there is one group of people who illustrate how easy it is to be one-sided in the possession of virtues, it is the Pharisees. They gave a tenth of their income – a good thing – but as Jesus pointed out, they neglected the more important matters – justice, mercy, and faithfulness. The tendency can be to focus on small details and miss the big.

John Wesley once took as his text Philippians 4:5 – 'Let your moderation be known unto all men' (KJV). Earlier we read that Handley Moule translated this verse 'Let your yieldedness be known to all'. Wesley went on to talk about people whose lives get tangled up over all kinds of matters, such as personal prestige, small hurts and resentments, but who miss the significant issues of life.

Similarly, I have met people who become so caught up in minor skirmishes over this, that, and the other – small things, petty things – that they lose the battles over major matters. It all comes back to what we concluded a few days ago when discussing assertiveness: our lives work best when we are wholly surrendered and wholly yielded to God. When a person is yielded to God then that person doesn't mind yielding to others over minor matters – matters that are not matters of principle, of course. But when a person is not yielded to God, not sure of the big, he or she makes an issue of every little thing. Every one of us ought to ask ourselves right now: Does a false sense of prestige keep me from yielding in matters where I ought to yield? Am I a big person as regards small matters, and a small person as regards big matters? Be sure of the big and the small things will take care of themselves.

Gracious and loving heavenly Father, I need a change of perspective. if I am to live the way You want me to live. Correct my vision so that I can see the big things as big and the little things as little. In Jesus' name. Amen.

Colossians 3:1–17; 2 Timothy 2:23–24
1. How should we relate to others?
2. What should we avoid?

Full Surrender

27 SEP

FOR READING AND MEDITATION – MATTHEW 4:18-22

'Come, follow me… and I will send you out to fish for people.' (v19)

We need to learn to yield to God before we can properly yield to others. Being yielded to God means that we are His and wholly His. Now be careful about this because although at the moment you may think you are yielded, in a few days' time you may discover that you are not as yielded as you thought you were. A situation may arise and your reactions may show that you need greater yieldedness.

Although justification may be instantaneous, sanctification is progressive. By that I mean, God brings about a change in you as you yield, but up ahead you discover that there is more to yield. Take, for example, the disciples in the passage before us. Peter and Andrew are seen casting their nets into the lake when Jesus calls them to be His disciples. Immediately they leave their nets and follow Him. Does this mean they were fully yielded? No. Later, Peter went back to his fishing nets even though he had been clearly called to leave them behind. He yielded, but not fully. Take also James and John. We read they were in the boat preparing their nets, and Jesus calls them; so they leave the boat 'and their father'. Note the words *'and their father'*. Does this mean they were fully yielded? It might seem so but we know from other parts of the Gospels that they still had some very unsanctified attitudes. On one occasion they wanted to call fire down from heaven on people who were not hospitable to Jesus (Luke 9:54).

It wasn't until Pentecost that the disciples appeared to offer their all, and when they did, God gave them His all – the Holy Spirit. I urge you, yield all to God today, and when you are fully yielded to Him, you will know how best to yield to others.

Father, I accept that before I can understand how to be yielded to others I must be fully yielded to You. I yield my all to You now. Help me to experience balance in both assertiveness and yieldedness. In Jesus' name. Amen.

Romans 6:13-23; 8:5-9; 12:1-2; James 4:7
1. How do we submit ourselves to God?
2. What happens when we do?

The Divine Optician

FOR READING AND MEDITATION – MATTHEW 19:16–30

'Love your neighbour as yourself.' (v19)

We come now to a pair of opposites which if not balanced can cause us a great deal of difficulty in life – self-concern and concern for others. Many are in trouble spiritually because they cannot integrate the two. They either focus on the spiritual life of others and pay no attention to themselves, or they pay attention to themselves and have no concern for others. We are intended to have both an inward and an outward focus; to be personal and social.

There is a verse in the book of Revelation that reads like this: 'In the centre, round the throne, were four living creatures, and they were covered with eyes, in front and behind' (Rev. 4:6). Moffatt translates this text thus: 'And on each side of the throne... four living Creatures full of eyes inside and outside...' They had eyes on the inside to see themselves and eyes on the outside to see others. Both are necessary. If you turn your eyes to continually focus on yourself to the exclusion of others, you can become morbidly introspective. And if you continue to do this and do it intensely, you could potentially become neurotic. On the other hand, if you look at others too much and never focus on what is going on in your own life, you could become overly critical and you will be known as a nit-picker.

I read this in one of Dr E. Stanley Jones' books – words that I think will strike a chord with all of us: 'Some Christians have cataracts on their 'inside' eyes and powerful bifocals on their 'outside' eyes. As we go periodically to have our spectacles adjusted, so we must go to the Divine Optician to have our inside and outside eyes corrected.'

O Father, deal with this tendency in me to look only in one direction. Help me to see through Your eyes and then I will see myself and others in the way I ought to see them. In Christ's name. Amen.

Mark 8:1–10; Luke 16:19–31
1. Contrast the attitudes of Jesus and His disciples to the crowd.
2. When did the rich man show concern for others?

Take Heed

29 SEP

FOR READING AND MEDITATION – HOSEA 7:1–10

'His hair is sprinkled with grey, but he does not notice.' (v9)

It is one thing to grow spiritually; it is another thing to grow up straight with no lopsidedness. Some become so self-focused that they don't look out to others, and some become so other-focused that they miss what is going on in their own lives. When I was being brought up I used to hear my father say over and over again, 'If some people were as good at telling themselves what is wrong with them as they are in telling others, they would be wonderful Christians. Now they are just wonderful Pharisees.' A self-focus is good – as long as it is in balance. Repeatedly in Scripture we are called to self-examination. Those who concern themselves with examining the lives of others and do not occasionally embark upon a few moments of self-examination, will wake up one day to discover that their virtue has become a vice.

Several years ago I did a study on how many times the New Testament encourages us to 'take heed to ourselves' (Authorised Version language). Here are just a few: 'Take heed to yourself and to the doctrine' (1 Tim. 4:16, NKJV). 'Take heed to yourselves and to all the flock...' (Acts 20:28, NKJV). 'Take heed to yourselves. If your brother sins against you, rebuke him; and if he repents, forgive him' (Luke 17:3, NKJV). There are many more. What these texts encourage us to do is to look at ourselves – to take an inside look.

Hosea chides the people of his time for having heads sprinkled with grey hair and not knowing it. Normally we are the first to spot greying hairs! But, just as normally, we are the last to spot signs of spiritual deterioration. That's Hosea's point. We think far too often that we are better than we are.

Father, I hear Your voice telling me to 'take heed'. I need this challenge. Forgive me if I am more concerned about taking out the speck in someone else's eye than the beam which is in my own. In Jesus' name. Amen.

Malachi 1:6–14; 3:6–16; Matthew 7:1–5
1. What did the people not realise?
2. What should we do before advising others?

Denial – My Trademark

30 SEP

FOR READING AND MEDITATION – LUKE 11:37–52

'You Pharisees clean the outside of the cup and dish, but inside you are full of greed and wickedness.' (v39)

We continue thinking about the imbalance that characterises us when we look at what is happening in the lives of others but give little or no consideration to what may be happening in our own life. The arguments that people use to avoid taking an inside look are many. One argument goes like this: 'I'm afraid to look at what may be going on inside me in case I become discouraged and overwhelmed.' But if problems are not faced, how can they be dealt with? The reason why God said to Eve in the Garden of Eden 'What is this you have done?' (Gen. 3:13) was not in order to find out why Eve had given Adam the fruit to eat but to give her an opportunity to identify what she had done. Only exposed problems can be dealt with.

The proper term for avoiding facing up to what is going on inside us is *denial*. I have talked a lot about this in my time, and every time I do people write to me and say, 'I didn't realise how deeply I was into denial until the Holy Spirit pointed it out to me through some words you had written.' One person even admitted this: 'Denial was my trademark.'

Jesus, you remember, kept some of His strongest criticism for the Pharisees, who made denial a way of life. They specialised in telling others how to live and pointing out their defects whenever they failed to meet the standards of Moses' law. Jesus called them hypocrites because they never paused to search their own hearts. They washed the outside of the cup but the inside was filthy. Little wonder that Jesus was not welcome in their midst. The principle Jesus was enunciating is this: before you look at how others are developing, take a long look at yourself.

O Father, if I am in denial, shake me out of it I pray, for I want no pretence in my life. Forgive me that so often I lament the faults in others when I am afraid to face my own. Amen.

1 Samuel 15:1–23
1. How did Saul excuse himself?
2. What was the consequence of his denial?

What to Look For

1 OCT

FOR READING AND MEDITATION – PSALM 139:17–24
'Search me, God, and know my heart…' (v23)

From experience I know that whenever I introduce the subject of self-examination, the question that comes into people's minds is this: but what do I look for? Exploring the soul is a complex business. Our heart, says Scripture, is 'deceitful above all things' (Jer. 17:9).

I have come to believe that the key thing we should look for in our hearts is motive. The older I get the more I realise how one can do things that appear to be spiritual when the real motive may be, for instance, a covert bid for attention, the itch to prove oneself or the desire for approval. When I think back to the early days of my ministry, with the advantage of hindsight (and some degree of maturity, I hope) I can see that much of what I did was motivated by self-interest rather than the glory of God. I wanted to be seen, to make a name for myself, and my deceitful heart was adept at finding ways that made my self-centred efforts look spiritual.

Once I talked with a young woman in Malaysia who told me that she wanted to invite an old boyfriend of hers to a meal in her home because, as she put it, 'I just want to show him that I bear no grudge.' I encouraged her to identify her real motive. She was open to the idea and after thinking it through she said, 'My underlying motive is not to show him I do not bear a grudge but to see if there may be a chance of us getting back together again.'

One thing I have learned in life is this: the human heart in its fallen state is an amazing instrument for self-deception. We are masters of the art. That is why we need regularly to take an inside look.

Father, I am just not able to search my heart in the way that You can. Let Your Holy Spirit shine into its inner recesses and bring to the light my true motives. In the name of Jesus Christ my Lord. Amen.

1 Samuel 16:7; Matthew 6:1–8; John 12:1–8
1. What were the Pharisees' motives in prayer and giving?
2. Why did Judas object to the woman's generosity?

Vision and Energy

2 OCT

FOR READING AND MEDITATION – COLOSSIANS 1:24–29

'To this end I strenuously contend with all
the energy Christ so powerfully works in me.' (v29)

We began this section with a reference to the four living creatures spoken of in Revelation who had 'eyes inside and outside'. They had eyes on the inside to see themselves and eyes on the outside to see others. The eyes on the inside were the first to be mentioned but the eyes on the outside were equally important. To have one without the other is to be unbalanced. Therefore the issue we face now is concern for others.

How concerned are you about the spiritual growth of others? I am referring, of course, to those with whom you have a close relationship. You can have a *general* concern for the development of the whole Body of Christ, but what is that concern like when it comes down to the *particular*? 'The Christian demand,' says a theologian, 'is two-fold: we are to be unbreakably given to Christ and unbreakably given to each other.' Paul knew the importance of that better than anyone. Read what he says in Galatians 4:19: 'My dear children, for whom I am again in the pains of childbirth until Christ is formed in you…' Put alongside that our text for today in which Paul talks about 'strenuously contend[ing] with all the energy Christ so powerfully works in me.' Two things are evident here: Paul had a vision for people to become mature, and he experienced an energy that worked through him towards that end.

When did you last focus your prayers on a Christian friend and pray for him or her to become mature? And when did you last feel a spiritual energy going through you to this end? It is not enough to be concerned about ourselves; we must be equally concerned about others.

Father, I have seen the importance of being concerned about my own growth; now help me be equally concerned about the growth of those who are close to me 'in Christ'. Give me Your vision and Your energy. Amen.

Ephesians 1:15–23; 3:14–19; Philippians 1:3–11
1. What concerned Paul?
2. What concerns you?

Giving Yourself to Others

3 OCT

FOR READING AND MEDITATION – 2 TIMOTHY 1:1–12

'Recalling your tears, I long to see you, so that I may be filled with joy.' (v4)

Yesterday we said that the apostle Paul demonstrated two things in his relationship with people: he had a vision for others and experienced the energy of Christ flowing through him as he related to them. These two things sum up what other-centredness is all about – having a vision for others and allowing Christ's energy to flow through you to them.

What kind of vision did Paul have for the people to whom he related? It was a vision for them to become mature in Christ. Do you have a vision like that for the people to whom you relate? Are you clear in your mind as to what maturity involves? How do you think Paul would reply if you could sit down with him and ask him a question like this: 'Paul, what is in your mind as you pray for Timothy? How would you like to see him develop?' I think he would say something like this: 'Ah, Timothy... he's a little fearful and somewhat self-conscious, especially about his youth, but I see him growing into a strong, confident leader in the Body of Christ.' That was his vision for him. But what about the energy? That came through him as he related to Timothy both in the letters he wrote and his personal contact with the young disciple.

Think now of your closest friend in Christ. It may be a husband, wife, son, daughter, neighbour, workmate. What comes into your mind whenever you pray for that person? In what ways do you feel he or she is in need of spiritual development? Do you focus on those matters in your prayer time and ask God to flow through you whenever you meet, so that His energy can come through you to them? That is what it means to give yourself to others.

Father, give me deep insight into the needs of those to whom I relate closely, so that I can see how to pray for them. And then flow through me with Your divine energy as we share Your love together. For Jesus' sake. Amen.

Luke 22:31–34; John 17:6–11,20–25
1. How did Jesus express concern for others?
2. How did Jesus express concern for you?

What is a Christian?

4 OCT

FOR READING AND MEDITATION – 1 CORINTHIANS 12:12–31

'Its parts should have equal concern for each other.' (v25)

We spend one last day emphasising the need to balance self-concern with concern for others. A woman sent me a letter some time ago after I had written about loving others as oneself, and took me to task for saying, 'We must take our eyes off people and put them on Christ. He alone is to occupy our attention.' In my reply I quoted the incident in John's Gospel when Peter asked, 'Lord, what about him?' and Jesus answered, '… what is that to you? You must follow me' (John 21:21–22). It seems to me that to be concerned about others is not to take our eyes off Christ but to look at others through the eyes of Christ. Those who are preoccupied with their own spiritual health but have no regard for the health and needs of others, grow lopsidedly.

When someone asked Baron Von Hügel, 'What is a Christian?' he replied: 'A Christian is someone who cares.' He went on to say that we can tell how far we are along the road towards maturity by how much we care for others.

A poet whose name I cannot trace put some of the thoughts I am sharing now into this poem:

> *If you've never felt the sorrow of another person's grief,*
> *If you've never felt an inner urge to want to bring relief*
> *To someone who's in trouble, with a kindly word or smile,*
> *If you've never loved your neighbour as yourself,*
> *with all your might,*
> *If you've never shed a tear drop at a pure and holy sight,*
> *If others have not been blessed by something you have said,*
> *You need have no fear of dying, Brother, you're already dead.*

Father, I simply must get these two issues in balance – concern for self and concern for others. Save me from erring in one direction and thus turning these virtues into vices. In Jesus' name. Amen.

Luke 10:25–37; Philippians 2:3–4
1. Who is our neighbour?
2. How can we love our neighbour?

Are You a CR?   5 OCT

FOR READING AND MEDITATION – MARK 7:1–13

'You have let go of the commands of God
and are holding on to human traditions.' (v8)

The next pair of opposites we examine are these: being conservative and being radical. By 'conservative' I mean having the tendency to conserve and maintain the status quo. By 'radical' I mean the inclination to question things and agitate for change. Those who demonstrate only conservative values tend to become reactionary and stuck in the mud. Those who manifest only radical tendencies can become obnoxious rebels and revolutionaries. Balanced Christians should be able to occupy both positions, to straddle both poles. They seek to conserve all that is right and good, but look also to overturn those things that need changing.

Our Lord Jesus Christ was both conservative and radical. He was balanced. He was conservative, for example, in His attitude to the ancient Scriptures. 'I have not come to abolish [the Law or the Prophets],' He said, 'but to fulfil them' (Matt. 5:17). No one was more fierce in their denunciation of those who wanted to change the Scriptures than Jesus. He did everything He could to conserve that which needed conserving. But He was radical too – as the passage before us today clearly shows. He supported His disciples when they were accused of eating food without having ceremonially washed their hands. He touched lepers on occasion, too (see Matt. 8:3), whereas the Pharisees made them keep their distance. He allowed a woman to pour on His head expensive perfume and reprimanded those disciples who said it was wasteful (see Matt. 26:6–13).

A disciple should not be above his teacher. If Jesus could combine radicalism with conservatism, so can we.

O Father, make me a balanced CR – a conservative radical. Sharpen my critical faculties so that I can see more clearly what needs to be conserved and what needs to be changed. In Jesus' name. Amen.

Matthew 5:27–45; 13:52
1. How did Jesus conserve the old in a radical way?
2. What is the attitude of mature disciples?

Here I Stand

6 OCT

FOR READING AND MEDITATION – 1 TIMOTHY 6:11–21

'Timothy, guard what has been entrusted to your care.' (v20)

Every Christian must be conservative. I am not talking now about political affiliation but about the need to conserve the good things that are ours from the past. In our text today Paul tells Timothy to guard what has been entrusted to him. Later he urges him to 'Guard the good deposit that was entrusted to you' (2 Tim. 1:14).

That advice is pertinent to our day too. We live in an age when the Bible's reliability is being questioned, not only by those outside the Church but by those inside it too. Often I meet young ministers who tell me they entered a theological college with great faith in God and in the Bible, only to come out of it with their faith in shreds. One young minister, knowing of my confidence in the Bible, said to me, 'I don't need a face lift but I do need a faith lift. I would like to sit down with you for a whole year for that purpose.'

His comment reminded me of a sign I saw outside a plastic surgeon's office during a visit overseas: 'Come in and have your face lifted.' Right next door to his office there was a church which had this on one of its posters: 'Come in and have your faith lifted.' Not all churches could put such a notice outside, for some have a crisis of confidence concerning the Scriptures. The task of the Christian Church is not to invent new gospels, new moralities, or new theologies, but to be a faithful guardian of the one and only gospel. There is need, I think, for another reformation, for all Christians to take their stand foursquare on the Word of God, as did Martin Luther, and say with him, 'Here I stand. I can do no other.'

Father, I see that our first task as Christians is to keep the good news of the gospel intact. Help me to form a strong conviction about this; not an opinion, but a conviction. In Jesus' name. Amen.

2 Thessalonians 2:13–17; 2 Timothy 3:14–17; Titus 1:7–9
1. What are the benefits of standing on the old?
2. What is the origin of Scripture?

Christian Conservationism — 7 OCT

FOR READING AND MEDITATION – JUDE 1–16

'I felt I had to write and urge you to contend for the faith that was once for all entrusted to God's holy people.' (v3)

The faith for which we are to contend, we must notice, was *once for all* entrusted to God's holy people. I like the way Eugene Peterson paraphrases this verse: 'Dear friends, I've dropped everything to write you about this life of salvation that we have in common. I have to write insisting—begging!—that you fight with everything you have in you for this faith entrusted to us as a gift to guard and cherish.' On this basis I say again: every Christian is called to be conservative. Our task is to conserve the revelation given to us in the sacred Scriptures.

A book was published many years ago, written by four different authors, entitled *Growing into Union*. One of the authors expressed the point I am making with great force: 'The Church's first task is to keep the good news intact. It is better to speak of the habit of mind which this calling requires as 'conservationist' rather than 'conservative' for the latter word can easily suggest an antiquarian addiction to what is old for its own sake, and for a blanket resistance to new thinking, and this is not what we are talking about at all. Antiquarianism and obscurantism are the vices of the Christian mind, but conservationism is among its virtues.'

I understand his desire to move away from the word 'conservative' to 'conservationism', but whichever word we prefer to use (mine is 'conservative'), it is clear that as Christians we are called to conserve, to guard, to protect the truth which has been handed down to us since the canon of Scripture was established. The Bible is changeless in its truth and authority. Changeless. It must not be altered in any way – either by addition or modification.

O Father, engrave this truth on the heart of Your present-day Church – the truth that we are to be guardians of Your Word, not questioners of it. In Christ's name I pray. Amen.

1 Timothy 4:1–16; 2 Peter 3:1–2
1. To what should Timothy be devoted?
2. What are we to recall?

Repairing the Lord's Prayer

8 OCT

FOR READING AND MEDITATION – PSALM 119:1–16

'Blessed are those who keep his statutes
and seek him with all their heart…' (v2)

If ever the Church needed conservative-minded men and women it is now. The Scriptures are being tampered with to such a degree that all kinds of new theories are being mooted.

I read about a church where the letters of the Lord's Prayer were inscribed in gold on one of its walls. The letters were in need of regilding, and so also were the words of the Ten Commandments and the Apostles' Creed. The decorator hired to do the task submitted his invoice in this form:

To repairing the Lord's Prayer: (x amount)
To three new commandments: (y amount)
To making a new creed: (z amount).

A number of people in today's Church like to set about 'repairing' some sections of the Word of God because they feel they are not in line with contemporary culture. But it is not that the Bible is out of step with culture; it is that culture is out of step with the Bible. Culture changes, Scripture never changes. At times, Christians can find themselves swimming against the tide of the 'If it feels good, do it' mentality. It's important, however, that we don't lose sight of core issues. We need to look at issues through the lens of Scripture (which contains generous amounts of compassion).

Remember this when you may be feeling like you are about to be washed out to sea by the tide of modern thinking: when you stand beside Scripture you stand beside God.

Father, help me to be fixed on the things that are fixed and not move from them no matter how plausible the arguments that are presented to me. Establish me in Your Word, for You are truth. In Jesus' name. Amen.

Luke 11:1–14; Romans 1:16–32
1. Why is the Lord's Prayer still relevant?
2. What happens when we reject God's truth?

As It Was in the Beginning... 9 OCT

FOR READING AND MEDITATION – ACTS 18:1–8

'From now on I will go to the Gentiles.' (v6)

We have been saying that every Christian must be conservative. But conservatism must be balanced by radicalism otherwise as we walk through the world we will veer in one direction. If our conservatism is not balanced by a *biblical* radicalism then it can degenerate into a vice. Some have pushed their conservative tendencies to such a degree that they are not just stuck in the mud; the mud has set like concrete. Paul's conservatism was balanced by a biblical radicalism, and when he realised that his ministry needed to change, he changed it. Others might have said, 'Stay exclusively with the Jews, that's what God wants', but Paul was radical enough to see that it was time for a change – an appropriate change.

An English duke is reported to have said, 'Any change at any time for any reason is to be deplored.' This is conservatism gone to extremes. Some lovers of change have as their slogan, 'Become a student of change. It is the only thing that will remain constant.' Conservatives hate change; radicals love it.

We must guard Scripture against the influences of our culture, but when culture is not antichristian then we can consider change – if appropriate. A balanced Christian, however, will scrutinise everything before change is made, and test his conclusions against Scripture. We must not cling to the past simply because it is part of the past. We cling to what is good and we change what is not good. No tradition (if it is not biblical) ought to be looked upon as sacrosanct and no institution as inviolable. We need to be conservative enough not to change for change's sake and radical enough to change when change is needed – sometimes even initiating it.

Father, do I need to be more radical? Has my conservatism got me stuck in the mud? If I am too conservative then help me move towards biblical radicalism. I don't want to be radical for its own sake but for Your sake. Amen.

Acts 15:1–21
1. How did the Early Church respond to change?
2. How did they reach a radical conclusion?

No Sacred Cows

10 OCT

FOR READING AND MEDITATION – ROMANS 12:1–8

'Do not conform to the pattern of this world,
but be transformed by the renewing of your mind.' (v2)

Today we ask ourselves: What really is biblical radicalism? It is the attitude of mind that questions things, reveres no sacred cows, and subjects traditions to careful scrutiny. In this sense Jesus was a radical, and so (as we saw yesterday) was the apostle Paul. I have just been reading the story of William Wilberforce, the man who did much to abolish slavery. His biographer said of him, 'There burned within him a passion to set men and women free from the evil chains of slavery. People called him a radical and a revolutionary. Thank God he was.' *Thank God he was.*

A radical, instead of lamenting change, will sometimes be in the forefront of it. Would to God there were more radical Christians when it comes to matters of changing our attitudes towards the poor both in our own country and overseas, fighting for the rights of disadvantaged individuals, and so on. Without realising it, many of us have become captive to the lifestyle and value system of the world. We need to question ourselves and 'root out' (the true meaning of 'radical') those things from our lives that we have embraced uncritically.

All our denominations reflect past cultures. We talk about Anglicanism, Presbyterianism, Methodism – all *isms*. Each is an historic form of Christianity, but each has its own cultural baggage. All of this should be subjected to careful examination to see whether it is culture being defended or Scripture. Not all traditions need to be swept away, of course. Extreme radicalism – simply getting rid of things because they originated in the past and for no other reason – is as foolish as extreme conservatism.

Father, I realise that I must be ruled not by culture but by Christ. Help me to subject everything to careful examination to see what is influencing me – the things of time or the things of eternity. In Christ's name. Amen.

Acts 11:1–18; Galatians 2:11–16
1. How did God radicalise conservative Peter?
2. Why did radical Peter revert to being conservative?

Time Again for a Check-Up — 11 OCT

FOR READING AND MEDITATION – LUKE 5:33-39

'And no one after drinking old wine wants the new,
for they say, "The old is better."' (v39)

We come back to what we said at the beginning of this section concerning conservatism and radicalism, namely that all Christians should be CRs – conservative radicals. Some might think that these two qualities are in opposition to one another, but they are not. One has only to look to Jesus and to the apostle Paul to see that there is no need for polarisation on this issue. It may not be easy to balance conservatism and radicalism, but with God's help it is possible. We are to be conservative in the sense that we cherish what has been handed down from the past, but radical in the sense that we question whether what we cling to comes more from culture than Scripture.

But even when Scripture encourages us to choose change, we are not to be what someone has described as 'mindless iconoclasts' – changing for change's sake. Sometimes, as Jesus tells us in our text for today, 'the old is better'. Like old wine, what is established has stood the test of time. What we must pray for is discernment – discernment to know when to be conservative and when to be radical. It is no good saying, 'Well I am conservative by nature and I leave it to others to be radical.' Biblical radicalism should be an integral part of everyone's development in Christ. If that balance is not there then, again – we will grow lopsidedly.

Take another look at your life today and ask yourself these pointed questions: Am I off-balance in regard to conservatism and radicalism? Am I stuck in the mud when I ought to get up and go? Or do I approach things so radically that I fail to see the value of conserving that which ought to be conserved? It is time again for a check-up.

My Father and my God, I have come a long way with You over these past few weeks. Help me to look at myself in this area too. Where I have been unbalanced, please bring about the necessary correction. Amen.

Malachi 3:6; Song of Songs 7:10-13; Jeremiah 31:31-36; Hebrews 13:8
1. What might new and old have in common?
2. Is God conservative or radical?

Two 'Trying' Sisters

12 OCT

FOR READING AND MEDITATION – 1 CORINTHIANS 15:1–11

'I worked harder than all of them – yet not I,
but the grace of God that was with me.' (v10)

Another pair of opposites that deserve attention are these: trusting and trying. It is a virtue to trust and it is a virtue to try but, again, if one virtue is not balanced with the other and held in tension, our growth will be one-sided. Some people's approach to the Christian life is all trust, and they do nothing to help themselves. Others are so taken up with 'working their passage to heaven' that there is little room for trust. Perhaps the great preacher C.H. Spurgeon summarised the matter correctly when he said, 'We pray as if it all depended on God, and we work as if it all depended on us.'

I like what the apostle Paul says in the verse before us today, where he points out that when it came to work he worked harder than anyone, 'yet not I, but the grace of God that was with me'. He tried harder than anyone, yet his trust was not in his own strength but in the strength given him by God. That's the secret – working hard, but working in God's strength and not our own. Recently I met a man who asked me to pray with him because he was unemployed. I offered to do so gladly but before praying I asked, 'What have you been doing about looking for a job?' 'Nothing,' he replied, 'I am trusting God to bring the right job to my attention.' In his case, trust needed to be married to trying.

When I was young I heard a preacher make a comment on a verse in Romans 16 which reads thus: 'Greet Tryphena and Tryphosa, those women who work hard in the Lord' (Rom. 16:12). He said he would like to rename these two 'Trying sisters' – 'Tryphena and Trust-phosa'. There is a place for trying and there is a place for trusting. And knowing the difference is crucial.

O Father, when do I trust and when do I try? Draw me so close to You that any misunderstanding I have on this issue will be resolved. In Jesus' name. Amen.

Nehemiah 4:1–23; Proverbs 3:5
1. How did Nehemiah combine trusting and trying?
2. Why should we not rely totally on ourselves?

Tired of Trusting?

13 OCT

FOR READING AND MEDITATION – GENESIS 16:1-16

'Sarai... took her Egyptian slave Hagar and gave her to her husband...' (v3)

Let's reflect together first on the tendency found in many Christians to veer more towards striving than trusting. I am most certainly in this class. For me, it is extremely hard to sit back, do nothing, and let God bring about the solution to a situation in His own time and way. There are occasions in my life (and in yours too) when this is the position to adopt. But trusting is not easy. As I write about trusting and trying I am aware that in this area, perhaps more than any other, I have grown lopsidedly. Some correction is needed, and with God's help I am dealing with it.

I have chosen our reading today because God has used it to pierce my soul recently, and I think He may well do that with some of you, too. Abram received from God a promise that through him and his wife Sarai would come a great nation. But Sarai fails to conceive and so she urges Abram to sleep with Hagar, her maid, and father a child by her. He responds to his wife's request, and sleeps with the maid, whereupon she conceives. How could Abram, the man whom God called His friend, act in this way? Why didn't he stand up to his wife and say, 'This is not the way to go; we must continue to trust God just as we have always trusted Him'? Probably because he was tired of trusting.

Can a child of God be tired of trusting? I'm afraid so. When God says 'Wait' but the situation appears to be getting out of control, it is tempting to take matters into our own hands. But that way always spells doom. Perhaps you are in that position at this very moment. Stop striving and trust. He will bring His purposes to pass in His own time.

O Father, I recognise this tendency in me to act precipitately when I am in trouble. Show me when I should take action and when I should wait for You to work. Amen.

Exodus 14:5-31
1. What did Moses advise the people?
2. What was the result?

Trust, not Negotiation

14 OCT

FOR READING AND MEDITATION – MATTHEW 18:15–35

'The servant's master took pity on him,
cancelled the debt and let him go.' (v27)

Throughout time Christians have found it difficult to learn to trust. Dr Cynddylan Jones, a famous Welsh preacher, once said, 'The middle verse of the Bible is Psalm 118:9, 'It is better to trust in the Lord than to put confidence in princes' (NKJV). I look at it every day, but still the biggest challenge of my life is to trust.' There is something in us all that wants God to come through for us in ways that do not demand our trust.

When Peter said to Jesus, 'We have left everything... What then will there be for us?' (Matt. 19:27), notice that our Lord replied by telling the story of the workers in the vineyard (Matt. 20:1–16). The vineyard owner hired men to work all day for the usual wage. Five times in all throughout the day he took on workers, but at the end of the day he paid them all exactly the same rate. Those who had laboured right through the day reacted strongly to the decision, but the owner said to them, 'Take your pay and go... Don't I have the right to do what I want with my own money?' (vv14–15).

On one level, this story emphasises the need for servants to trust their master to do what is right. So often, like Peter, we talk trust but practise negotiation. We come to God believing that 'he rewards those who earnestly seek him' (Heb. 11:6), but then we insist on being rewarded in the way we think we deserve. Where is trust in this? If trust means anything, it means coming to God and saying, 'Whatever You think is best is fine with me.' It doesn't mean that we have to stop asking for everything our hearts desire (as children do at Christmas), but it does mean being willing to remain content with whatever He chooses to do.

Father, help me understand that You always give the best to those who leave the choice to You. I want Your best and to be the best. In Christ's name. Amen.

Genesis 28:20–22; Philippians 4:10–13; 1 Timothy 6:6–8
1. Was Jacob's vow based on trust or negotiation?
2. What secret had Paul learnt?

Careless in God's Care　　　15 OCT

FOR READING AND MEDITATION – MATTHEW 6:25–34

'Look at the birds of the air; they do not sow or reap…
and yet your heavenly Father feeds them.' (v26)

George MacDonald, the Scottish novelist, said, 'It is a greater compliment to be trusted than to be loved.' If that is so, then what sort of compliment are we paying God? We say we love Him, but do we trust Him? I have often thought how different life would be if God would say something like this in times of confusion: 'Look, this is what is happening. I am working on a person who can help you with your difficulty, but it will take two weeks before they are ready to move in the way I want them to move. However, at the end of two weeks they *will* move, and then your situation will be resolved.' But God doesn't show us what He is planning. He simply says, 'Trust.'

The verse before us today has been a great comfort to me when I have needed to trust. Eugene Peterson's *The Message* words it like this: 'Look at the birds, free and unfettered, not tied down to a job description, careless in the care of God. And you count more to him than birds.'

I am reminded of the true story of a contractor who was commissioned to remove several trees from a street that was to be widened. He and his workmen discovered a bird's nest in one of the trees, with a mother bird sitting on her eggs. They decided to leave the work until a week or two later. When they returned they found the nest occupied by five widemouthed baby birds. So they waited a few more weeks until the birds had flown the nest. The whole enterprise was held up for several weeks and at some commercial cost. When a workman looked into the empty nest something caught his eye: a soiled little white Sunday school card. On it were the words 'We trust in the Lord our God.'

O Father, how often do Your Word and my need fit together. My trouble is I want to trace You rather than trust You. Forgive me for this, and help me be a more trustful person. In Jesus' name. Amen.

Philippians 4:4–7; 1 Peter 5:6–7
1. What should we do with our cares?
2. What will be the result?

Time to Mop

16 OCT

FOR READING AND MEDITATION – ACTS 27:27–44

'They dropped four anchors from the stern and prayed for daylight.' (v29)

We have been reflecting on the importance of trusting; now we turn our attention to the importance of trying. Trust has to be balanced by trying or working, otherwise there is an imbalance. Not long ago I heard a story concerning an incident in the life of the eminent American philosopher John Dewey. The great man was called by his ten-year-old son to the bathroom. The tap had got stuck and there was water all over the floor. The professor stood there for a few moments looking, thinking, attempting to take in the situation and come up with a way of dealing with it. His son looked at him in amazement and burst out, 'Father, this is not the time to philosophise, this is the time to mop.' There are times when trust has to give place to action.

In the passage before us today we read of a storm of hurricane force which threatened the life of Paul and his companions. An angel had appeared to Paul and told him not to fear for no one would be lost in the storm (vv23–24). As the hurricane continued to blow and the ship was being driven towards the rocks, we read, 'they dropped four anchors from the stern and prayed for daylight' (v29). Why didn't Paul just say to his shipmates, 'Look, God has told me no harm is going to come to any of us, so forget about trying to save yourselves and just trust God'? Because Paul knew that trust needed to be wedded to action, he gave them some practical advice on how to handle the situation (vv31–36).

St Bernard of Clairvaux, when preaching on this passage, ended his sermon with these words: 'He who labours as he trusts lifts his heart to God with his hands.' He does.

Father, how grateful I am that You have given me in Your Word so many illustrations of Your truth. They hedge me in and show me not just what to do but how to do it. Amen.

John 9:1–7; James 2:14–26
1. When did the man receive his sight?
2. How did Abraham wed faith to action?

God Helps Those...

17 OCT

FOR READING AND MEDITATION – JOHN 9:1–12

'As long as it is day, we must do the works of him who sent me.' (v4)

J.G. Holland, a Christian preacher and writer, was close to the mark when he said this while talking about the need to balance trust and action: 'God gives every bird its food but He does not throw it into the nest.'

Earlier I mentioned that during my developmental years I found study hard going. My parents, who were both devout Christians, prayed regularly for me, but their prayers didn't seem to accomplish very much. I remember saying to them one day, 'Why doesn't God give me the ability I need?' My mother replied, 'God helps those who help themselves.' No doubt you have heard that statement many times, but it was the first time I had come across it, and it acted, as the Americans say, 'like a burr in my saddle'. I realised that I was waiting for God to work a miracle while He was waiting for me to knuckle down to some serious study and apply my mind to what I should be doing, instead of using it to fantasise about this, that, and the other.

A pastor was called to take over a church where the congregation had sunk into a low state spiritually. They believed that if they trusted God, people would come into the church without any effort on their part. The pastor thrilled the congregation with his first sermon, based on our text for today – 'As long as it is day, we must... work...'. The next Sunday he preached the same sermon. When, on the third Sunday, he preached the same ringing message and on the same text, one of the deacons felt something should be done. 'Pastor,' he said, 'don't you have more than one sermon?' 'Oh, yes,' he said quietly, 'I have quite a number. But you haven't done anything about the first one yet.'

Lord, I continue to be grateful that You insist on my being balanced. You demand nothing of me that I cannot attain – by Your Spirit's help. Teach me when to trust and when to try. For Your own dear name's sake. Amen.

Exodus 16:11–26; Proverbs 24:30–34
1. Why did the manna not come precooked?
2. Why may a lack of action indicate laziness rather than trust?

I Did Help You

18 OCT

FOR READING AND MEDITATION – JOB 13:1-12

'Would it turn out well if he examined you?' (v9)

Take a moment now to ask these questions of yourself: How balanced am I in relation to trusting and trying? Do I find it difficult to trust, preferring to rush in and do something instead of waiting for God? Or am I the kind of person who tends to want to trust God to bring about the resolution of certain situations, when perhaps the appropriate thing to do is to exert some effort?

An apocryphal story goes like this. A small town was struck by a fierce storm and soon many of the streets and homes were flooded. One man had to climb onto the roof of his house for safety. A helicopter came along, dropped a rope, and a voice said, 'Grab the rope and we will haul you to safety.' 'No,' said the man, 'it's all right. I'm going to trust the Lord.' The helicopter moved away and later along came a speedboat. 'Jump into the water,' somebody shouted, 'we'll pick you up and take you to safety.' 'No,' said the man, 'I am going to trust the Lord.' The storm grew stronger and the man was swept away and drowned. When he arrived in heaven he complained to the Lord: 'Why didn't You help me? My trust was in You.' 'I did help you,' said the Lord. 'I sent you a helicopter and a speedboat, but you refused to use them.'

The truly balanced Christian is trustful and active, not now and again trustful, and now and again active, but trustful and active at one and the same time. Jesus demonstrated the right balance of trust and effort. He said: '... the Son can do nothing by himself...' (John 5:19) – trust. And again: 'My Father is always at his work... and I, too, am working' (John 5:17) – effort. The two were beautifully balanced.

Father, I am on a quest for maturity, but now I want to make the quest specific: help me be balanced in this area of trust and effort. Save me from trying when I should be trusting, and trusting when I should be trying. Amen.

---

2 Kings 3:14-26; Mark 16:15-20
1. How did the Israelites wed trust and action?
2. When would God work miracles?

Wise Words

19 OCT

FOR READING AND MEDITATION – MATTHEW 10:1-16
'Freely you have received; freely give.' (v8)

Yet another sphere of life where we may discover an imbalance is that of experience and expression. Some concentrate on experiencing God but fail to express what they have experienced. Others concentrate on the expression of their spiritual life but do not have much experience of God, and thus have little to express. It is only when we learn to occupy both camps that we exhibit a healthy biblical balance. Unfortunately, many of us push other people over to one extreme position while keeping the opposite position for ourselves, foolishly believing that ours is the best.

No one ever warned me more clearly of this danger than John Wallace, the principal of the college I attended when preparing for the ministry. He said, 'You will be tempted to take up extreme positions when you go out into the Christian ministry. You will say, 'I believe in the sovereignty of God', and claim to be a Calvinist. Or you will say, 'I believe in the freedom of the will', and claim to be an Arminian. But you will not be a balanced person unless you can harmonise the sovereignty of God and the freedom of the will. If you do not emphasise the freedom of the will you have nothing to save; if you do not emphasise the sovereignty of God you have nothing to save with.' Wise words.

On one occasion I met a man who told me that he was able to harmonise the Calvinist and Arminian views by being a Calvinist one day and an Arminian the next. He thought he was balanced; I thought he was barmy. We are not to be one thing one day and another thing the following day. We are to blend opposite virtues and make them one.

Father, I am so thankful for the experience I have of You. Help me to express what I have experienced so that it does not become stale and musty. This I ask in Jesus' name. Amen.

Luke 8:26-39; John 4:28-30,39-42
1. What instruction did Jesus give to the healed man?
2. Why did many believe in Jesus?

What is 'Life'?

20 OCT

FOR READING AND MEDITATION – JOHN 1:1–14

'Yet to all who did receive him, to those who believed...
he gave the right to become children of God...' (v12)

We continue to explore together the matter of experience and expression. Some, we said, concentrate on building up their experience of God but are not good at expressing it – giving out to others. Then others are good at giving out but not at taking in; they fail to deepen and develop their knowledge and experience of God. Whatever language we use – experience and expression, receptivity and response, taking in and giving out – it is clear that they are as integral to each other as an unborn baby is to its mother. Before we can give we must receive.

John sums up this thought in the words of our text today: '... to all who did receive him... he gave the right to *become*...'. How do we get the power to become? First by receptivity: 'to all who *did receive* him' (my emphasis). How does a plant get power to become? By surrendering, adjusting, receiving. Then and only then is it able to give. Suppose a plant tried to give out without receiving – if such a thing were possible. What would happen? It would shrivel up and die. No receptivity, no response. No assimilation, no expression.

A scientist has defined life as 'receiving from one's environment'. You and I live physically because we receive from our environment food, water, air, and so on. In the same way we live spiritually by taking in from our spiritual environment, the kingdom of God. What happens if we do not receive physically? We languish and die. What happens if we do not receive spiritually? Spiritual death creeps over us. No matter how naturally self-expressive and outgoing you are, you need to take in daily the resources of heaven if you are to remain a balanced Christian.

Father, You are leading me towards a more balanced life. For I cannot be mature without balance. Help me not to be like a dammed-up stream, with plenty flowing in but nothing flowing out. In Christ's name. Amen.

2 Samuel 18:19–33; Ezekiel 17:5–8

1. Contrast the two messengers.
2. Why would the vine flourish?

Time Alone! 21 OCT

FOR READING AND MEDITATION – MATTHEW 6:1–14

'But when you pray, go into your room,
close the door and pray to your Father…' (v6)

We ended yesterday with the statement: No matter how naturally self-expressive and outgoing you are, you need to take in daily the resources of heaven if you are to remain a balanced Christian. This means: be willing to spend time alone with God.

Introverts reading this will say (to themselves) 'Amen'. Extroverts might say (to others) 'Ouch', for extroverts draw a lot of their energy from being with people, and often need interaction to discover what they think. I sympathise with your temperamental difficulty if you are extrovert, but if you are to express through your extrovert nature the power of God, you need to draw from His resources, otherwise it is natural energy that is coming through – your energy and not the energy of Christ.

Listen to these powerful words of James Russell Lowell (1819–1891), which make this point clearly:

> *If the chosen soul could never be alone*
> *In deep mid-silence, open-doored to God,*
> *No greatness ever had been dreamed or done,*
> *The nurse of full-grown souls is solitude.*

The cause of many of our problems, said Blaise Pascal, arises from the fact that we cannot sit still in a quiet room for an hour. But if we can, and if in that hour we make contact with God – what then? We will rise to go out into life with something to give other than our natural energy. We will go with God and we will give out God.

My Father and my God, You are offering to me breathtaking advice and breathtaking power. Help me humbly to take in and give out, to experience You and to express You. In Jesus' name. Amen.

Matthew 14:23; Mark 1:35–39; Luke 5:16
1. What did Jesus do often?
2. How did He combine experience and expression?

Now Let Him Out

22 OCT

FOR READING AND MEDITATION – HEBREWS 13:7–21
'And do not forget to do good and to share with others...' (v16)

We have been emphasising the need to build up and develop our experience of God, for without experience we have little to express. Yesterday we considered those people who are extrovert in nature, who struggle to seek out solitude in order to meet with God. But what about those on the other end of the scale who have a rich experience of God but do not express it? That's what we must get to grips with now.

A poet whose name I have not been able to trace once wrote these words:

Every morning lean thine arm awhile
Upon the window sill of heaven
And gaze upon thy God,
Then with the vision in thy heart
Turn strong to meet the day.

You can't 'turn strong to meet the day' unless you have the vision in your heart. And what is this 'vision'? It is the vision that comes from experiencing God.

Experience is wonderful, especially the experience of God, but the experience is not an end in itself; it must end in expression. It is one thing to have a beautiful experience of God, but it is another to share that experience with others. There must be inflow and outflow, otherwise the inflow will dry up. Billy Graham, when speaking about the Holy Spirit, said, 'The Holy Spirit is like electricity; He won't come in unless He can get out.'

You have the Holy Spirit within you. That is your experience. Now let Him out. That will be the expression.

Father, I am so thankful for the privilege of looking into Your face each day, reading Your Word and reflecting on all You say to me. Help me to go with You into the day and give out for You. In Jesus' name. Amen.

Acts 2:1–4,14; 3:1–10; 4:1–4
1. How did Peter express his experience?
2. What were the results?

An Infallible Spiritual Law 23 OCT

FOR READING AND MEDITATION – NUMBERS 10:29-36

'If you come with us, we will share with you
whatever good things the Lord gives us.' (v32)

For one more day we discuss the need to express our experience of God. If we are to be balanced then we must discipline ourselves to do this. There should be as much discipline in giving out as there is in taking in. Many Christians fail to share what they have received from God and thus what they have tends to go stale. We need to sit down with one another more frequently and say, 'What has the Lord been telling you recently? Tell me about what you are hearing from God in your reading of His Word or in your personal prayer times.' There is a verse in the Old Testament that goes like this: 'Then those who feared the Lord talked with each other…' (Mal. 3:16).

A man told me that while he was standing in the foyer of his church he overheard two other men talking. One commented, 'I heard a wonderful sermon when I was on holiday.' The other said, 'I did too.' And that, apparently, was the end of the conversation. Some are earnest and regular in their Quiet Time and concentrate on building up their experience of God, but they are not as earnest or regular in their expression of it. They have never disciplined themselves to share. If someone engages them in conversation and jolts it out of them, then they share, but the sharing seems to depend on accident more than on choice – whim rather than will.

How are you doing in relation to this matter of experience and expression? Does your experience of God flow out in your expression of God? What God gives you is like bread. If it is not broken and shared it grows mouldy and goes bad. The more you share the more you will have to share. It is an infallible spiritual law.

O Father, help me not to become weary with the challenges. Show me clearly that not only do You lift the standards high but You supply the power by which I can reach up to them. Amen.

Exodus 16:13-20; 2 Timothy 1:5-13; 2:1-2
1. What happened when the Israelites did not use what God had given?
2. Of what process was Timothy a part?

I Say This in Love

24 OCT

FOR READING AND MEDITATION – EPHESIANS 4:1–16

'Speaking the truth in love, we will grow to become
in every respect the mature body of him…' (v15)

We come now to the last pair of opposites – truth and love. Scripture holds these two in balance, and so must we. Some people are so focused on promoting love in their lives that they overlook the importance of truth. Have you ever heard this argument: 'Let's forget our doctrinal differences in the interests of Christian love'? The idea sounds very plausible, doesn't it, but it is not biblical. Scripture commands us to love, but it also commands us to abide by the truth. Others adopt the attitude that truth is all-important and pursue it at the expense of love. So dogged is their zeal for truth that they become harsh, rude, and sometimes downright obnoxious.

I have often heard one person say to another, 'Now I'm telling you this in love', and yet I could tell by their tone of voice and the angry look on their face that though there was evidence of truth there was little evidence of love. Love that is not undergirded by truth can become sickly sentimentalism, and truth that is not shot through with love can become steel-like and hard. Let those who say it does not matter what you believe as long as you love, go back once more to their Bibles, for everywhere the Scripture binds truth and love together. They are like conjoined twins. And let those, also, who say the manner in which you raise a matter with another person is unimportant as long as you speak the truth, open up their New Testaments once again and read words such as those at the top of this page today: 'speaking the truth in love'.

It should not be difficult for Spirit-filled believers to maintain this biblical balance, for the Holy Spirit is Himself 'the Spirit of truth' whose first fruit is 'love'.

Dear Father, burn these words into my heart so that I shall be as truthful as I am loving, and as loving as I am truthful. Help me see that my way of life will not work unless it works Your way – the way of truth and love. Amen.

James 2:15–17; 1 John 4:7–21
1. How did James explain that truth and love should combine?
2. Why may saying 'I love God' be inadequate?

The Highest Emphasis

25 OCT

FOR READING AND MEDITATION – 2 CORINTHIANS 5:11–21

'For Christ's love compels us, because
we are convinced that one died for all...' (v14)

There are those in the Church who are determined to maintain the truths of God's Word, come what may. For that we must be thankful. But so often their pronouncements of truth are visibly lacking in love; thus the truth has little impact. I would say to those whose truth-telling is not balanced by love that you are not following in the footsteps of the Master, nor indeed of one of His greatest servants, the apostle Paul. Jesus' love was a central aspect of His life, and He insists that it is in ours also. Did Jesus pass on the torch of love to His disciples? He most certainly did. Peter talked about it as being supremely important. So did John. And so did Paul.

You will have gathered from the Acts of the Apostles, I am sure, that Paul was a fighter. When we first meet him in Scripture, He was ready to kill people to make them love God. Then came an amazing change. He was visited by the risen Christ on the road to Damascus and the germ of God's love got into his spiritual bloodstream, so much so that from that day to the day he died he was like a man burning with a raging fever – the fever of God's love. When writing his first letter to the Corinthians, he made love his highest emphasis, as we see from 1 Corinthians 13. And when writing his second letter he tells them that he was *compelled* by Christ's love.

Those who are prepared to do battle whenever they think the truth of God is being compromised need to remember that though it is right to stand up for the truth, it is wrong if it is not done in a spirit of love.

O Father, I am grateful for the words of Your servant Paul, for he could not have uttered them unless Your Spirit was speaking through him. As he held the torch of love aloft, so must I. Help me do just that, dear Father. Amen.

John 1:16–17; 1 Corinthians 13:1–13
1. Contrast Moses and Jesus.
2. Why is love the greatest?

A 'Fallen' Church

FOR READING AND MEDITATION – 1 TIMOTHY 1:1–11

'Stay there in Ephesus so that you may command
certain people not to teach false doctrines any longer…' (v3)

The Ephesian church had a marvellous beginning when the Holy Spirit came upon them (Acts 19:1–7), and such was the impact of the Spirit on the community that people who practised magic arts came and publicly burned books worth 50,000 pieces of silver. 'In this way the word of the Lord spread widely and grew in power' (Acts 19:20). It was a great beginning, but it was not long before some got off-track in their teaching. Paul asks Timothy to set things straight. So, what happened after this?

By the time John writes to the Ephesians in Revelation 2:1–7, we read that although they became sound in their doctrine, something vital was missing: 'I know your deeds, your hard work and your perseverance… [but] you have forsaken your first love.' Then he continues: 'Consider how far you have fallen! Repent… If you do not repent, I will come to you and remove your lampstand from its place.' Later these words are added: 'You hate the practices of the Nicolaitans, which I also hate.' The problem with the Ephesian church was that they were better at hating than loving, a problem which some churches have today. I know communities of God's people who are strong at hating evil but not strong at loving. The Ephesian church was a top-notch church in the eyes of many – busy and industrious – but in the eyes of Christ they had 'fallen'.

By that standard I would say many contemporary churches have 'fallen' – correct in doctrine, beautiful in ritual, eloquent in preaching, rich in culture, but lacking in love. Such churches should be careful, for if this lack of love is not repented of, Christ will come and remove His lampstand from their midst.

Lord Jesus Christ, Your relentless but loving eyes see where we are ailing. Help us not to dodge the issue or make excuses. We repent, so give us another chance – another chance to love. For Your own dear name's sake. Amen.

1 Corinthians 4:14–21; 2 Corinthians 2:1–11
1. How did Paul relate to the Corinthians?
2. What were his concerns?

The Power of Love

27 OCT

FOR READING AND MEDITATION – 1 PETER 1:13–25

'Love one another deeply, from the heart.' (v22)

Today we ask: is the way of love a practicable way to live? If I were to select the most outstanding characters in the New Testament, I would choose the following: Jesus, Stephen, Paul, and John. Why these four? Because they were all masters of the art of loving.

Jesus died with the word of love upon His lips: 'Father, forgive them, for they do not know what they are doing' (Luke 23:34). And Stephen did the same: 'Lord, do not hold this sin against them' (Acts 7:60). Paul said: '… everyone deserted me. May it not be held against them' (2 Tim. 4:16). And some of the last words of the apostle John were these: '… we ought to lay down our lives for our brothers and sisters' (1 John 3:16).

A story I love to remind myself of whenever I think about the power of love was first told in a magazine called *Fellowship*. It concerns an American missionary to China who, during the difficult war years, refused to hand over the keys of an abandoned American university to the Japanese officer demanding them. The officer threatened the missionary with death by a firing squad if he did not obey him. Still the missionary refused, and three soldiers were selected and lined up to shoot him. As they pointed their guns at him, the missionary smiled his broadest and most loving smile. They stood there sheepishly, lowered their guns and refused to shoot. An onlooker said the Japanese officer was so amazed that he did not discipline the soldiers. He too melted under the power of love. Later, the missionary made tea for the officer and his soldiers before they went on their way. Love conquered. There is no greater power.

O God my Father, make me a more loving person, for this is the only way life will work. Teach me to launch out in love, and let it be my only attitude. In Jesus' name I pray. Amen.

2 Kings 6:8–23; Matthew 5:44; 1 Thessalonians 4:9–10
1. Contrast Elisha and the king of Israel.
2. What does God teach and inspire us to do?

Stand Up and Be Counted

28 OCT

FOR READING AND MEDITATION – REVELATION 2:12–17

'To the one who is victorious, I will give some of the hidden manna.' (v17)

We have seen that without love, truth becomes hard and steellike. Christians whose noses begin to twitch whenever they sense truth is being compromised and who are all set to fight but show no evidence of love, need to repent. Christ may come and remove His lampstand from their midst. But what if love is present but there is no passionate concern for truth? That also is an issue, and one we must examine now.

Those who are prepared to demonstrate brotherly love to all, but are not prepared to stand up for truth when it is being compromised, are also off-balance. I began this section, you remember, by saying that our Lord Jesus Christ is deeply concerned for the preservation and propagation of the truth. Our reading today tells the story of the church at Pergamum – a church where truth was being compromised. They were not lacking in love but they were lacking in a willingness to deal with the error that was circulating among them. In the name of love they were too tolerant of the false prophets who were part of their fellowship.

The privilege of guarding the truth which has been vouchsafed to us through the Scriptures, should be of great concern to every Christian. It certainly is of great concern to our Lord, for here He takes the leaders of the church to task for not confronting those in error. He wants us to love Him, but He also wants us to guard and preserve the truth He has given us. Those who think that it is possible to overlook error in the interests of love need to think again. In fact, they need to repent, because this too could bring our Lord into their midst not to bless but to judge.

O God, forgive me if I have been too tolerant of error. I see that I am called as part of Your Church to guard and preserve true doctrine. Help me hold the truth in love, and love others in the truth. In Jesus' name. Amen.

1 Corinthians 5:1–13; Galatians 5:1–12
1. How did Paul respond to sin and false doctrine?
2. What was his wish for false teachers?

The Irreducible Minimum

29 OCT

FOR READING AND MEDITATION – ROMANS 10:1-13

'If you declare with your mouth, "Jesus is Lord,"
and believe in your heart...' (v9)

If we are to stand up for truth then we must understand what truth really is. The question 'What is truth?', you remember, was one which Pilate asked Jesus (John 18:38). But in the famous words of Bacon: 'He did not stay for an answer.' There are many things about which Christians may disagree – as long as we disagree without being disagreeable. There are two things, however, about which there should be no disagreement, and anyone who does not subscribe to them ought to be deemed as being in error. This does not mean that such people should be treated as pariahs, but it can be made clear to them that close fellowship cannot be maintained when these matters are not accepted. The two issues I refer to are these: the authority of the Bible, and the Person of Christ. Speaking personally, these two issues have been the touchstone by which I have always agreed to have fellowship or not to have fellowship with others.

Take first the Person of Christ. One great preacher said, 'Christianity *is* Christ.' To be a Christian means accepting Him as Saviour, as Lord, and as the second Person of the Trinity. Anyone who denies this truth cannot be a Christian and therefore cannot be accepted as being in fellowship in the Christian Church.

The second belief to which every Christian should subscribe is the authority of the Bible. If we do not believe its truths, bring ourselves under its authority, and obey its commands, we cannot call ourselves Christians. We may describe ourselves as moral or respectable, but true believers are Bible people who guard what has been entrusted to them – earnestly contending for the faith and holding the truth in love.

Father, I know I must be tolerant, understanding, and respectful of other people's beliefs, but never let me become so tolerant that my convictions are compromised. In Christ's name I pray. Amen.

2 Timothy 3:16; 2 Peter 1:20-21; 1 John 4:1-3; Jude 3-4
1. Why is the Bible not just a collection of religious sayings?
2. Why is the deity of Christ so important?

Strong Yet Weak

30 OCT

FOR READING AND MEDITATION – JOHN 15:1–7
'You are already clean because of the word I have spoken to you.' (v3)

During these meditations on the theme of unbalanced virtues it will have become clear to many that though they are strong in certain virtues, those virtues may, without them even realising it, easily become vices. I wonder, have some of you been talking to each other as you have followed me day by day in these meditations? I feel like saying to you as our Lord said when He joined the two disciples on the way to Emmaus, 'What have you been discussing together?' (see Luke 24:17).

The Lord is asking you a similar question right now: what have been your thoughts as you have journeyed over these past weeks? Perhaps you have been thinking: 'I am strong in some virtues but weak in others.' These weaknesses must be brought to the Lord for His balance. But keep in mind also that our strengths as well as our weaknesses need to be brought to Him. We tend to think that it is only our weaknesses that get us into trouble, but often it is our strengths that do that. Peter's downfall resulted from his loyalty – which was his strength. He said to Jesus, 'I will never leave You', but he finished up denying his Lord and insisting that he had never known Him (see Matt. 26:69–75). His loyalty was not counter-balanced by humility, so the driving force of loyalty pushed him towards spiritual pride, and his pride went before his fall – as it always does.

Surrender both your strengths and weaknesses into Christ's hands right now and trust Him to work within you to bring about a better balance. He stands ready to steady your life, and all He needs is your consent and co-operation. You give Him your willing heart and He will give you His wonderful power.

O God, set a watch not only at the place of my weakness, but also at the place of my strength. I dread to think that any light in me may become darkness. In Christ's name. Amen.

Isaiah 40:28–31; 2 Corinthians 12:7–10
1. What happens to those who hope and wait on the Lord?
2. Why did Paul boast in his weakness?

The Last Word

31 OCT

FOR READING AND MEDITATION – MATTHEW 1:18-25

'You are to give him the name Jesus,
because he will save his people from their sins.' (v21)

As we end this series of meditations we take a brief backward glance at the road we have travelled together. We began by making the point that virtues which are not balanced can easily become vices. In order to be a fully developed person, one's virtues must be held in tension by other virtues, for it is in that very tension that strength is to be found. There are many pairs of opposites we could have looked at, but space allowed us to consider just eight: speech and actions, the mental and emotional, assertiveness and yieldedness, self-concern and concern for others, being conservative and being radical, trusting and trying, experience and expression, and love and truth.

But what is to be my last word? It is based on our text for today: 'You are to give him the name Jesus, because he will save his people from their sins.' This was the text of the first sermon I ever preached. In these words lies our hope. During that first sermon I said, 'There are two things we need – light to help us understand the mystery of life, and power to give us mastery in life' (I have always loved alliteration!). In Jesus these two needs are met. He illuminates life by having come to this world and shown us how to live. But more, He gives power for the mastery of life. He saves us from our sins and from the things that have the potential for sin – such as unbalanced living.

Over these past weeks He has thrown some light on the unbalance that may be present in our lives; now He wants to supply the power so that we can walk through life without a limp. We have found Him as light, now let us go on to find Him as power.

Lord Jesus Christ, I am thankful that You save me from all sin, and also from those things that can quickly become sin. You have given me light. Now give me power – power to become. For Your own dear name's sake. Amen.

2 Peter 1:1-11; Colossians 3:1-14

1. For what should we be eager?
2. How should we live?

PRAY IT FORWARD ▶▶▶

Father, You hold all things together. Teach me to walk in balance - work and rest, prayer and action, grace and truth - so that my life reflects the harmony of Your kingdom. Amen.

PAY IT FORWARD ▶▶▶

At Waverley Abbey, we help people find God in the midst of life's pressures. Whether through retreats, resources, or mentoring, we guide others into rhythms that restore and renew. **Your donation enables us to make room for many more people to encounter God.**

Visit **waverleyabbey.org/donate-to-edwj** call **01252 784700** or scan the **QR code** ▶

NOVEMBER & DECEMBER

SHARING YOUR FAITH

INTRODUCTION

At the heart of the Christian life is a calling not only to believe, but to share what we believe. In this theme, Sharing Your Faith, we are reminded that the gospel is not a private treasure to be hoarded, but a life-giving truth to be shared.

Many believers struggle with fear, hesitation, or a sense of inadequacy when it comes to witnessing – but as Selwyn Hughes shows, sharing our faith is not about being eloquent or forceful, but about being authentic and obedient.

These devotions encourage us to see evangelism as a natural overflow of our relationship with Christ, and they equip us with the biblical perspective and spiritual confidence we need to speak of Jesus with courage, compassion, and clarity.

Lift Jesus Higher

1 NOV

FOR READING AND MEDITATION – JOHN 12:23-36

'And I, when I am lifted up from the earth,
will draw all people to myself.' (v32)

The world is waiting for good news. Anxiously men and women scan the headlines searching for some glimmer of light in the slow dark development of international politics. To say that the men and women of this age are unhappy is to say the least. They are sick. For too long humanity has been fed upon a diet of extreme optimism and despairing pessimism. There is need for a change. Where then can we turn for a glimmer of hope in the present world situation?

Is it on the chair of the scientist, the philosopher, or the politician? No. World leaders have had their chance. The only hope for this planet is to hear, from the lips of those who have experienced Christ's transforming power, the good news of the gospel. Next to worship, the bold proclamation of our faith is, therefore, the highest priority of the Christian Church. As we consider this topic in these next two months of *Every Day with Jesus* we must commit ourselves to the task of proclaiming the message of the gospel with boldness and enthusiasm to those in our neighbourhood and circle of friends. It is entirely possible that you could be entering a season that is as penetrating and rewarding as you have ever known.

Christ's gospel is only effective as it is proclaimed. It must not be apologised for, watered down, or adjusted to suit the interests of this modern age – not even disguised so that it gets past an unbeliever's guard. On this, the first day of this series, let us dedicate ourselves to the task of lifting Jesus higher and, by every means available, spread abroad His fame. We must say with Charles Wesley, *'O let me commend my Saviour to you'*.

O Father, help me to have a new encounter with You and with Your Son. And then help me to do something about sharing it. In Jesus' name. Amen.

Luke 10:1-20; Exodus 4:12; Acts 10:42; 22:15
1. Write three definitions of the word 'evangelism'.
2. In what current efforts of evangelism are you involved?

The Great Commission

2 NOV

FOR READING AND MEDITATION – MARK 16:15–20

'He said to them, "Go into all the world
and preach the gospel to all creation."' (v15)

We began yesterday by affirming that, next to worship, the highest priority of the Christian Church is the bold proclamation of our faith. This is a fact which applies to every generation of the Church's existence on this earth. Let us be quite clear about this before going any further – the urgency of evangelism does not arise from the call of Christian leaders for they only repeat and re-echo what Christ first said. The word, 'Go', is chiselled into the bedrock of the Christian Church by its Master-Builder and, no matter what happens, they can never be obliterated or removed. If words mean anything then it is quite clear from what Jesus is saying here, in our text today, that He intended the *Great Commission* to take precedence over every other form of Church activity.

When a proposal to evangelise non-Christian nations was brought before the Scottish Church in 1796, it was met with a resolution stating that to spread the gospel to such nations is 'highly preposterous – philosophy and learning must take precedence.' Upon hearing this, Thomas Erskine called out to the Moderator, 'Pass me that Bible.' Turning to the sixteenth chapter of Mark's Gospel, he read to the whole assembly the words which appear in our text, but in an older translation, 'Go ye into all the world, and preach the gospel.' Observers said that, such was the force and power of Erskine's reading, the words of the Great Commission burst over their heads like 'a clap of thunder'. I hope, with all my heart, that these words will burst with the same explosive force in every section of Christ's Church this very day.

O God, having put my hand to the plough I do not intend to look back. This shall be no halfway business. You command and I obey. Show me how to share my faith with ever-increasing effectiveness. In Jesus' name. Amen.

Joel 1; Matthew 9:37–38; John 4:35–38; Galatians 6:9
1. Compare Joel 1 with the condition of our nation.
2. How can we be sure of reaping a harvest?

Christian Contagion

3 NOV

FOR READING AND MEDITATION – PHILIPPIANS 1:1–21

'Being confident of this, that he who began a good work in you will carry it on to completion until the day of Christ Jesus.' (v6)

We are seeing that the urgency and importance of evangelism does not arise simply from the call of Christian leaders but from the very words of Christ Himself. Evangelism is not an imposition – something imposed on us by zealous ministers and priests – but an exposition – something exposed out of the very facts of Christian experience. Paul puts it this way: 'I always pray with joy because of your partnership in the gospel from the first day until now, being confident of this, that he who began a good work in you will carry it on to completion until the day of Christ Jesus' (Phil. 1:4–6). From the very first day they stepped into the kingdom of God, they began to contribute to it – to spread it. It was not something they learned; it was instinctive. It was as natural as a baby's cry at birth.

Whilst we are thankful when Christian leaders call their churches to commit to evangelism, the work of evangelism must not be seen as an imposition. Anyone who starts to get excited by the privilege of sharing their faith will want to make it a lifestyle. And why? Because once we begin to share our faith then our faith begins to mean something more to us. Christianity, you see, is not merely a conception – it is a contagion. And when the contagion is lost, the conception, too, is lost. It is a law of the mind that that which is not expressed soon dies. Nothing is really ours until we share it. The expression of our faith is of the essence of our faith.

O God, You have given me the greatest work in the world, the work of bringing others to You. Help me, not only to dedicate myself to that task but to be faithful to it. For Jesus' sake. Amen.

John 3; Matthew 10:27; John 5:24
1. When was the last time you shared your faith?
2. What does John 3 tell us about sharing our faith?

The Impulse to Share

4 NOV

FOR READING AND MEDITATION – ACTS 6:1–8

'Brothers and sisters, choose seven men… full of the Spirit and wisdom. We will turn this responsibility over to them… They chose… Philip…' (vv3,5)

The conclusion to which we are coming, in these first few days of our studies, is this – evangelism is not something imposed on the Church; it is something inherent. The work of winning men and women to Jesus Christ is not merely an occupation but an outcome – it is the outcome of the nature of life itself. Inherent in all life is the impulse to create – life produces life. If it doesn't create it dies. The impulse to share life is wonderfully illustrated in the life of Philip. He was given a task by the Early Church which was not intended to be evangelistic. In fact, the apostles gave up the work of serving tables so that they could give more of their time to evangelism.

But, strangely enough the only man who had the title of 'Evangelist' in the Acts of the Apostles was the man who had a layman's task imposed upon him and who was not supposed to get involved in evangelistic work. The impulse to share Christ, however, was greater than the imposition. The reach of his soul went beyond the reach of his hand and, although delegated to share out the goods and serve tables, he became involves also in sharing the gospel and became known affectionately in the Scriptures as 'Philip the evangelist' (Acts 21:8). In fact, this lay evangelist became so active that he kept the apostles on the trot following up his ministry. 'When the apostles in Jerusalem heard that Samaria had accepted the word of God, they sent Peter and John to Samaria' (Acts 8:14).

I say again, evangelism is not something imposed; it is inherent. We cancel the power of the gospel in ourselves unless we pass on itspower to others.

O God, if the expression of my faith is the essence of my faith then help me to so live that my faith becomes contagious, convincing, and compelling. In Jesus' name. Amen.

Genesis 1; John 15
1. What was God's first command to Adam and Eve?
2. What is Jesus teaching about fruitfulness?

No Private World

5 NOV

FOR READING AND MEDITATION – 1 PETER 3:8–22

'Always be prepared to give an answer to everyone who asks you to give the reason for the hope that you have. But do this with gentleness and respect...' (v15)

We are studying together the urgency and importance of evangelism. There are three cardinal signs indicative of the new life in Christ: (1) The desire to pray and read Scriptures; (2) The urge to join others in Christian fellowship; (3) The desire to bring others to Jesus Christ. Some have even gone as far as to say that without the last-named there is no new life. Bishop Stephen Neill once said, 'It is not for any minister to say, "I am not an evangelist." The minister has been ordained for the purpose of winning men and women to Jesus Christ and if he is not doing it then it ought to be questioned whether he ought to be in the ministry at all. So with a layman; if he is not willing to be a witness it is time he gave up calling himself a Christian.'

Strong words, but they are words the need to be said. Any why? Because if the Church fails to win others to Christ then quite simply there will be no Church in the future. This is not the main motive for evangelism, of course, but it is a face that cannot be overlooked nevertheless. When we of the Church today die, the Church dies with us – unless the Church of tomorrow has been won in the meantime.

If you, as a member, are unable to share your faith with others, you contribute – however unintentionally – to the decline of the Church. If this continues collectively, the Christian Church may not exist a hundred years from now. The idea that a Christian can live entirely in a private world, disconnected from others, is misleading. But in truth, there are no fully private worlds – we are connected, and we bear responsibility for one another, for better or worse.

O God, give me the will to share my faith for I know if I have the will then it won't be long before I have the opportunity. In Jesus' name. Amen.

Luke 24:36–53; Acts 10:34–43; 1:8
1. Of what are we to be witnesses?
2. How were the disciples to become witnesses?

All of Us – Evangelists

6 NOV

FOR READING AND MEDITATION – JOHN 3:25-36

'He must become greater; I must become less.' (v30)

We said yesterday that there are no private worlds – we belong to each other for good or ill. Although we may not realise it every one of us is, in a sense, an evangelist. We are all involved in propagating something. 'Out of the abundance of the heart the mouth speaks' – speaks something (Matt. 12:34, NKJV). Some propagate bitterness and ill-will. It spills over onto those whom they meet and douses them with negative feelings. That is their evangelism. Others propagate themselves. They introduce 'self' into every conversation, at every opportunity, and in every situation. Simon Peter, at one time in his life, was like this. He said, 'Lord, we have left everything to follow you!' (Mark 10:28). Everything – except himself. But he was not the only disciple to have this fault. Remember James and John? They once said to Jesus, 'Let one of us sit at your right and the other at your left in your glory' (Mark 10:35-41). With Jesus standing right beside them, they were involved in preaching the gospel of themselves.

All of us are evangelists of something. We propagate the attitudes and ideas that lie deep within our hearts. If this is so then let us choose here and now to become evangelists of Jesus. We don't have to be saints to share Him with the world, but we do have to be sincere. We are imperfect proclaimers of a perfect Saviour. But in proclaiming the Perfect, we, ourselves, tend to become more perfect.

Gracious Father, I point to everything on this earth with hesitation – except to Your Son. With Him my hesitations drop away. He is the sinless, spotless Lamb of God and in pointing I, too, am perfected. Thank You, Father. Amen.

James 3; Matthew 12:34-37; Job 6:25
1. What major tool does God use in evangelism?
2. List five other avenues He uses to spread His Word.

Save – and Be Saved!

7 NOV

FOR READING AND MEDITATION – EZEKIEL 33:1–16

'But if the watchman sees... and does not blow the trumpet...
I will hold the watchman accountable for their blood.' (v6)

We have seen over this past week that from the moment we share our faith with someone else then it begins to mean something more to us. A Jewish Rabbi said, 'All religions, from time to time, are glad to have enquirers come to them, but Christianity is different – it does not wait for people to come and ask questions but goes and seeks them out. It goes to the lowest, the undeserving and the sinful.' We might add that if it didn't then it would sink back into Judaism from whence it came. When Christianity loses its fervour then it is not long before the facts of the gospel become faded and lose their glow. This is why we have so many Christians in our churches to whom the facts of the gospel are not alive – they fail to share their faith and thus their faith begins to fade. We cannot truly be evangelical without being evangelistic, and we cannot be evangelistic without being more evangelical.

A church I preached at in South Korea would admit no one as a member until they had won someone else to Jesus Christ. I tell you the atmosphere in that church was something I have not encountered in any other part of the world. These people are in the authentic tradition of the Christian faith which Harnack says, 'won all its early conquests through informal missionaries'. I once took an American friend around Westminster Abbey and in a loud voice he enquired, 'Anyone been saved here lately?' It was a good questions for 'no heart is pure that is not passionate, no virtue is safe that is not enthusiastic'. And no life is truly Christian unless Christianising. Save and be saved!

O God, help me to make my priorities Your priorities and deepen the growing conviction within me that the greatest task I can ever accomplish on this earth is to introduce someone to Your Son. Amen.

Luke 15; 19:10
1. What is the message of Christ in Luke 15?
2. What is taught here concerning seeking the lost?

An Angel at Its Heart

FOR READING AND MEDITATION – MATTHEW 28:1–8

'The angel said to the women… "He is not here; he has risen…"' (vv5–6)

Having considered over the past week the importance and urgency of evangelism, it is time now to break open the word and ask ourselves: what do we mean by 'evangelism'? The word 'evangelism' was in use long before New Testament times and was used mainly to describe some welcome announcement from the Emperor proclaimed in the Greek-speaking provinces of the Roman world. Evangelism is, therefore, the proclamation of good news. There is a charming story told of the famous painter and sculptor Michelangelo, which tells of how once, while visiting a friend, he pointed to a huge block of marble and said, 'An angel is imprisoned in that stone and I am going to let him out.' The word 'evangelism' is rather like that block of marble. There is an angel at its heart. Subtract the first and last syllables and what do you have left? 'Angel'. To evangelise is quite literally to 'play the angel'. The announcement of the good news that Christ was born in Bethlehem, given by the angels in Luke 2:10, was true evangelism.

The best modern definition of evangelism is no doubt that of the *Lausanne Covenant* drawn up in 1974 which says, 'Evangelism is the proclamation of the historical, biblical Christ as Saviour and Lord, with a view to persuading people to come to Him personally and so be reconciled to God.' Although the word 'evangelism' is used in Christian circles to describe almost any endeavour of the Christian Church, I shall limit the word in these studies to the proclamation of the good news of God in Jesus Christ to those who do not know Him.

Loving, heavenly Father, how can I be silent about You? If I were, the very stones would cry out. Save me from silence when so much is at stake. In Jesus' name. Amen.

Acts 2:14–47; John 15:27; Acts 22:14–15
1. List five important characteristics of Peter's proclamation.
2. List ten results that followed.

Love in Action

9 NOV

FOR READING AND MEDITATION – 2 CORINTHIANS 10:7–18

'So that we can preach the gospel in the regions beyond you. For we do not want to boast about work already done in someone else's territory.' (v16)

Those of us who like to have biblical authority for everything we believe concerning God, Christ, and His Church, will be surprised to discover that the word 'evangelism' does not appear anywhere in the Scriptures. Nor does the word 'evangelist' often occur in the Bible – just three specific occasions. Philip, the deacon, was called an evangelist (Acts 21:8). Timothy was told to do the work of an evangelist (2 Tim. 4:5), and Paul describes the evangelist as one of Christ's gifts to His Church (Eph. 4:11). However, the verb form of the word appears more than fifty times. Dr Leighton Ford suggests that the Bible, by using verbs to talk about evangelism, puts the emphasis on *action*.

A careful examination of the fifty-two occasions where the verbs appear in the New Testament show in every instance a picture of intense care and concern on the part of an individual to share the good news of the gospel. Take the example before us in our reading for today. Here Paul's heart is on fire. Such is the passion that burns in his heart that he cannot remain satisfied with preaching the gospel in the regions around – he must preach it in the regions *beyond*. No sooner had Paul planted a New Testament Church than something inside him said, 'Now carry the message still further.' Something blazed inside this great soulwinner. What was it? It was the constraining love of Christ which so monopolised his life that he ached to share that love with others.

Evangelism is love in action. I like the way Dr Paul Little put it: 'Evangelism is one beggar telling another where to find bread.'

O God, show me that if I am vocal about other things but silent about You then all my values are twisted. Help me to have as my motto, 'Freely have I received so freely do I give.' For Jesus' sake. Amen.

Luke 10:25-37; 1 John 3:1; Romans 5:8; Ephesians 2:4-5
1. What is Luke 10 teaching about our responsibility to the lost?
2. What motivated the Samaritan to become involved?

The Starting Point

10 NOV

FOR READING AND MEDITATION – MATTHEW 28:9-20

'Then Jesus came to them and said, "All authority in heaven and on earth has been given to me. Therefore go and make disciples…"' (vv18-19)

Although most Christian would agree that evangelism means the sharing of the good news of God in Jesus Christ, there is not the same agreement on the means by which that good news should be spread. And let's face it, there is room for a wide difference of opinion here. Some believe that the best way of witnessing to an unbelieving world is to put on large evangelistic rallies in football stadiums. Others believe the best way is by individual witness. Still others believe all evangelism ought to be channelled through the local church. One minister I know says (and he has a point): 'Para-church organisations are not God's way of winning people to Himself. We must move as one body of people (the local church) into the local area around us, and this means no one must go off on their own and do their own thing evangelistically.'

We all have different views and opinions on how best to go about the work of evangelism and, as I have said, there is room in the Christian Church for these differences of opinion. Having said that, however, there are two things on which there can be no difference of opinion if our evangelism is to be considered as biblical evangelism. They are a kind of *starting point* and *finishing point* – two issues about which no division can be tolerated. And what are they? Jesus announces them in the passage before us today. He says: (1) 'All authority is given to me' and (2) 'Go and make disciples.' Our starting point is, therefore, quite clear. We begin our evangelism at the same point the early Christians began it by affirming clearly and categorically that 'Jesus is Lord'.

O God, help me to begin where the gospel begins – with submission to Your authority as Lord. Show me that unless I crown You Lord of all then I do not crown You Lord at all. Amen.

Acts 26; 10:36; 1 Timothy 6:15
1. What steps did Paul follow when sharing his testimony?
2. What was his central theme?

Is Jesus Lord?

11 NOV

FOR READING AND MEDITATION – 1 CORINTHIANS 12:1–3

'No one can say, "Jesus is Lord," except by the Holy Spirit.' (v3)

We said yesterday that whilst there is room in the Church for differences of opinion on the means and ways by which the good news of God in Jesus Christ is made known, no differences can be tolerated regarding the starting point and finishing point – namely the authority of Christ and the making of disciples. Evangelism *begins* in submission to the fact that Jesus Christ is Lord. Why is this so necessary? What does the authority of Jesus have to do with the sharing of our faith? It means firstly that we do not see *ourselves* as saviours.

The temptation we fall into when we begin to share Christ is to draw attention to ourselves and thus become reformers rather than evangelists. Submission to Christ's authority means that we see ourselves as servants and not masters. We are not better than others – although, of course, better off. We are not cleverer than others. We are not superior to others. Paul said, in writing to the Corinthians, 'Unlike so many, we do not peddle the word of God for profit. On the contrary, in Christ we speak before God with sincerity, as those sent from God' (2 Cor. 2:17).

The phrase 'peddle the word of God' is arresting. Peddlers peddle their wares for their own ends. How many Christians peddle God's Word to gain attention, to put themselves in the limelight or to satisfy their ego? There is just enough truth in this to make it sting. We cannot go any further until each one of us personally settles this issue. How can I ask other people to make Jesus the centre of their lives if He is not the centre of mine? I must ask myself: who is in charge of my life – me or Christ?

O God, save me from becoming a peddler of Your Word, someone using Your gospel for self-centred ends, but make me a proclaimer of it- someone who, in proclaiming the Perfect, becomes more perfect. Amen.

Luke 24:13–35; Acts 10:36–48
1. What was the real problem of the Emmaus Road disciples?
2. Why was Peter's sermon successful?

Christ Put Me Here

12 NOV

FOR READING AND MEDITATION – ACTS 10:34–43

'He commanded us to preach to the people and to testify that he is the one whom God appointed as judge of the living and the dead.' (v42)

We must spend another day in discussing the question of what the authority of Christ has to do with the subject of sharing our faith. We said yesterday that unless we acknowledge Jesus as Lord then our evangelism simply becomes the peddling of God's Word in which we use spiritual things as a means of satisfying our selfish ego. A missionary tells how he saw a bird settle on a cross of a church and make it a base of operation. The bird would sit on the cross until an insect came near and then would dart out and gobble it and return to the cross. It was a base for foraging. We can so easily use the Christian message for our own glorification.

The acknowledgement of Christ's total authority means that we are committed to Him using us, not us using Him. The second thing that the authority of Christ has to do with the sharing of our faith is that it makes it not a matter of choice, but a matter of requirement. As our text says, we are 'commanded' to present Christ to the world. It is not an elective; it is a commission.

Leighton Ford, in his book *Good News is for Sharing,* tells how one day he landed in Dakar, West Africa, at a small airport and, whilst there, met a missionary who came over to talk to him. He discovered during the conversation that the missionary had worked in the Muslim area for ten years and had seen no more than two or three people converted. A member of Mr. Ford's party said, 'Why do you stay here?' The man looked surprised at the question. 'Why do I stay here? Jesus Christ put me here. That's why!'

O God, I see that it's not so much where I am but what I am that is important to You. Help me to share my faith in the place You put me, today. For Jesus' sake. Amen.

John 13:1–17; 12:26; Philippians 2:1–11
1. What was Jesus demonstrating to the disciples?
2. In what way is servanthood related to authority?

The Ultimate Goal

13 NOV

FOR READING AND MEDITATION – JOHN 15:1–11

'This is to my Father's glory, that you bear much fruit,
showing yourselves to be my disciples.' (v8)

Having examined over the past few days the starting point of all evangelism – the authority of Christ – we move on now to consider the *goal* of evangelism: turning converts into disciples. The ultimate aim of all biblical evangelism is to 'make disciples'. Jesus Christ has not called us primarily to put up buildings, publish magazines, or organise special Christian events. These things may well be necessary but they are not our *primary* task. The specific command Christ gives us here means that we are not to be content with simply seeing people come to Christ, but we are to follow their progress with the utmost care and concern until their lives reflect the glory of God and the character of Jesus Christ.

A few years ago a dear friend of my wife's and mine brought a young married couple, living in the wealthy 'stockbrokers' belt' in Virginia Water, Surrey, to Christ. Not satisfied with simply leading them to Christ, she followed their progress with deep, prayerful concern. When, after a little while, they moved to the United States, she emphasised to them the need of finding a 'live' Christian church and of going on with Christ. Daily she prayed for them until news came that they had found a church and were growing in leaps and bounds in the things of God. Not so long ago I spent a little time in their beautiful home near Washington DC and I could not help but marvel at the way they had grown in Christ and were now reaching out to share their faith with others. They were now more than just 'converts' – they were well and truly 'disciples'.

Evangelism is not complete until the evangelised become evangelists.

Gracious God and loving, heavenly Father, thank You for showing me that the end of all evangelism is that the evangelised become evangelists. Help me not only to save a soul but to make a disciple. In Jesus' name. Amen.

Matthew 5–7; John 8:31; 15:8
1. How did Jesus make disciples?
2. List ten characteristics of discipleship from Matthew 5–7.

The Sustaining Assurance

14 NOV

FOR READING AND MEDITATION – MATTHEW 28:16–20

'And surely I am with you always, to the very end of the age.' (v20)

If God expects each Christian to be involved in the task of making disciples then we must stop thinking of evangelism as an elitist activity – something undertaken solely by ministers, priests, and itinerant preachers. Most Christians, whenever they hear the word 'evangelist', think of someone like Billy Graham who travelled from place to place bringing people to a point of decision, and then moving on. This kind of ministry is quite valid, of course, for God has put certain people in the Church for this purpose.

You may not be called to this type of ministry but you are most certainly called to the ministry of making disciples. How do we make disciples? We make disciples by telling others the story of Jesus Christ, by helping them come to a point of decision, by encouraging them to become linked with a live Christian church, and by demonstrating to them, by our love and by our actions, the reality of life in the kingdom of God. If you are about to wilt under the enormity of the task, take heart. Jesus Christ says, 'And surely I am with you always, to the very end of the age.' Roland Allen says of this phrase, 'The promised presence of Christ is not a reward offered to those who obey, but rather the assurance that those commanded *will* be able to obey.'

Get rid of the idea that evangelism is something we do for Jesus Christ. It is not. It is something He does through us. He does not say, 'Go out into the world and do something for Me.' Rather He says, 'As you go into the world, to work, to school, to play I am with you and in you making my authority known throughout the earth.'

Father, I am relieved that evangelism is not just a commission but a co-mission. I may be ordinary but with You I am extra-ordinary. Together we can change the world. Amen.

Matthew 10; John 1:38–51; Mark 3:13–19
1. List the types of people Jesus called as disciples.
2. Give ten characteristics of a disciple from Matthew 10.

Personal Experience

15 NOV

FOR READING AND MEDITATION – HEBREWS 3:7–19

'Today, if you hear his voice, do not harden your hearts...' (v15)

We come now to a week in which we shall examine together some of the reasons why Christians do not share their faith. If, as we have seen, the New Testament places so much emphasis on the need for personal evangelism, why are so many indifferent to this great demand? When one thinks of a convinced Communist or the hot enthusiasm of the soap box orators running around with their latest nostrum for curing the world's ills, how sad it is that so many churchgoers are tepid in this vital task.

There are, of course, many explanations for this lack of zeal. *Perhaps it's because of a lack of a deep personal experience of God.* You attend church regularly, participate in all its functions, even teach in the Sunday School, yet you lack a personal relationship with God and His Son, Jesus Christ. You travel along on the strength of last Sunday's sermon or the last good inspirational service, but as far as a daily relationship with God, through prayer and Bible reading, is concerned, you know nothing of that. Consequently, having no personal relationship with God, you have nothing to give away.

If I am accurately describing your condition, then the first step you should take after finishing this page is to put down this book, kneel before God in prayer, and invite Jesus Christ into your life as Saviour and Lord. Say, 'Lord Jesus Christ, I am sorry that for so long I have tried to run my life on my terms. Now I invite You in. Forgive my sin and help me live for You day by day.' Believe me, if you will do this then it will not be long before Your life becomes contagious and compelling.

O God my Father, I see so clearly that the effective proclamation of the Christian faith flows out of a personal encounter with You. Help me to experience this today. And if I have experienced it, then let its wonder deepen from this very moment. In Jesus' name. Amen.

Acts 9:1–31; 26:19; 2 Timothy 1:6–8
1. What were the characteristics of Paul's commission?
2. What was his response to God's voice?

Not Enough Bible Knowledge

16 NOV

FOR READING AND MEDITATION – 2 TIMOTHY 3:12–17

'All Scripture is God-breathed and is useful for teaching, rebuking, correcting and training in righteousness…' (v16)

We continue examining some of the major reasons why so many of us fail to actively share our faith with the world. A second reason why people fail to witness for Christ is *because they feel they do not have enough Bible knowledge.* If we wait to share Christ until we have a degree in theology or we have spent time researching answers to every conceivable question then we will probably go through life without ever once testifying to our faith.

Even spiritual 'babies' can share what they have experienced. Remember the blind man who was healed by Jesus in John 9? Some critics tried to stump him with some pretty heavy theological questions but he replied, 'One thing I do know. I was blind but now I see!' (v25). The Christian singer George Beverly Shea was asked by a friend, 'How much do you know about God?' 'Not very much,' replied Bev, 'but what I do know has changed my life.'

This does not mean, of course, that we should be content with our ignorance. The fact that God can use us with a minimum of knowledge does not mean that we can ignore the scriptural command to 'grow in the grace and knowledge of our Lord and Saviour Jesus Christ' (2 Peter 3:18). I would suggest three steps for getting to know the Bible: (1) *Read it every day.* Apart from the reading in this devotional aid, go through the Bible systematically, book by book; (2) *Attend a weekly Bible study.* If you don't have an in-depth Bible study group in your church then find one elsewhere and join it; (3) Consider a course such as *The Bible Course* from the Bible Society. These courses give accessible overview of the whole Bible and help you see how the story fits together, making personal study more rewarding.

Heavenly Father, help me to strike a balance in this matter. To share my faith I need not wait until my Bible knowledge is perfect but, at the same time, I must study to be one 'who correctly handles the word of truth' (2 Tim. 2:15). Please help me. Amen.

Psalm 119; 2 Timothy 2:15; Acts 17:11
1. List ten things that God's Word will do.
2. How much time do you spend studying God's Word?

Not a Salesman — 17 NOV

FOR READING AND MEDITATION – EXODUS 4:6-17

'Moses said to the Lord, "Pardon your servant, Lord. I have never been eloquent… I am slow of speech and tongue."' (v10)

Another reason why people fail to share their faith is because (so they say) *they do not have the right temperament for talking to people.* A man said to me the other day, 'I do not have the personality for witnessing. I leave that to the "salesman" types.' Brother Lawrence tells how one day, sitting under a tree, he discovered a wonderful Christian secret. For some time he had been struggling to be an effective Christian but as he looked at the tree, he thought to himself, 'In the cool of winter the tree is barren and unfruitful. As spring comes new life comes and buds appear. Then in summer the fruit comes.' He concluded that the tree before him was like his life, and there was no way he could make himself into a super personality for God to use. He could only trust God, in His own timing, to work through him and shape him into the person He wanted him to be. From that time onwards, Brother Lawrence rested in what he called 'the practice of the presence of God'.

Your weakest place can become your strongest place. John R. Mott says that the phrase he has repeated most in his life is, 'You can become strongest in your weakest place.' Jeremiah, when the call of God came to him, pleaded, 'I do not know how to speak; I am too young.' (Jer. 1:6). But he offered that trembling hesitation to God and when he did speak, how mighty was his word. When God called Moses he, too, pleaded that he was 'slow of speech'. But God met him at his weakest place, loosed him from his affliction and, when he got started, he made a speech that covered the whole book of Deuteronomy. He became strongest at his weakest place.

O God, if this is so then, from today onwards, I shall approach life with a new perspective. My weakness serves only to show up Your strength. In Your Name I say goodbye to my weakness and take instead Your omnipotence and strength. Amen.

Matthew 26:30-51; Acts 2; Hebrews 11:34
1. What sort of temperament did Peter have?
2. What changed him?

True to Oneself

18 NOV

FOR READING AND MEDITATION – MATTHEW 5:13-20

'You are the salt of the earth… You are the light of the world.' (vv13-4)

A further reason why some Christians fail to witness is *because of the weight of their own personal problems.* 'I have so many problems of my own,' they say, 'I would feel a hypocrite telling others that Christ can solve all their problems.' John White, a Christian psychiatrist in the USA, writes, 'Has it never dawned upon you that the essence of witnessing is just plain honesty? You are salt – whether you feel like it or not. You are not told to act like salt but to be what you are. You are a light. God has done a work in your life. Don't try to shine. Let that light God has put there shine out. Letting your light shine demands no more than honesty before unbelievers. In fact such honesty is in itself 90 percent of witnessing. Witnessing is not putting on a Christian front so as to convince prospective customers. Witnessing is being honest, that is, being true to what God has made you in your speech and in your day to day behaviour.' Unbelievers know we are not perfect and if we pretend we have no problems, when we do, they will soon detect our dishonesty.

Let's be honest with the world. Coming to Christ does not mean that our problems disappear. It does mean, however, that we have Someone to steer us through our problems and turn them into possibilities.

O God, in my efforts to become an effective witness, help me not to put on a phoney front but to live out my life honestly, sincerely, and convincingly. This I ask in Jesus' name. Amen.

Matthew 5:1-16; 2 Corinthians 11:22-33; 12:9
1. List the problems Paul faced in his life.
2. What did Christ promise to His followers?

Fear of Rejection

19 NOV

FOR READING AND MEDITATION – MATTHEW 5:1-12

'Blessed are those who are persecuted because of righteousness, for theirs is the kingdom of heaven.' (v10)

One of the biggest reasons why people fail to share their faith *is the fear of being rejected*. And let's face it, rejection by others can be a very real possibility whenever we begin to witness for Christ. In fact, as someone has pointed out, this possibility is implied in the very word *witness*. The word 'witness' in the Greek is *marturia* which is the root of our word *martyr*. 'An authentic witness,' claims one preacher, 'always carries the seed of the martyr.' Jesus made it quite clear that if we are going to follow Him then we must expect some rejection. After all was He not 'despised and rejected by mankind'? (Isa. 53:3). 'He came to that which was his own, but his own did not receive him' (John 1:11).

One of the first things we should teach a new Christian is to expect, whenever they share their faith, a certain amount of rejection. This will not serve to put them off but it will help deepen their commitment. They will then reason thus: 'Am I committed enough to Jesus Christ to be willing to let people know that I am a Christian even if it means the loss of my relatives and friends?' Of course, whenever we face opposition or rejection as a result of our witness, we will feel a degree of fear. The question we must then ask ourselves is this: 'Who or what is going to rule my life – fear or Jesus Christ?' I once said to a woman who told me she was afraid to witness, 'I believe you are a coward.' I waited for the explosion but it never came. Instead she said, 'You are right. From now on it will not be cowardice but courage.' 'And courage,' said someone, 'is just fear that has said its prayers.'

O God, You know the biting hesitation and doubt that fill my heart when I feel rejected by those I love. But I hear You calling me to a deeper commitment. Help me to come out on Your side in this issue. In Jesus' name. Amen.

Genesis 3:10; Matthew 25:14-30; 2 Timothy 1:7
1. How does Satan prevent us from evangelising?
2. What does Matthew 25 teach us?

He Kept Looking Down

20 NOV

FOR READING AND MEDITATION – DANIEL 12:1–13

'Those who are wise will shine like the brightness of the heavens, and those who lead many to righteousness, like the stars for ever and ever.' (v3)

Some Christians look upon their faith and experience as something so sacred that it should be kept secret. Suppose a mother should say to her children, 'Now, children, food is such a sacred thing I cannot talk to you about it, nor can I invite you to partake of it.' Or the teacher says to the pupils in the class, 'Now knowledge is a very sacred thing. I cannot talk to you about it so there will be no classes today.' Absurd? Well, no more absurd than the unnatural attitudes that some Christians hold concerning the most precious possession in the universe – the good news of the gospel of Jesus Christ. Why, the impulse to share something good is inherent even in animals.

Rags, an Airedale, missing for three days, was discovered when a faint barking was heard from a disused mineshaft. A man was lowered into the mine and found the dog, weak, hungry, but uninjured. The man put Rags in a sack and, in doing so, he felt something brush against his leg. He found that a large rabbit had fallen into the mine, too. The rabbit was also put in the sack but, on the way up, the sack opened and the rabbit fell back into the shaft. When Rags arrived at the surface he eagerly consumed the food and water that was brought for him by his owners but, when they wanted him to go home, he refused to budge from the mouth of the shaft. He kept looking down. So someone went down and brought up the rabbit, whereupon Rags sniffed it affectionately then headed for home.

The true impulse in the heart of every person who has come to Christ, is to see others brought up from the pit from which they have been rescued.

O God, like Rags I, too, am not content to be rescued alone. I shall be content only when those who have shared my pit have also been rescued. Help me to do my part towards that task. For Jesus' sake. Amen.

Romans 10; Acts 13:47; Ephesians 5:8; Philippians 2:15
1. What are our awesome responsibilities?
2. Is there such a thing as a secret disciple?

When There is No Obvious Response   21 NOV

FOR READING AND MEDITATION – 1 CORINTHIANS 3:1–11

> 'So neither the one who plants nor the one who waters is anything, but only God, who makes things grow.' (v7)

We have been looking over the past week at some of the reasons why Christians fail to share their faith. Today we come to the last of these which is *discouragement due to no obvious results.* Such a person says, 'I have tried to witness but it doesn't seem to accomplish anything. So what's the use?' This attitude stems from the fact that one feels inwardly compelled to come up with results. *Evangelism is not defined by a positive response on the part of those to whom we witness.* God has called us to do two things: (1) Proclaim the good news and (2) disciple those who respond for Christ. The actual producing of results is always in God's hands. The text for today spells this out quite clearly. Look at it again. 'So neither the one who plants nor the one who waters is anything, but only God, who makes things grow.'

What God expects from each one of us is faithfulness, obedience, and reliability. 'It is required that those who have been given a trust must prove faithful' (1 Cor. 4:2). If our efforts do not yield results, it may be right, of course, to ask ourselves whether or not our approach is right or whether our evangelism is biblical. If we are sure that we are doing everything God expects of us then we leave the matter with Him, and carry on witnessing whether we see results or not.

Remember, too, that your witness may be an important link in God's chain. I led a man to Christ some years ago who told me that ten years earlier someone witnessed to him in Hyde Park Corner and invited him to come to Christ. He refused but he confessed that he had been waiting for ten years for someone else to ask him.

Gracious Father, thank You for reminding me that evangelism is more than just a responsibility but my response to Your ability. It is mine to speak but Yours to save. I am so thankful. Amen.

1 Kings 19; Isaiah 40:31; Galatians 6:9
1. What was the real cause of Elijah's discouragement?
2. What are God's promises to our hearts?

An Enlarged Heart

22 NOV

FOR READING AND MEDITATION – 2 CORINTHIANS 6:1–11

'We have spoken freely to you, Corinthians,
and opened wide our hearts to you.' (v11)

I suppose, if we are really honest, most of the reasons we have looked at over the past week, as to why Christians fail to share their faith, are not really reasons, but excuses. If we were really gripped by God then many of the issues we have discussed would dissolve as easily as the morning mist before the warmth of the rising sun. This is why I feel it is time now to bring the whole subject of evangelism into an intensely personal perspective by inviting you to ask yourself this question: *how much of a grip does God have upon me?* We are about to engage on a week of evangelistic effort, not to the hearts of the unconverted, but to our own hearts. The reason for this is because no one can be successful in evangelism until their own heart has first been evangelised by the Master. The poet put it thus:

I know a bosom which within
Contains the world's sad counterpart
Tis here the reign of death and sin
O God evangelise my heart!

Evangelise my heart! What an exciting thought! Is not this exactly what we need? Assuredly it is, but in what way can God answer that prayer? He does it by flowing into our beings with such an inrush of His life and power that our hearts actually become enlarged. Not physically, of course, but enlarged in sympathy, empathy, and spiritual concern. Paul, as we see from our text, had a heart like that. Let me put it to you now. Is your heart like the apostle's – large enough to take in others? If not, then let God perform the operation that will bring about an enlargement of your heart.

O God, Your Word is as sharp as a surgeon's knife and just as saving. Open up my heart, I pray, and enlarge it until it is big enough to take in the whole wide world. In Jesus' name. Amen.

Luke 14:15–35; 2 Corinthians 6:2; James 4:13–14
1. How did Jesus link His parable to discipleship?
2. Why did He exhort His listeners to count the cost?

Have You Room for One?   23 NOV

FOR READING AND MEDITATION – MATTHEW 23:34-39

'Jerusalem, Jerusalem… how often I have longed to gather your children together… and you were not willing.' (v37)

We ended yesterday by saying that one of the most important operations the Holy Spirit can perform upon us is that of enlarging our hearts. John Wesley knew something about this. Time and time again in his journals one comes across an entry like this, 'preached with great enlargement of heart.' And it is told of George Whitefield that when, during the revival of the eighteenth century, he addressed the miners of Bristol, whose soot-covered faces were stained with veins of white as the tears coursed down their cheeks, he cried, 'O men of Bristol, my heart is enlarged toward you.' The psalmist prayed similarly: 'I will run the way of thy commandments, when thou shalt enlarge my heart' (Psa. 119:32, KJV).

When we comb the record of our Lord's life on this earth we find that there was never anyone with a heart so large as His. As He moved across the ancient land of israel, He had time and concern for everyone He met. Whether, like Peter, they smelt of the sea or, like the woman of Samaria, they bore the name of a harlot, He had room in His heart for them all. In the Praetorium, when facing death by crucifixion, His thoughts were so taken up with others that He calmly discussed with Pilate His mission in the world. On His way to Golgotha, He turned to the weeping women and said, 'Weep not for me, but rather for yourselves and your children.' And when finally He stretched His weary body on the cross, He prayed, not for Himself, but for the murderers who crucified Him, and asked that they might be forgiven. Christ carried the whole world of lost humanity in His heart. Have you room for one?

O Father, You are so skilful in dropping the seed of Your Word in my heart and that seed soon brings about a revolution. Help me to start by loving just one person the way You love them and then open up my heart until there is room for many others. Amen.

Ephesians 3; 2 Samuel 22:37; 1 Kings 4:29; Isaiah 54:2
1. What is the definition of the Bible's use of 'heart'?
2. What steps can be taken to enlarge our 'hearts'?

Ours for the Asking

24 NOV

FOR READING AND MEDITATION – PHILIPPIANS 2:1–13

'In your relationships with one another, have the same mindset as Christ Jesus: who, being in very nature God… made himself nothing…' (vv5–7)

Today we begin with a pointed question: *how does God go about the task of expanding a Christian's heart*? Firstly, He does it *by giving us a great love for all humanity*. Many of us spend our lives in compartments. We move amongst people of our own social status. We talk most freely with those who are our equals and, more often than not, we avoid the company of those whom we consider are beneath us in dignity, education, and background. Love is the answer. A love that is deep, strong, and true, and loves even when it cannot like. Christ is able to bring into our lives a stream of love for the lost that provides us with the power to go on loving even though we are rebuffed, rejected, and reviled. It is almost impossible to love someone who constantly loses their way and ends up in a bad place; a natural reaction is to turn away in disgust.

But such is the love that Christ plants in our hearts (in response to prayer) that there is no situation we will ever face that cannot be answered by that love. In the *Letters of James Smethan*, it is recorded, 'Christ takes your view of things and mentions no other. He takes the old woman's view of things and shows a great interest in washing powder; Sir Isaac Newton's view of things and wings with him among the stars; the artist's view of things and feeds among the lilies; the lawyer's view of things and shares his sense of justice. But He never plays the lawyer or the philosopher or the artist to the old woman. *He is above the littleness*.' The skill Christ has in relating to men and women He passes on to us. It is ours for the asking.

O God, if this skill which comes from You is mine for the asking then I ask for it today. Help me to use it to bring others to You. Amen.

Mark 14–16; Deuteronomy 10:19; Matthew 22:39; John 15:13
1. List ten ways in which Christ demonstrated His love for humanity.
2. List ways in which Christ's love is demonstrated through your life.

Sheep Without a Shepherd

25 NOV

FOR READING AND MEDITATION – MARK 6:30–44

'When Jesus landed and saw a large crowd, he had compassion on them, because they were like sheep without a shepherd.' (v34)

Another way in which Christ proceeds to enlarge and expand our hearts is *by showing us what people really need.* Bishop Taylor Smith, when responsible for the selection of chaplains for the Armed Forces, was once approached by a clergyman who asked to be considered for the job of chaplain. The bishop looked at him, pulled out his watch and said, 'I am a soldier dying on the battlefield with three minutes to live – what have you to say to me?' Utterly taken aback, the man had nothing to say and, because he had no message for a dying man, his application was dismissed. If all of life was suddenly reduced to three minutes, it would be easy to see what people *most* needed. There would be hardly any doubt in a Christian's mind – *Christ!* Because life goes on and no one knows the exact moment eternity will call, it does not mean that people's needs are different. Christ is still the greatest need of all those who do not know Him and, as we draw close to Christ's heart, this single fact is brought fully into focus. When Peter and the rest of the disciples stepped out of the upper room on the Day of Pentecost, they moved with tremendous urgency among the people. And why? Because they saw the people as Christ saw them – as sheep without a shepherd. When Christians get near to Christ's heart then they show the same emotion as F.W.H. Myers (1843–1901), who wrote:

> *Then with a rush the intolerable craving*
> *Shivers through me like a trumpet call*
> *O to save these! to perish for their saving*
> *Die for their life, be offered for them all!*

O God, as I ponder this great fact, that the greatest need of my friends and family is Christ, let it burn within me until it catches fire. Then help me to share Christ with them – with love, with enthusiasm and with compassion. In Jesus' name. Amen.

John 9; 4:1–30; Luke 19:1–10
1. What was Jesus' approach to the sinner?
2. Did Jesus see people as more than lost souls?

Ambassador on Special Mission

26 NOV

FOR READING AND MEDITATION – 2 CORINTHIANS 5:10-21

'We are therefore Christ's ambassadors, as though God were making his appeal through us. We implore you on Christ's behalf: be reconciled to God.' (v20)

Yet another way in which Christ enlarges our hearts and expands our vision for those who are lost is *by conferring on us the dignified title of one of His ambassadors.* 'Now,' says Paul, '*we* are ambassadors for Christ,' personal representatives of our heavenly King. Lord Templewood in his intriguing book *Ambassador on Special Mission,* tells the story of his despatch at a crucial part of the Second World War with special instructions to keep Franco out of the struggle. To read his gripping account of the twists and turns of ambassadorial policy is to sense the tremendous privileges and responsibilities of an ambassador's life. Lord Templewood was not an ordinary ambassaador. The King had sent him on a *specific* task.

We, too, as Christ's ambassadors, have a special mission. Indeed, egotism aside, there are none so special as we! And what is our task? Paul puts it succinctly when he says, 'We implore you on Christ's behalf: be reconciled to God.' What a task! Every true believer is commissioned by Jesus Christ to stand before an unbelieving world and say, 'I am an ambassador of the King of Kings. I have been commissioned from another world to tell you that the Ruler I represent is willing to be reconciled to you. Though you offended Him, He is willing to take the initiative and He wants me to tell you that, providing you accept the atonement of His Son, there can be complete reconciliation.' You would not use that *language,* of course, but in your own words, words adapted to the person to whom you are speaking. Your specific task, as an ambassador on special mission, is to tell people they can be reconciled to God.

O God, my Father, what a dignity and what a responsibility You have given me by making me one of Your ambassadors. Help me to walk through this world each day of my life with an ever-growing consciousness of my high and important status. Amen.

Romans 5; Colossians 1:20; Hebrews 2:17
1. What does it mean to be reconciled?
2. List the stages of reconciliation.

No Other Plan

27 NOV

FOR READING AND MEDITATION - ROMANS 10:13-21

'And how can they believe in the one of whom they have not heard? And how can they hear without someone preaching to them?' (v14)

We continue meditating on the ways by which God seeks to evangelise our hearts, thus expanding our vision and enlarging our concern for a world lost in sin. He does this by reminding us that unless the good news is shared by those of us who have tasted it and experienced it, *there is no other way it can be made known.* God has no alternative plan! In his book *The Master Plan of Evangelism,* Robert E. Coleman shows how God's plan for the evangelisation of the world centres on what he calls, 'the redeemed winning the unredeemed'. In other words, the only valid messengers of the gospel are those who have themselves experienced its transforming power in their lives. Angels would vie with archangels for the privilege of telling the good news to the world but, having never tasted it, they cannot properly tell it.

A story I heard many years ago (the source of which I have been unable to trace) tells how Christ, having ascended to His Father from the Mount of Olives, was immediately surrounded by a group of excited angels. Now that His mission was finished, they were eager to discover if they were to have any part in making the good news known. Christ explains to them that this part of the task He has left to His disciples. 'But what if they fail?' asked one of the angels. 'Didn't they prove untrustworthy in the past? Surely, Master, you can't leave the responsibility of making the message known solely to those disciples?' Christ looked at the angel solemnly, and quietly said, 'I have no other plan.'

Let the truth take hold of you now. If you and I don't spread the Word then quite simply the task will not get done. God has no other plan.

O God, my Father, with one stroke You bring everything out into the open and put it in perspective. In the light of Your Word to me, today, I ask myself: what my heart has experienced, shall my tongue refuse to tell? Amen.

1 Corinthians 1; John 15:16; Acts 9:15
1. List the types of vessels God uses.
2. What sort of vessel are you?

Power for the Task

28 NOV

FOR READING AND MEDITATION – ACTS 1:1–14

'But you will receive power when the Holy Spirit comes on you; and you will be my witnesses in Jerusalem… Judea… Samaria, and to the ends of the earth.' (v8)

Finally, another way in which Christ evangelises and enlarges the hearts of His children is *by imparting to them a special supply of divine power.* No one can expect to have a great deal of success in reaching men and women for Christ until they have been filled with the power that makes effective evangelism possible. This power is expressly promised by Christ to all His children and is, in fact, the biggest single factor to producing an enlarged heart. Watch how it operated in the lives of the disciples. Before they received this power, they sat like frightened sheep in that upper room at Jerusalem 'for fear of the Jews'. Then suddenly there burst into the room the supernatural power of the Holy Spirit which, upon entering their personalities, transformed them from shy, timid, and hesitant disciples into men who were ablaze and invincible. No longer were they afraid of people's opinions. In fact, after Pentecost, they were the ones that largely shaped public opinion and, by their words and deeds, did much to change the trends of their day and generation.

When you examine the lives of the disciples prior to Pentecost, you cannot help but be struck by the fact that they had little interest in reaching the multitudes. They tried to keep Christ for themselves. On the Mount of Transfiguration Peter seemed to be saying, 'Let's build three tabernacles and stay right here.' But all this is reversed at Pentecost. The power they received enlarged their hearts not only to take in Jerusalem but Judaea also and Samaria… until ultimately they took in the whole of the then known world.

Gracious God, I see that, in giving me the gift of the Holy Spirit, You made it possible for me to meet the impossible. Help me to walk in the light of the fact that the task ahead of me is never as great as the power behind me. In Jesus' name. Amen.

Acts 8:26–40; John 15:26–16:15
1. What is the main ministry of the Holy Spirit?
2. How did this apply to Philip?

The Master Soulwinner

29 NOV

FOR READING AND MEDITATION – JOHN 3:1–13

'Very truly I tell you, no one can see the
kingdom of God unless they are born again.' (v3)

We come now to an important and practical section of our studies – *getting the message through*. Over the next week we shall endeavour to collect some of the important guiding principles we need to know when attempting to lead a person to new life in Christ. And where better to gather these principles than from watching the Master Soulwinner at work – Jesus Christ Himself. 'Jesus,' said a little boy, 'is the gospel in living colour.' He is! Almost everything our Saviour did, while He was here on earth, was directed towards the end of winning men and women to His Father's kingdom.

Someone has pointed out that every parable Christ spoke was a soulwinning parable. Although the four Gospels record only about *fifty* days in the life of our Lord, those days are filled with incidents, accounts, and words that are directed towards helping people find hope and salvation in God. As we listen to His words, watch His acts, and see His spiritual expertise, we build up a picture of One who strode through this life with one dominating passion filling His being – the passion of sharing the love of His Father with a soiled and sin-stained world. On one occasion the Scriptures said of Him that, as He made His way to Jerusalem for the last time to face the cross, He came 'journeying and teaching'. Many of us would have nursed our coming pain. But He had the inward compulsion to teach the love of God to others – on the way to die!

If this Christ doesn't get into our blood and raise our spiritual temperature then we ought to wonder why.

Lord Jesus Christ, I come to You to put my life alongside Yours, to be guided, directed, and taught by You this day. Amen.

John 10; Matthew 13
1. What was Christ's major method of sharing His message?
2. List six symbols He used in describing Himself (e.g. bread).

No Proselytism

FOR READING AND MEDITATION – JOHN 4:1–10

'Now Jesus learned that the Pharisees had heard that he was gaining and baptising more disciples than John… So he left Judea and went back once more to Galilee.' (vv1,3)

We said yesterday that in order to get some guiding principles to help us win others to the new life, we are going to watch the Master at work. I know of no greater illustration of how to lead a person to faith and trust in God than the story of our Saviour's encounter with the woman at the well. So, as an apprentice stands at the side of his Master to watch and learn how a task is done, we come alongside our Lord in this gripping story and learn step by step as we go. The first principle that becomes clear is that Christ was not interested in proselytising but in bringing about a true change in human nature. The account says, 'Now Jesus learned that the Pharisees had heard that he was gaining and baptising more disciples than John… So he left Judea and went back once more to Galilee' (John 4:1,3). He would not allow Himself to become involved in a struggle for numbers – so He left at high tide.

This account of the Samaritan woman is not in the context of proselytising but of true conversion. Proselytising is influencing someone to change from one group to another without any necessary change in character and life. The Christian convert in the New Testament is never called a 'proselyte' – there were Jewish proselytes, but no Christian proselytes. The gospel produces not a change of label, but a change of life.

Those of us who may hesitate to throw ourselves into this movement towards evangelism, that is now beginning, because we don't want to become involved in just a scramble for numbers, are re-assured here – this is deeper; it is a move to produce conversion.

O Father, help me to keep before me the fact that, in bringing someone to You, I am helping them not merely to change their label but to change their life. In Jesus' name, I ask it. Amen.

Matthew 18; 3:2; Luke 13:2–3
1. What was the main message of Jesus?
2. What other aspect is Jesus emphasising in Matthew 18?

Using the Inevitable 1 DEC

FOR READING AND MEDITATION – JOHN 4:4–14
'Now he had to go through Samaria.' (v4)

We continue studying the thrilling account of our Saviour's meeting with the Samaritan woman. The Scripture says, 'Now he had to go through Samaria.' As Jesus left Judaea on His way to Galilee, He made His way through Samaria as it was the shortest and most direct route. Most Jews, because of their intense hatred and dislike for the Samaritans, would go by a more circuitous route along the Jordan valley thus adding sixty or seventy extra miles to their journey. Jesus, however, banished such bigotry, took a straight course, and thus found His evangelistic opportunity in something that was inevitable. Doing the right thing is always the right thing to do. Jesus found His opportunity of getting His message across in the everyday inevitabilities of life.

There are certain things in your life and mine that are right to do and inevitable – we have to go to the office, to school, to the workshop, or perhaps attend to home duties. Evangelise that inevitable situation – find your opportunity in the inevitable contacts of the day. Evangelism is not something imported into special weeks, special days, or special occasions – it must become as natural to us as breathing. A businessman told me that he couldn't do evangelistic work as too many people came to him each day with their problems. I suggested to him that he might find his evangelistic opportunity right there – and he did. Once we have the will to evangelise then it won't be long before God gives us the opportunity. Then no day is ordinary as all contacts become redemptive. Nothing – absolutely nothing – is more important under heaven than just that.

Gracious God and heavenly Father, give me an alert heart and a responsive will so that I may discover an evangelistic opportunity in all my daily contacts. In Jesus' name, I ask it. Amen.

Mark 10:46–52; Luke 7:11–17; 8:49–56
1. List ten other instances when Jesus had personal encounters with people.
2. How many times have you shared Christ person to person recently?

The Dominant Interest

FOR READING AND MEDITATION – JOHN 4:9–13

'Jesus answered, "Everyone who drinks this water will be thirsty again..."' (v13)

As the first step in opening a conversation is the most difficult, today we shall examine just how Jesus overcame this problem. He began at the woman's dominant interest and led her along the line of that dominant interest. He began at the thing she came for – water – and then went from natural water to spiritual water. Is a young man interested in athletics? Then talk to him about a strong body and the necessity of purity if that body is to be at its best. It is part of the dynamic of the gospel to enable a person to become pure not only in body but also in mind. Is a parent wrapped up in his or her children? Then it becomes a simple thing to show them how, if they want to pass on to their children a good heritage, they can best do it, by accepting Christ and letting Him become involved in their family relationships.

One minister tells a story of how, as a young evangelist, he stopped one night by a fence where the town drunk was working in his garden. The evangelist complimented the man on his fine garden and then gradually brought the conversation around to whether he had got the weeds out of his own heart. This remark, said tenderly and appealingly, got right into his soul. He became a Christian. The late Dr W. E. Sangster said that he knew a man in his sixties who took up keeping guinea pigs in order to reach the heart of a boy. It might seem absurd and quixotic but it proved effective. The boy, himself, became a fisher of men. When you show an interest in what people are interested in, they will probably respond and be interested in what you are interested in.

O Father, give me Your skill and insight to see what people want, and then to lead them from that want to what they ought to want. For Jesus' sake. Amen.

Revelation 22; Isaiah 44:3; 55:1–3; John 4:14
1. List the simple steps Jesus followed in John 4.
2. Apply this strategy when you next witness.

The Higher Issue   3 DEC

FOR READING AND MEDITATION – JOHN 4:9–15
'Whoever drinks the water I give them will never thirst.' (v14)

When Jesus found the dominant interest in the Samaritan woman's mind and opened up the conversation at that point, the woman reacted by putting up a barrier. This is natural and instinctive – the instinct of self-preservation. Many Christians would have stopped right there, but they would have stopped too soon. If you hang around, a second instinct comes into operation – the instinct of self-revelation. If the first instinct is to shut people out, the second one is to open up. But to do this a person has to feel that the one to whom they are talking is genuinely interested, truly sympathetic, and warmly understanding. So don't be discouraged when you meet this instinct; wait for the working of that deeper instinct of self-revelation. Now how did Jesus get rid of the clash between Jew and Samaritan which came into the picture at this point? 'You are a Jew and I am a Samaritan woman. How can you ask me for a drink?' He did it by a simple technique which He used all the way through the conversation – He raised a higher issue: 'living water'. When He focused her attention on that higher issue the smaller issue faded into the background and was forgotten.

Fix that as a principle in an evangelistic conversation. Don't pick up subordinate issues and debate them; you will get tangled up in the little and the irrelevant. Raise the higher issue and the lesser issue will fade out. This does not mean, of course, that you ignore a genuine objection. But as the issue you are raising – eternal life – is the greatest issue of all time, keep moving towards your goal, not theirs.

O God, help me to be a guide who directs others towards Your goals. Help me to be too big to be caught up in little issues when larger ones await me. Amen.

Luke 24:13–36; Mark 4:34; Matthew 5:2
1. What was Jesus' approach to the Emmaus Road disciples?
2. How did He focus their minds on the real problem?

The Delicate Moment

4 DEC

FOR READING AND MEDITATION – JOHN 4:9-23

'The woman said to him, "Sir, give me this water…"' (v15)

Jesus expressed an amazing confidence in this woman of Samaria: 'If you knew the gift of God and who it is that asks you for a drink, you would have asked him…' – i.e. if you can see what I am talking about, you will want it. Jesus believes in people when they cannot believe in themselves. We must believe in people in spite of what they are if we are to influence them. If we become cynical about people we become powerless to help them. At this stage the woman raised a further controversy, 'Are you greater than our father Jacob…?' Jesus could have said 'Jacob was a scheming liar and lost his birthright.' To have done so, however, would have raised an argument. How did Jesus get rid of Jacob? Once again He raised a higher issue: 'a spring of water welling up to eternal life'. She got her eyes on that and Jacob vanished out of the picture. It was then that Jesus came to the root cause of her difficulties – her moral problem.

Take it as an axiom in dealing with the unconverted that there is a moral problem in everyone's life. This is the decision point from which people move towards deeper darkness or towards the light. How did Jesus get to the moral problem without seeming to invade sanctities? He did it delicately. He did not say, 'You are an adulterer,' but, 'Go, call your husband and come back.' She then responded by saying, 'I have no husband.' The words mean more than they seem. It was an admission of guilt in itself. It is not enough to point out people's sins; they must be led to point them out themselves. Then, and only then, are they on the road to getting rid of them.

O God my Father, help me to love love out of the loveless and when I come to that delicate moment of sin exposure, give me the sure word that points to the sin exit – You. Amen.

John 8:1-11; 5:1-16; Luke 23:32-43
1. What was Christ's main interest as shown in the above passages?
2. What characteristics did He display in these accounts?

The Goal

5 DEC

FOR READING AND MEDITATION – JOHN 4:24-30

'Come, see a man who told me everything I've ever done. Could this be the Messiah?' (v29)

We must spend one last day in looking at this marvellous encounter of Jesus with the woman of Samaria. We left the woman yesterday having come face to face with her sins. Feeling uncomfortable (as everyone does when they come face to face with their sin) she sought to divert the conversation into an abstract religious issue: 'Where must we worship?' Beware of the attempt to pull you off the real thing by using the red herring of religious issues. Hold to the moral problem. Did Jesus answer her question? He did, but He was soon back at the central issue. We must not dodge questions or treat them as trivial but keep the conversation moving towards the central issue – how a person can get rid of sin and find moral and spiritual deliverance. The moral problem is always central.

We now ask ourselves: what was the end of this conversation, the goal towards which it all moved? It was this – 'I, the one speaking to you – I am he.' The goal was the unveiling of Himself as Saviour and Lord. The end of our work in evangelism is to get people to see Jesus. But there is one final step I want you to notice before we leave this matchless story. The woman left her waterpot, went into the city, and said, 'Come, see a man who told me everything I've ever done.' The end of evangelism is to produce an evangelist. Someone said, 'You haven't got them in until you get them out.' The account says: 'Many of the Samaritans from that town believed in him because of the woman's testimony...' Jesus must have rejoiced that day that He had put the graft of a higher life into a human soul. That was the will of God for Him – it is also for us.

O God, help me to keep my life moving towards this central necessity and give me the ability to put the graft of Your life into other lives. For Jesus' sake, I ask it. Amen.

Acts 3 & 7
1. How did both Peter and Stephen handle the religious problem?
2. What contrasts did they draw?

A Worldwide Task Force

6 DEC

FOR READING AND MEDITATION - ACTS 11:19-30

'Now those who had been scattered... travelled as far as Phoenicia, Cyprus and Antioch, spreading the word...' (v19)

We turn now to consider the important subject of lay witness. Following a gathering of the Lausanne Conference on Evangelism, the executive secretary of the Continuation Committee was asked by an interviewer just how he proposed to go about raising the task force necessary to carry out world evangelism in the present day. He replied that the task force already exists amongst the rank and file of the multitudes who are committed to Jesus Christ. An evangelistic task force exists; the problem is how best to mobilise it. Without an effective lay witness, the Christian Church will never be able to meet the challenge of its generation.

Some years ago I spoke to a small group of people in a village in Sweden, on the importance of lay witness and lay evangelism. At the end of the evening they were all fired up to witness but, being in an isolated area, they had no one to whom they could go. One of them said, 'Let's pick up the telephone and tell someone about Jesus.' Feeling this to be the Spirit's prompting, they selected a number and made the call. As soon as the person on the other end picked up the phone they began to sing in Swedish, 'Jesus in the answer, let Him in today.' When they had finished they paused to see what reaction their song had brought. They heard deep sobbing and, when later the person could speak, he said, 'I was just about to end my life when the phone rang. Your song has touched me deeply. Please tell me how I can find Jesus.' You don't need to be a minister, priest, or preacher to share Christ. Follow the Spirit's guidance and you will find open doors everywhere.

O God, I see clearly today that the task force to win the world for You is already in its place. The problem is that we are not properly mobilised. Here I am, Lord. Start with me. Get me going and then use me to get others going. For Jesus' sake. Amen.

John 17; Mark 16:14-20; Acts 1:8
1. What was Christ's prayer for believers in relation to the world?
2. List six specific requests Christ made in His prayer.

Equipping the Laity　　　　　　　　　　7 DEC

FOR READING AND MEDITATION – EPHESIANS 4:1–15

'So Christ himself gave [some]… to equip
his people for works of service…' (vv11–12)

It is time now to give our minds to the question of what part each local church plays in this vital and important matter of evangelism. In a day of rugged individualism and the plethora of what we call para-church organisations, we must not forget that the community of God's people, who form a local church, lies at the centre of His purposes. Regrettably many local churches (not all) are suffering from a severe case of identity crisis. Dr Howard Hendricks says, "The contemporary Christian church is like an amnesia victim trying to find out 'Who am I?' " There are many reasons why the Church fails to function in the way God desires, but I believe the major one is this – God's people have not locked into God's 'Game Plan' which He has outlined in Ephesians 4:11–12.

Imagine for a moment you are standing on the sidelines of an English football game. Suddenly, instead of the eleven players you expect from your home team, just one person appears – the coach. Someone says that as this person has a lot more experience than the others, they are going to play the other team all by themselves. Ridiculous? Well, isn't this the kind of picture many Christians have of the Church? The members expect the minister to do all the preaching, praying, and witnessing because, as they say, 'That's what he or she is paid for.'

The Church will not move forward until everyone recognises that God gives leaders to the Church not to do all the work but to help the rest of God's people do it. Lay people are not in the Church simply to pay pastors, evangelists, and teachers to do the Lord's work. Rather, pastors, teachers, and the other leadership are there to equip the so-called 'lay' people to be ministers.

O God, bring Your Church to the realisation of Your perfect plan as outlined so clearly in Your Word, the Bible. Use those in spiritual authority over me as a tool in Your hand to make me more useful and effective for You. In Jesus' name. Amen.

Romans 12; 1 Corinthians 12
1. List the different ministries God has placed in His Body.
2. What ministry do you have in the Body of Christ?

Keepers of Aquariums   8 DEC

FOR READING AND MEDITATION – JOHN 15:5–16
'I chose you and appointed you so that you might
go and bear fruit – fruit that will last...' (v16)

We ended yesterday by saying that lay people are not in the Church to pay pastors, teachers, and evangelists to do the Lord's work – rather, pastors, evangelists, and teachers are there to equip so-called lay people to be ministers. Someone has described the Church as being like a football match in which '11 men on the field, desperately in need of a rest, are watched by 11,000 in the stands desperately in need of exercise.' If your church is not functioning in the way described in Ephesians 4:11, where the leaders train, equip, and teach you to be an effective witness and worker in Christ's Body then, believe me, your church is in big trouble. The Church is supposed to be Christ's Body – His hands, His feet, His voice – by which He carries out His purposes in the world.

The Christian life was never intended to be lived only in church for a few hours on a Sunday and perhaps an occasional mid-week prayer meeting or Bible study. It's meant to be lived in the factory, the office, the school, the neighbourhood – seven days a week. We must have worship, of course – in fact that is the very first priority. But after that comes study and training so that every believer can discover their basic gift and develop it for effective service, firstly in the Church and then to the world around. Let's face it, many churches are like exclusive clubs rather than workshops where men and women are trained for effective service. We are more inward looking than outward looking and become, as Dr David Seamands says, 'keepers of aquariums rather than fishers of men'.

O Father, I see that the deepest need of Your Church at this time is to be more outward looking. Help me to remember that 'no virtue is safe that is not enthusiastic and no life is Christian that is not Christianising'. For Jesus' sake. Amen.

Acts 20:17–38; Ephesians 4 & 5
1. What was Paul's charge to the Ephesian elders?
2. What was his charge to the Ephesian church?

Without Love – a Sounding Brass

FOR READING AND MEDITATION – JOHN 15:17–27
'This is my command: love each other.' (v17)

We continue facing the strong challenge of Ephesians 4:11–12 which describes the Church as a community where its leaders equip the so-called laity for maximum effectiveness in Christ's Body. I realise, of course, that some will now begin to take what I am saying and start making comparisons with their own local church. If you find yourself in a church where there is no systematic training or teaching programme designed to help you discover and develop your basic spiritual gifts, do not go off the deep end and start taking pot shots at the minister or the church council.

Firstly, pray about it. It may be that your minister has not quite caught the vision of this section of the Scriptures. Prayer can change things. Whatever you do, do not criticise, grumble, or complain. This will only make you part of the problem and not part of the solution. Constructive change can only come about in any church when it is done in a spirit of love. Remember, no evangelism is effective when expressed through any local church, either by its individual members or as a corporate act, unless conducted in a spirit of genuine Christian love. 'We Christians,' says Dr Leighton Ford, 'talk about "winning the world to God."'

We know the whole world will not be converted but what if it were? What would a world won to Christ be like? Would its personal relationships be like those in your church? Would its educational system be patterned after your Sunday School? Would its political system operate like your church board? If God's total Church is the agent for evangelism then, remember, it can only be effective when it flows out of a spirit of love.

Lord Jesus, today You have touched the nerve centre of my problems. You know my tendency to criticise, grumble, and complain. Sweep into my soul today with a fresh glimpse of Your love; for to love more I must first see how much You love me. Amen.

1 Corinthians 13; 1 John 3; John 15:13
1. How is the gospel demonstrated in the Church?
2. How does this relate to preaching the gospel?

The Church is Christ's Church

10 DEC

FOR READING AND MEDITATION – EPHESIANS 1:15-23

'And God... appointed him to be head over everything for the church, which is his body, the fullness of him who fills everything in every way.' (vv22-23)

We are seeing that there is a desperate need to reexamine the structure and function of the Church so as to bring it in line with God's original purpose as outlined in Ephesians 4:11-12 and other passages of Scripture. The Church is not an institution run by a spiritual hierarchy and paid professionals but a community where everyone has a part to play in making Christ known to the world. In his book, *The Reconstruction of the Christian Church*, the late Dr E. Stanley Jones claimed that one of the reasons why the Church has not developed in the way it should, is because it has modelled itself on the church in Jerusalem rather than the church in Antioch. It was at Antioch, he believed, that the Church really came into its own. Is he right? I believe (with some reservations) that he is right. This is an area of discussion that is, of course, strewn with the scalps of many a theological gladiator, but let's press on.

For centuries the Church has patterned itself after the church in Jerusalem and called itself an 'Apostolic Church'. Whilst, in a sense, this is so, as, according to Scripture, it was 'built on the foundation of the apostles and prophets' (Eph. 2:20); it is also true that Jesus said, 'On this rock I will build my church' (Matt. 16:18). The Church is Christ's Church. When the groups at Corinth began to say, 'I follow Paul' and 'I follow Apollos' (1 Cor. 1:12), Paul reminded them that they belonged not to men but to Christ. Here Paul broke the nexus of loyalty to men and fastened it on Christ. He was saying, in effect, glance at men but focus your gaze only on Christ.

Father, whilst I am thankful for the ministry of the apostles who founded the Early Church, help me to understand that it is not theirs but Yours. And because it's Yours it will never perish. I am so thankful. Amen.

Acts 2 & 3

1. What were the four characteristics of the earliest church?
2. Who was involved? What was the result?

The Laymen of Antioch   11 DEC

FOR READING AND MEDITATION – ACTS 13:1–3
'Now in the church at Antioch there were prophets and teachers:
Barnabas, Simeon... Lucius... Manaen... and Saul.' (v1)

In putting the emphasis on the fact that the Church is Christ's Church and not the Apostles' Church, we are not seeking to devalue the great work which the first apostles did in founding the Christian faith. They founded it, but they were not its foundation – Christ was and is. Whilst Christianity got underway through the dynamic ministry of the first apostles at Jerusalem, it did not really come into its own there for two main reasons: (1) it was too racial and (2) it was too authoritarian. The graveclothes of Judaistic outlook and customs still clung to the movement. The Jews tried hard to enforce their customs on the Gentile converts until God scattered the movement and allowed it to come into its own in Antioch. The Christian movement could not be universalised from the model in Jerusalem. It needed a new matrix so that the future ages could see just what kind of church God wanted His Church to be. At Antioch the Christian Church was free to express its nature and purpose.

One of the most important features about it was the fact that laymen made a vital contribution to its function and operation. Although the leadership ministries, as outlined in Ephesians 4:11, pastors, teachers, evangelists, etc, have a vital part to play in the growth and development of the Church, the cutting edge of the Christian movement is really in its laity.

It is important to see this as we need to see a great spiritual advance come through the laity where it may have hitherto been focused on ministers and priests. Change is needed. And, believe me, greater changes are ahead.

O God, help me to take my place among the millions today who will seek to share Your love with the world, and help me to witness with a quenchless joy. For Jesus' sake. Amen.

Acts 11
1. List the characteristics of the church at Antioch.
2. Are these characteristics found in your church?

The Key to the Future

12 DEC

FOR READING AND MEDITATION – 2 TIMOTHY 2:1–15

'And the things you have heard me say… entrust to
reliable people who will also be qualified to teach others.' (v2)

We ministers, priests, missionaries, and evangelists are never by ourselves going to make a great impact upon the world. We are too few to do it, and, even if we could do it, it would be counter-productive for it would take away from the laity that spiritual growth and development which comes through sharing one's faith. At Pentecost the Holy Spirit was not given merely to the apostles but to the 120. A Roman Catholic priest was asked, 'What is the Church?' He replied, 'The people of God.' He was then asked, 'Not the hierarchy?' His reply was the same, 'No, the people of God.' He was right. The word for 'laity' comes from the Greek *laos* and means just that – the people of God.

The whole purpose of what some people call the hierarchy is to 'equip God's people' for the work of the ministry. Not for merely taking up collections, showing people to their seats, and sitting on committees (these are necessary and important tasks, of course) but far more than that – training the people of God to be efficient and effective ministers.

The chief business of leaders in Christ's Church is to be the guides, coaches, and stimulators of a powerful lay movement, for lay witnessing is the key to the future. Jesus was a layman. The religious system' of His day gave Him no credentials. His call was from God and not from man. He was not ordained in the ordinary sense by the laying on of hands. His credentials were the changed people that surrounded Him. You, too, may have no credentials and no ordination but, as a member of Christ's Body, you are part of His purposes in bringing men and women to the Master's feet.

O Father, I am seeing so clearly that in Your Church everyone is expected to be a minister. Though some have more gifts and greater responsibilities, all are expected to serve. Minister to me so that I may minister to others. For Your own Name's sake. Amen.

Titus 1; 1 Corinthians 7:17

1. What are the qualifications for spiritual leadership?
2. Pray for your church leaders today by name.

An Evangelistic Lifestyle

13 DEC

FOR READING AND MEDITATION – 1 PETER 2:1–16

'Live such good lives among the pagans that, though
they accuse you of doing wrong, they may see your
good deeds and glorify God on the day he visits us.' (v12)

Our thoughts over the corning week are to be centred on the need to develop what we are going to call *an evangelistic lifestyle.* We begin with a pointed question: is our evangelism something we keep for Sundays and special occasions or is it something that permeates all our actions and activities? Some Christians think of evangelism as something that fits into their lives like sections in a news magazine. There are headings such as sport, fashion, education, religion, and so on but nothing really ties or integrates these different sections except the staples and the cover. They feel that unless the activity in which they are engaged happens to fall under the section of religion then it is not appropriate to mention their faith or their allegiance to the Lord Jesus Christ. Evangelism (for them) is seen as something done at a particular time and on special occasions. Although familiar with the words of Jesus: 'You are the light of the world' (Matt. 5:14), they interpret that to mean, 'when and where I want to be.' Evangelism, if it is to be biblical, must be a lifestyle.

Let me remind you once again of what the Christian psychiatrist, John White, has said, 'Witnessing is not putting on a Christian front so as to convince prospective customers. Witnessing is being honest, that is, being true to a God who had made you in your speech and in your day-by-day behaviour.' If we Christians are to be the salt of the earth then we must get out of the salt shaker. Salt in the shaker never flavoured anything. And too much salt in one place tastes terrible and makes one sick.

Father, I see so clearly that the dominant impression I leave on people is my evangelism. Help me to make that dominant impression one that leaves my contacts with the feeling that they have been in touch with an ambassador of Jesus Christ. Amen.

Galatians 5; Luke 6; Ephesians 5:18
1. List the Christlike qualities the world needs to see.
2. What does Paul underline as the key to these?

Still in the Pencil

14 DEC

FOR READING AND MEDITATION – ACTS 5:33-42

'Day after day, in the temple courts and from house to house, they never stopped teaching and proclaiming the good news that Jesus is the Messiah.' (v42)

We ended yesterday by saying that if we Christians are to be an influence in the world then we must get out of the salt shaker and allow Christ's love to flow through us to everyone we meet. In other words, we must begin to develop an evangelistic lifestyle.

How do we begin? Do we start by determining in our minds that every non-Christian we come across, we will ask them point-blank, 'Are you saved?' No. First, *we begin by making sure that we have a deep, rich, ongoing relationship with Christ every day of our lives.* This point has been strongly emphasised in one of our readings a few weeks ago but it will bear repeating here. Professor Chad Walsh in his book, *Early Christians of the First Century,* said, 'I suspect that Satan has called off his attempt to convert people to agnosticism. After all, if a man travels far enough away from Christianity he is liable to see it in perspective and decide that it is true. It is much safer, from Satan's point of view, to vaccinate a man with a mild case of Christianity so as to protect him from the real disease.' No one could accuse the Early Church of being 'vaccinated with a mild case of Christianity.' They had the real disease and, believe me, they made it communicable. A little girl was asked by her teacher where the dot was that should have gone over the 'i' in her composition. The little girl replied, 'Oh, that's still in the pencil.' Perhaps you have been withholding your witness far too long – it is still in you. Then get it out quick, for if you do not you will probably have little to witness to.

O Father, make my tongue a dedicated tongue–dedicated to the highest possible use: of witness for You. This, I ask, in Christ's name. Amen.

Colossians 1-3

1. Give ten ways for developing an evangelistic lifestyle.
2. What is the key? (1:27) What does this mean?

God's Conversationalist

15 DEC

FOR READING AND MEDITATION – PSALM 107:1–15

'Let the redeemed of the Lord tell their story…' (v2)

We continue examining the steps we need to take if we are to develop an evangelistic lifestyle. 2. *Be alert to sharing Christ through your everyday conversation.* In an age where conversation is so superficial, it is simply amazing the number of people who are willing to talk deeply about spiritual things providing they can do so with someone who speaks in a normal tone of voice and does not embarrass them with a style of language about which they know nothing. A preacher tells of overhearing a woman witness for Christ to a London beggar. Fragments of her speech floated to him thus: 'It must be "yea" and "amen" to the promises of God… I suspect you are still under the old dispensation… Do you understand the difference between natural and effectual faith?… You need to experience a mighty outpouring of the Spirit…' The beggar's reply to all this was interesting. 'Okey dokey,' he said. The preacher said, 'I felt two worlds had met in those two persons – and they had not intersected.'

Billy Graham, although a pulpit evangelist, was also a master of the art of bringing Christ into his everyday conversation. Leighton Ford, his brother-in-law, said of him, 'We might be sitting at a table with some people and Billy will say, "Last week I was talking with someone about this very same thing. I said…" He then lets the rest listen in on a conversation he had with someone else. He gets the message home without people feeling he is preaching.' Remember the use of questions in opening up conversation. 'What do you think is wrong with the world?' 'What's your goal in life?' Let's begin today to grasp the opportunities that come from being a conversationalist for God.

O God, give me, I pray, the skill that puts You right at the centre of my conversation and in a way that impresses not embarrasses those with whom I speak. In Jesus' name. Amen.

1 Corinthians 1:17–25; 2; 9:16, 2 Corinthians 4:5; 2 Timothy 4:2
1. What was Paul's burning desire?
2. What does the word 'preach' really mean?

The Use of Literature

16 DEC

FOR READING AND MEDITATION – PSALM 126:1-6

'Those who go out weeping, carrying seed to sow,
will return with songs of joy, carrying sheaves with them.' (v6)

Step three in developing an evangelistic lifestyle is that of *sharing Christ through carefully selected literature.* Multitudes of men and women will be in heaven through reading a book that was given to them by someone deeply concerned about the salvation of their soul. I said to a university lecturer many years ago, who, whenever we met, seemed to always want to argue with me about the story of Christ's resurrection, 'Here's a book I'd like you to read; when you get through, I'd be interested in knowing your impressions.' He read it and was immediately converted. He told me later, 'I was really wanting to hear my own voice and my skill at sustaining an argument. The book you gave me gave me no real opportunity to do that so I just sat back and let Christ save me.'

In one of the Christian Counselling courses at Waverley Abbey College, a lady said that she spent between one and two pounds a week on evangelistic literature for her non-Christian friends. Her technique was this – she waited until she discovered someone's dominant interest – politics, education, science, etc – then selected a book written by a Christian that presented Christ in the context of that subject. She told us that she aimed to do this for about thirty to forty of her non-Christian friends each year. Someone asked her what results she got from this. She said that she knew for a certainty that around ten people each year were brought to Christ through this simple but effective ministry. Discover the dominant interest of a non-Christian friend and then pass on a book written from a Christian perspective on that subject. It may be the means in God's hands of winning them to Christ.

O God, give me a creative mind and imagination in order to help me win my friends to You. Guide me to the right seed for I intend to be a sower, sowing beside all waters. For Your own Name's sake. Amen.

Romans 10; Psalm 68:11; Mark 13:10; Acts 13:49
1. When was the last time you gave out some gospel literature?
2. How do you 'publish' God's Word in your life?

For His Sake

17 DEC

FOR READING AND MEDITATION – COLOSSIANS 3:16–25

'And whatever you do, whether in word or deed, do it all in the name of the Lord Jesus, giving thanks to God the Father through him.' (v17)

Another step we can take in developing an evangelistic lifestyle is to share Christ through our daily work. Unfortunately, many Christians never realise that their work is a major area of Christian stewardship. Sloppiness and slipshod attitudes towards our work will serve to bring on ridicule and scorn whenever we attempt to openly share the gospel. 'The Christian workman,' says one writer, 'is not an ordinary workman, extraordinary only because he goes to church and not to the cinema on a Sunday evening. He is a different workman. The Christian employer is not an ordinary employer who happens to give large sums to the Church. He is a different employer.'

In humble and exalted positions, we Christians must see life from the standpoint of Almighty God and seek to share Him in every situation. Are you a doctor? Then every time you take someone's temperature, do it with the tenderness and compassion of Christ. Are you a nurse? Then show God's love to everyone on your ward – including that cantankerous person in the end bed! Are you a schoolteacher? Then show by your demeanour before your class that you are not only an educator but an ambassador for the Lord Jesus Christ. Are you an office worker? Then show by the way you tot up the columns or type a letter that you are working not merely for an earthly employer but that you are in the direct employ of the King of Kings. A lecturer in a teachers' training college was asked by one of his pupils what was different about him from the others. 'Perhaps,' he said, 'it's because every lecture I give I know there sits in my audience the Lord Jesus Christ.'

O Father, my destiny is so clear. I am to live for You and not for myself. Help me to represent You before everyone I meet and in everything I do today. For Jesus' sake. Amen.

1 Peter 2; 2 Corinthians 3:2–3; Colossians 3:22–24
1. List five ways you can be a better Christian on the job.
2. What should our attitude be to our employers?

A Ready Listener

18 DEC

FOR READING AND MEDITATION – JAMES 1:16–27

'My dear brothers and sisters, take note of this:
everyone should be quick to listen…' (v19)

Another way we can go about developing an evangelistic lifestyle is by *learning how to be a good listener*. This aspect of sharing our faith has been greatly neglected. Instead of listening sensitively to what a person is saying, we wait for an opportunity to proclaim the truth. And the result? The truth we try to communicate fails to penetrate deeply into other people's lives. Someone has described this as the 'Evangelical disease which affects so many modern-day Evangelicals; it's the habit so many of us have fallen into of giving answers before we have properly listened to the question.'

Dr Paul Tournier, the famous Swiss psychologist, says, 'It is impossible to over-emphasise the immense need human beings have to be listened to… in most conversations, although there is a good deal of talking, there is no *real* listening; such conversations are no more than a dialogue of the deaf.' It's not easy to be a good listener. Most of us, when talking to someone, want to offer advice or tell them as quickly as we can that they need Christ. Although it may be hard for some to understand, the more time we give to listening to someone, the easier it is for them to respond when we share with them the true solution to all their problems – Christ. The Bible says in Proverbs 15:23, 'A person finds joy in giving an apt reply…' and later on in verse 28, 'The heart of the righteous weighs its answers'.

Remember, sharing your faith does not always mean *talking*. Perhaps, as someone said, this is why God gave us two ears and only one mouth; He might want us to do twice as much listening as talking.

Heavenly Father, make me a real listener – one who can rub a spiritual finger along the edge of a person's soul and discern the real needs. Make me sensitive and not obtrusive. For Jesus' sake. Amen.

Job 10–13; Psalm 115:6; Matthew 11:15; Revelation 2:7
1. What was Job's complaint against Zophar?
2. How can we be guilty of this?

More about the art of listening can be found at howtolistenwell.co.uk

A Dedicated Tongue

19 DEC

FOR READING AND MEDITATION – PSALM 45:1–8

'My heart is stirred by a noble theme as I recite my verses for the king; my tongue is the pen of a skilful writer.' (v1)

Over the past week we have been seeking to answer the question: *is our evangelism to be confined to certain periods and special occasions or is it to be a constant lifestyle?* I believe the answer is inescapable. Christ wants us to carry our witness with us everywhere we go and to everyone we meet. This does not mean, of course, that we have to buttonhole everyone we meet and ask them, 'Are you saved?' But it does mean that by using every non-verbal means we can, we share with them the fact that Christ lives in us and that we are the adopted children of a heavenly King. To do this effectively means that we have to develop a certain amount of creativity in our relationships with those who are not yet Christians.

God has gifted us with a great deal of creativity and where better to use it than in thinking up ways to make Christ meaningful to the men and women we meet. We said yesterday that listening is important but there are times when listening is not enough. We must *tell* men and women about Christ – clearly and convincingly. Let me put it this way. Suppose you had a fatal disease from which happily you were delivered through the efforts of a certain doctor. One day you meet someone with exactly the same symptoms as you once had. Would you simply listen and say, 'Oh, I'm so sorry. You have my deepest sympathy'? To do so would be almost criminal. No, instead you would say, 'I had the very same disease – would you like to know how I was cured?'

When people meet us they get a dominant impression – an impression of self-centredness or an impression of Christ-centredness. What sort of impression are people getting from you?

Lord, help me to be more than a half-witness, someone who acts and does not speak or someone who speaks and does not act. I want to be a whole witness and witness with my total life – deeds and tongue. Amen.

Colossians 4:1–6; Ecclesiastes 3:7; 2 Timothy 1:13; Job 6:25
1. What should be the characteristics of our speech?
2. Practise giving your testimony in two minutes.

A Picture of Evangelism

20 DEC

FOR READING AND MEDITATION – JUDE 17–25

'Save others by snatching them from the fire; to others show mercy, mixed with fear – hating even the clothing stained by corrupted flesh.' (v23)

Much of what we have been saying over the past seven weeks has been confined to the theory of evangelism. It is time now to turn to more practical things. 'Philosophers,' wrote Karl Marx, 'have only interpreted the world differently; the point is, however, to *change* it.' We can never expect to change the world by focusing merely on the theory of evangelism; what we have learned must now be put to work.

An artist once set out to capture on canvas the meaning of evangelism. He painted a picture of a storm at sea. Black clouds filled the sky and, illuminated by a flash of lightning, was a little boat being dashed against a reef by the pounding seas. In the water sailors could be seen struggling for their lives. The only glimmer of hope was in the foreground. There a huge rock jutted out of the sea and clinging desperately to it with both hands was a lone seaman. It was a moving scene but after the artist stepped back to admire his work, he sensed that he had missed the point. So putting aside the painting, he immediately started work on another. It was the same scene, the same black clouds, the same flash of lightning, the same ship and the same lone seaman clinging to a rock. But now the artist made one change. This time the lone seaman was holding on to the rock with just one hand and with the other was reaching down beneath the waves to lift up a sinking friend.

That is the New Testament picture of evangelism – with one hand we hold on to Christ and with the other we reach down beneath the swirling waters of sin to help lift up a friend.

Father, I'm available. Use me to lift someone from the seas of sin. Take over my whole being and turn me from theory to practice. In Jesus' name. Amen.

Acts 8; John 1:45–51; 12:21–22
1. What two forms of evangelism are found in Acts 8?
2. What was Philip's attitude and approach?

Prayer and Evangelism

21 DEC

FOR READING AND MEDITATION – MARK 11:12–26

'Therefore I tell you, whatever you ask for in prayer,
believe that you have received it, and it will be yours.' (v24)

We are seeking this week to turn theory into practice and to discover what practical steps we can take in attempting to win our acquaintances, friends, and relatives to the Lord Jesus Christ. 'The best way to begin to witness,' said someone, 'is to begin to witness.' For those who are aren't actively engaged in evangelism, let me lay down some guidelines to help you get started. Remember, however, that these are guidelines and not rules. It may be, as you think them through and pray over them, that God will show you something different. *Prayerfully draw up a list of people whom you know are not Christians and begin to pray daily for their conversion.*

George Müller of Bristol, the famous man of faith and prayer, once did this. He prayerfully selected five friends whom he wanted to see become Christians and began to pray for them every day. Within about five years, two of them came to Christ. Twenty years later one more came. He kept on praying for the other two day after day for forty years until he died. Both of the two remaining men on his prayer list became Christians within two years of his death! If the people you select live close to you then you can consider inviting them to a Christian event such as an evangelistic festival or concert. You might like also to consider giving them a Christian book, or plan a day out with them on some friendship activity, where you share with them something about your Christian faith. What is most important is to begin right away.

Ask God to show you those for whom He wants you to pray – then go to work in daily intercession for their salvation.

Thank you, Father, for reminding me again of the power of prevailing prayer. I shall, as one great servant of Yours once said, 'Ask great things from God, expect great things from God, attempt great things for God.' Help me, I pray. Amen.

Acts 16; 1 Corinthians 14:15; 1 Timothy 2:8
1. What was Paul's strategy for the evangelism of Philippi?
List eight results.
2. List unconverted friends and pray specifically for them.

Your Own Personal Story

22 DEC

FOR READING AND MEDITATION – ACTS 26:1-20

'King Agrippa, I consider myself fortunate
to stand before you today as I make my defence...' (v2)

We continue looking at practical ways by which we can win our friends, acquaintances, and relatives to faith in the Lord Jesus Christ. Today we consider the importance of learning to tell our own personal story. Not only did the early Christians tell the story of Jesus but they told their own story. Paul did this with great effect on at least two occasions (Acts 22 and 26). The early Christians did not, of course, advance their experience as the main reason why others should believe.

Our experience is not the basis of our faith; it is the validation of our faith. Sharing Jesus consists first of telling His story and then our own story. People who are unconvinced by the theoretical are often moved by the personal. A close observer of Billy Graham says that whenever he struggled to put some point across, he stopped preaching and began to relate how, as a young boy of seventeen, he came to know Jesus Christ. The observer writes 'Almost always a hush seemed to fall over the audience.'

Each one of us has a story that is worth sharing because every person is different and, from the heart of your uniqueness, God wants to bring forth a testimony to His Son. Every Christian should think through his own conversion story and tell it clearly, effectively, and concisely in about ninety seconds. A testimony to Christ should underline four themes: (1) Your attitudes to life before you came to know Christ; (2) How you came to feel your need of Him; (3) How you came to know Him; (4) What has happened since – what Jesus Christ means in your life at this present moment.

Lord, I am so grateful for my own uniqueness. No one else in the universe has a story quite like mine. Help me to tell it convincingly and compellingly. For Your own dear Name's sake. Amen.

1 John 4-5; Acts 20:24
1. Write the account of your commitment to Christ in 300 words.
2. Ask God to lead you to someone with whom to share it today.

Stress Repentance

23 DEC

FOR READING AND MEDITATION – MARK 1:14–18

'Jesus went into Galilee, proclaiming… Repent…' (vv14–15)

Some Christians, although they are able to relate their own personal story of how they found Christ, find it difficult to summarise their faith in a scriptural setting. You do not need to know the whole Bible in order to lead a person to Jesus Christ but there are some basic things which need to be firmly embedded in your memory. These basics are illustrated for us in the passage before us today and show us clearly the three things that one needs to know in order to become a Christian.

The first is repentance. 'Repent and believe the good news!' Do not be afraid of this word when talking to your non-Christian friends, for evangelism to be effective must tell 'the truth, the whole truth and nothing but the truth'. Repentance means 'agreeing with God'. When I repent I recognise that God made me for Himself, for Him to live and reign in the centre of my being, and that I have no right to manage my life on my own terms. Many people think repentance involves great emotion. It can do, of course, but primarily it is an attitude of mind whereby I stop trying to manage my life on my own terms and allow Jesus Christ to be my rightful Lord. Don't sugar-coat or try to soft-sell this issue.

People who come into the Church without experiencing true repentance are full of problems. Explain to them that repentance is like driving down life's road in your car when suddenly Christ confronts you. You realise you are going the wrong way so you move over and let Him come in, take the steering wheel, and make a 'U' turn. That way you start heading in a new and different direction.

O God, impress deep into my spirit today the profound importance of this truth that to become an effective Christian one must first step through the door of true repentance. Help me to make this clear to everyone to whom I witness. In Jesus' name. Amen.

Luke 18:9–27; Matthew 3:2; Luke 13:2–3; Acts 3:19
1. Write out your own definition of 'repentance'.
2. What can we learn about repentance from Luke 18?

Focus on Christ's Person

24 DEC

FOR READING AND MEDITATION – MARK 1:14–18

'Jesus went into Galilee, proclaiming the good news of God... "Repent and believe the good news!"' (vv14–15)

We continue examining the basic requirements which a person needs in order to receive Christ and become a true Christian. The first thing (as we saw) is repentance. What then is step 2? This. 'Believe the gospel.' The gospel is basically the good news – that God has done in Jesus Christ what we could never do for ourselves. To believe is to put our full trust and confidence in the message of God's Word.

How do we convey this? We need to stress three very important points all focusing on the uniqueness of our Lord Jesus Christ. (1) *He is unique because He is the 'only begotten Son'* (John 3:16; 5:18 and 10:10–30). This makes Him not only the Son of God but God, the Son. In a day when there are so many self-appointed saviours, gurus, and so-called prophets, take time to impress upon the person to whom you are walking the fact that Jesus Christ alone is *the* Son of God, and not *a* Son of God. (2) *He is unique because only He could take our place on Calvary and pay the atonement for our sin* (Matt. 26:28; 1 Cor. 15:2–4). Christ actually became man for our sakes so that He could take our place on Calvary's tree, substituting His righteousness for our guilt so that He might bring us back to God (1 Peter 3:18). (3) *He is unique because He rose from the dead* (Luke 24:36–48).

No sceptic has been able to explain how the first Christians who were so defeated when Jesus died, suddenly became triumphant witnesses. The change can only be explained by the fact that He rose from the dead to live His life within the personalities of His disciples.

O Father, help me to get this clearly in my mind so that I, in turn, can make it clear to others. Impress it upon me so that, when I share it with others, I will be able to impress it upon them. Amen.

Hebrews 11; Mark 9:23; John 1:7; 14:1
1. Write out your own definition of 'faith' and 'belief'.
2. Why does God require faith at the beginning of our Christian work?

Christmas Day – A New Beginning*   25 DEC

FOR READING AND MEDITATION – JOHN 1:1,9,14
'The Word became flesh and made his dwelling among us.' (v14)

Christmas Day greets us not just with carols and candles, but with the echo of eternity breaking into time. 'In the beginning...' John writes, drawing us deliberately back to Genesis. No first-century Jew would have missed the force of that phrase – *bereshit* – 'in the beginning'. It signals not merely the start of a story, but the beginning of something entirely new. A new creation is at hand.

And at the centre of this new beginning is the Word. Not an idea. Not a distant deity. But a Person – One who was with God, and who was God. On this day, we celebrate not merely the birth of a child, but the advent of God Himself into human history.

Whenever we use words, we express something of ourselves – our thoughts, emotions, convictions. But when God speaks, He expresses not part, but the whole of Himself. He speaks not a sentence, but a Person. Jesus is the full expression of God – God from God, Light from Light, True God from True God.

The Word became flesh. Not in metaphor, but in reality. He stepped into our dust, our darkness, our brokenness. He didn't come simply to dwell among us but to dwell with us – Emmanuel. He embraced our humanity so we might share in His divinity.

This is Christmas: not just the start of a story, but the start of everything new. In Jesus, the Creator has begun His re-creation – one heart at a time. And that includes yours.

Whatever your past, Christ brings a new beginning. Today is not just Christmas – it is the first day of new creation.

Lord Jesus, Word made flesh, thank You for coming to dwell with us. Be born anew in my heart today. Let Your light shine in every corner of my life, and may this Christmas mark a new beginning with You. Amen.

Colossians 1:15–17; Hebrews 1:1–3
1. Find a quiet moment today to reflect on one area of your life where you long to see Christ's light and love break through afresh.
2. Write a short note to Christ – as a prayer or journal entry – thanking Him for becoming flesh and entering your story.

*Written by Jason Swan Clark.

Encourage Personal Commitment   26 DEC

FOR READING AND MEDITATION – MARK 1:14–18

"'Come, follow me,' Jesus said, "and I will send you out to fish for people."' (v17)

The third basic essential a person needs to know in presenting a clear picture of salvation to someone who does not know Christ is this – 'Follow Me.' Conversion means more than just an intellectual assent to what Jesus said and did; it is a personal relationship with Him in the here and now. Someone put it this way: 'In becoming a Christian there is not only something to believe, but also Someone to receive.' Some like to compare it to marriage. Marriage is more than a philosophy or an institution. I may spend years studying the social implications of marriage but unless I have a partner to whom I am personally related then marriage is merely a theory and not a fact.

A person may well study Christianity for years and yet have no personal relationship with Jesus Christ. This fact then must be stressed – that Christianity is not just an attachment to a formula or a creed but a vital contact with a living Person. One of the most delightful experiences life can offer us is to be on hand when God breaks creatively into someone's life in true conversion. It's like observing the birth of a child! We need to think of ourselves as 'spiritual midwives' and watch for those whom God is drawing to Himself so that we may aid them. In helping a person come to Christ we ought to avoid manipulating them or playing on their emotions.

Don't try to persuade people in a way that restricts their freedom. We must urge people lovingly, persuade them with all the conviction of our being, but we must watch for God's moment and be sure not to push people until they are ready.

O Father, make me sensitive to the fact that fruit cannot be picked until it is ripe. Give me insight and understanding so that my efforts coincide with Yours, not contradict them. In Jesus' name. Amen.

Luke 9:57-62; Matthew 4:19; John 12:26; Matthew 16:24-26
1. What was Jesus teaching about commitment?
2. What do you understand by the word 'deny'?

Getting the Decision

27 DEC

FOR READING AND MEDITATION – ROMANS 10:1-13

'As Scripture says, "Anyone who believes
in him will never be put to shame."' (v11)

What if, after witnessing to someone about the gospel and the need for faith in the Lord Jesus Christ, they say, 'I would like to become a Christian – can you help me?' The first person I witnessed to, about a month after my conversion, did just that – he said, 'I would like to become a Christian; how do I go about it?' I was scared out of my wits. I began to physically tremble and stutter but somehow, as we say, I 'got him in'. Let me encourage you to step out in faith and let God use you. There is no joy in this world that exceeds the joy of leading someone to the Lord Jesus Christ. There are several ways this can be done.

Firstly you can suggest the person gets alone some place, tell them the kind of prayer they should pray, and then invite them to tell you about it afterwards. *Secondly* you can introduce your friend to someone else who can pray with them and lead them to Christ – but this ought to be done only if you feel utterly inadequate and unable to deal with the situation. *Thirdly,* and this is without doubt the most rewarding way, get the person to pray with you, in your presence. If the person shows some hesitancy in praying then you can lead them into a prayer – pausing, and letting them repeat the words themselves. It is best if this prayer is prayed out loud because the ear then comes to the aid of the mind and helps to clinch the decision in an important way. Then, when this is over, ask the person a pointed question such as this, 'What has happened here today?' This will gently press them to make their first confession – 'I have taken Jesus Christ to be my personal Saviour.'

O God, make me ready so that soon I can personally become involved in experiencing one of the greatest joys a Christian can know – the joy of leading someone to new life in You. For Jesus' sake, I pray. Amen.

Matthew 10; Romans 14:11; Luke 12:8; Philippians 2:11
1. What is the importance of a verbal confession of faith?
2. When was the last time you led someone to a verbal confession of faith?

A Seven-Step Ladder

28 DEC

FOR READING AND MEDITATION – PSALM 51:10–19

'Restore to me the joy of your salvation and grant me a willing spirit, to sustain me. Then I will teach transgressors your ways, so that sinners will turn back to you.' (vv12–13)

With only four days left before we come to the end of this topic, I want to spend the time recapitulating what we have said, and looking once again at some of the more salient issues so that they will not be overlooked or forgotten. We shall build, over these next four days, what we are going to call *a ladder to a contagious life.* To have the qualities of Christ in our being is not enough unless we have also the quality of contagion. For contagion makes these qualities outgoing and places them at the disposal of others. Remember what we said? 'No virtue is safe that is not enthusiastic; no heart is pure that is not passionate; no life is Christian that is not Christianising.'

We must deliberately set ourselves to be spiritually creative. If we climb the following seven steps, they will, I believe, help us towards a contagious life. (1) *We are made in the inner structure of our beings to be creative.* You and I are made in our innermost being for achievement, to be outgoing, to create. If we are not positively creating and producing, the machinery of life will get out of gear for we are geared to creation. (2) *To win others to the new life is the highest form of creative activity.* In widening the circle of faith so that it includes more and more people who have trusted Christ as their Saviour, we have a chance to be creative where it counts most. Although physical creativity may be denied us, spiritual creativity is an ever-open door. No Christian is denied spiritual creativity unless, of course, they deny it to themselves.

O God, I bring my non-creative life to You today so that You can release it into creativity. Flow into my imagination so that I will be alert and open to ways by which I can win others to You. In Jesus' name. Amen.

1 Corinthians 9; Proverbs 11:30; Daniel 12:3; Jude 23
1. What is Paul teaching about winning the lost?
2. What dangers does he point out?

Throwing Off All Reserve

29 DEC

FOR READING AND MEDITATION – ACTS 3:1-11

'Then Peter said, "Silver or gold I do not have,
but what I do have I give you."' (v6)

We continue climbing the ladder to a contagious life. (3) *Nothing is really ours until we share it with others.* All expression deepens impression. It is a law of the mind that that which is not expressed dies. If there is no outflow the inflow automatically stops. There are two seas in the Holy Land. One is the fresh and fruitful Galilee, the other, the Dead Sea – bitter and barren. Why the difference? Galilee both takes and gives. The Dead Sea has no outlet. The passage before us today reminds us that 'to have' is not enough. 'What I have,' said Peter, 'I give to you.' My possessions become my debt. I do not *own* them; I *owe* them. I must share them. (4) *We shall have the will to evangelise.* Up until now the desire to evangelise has been mostly in our minds and in our emotions; now it must get into our wills.

We must decide to share with others what others have shared with us. We are at a place in our spiritual lives today similar to that of the early disciples in Acts 13:44-52. The apostles had gone to the Jews alone and had acted as if the gospel was Jewish – from Jews to Jews. The Scripture says, 'Then Paul and Barnabas answered them boldly: "We had to speak the word of God to you first. Since you reject it and do not consider yourselves worthy of eternal life, we now turn to the Gentiles."' (v46). The early disciples had a larger gospel in their hearts than they were proclaiming.

Today a similar crisis has arisen. We have a larger gospel in our hearts than we are proclaiming. We have acted on less than the whole. Now this challenge of the past two months is pressing us to throw off all reserve. Then our evangelism from here on will be contagious, continuous, and compelling.

Gracious God and heavenly Father, help me, from this very moment, to throw off all reserve and to act on the larger implications of the gospel that I know are in my heart. For Jesus' sake. Amen.

Acts 5; Romans 10:1; 1 Corinthians 9:16; Acts 2:40; John 9:4
1. What was the apostles' attitude to sharing the gospel?
2. What can we learn from this?

The Gentle Inner Push   30 DEC

FOR READING AND MEDITATION – ROMANS 2:1-16

'They show that the requirements of the law are written on their hearts, their consciences also bearing witness, and their thoughts sometimes accusing them and at other times even defending them.' (v15)

Today we come to step 5. *If we are afraid of being snubbed or rejected we will remind ourselves that we have a secret ally in every heart.* Victor Frankl, the famous psychiatrist, said that the God urge is native to man, as native as the other urges. If you suppress God in your life, he said, you will get a complex just as you do when you suppress other urges. He believed that about fifty percent of his patients were suffering from the suppression of the God urge in their lives. If that is true, it means that in every human heart we have an ally when we approach it and claim it for Christ. Deep down in every man and woman is that something which waits for somebody to give the inner gentle push that will lead to Jesus Christ. All that keeps some people away from Christ is that they have never been asked.

(6) *Our motive in winning people to Christ will not be to exploit our need for achievement but we will do it for Jesus' sake.* A nurse on the mission field stood washing the sores of a person suffering from leprosy. A visitor from the West stood watching her and remarked, 'I wouldn't do that for a million pounds.' 'Neither would I,' said the nurse. 'But I will do it for Jesus' sake.'

When we look into the face of Jesus and then into the face of humanity's need, we realise more fully the need to spend the balance of our days trying to bring them together. (7) *If we fail we shall fail in doing what we should do.* But perhaps the greatest failure is the failure to do anything. If our efforts falter perhaps it will give God the greater chance to work. When we speak haltingly it may be that He will speak most clearly.

O God, help me, as I go through life, to be used by You in giving that gentle inner push to someone which will bring them to Your feet. For this is where the world belongs–at your feet. I am there now. Yours–to be used. Help me, dear Lord. Amen.

Revelation 2:1-7; 2 Corinthians 5:14; Matthew 9:3-6; 20:34
1. What must be our motivation for winning the lost?
2. How is your first love related to winning the lost?

The Divine Equation

31 DEC

FOR READING AND MEDITATION – JOHN 20:19–31

'As the Father has sent me, I am sending you.' (v21)

On this last day of a two-month period in which we have been looking at the tremendously important subject of *Sharing Our Faith,* we must sum up what we have been saying in the form of a single conclusion. And our conclusion is this. It is not enough to tell people Jesus is the answer. We must be willing to say, 'Jesus – *be* the answer through me.' Is not this what our text is saying to us today? 'As my Father sent me... so send I you.' The words are in the form of a divine equation. As... So. As God wrapped His love in the personality of Jesus Christ, so He wants to wrap His love in us today. He could have put His message for humankind in fiery flashes of lightning and scattered them across the sky. He could have organised a troop of singing angels to have gone from one end of the world to the other so that all humankind could hear. Instead He compressed Himself into the body of a Man, walked the hot, dusty roads and endured the agony of a cross so that humankind could not only hear but *see* the measure of His love.

Today, as in those distant centuries close on 2,000 years ago, He still chooses to spread His message through a human personality. He chooses to walk the streets of Great Britain, of the United States of America, indeed of every country in the world, through interpreters of His gospel such as you and me. I trust that soon everyone who has shared in these daily meditations will have the privilege of saying to another person, 'I would like to introduce you to Jesus Christ', and of seeing that transforming friendship begin.

O God, I have looked into Your heart of love over these past two months and I can never be satisfied until I can get others to look into Your heart. I commit myself, in these coming days, to getting others committed to You. Help me to succeed. For Your own dear Name's sake. Amen.

Philippians 2:1–16; Matthew 22:9; John 7:37; Romans 10:12; Revelation 22:17
1. What was the mind of Christ?
2. What is Paul's challenge in the light of this?

PRAY IT FORWARD ▶▶▶

Holy Spirit, give me boldness and gentleness as I share the hope I have in Jesus. Open doors for conversations, and let my life shine with Your light so others may be drawn to You. Amen.

PAY IT FORWARD ▶▶▶

The gospel is too good to keep to ourselves. At Waverley Abbey, we inspire and equip believers to share their faith through teaching, writing, and community initiatives.
By giving today, you help us spread the gospel further than we ever could alone.

Visit **waverleyabbey.org/donate-to-edwj** call **01252 784700** or scan the **QR code** ▶

WAVERLEY ABBEY
ANCIENT SPARK NEW FIRES

A New Abbey for a New Generation

God is moving across the nation and we're ready to serve it.

Waverley Abbey is a new spiritual home for a rising generation, based in one of England's oldest places of Christian prayer, mission and justice. Today, we equip believers and leaders to play their part in the the renewal of faith in the nation.

 A House of Prayer

 **Practical Education**

 **Exceptional Hospitality**

 Innovative Enterprise

📍 Farnham, Surrey GU9 8EP
🌐 waverleyabbey.org • 📷 @waverleyabbey